T0211235

Lecture Notes in Computer Science　　　10437

Commenced Publication in 1973
Founding and Former Series Editors:
Gerhard Goos, Juris Hartmanis, and Jan van Leeuwen

More information about this series at http://www.springer.com/series/7408

Marco Bozzano · Yiannis Papadopoulos (Eds.)

Model-Based Safety and Assessment

5th International Symposium, IMBSA 2017
Trento, Italy, September 11–13, 2017
Proceedings

 Springer

Editors
Marco Bozzano (iD)
Fondazione Bruno Kessler
Trento
Italy

Yiannis Papadopoulos (iD)
University of Hull
Hull
UK

ISSN 0302-9743   ISSN 1611-3349 (electronic)
Lecture Notes in Computer Science
ISBN 978-3-319-64118-8   ISBN 978-3-319-64119-5 (eBook)
DOI 10.1007/978-3-319-64119-5

Library of Congress Control Number: 2017946700

LNCS Sublibrary: SL2 – Programming and Software Engineering

Printed on acid-free paper

This Springer imprint is published by Springer Nature
The registered company is Springer International Publishing AG
The registered company address is: Gewerbestrasse 11, 6330 Cham, Switzerland

Preface

This volume contains the papers presented at IMBSA 2017: the International Symposium on Model-Based Safety and Assessment, held during September 11–13 in Trento.

The International Symposium on Model-Based Safety and Assessment (IMBSA) was held for the fifth time. Since the first edition in Toulouse (2011), the workshop has evolved to a forum where brand new ideas from academia, leading-edge technology, and industrial experiences are brought together. The objectives are to present experiences and tools, to share ideas, and to federate the community. To foster academic and industrial collaboration, in addition to more traditional talks reporting on novel advances on hot research topis, the program featured two poster and demo sessions, where speakers had the opportunity to present ongoing research and industrial experiences, and demonstrate their tool interactively.

We believe that a mixture of conventional talks about the newest achievements, the presentation of practical experiences, and interactive learning facilitates fruitful discussions, exchange of information, as well as future cooperation. Therefore, following the previous edition of IMBSA in Munich (2014), an important focus of this year's edition in Trento was placed on tool demonstrations. Nevertheless, the main scientific and industrial contributions were presented in traditional talks and are collected in this volume of LNCS.

For IMBSA 2017, we received 29 regular submissions from authors of 12 countries. The best 17 of these papers where selected by an international Program Committee to be published in this volume. In addition to this LNCS volume, IMBSA 2017 also published separate online proceedings for poster and demo contributions.

As program chairs, we want to extend a very warm thank you to all 32 members of the international Program Committee. Each submission was reviewed by at least three Program Committee members. The comprehensive review guaranteed the high quality of the accepted papers. We also want to thank the local organization team at Fondazione Bruno Kessler (Italy), and our fellow members of the Steering Committee: Leila Kloul, Frank Ortmeier, Antoine Rauzy, and Christel Seguin.

Finally, we wish you a pleasant reading of the articles in this volume. On behalf of everyone involved in this year's International Symposium on Model-Based Safety and Assessment, we hope you will be joining us at the next edition of IMBSA.

June 2017

Marco Bozzano
Yiannis Papadopoulos

Organization

Program Committee

Jean-Paul Blanquart	Airbus Defence and Space, France
Marc Bouissou	EDF and Ecole Centrale Paris, France
Marco Bozzano	Fondazione Bruno Kessler, Italy
Jean-Charles Chaudemar	ISAE, France
Regis de Ferluc	Thales Alenia Space, France
Jana Dittmann	Otto von Guericke University Magdeburg, Germany
Marielle Doche-Petit	Systerel, France
Peter Feiler	Software Engineering Institute, CMU, USA
Francesco Flammini	Ansaldo STS, Italy
Lars Fucke	Boeing, Spain
Lars Grunske	Humboldt University Berlin, Germany
Matthias Güdemann	DiffBlue, UK
Brendan Hall	Honeywell, USA
Michaela Huhn	Ostfalia, Germany
Kai Höfig	Siemens, Germany
Tim Kelly	University of York, UK
Leila Kloul	Universite de Versailles, France
Agnes Lanusse	CEA LIST, France
Timo Latvala	Space Systems Finland, Finland
Till Mossakowski	Otto von Guericke University Magdeburg, Germany
Juergen Mottok	LaS, OTH Regensburg, Germany
Thomas Noll	RWTH Aachen University, Germany
Frank Ortmeier	Otto von Guericke University Magdeburg, Germany
Yiannis Papadopoulos	University of Hull, UK
Antoine Rauzy	Norwegian University of Science and Technology, Norway
Wolfgang Reif	University of Augsburg, Germany
Jean-Marc Roussel	LURPA, ENS Cachan, France
Christel Seguin	ONERA, France
Pascal Traverse	Airbus, France
Elena Troubitsyna	Åbo Akademi, Finland
Marcel Verhoef	European Space Agency, The Netherlands
Marc Zeller	Siemens, Germany

Additional Reviewers

Bandur, Victor
Gonschorek, Tim
Knapp, Alexander
Leong, Chris
Leupolz, Johannes

Lisagor, Oleg
Pereverzeva, Inna
Pfähler, Jörg
Prokhorova, Yuliya
Rauf, Irum

Contents

Safety Process

Building Models We Can Rely On: Requirements Traceability for Model-Based Verification Techniques

Marco Filax[✉], Tim Gonschorek, and Frank Ortmeier

Chair of Software Engineering, Otto-von-Guericke University of Magdeburg,
Magdeburg, Germany
{marco.filax,tim.gonschorek,frank.ortmeier}@ovgu.de

Abstract. Proving the safety of a critical system is a complex and complicated task. Model-based formal verification techniques can help to verify a System Requirement Specification (SRS) with respect to normative and safety requirements. Due to an early application of these methods, it is possible to reduce the risk of high costs caused by unexpected, late system adjustments. Nevertheless, they are still rarely used. One reason among others is the lack of an applicable integration method in an existing development process.

In this paper, we propose a process to integrate formal model-based verification techniques into the development life-cycle of a safety critical system. The core idea is to systematically refine informal specifications by (1) categorization, (2) structural refinement, (3) expected behavioral refinement, and finally, (4) operational semantics. To support modeling, traceability is upheld through all refinement steps and a number of consistency checks are introduced.

The proposed process has been jointly developed with the German Railroad Authority (EBA) and an accredited safety assessor. We implemented an Eclipse-based IDE with connections to requirement and systems engineering tools as well as various verification engines. The applicability of our approach is demonstrated via an industrial-sized case study in the context of the European Train Control System with ETCS Level 1 Full Supervision.

Keywords: Traceability · Verification · Practical experiences

1 Introduction

Developing safety critical systems is a complex and complicated task because malfunction imposes high costs or even endangers human lives. Therefore, safety critical systems are specified with an increasing amount of functional and non-functional requirements, to reduce the risk of malfunction and hazardous behavior.

Further, it has to be ensured that the system adheres to specific safety norms and standards, e.g., EN 50128 for railway, DO-178C for avionics or ISO 26262

© Springer International Publishing AG 2017
M. Bozzano and Y. Papadopoulos (Eds.): IMBSA 2017, LNCS 10437, pp. 3–18, 2017.
DOI: 10.1007/978-3-319-64119-5_1

for automotive applications. Before the developed safety critical system can be put into operation, it must be certified by a governmental authority according to the relevant safety norm. It must be shown that all normative and safety requirements have been met for the system.

The fulfillment of safety requirements covers the complete safety lifecycle of the system. It is desirable to detect possible malfunction and hazardous behavior as early as possible because unexpected, late system adjustments would impose even higher costs. To detect hazardous behavior a complete, consistent and correct System Requirement Specification (SRS) that adheres to all normative and safety requirements, is required. However, proving the fulfillment of all these requirements is a challenging task.

Formal verification techniques can help proving normative and safety requirements. Thus, almost all norms recommend the use of formal verification techniques to prove functional safety properties [9,15,16] depending on the required safety integrity level (SIL). The application of formal methods during the requirement specification phase is recommended for systems with SIL 2 and higher and highly recommended for systems with SIL 4 [15].

However, IEC 61508 acknowledges[1] that using formal methods may be challenging [15]. In our point of view, one reason is that none of these norms suggest an integration into the lifecycle. Additionally, they do not emphasize requirements traceability during the implementation of the formal model. As traceability is an issue for traditional methods, it is an enormous problem for formal verification techniques: formal models, which describe the complete behavior of a safety critical system mathematically, might be challenging to understand by others without a strong formal background. In our point of view, this increases the hurdle for applying formal verification techniques during the requirement specification phase. However, if every element of the formal model would be linked to the requirements, this hurdle is negotiated.

We collaborated with the German Federal Railroad Authority (EBA) and an accredited assessor to develop a structured workflow supporting safety engineers in integrating formal model-based verification techniques into the safety lifecycle of critical systems. The core idea is to systematically refine informal specifications by (1) categorization, (2) structural refinement, (3) exemplary behavioral refinement, and finally, (4) operational semantics. We rely on our previous work [11] on transforming informal natural language requirement via semi-formal UML models into a formal interpretation. Traceability is upheld through all refinement phases with the explicit need for linking requirements (e.g. the resulting formal model). We introduce some (semi-)automatic consistency checks and provide adequate tool support for the proposed process. Developing the formal model with the proposed process, which supports the usage of formal methods in a traceable, well-defined, reliable and understandable manner, increases the acceptance of the formal verification results.

In the following section, we present an overview of the proposed process and describe how to integrate it into a typical development process. We rely on

---

[1] Acknowledged in IEC 61508-7 section B2.2.

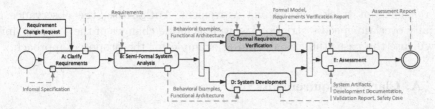

Fig. 1. Five phases of the safety lifecycle: the phases A, B, D, E represent state-of-the-art actives. In this paper, we integrate phase C: *Formal Requirements Verification* into the development process. Solid lines represent control flow whereas dashed lines represent object flow.

state-of-the-art methods to determine a semi-formal UML model (cf. Sect. 3) based on the SRS. We then summarize the different steps to derive the formal model from the UML and the requirements in Sect. 4. Throughout the whole paper, we demonstrate the feasibility of the approach on a case study. At the end of this paper, we point out future directions.

2 Building Reliable Formal Models

The proposed approach to integrating formal verification techniques into the safety lifecycle is summarized in Fig. 1. Given a SRS we distinguish five phases: *A: Clarify Requirements, B: Semi-Formal System, C: Formal Requirements Verification, D: System Development*, and *E: Assessment*. The phases A, B, D, and E summarize state-of-the-art activities to develop a safety critical system. In the following we describe how to integrate phase *C: Formal Requirement Verification* in this typical development process. We also summarize activities of the other phases and specify extensions if necessary.

The different phases of the proposed process are implemented in the Verification Environment for Critical Systems (VECS). VECS supports the efficient development of formal models and gives the possibility to check the formal models in different model checking tools, without switching from one to another. The results can be analyzed directly in VECS. Further, we developed a plugin for a state-of-the-art UML modeling tool to enhance the integration in our formal verification tool. VECS enables the modeler to trace generated elements directly to the UML model what helps to validate that the generated formal elements are corresponding to the UML model. Additionally, we implemented traceability reports to analyze and document the coverage and linkage of requirements in UML.

We evaluate the proposed approach by formalizing the SRS of the European Train Control System (ETCS) Level 1 Full Supervision. For this, we modeled all requirements necessary for the verification corresponding to a reference track defined by the EBA[2]. This contains the communication via Eurobalises, locking

---

[2] Available online: https://cse.cs.ovgu.de/vecs/index.php/product/achievements/casestudies/etcs.

and releasing of track sections via Movement Authorities, the observance of partially overlaid speed restrictions as well as mode changes of the onboard unit. We will use the case study as a running example for the proposed approach.

2.1   A: Clarify Requirements

Informal requirements often are neither complete nor organized in a way that they can be processed in a structured manner. Hence, a system analyst must clarify the requirements and therefore split them into atomic statements as illustrated in Fig. 1. These atomic statements can be sorted into different categories, defined by a requirement pattern, to support following phases. There already exists a variety of successfully applied requirement patterns [20]. However, the final domain-specific needs of the system typically require an adoption of the used pattern.

A requirement pattern decreases the complexity of following phases for two reasons: On the one hand, the set of requirements becomes structured since for certain phases only specific categories are required (e.g. for the functional architecture we only need architectural requirements). On the other hand, the set of requirements becomes reduced since particular requirements could occur in several statements but can be combined into a single atomic statement.

As the system analyst splits requirements into atomic statements and categorizes them afterward, changes need to be documented. Changes in the requirements might occur in later phases of the process, e.g., when an error in the specification is detected and needs to be corrected. Such change requests may occur at any process phase (cf. *Requirement Change Request* in Fig. 1).

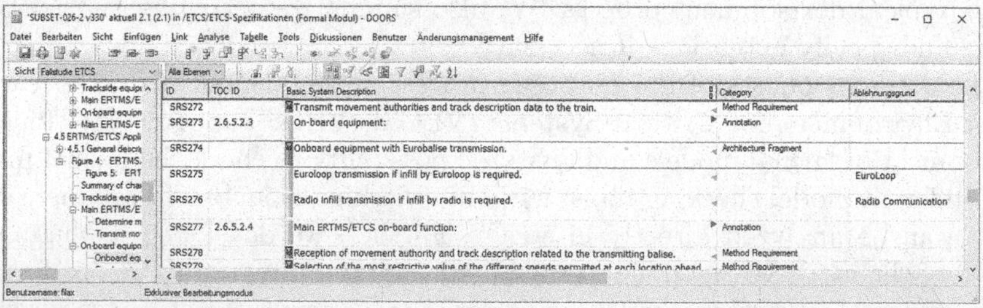

Fig. 2. An excerpt of requirements from the functional specification of the ETCS. Note that these requirements have been clarified: Requirement 2.6.5.2.3 was split into four atomic statements. The requirements have been categorized and some are rejected as they are not in the scope of the case study.

We applied the requirement pattern presented in [8], adopted in our previous work [10], because it had been applied to this domain successfully. Our pattern contains eight categories: *Method, Sequence, User, State* and *Safety requirements*,

Architecture and *Glossary fragments* and *Annotations*. Figure 2 depicts an exemplary application of the requirement pattern. The requirements are already clarified and split into atomic statements. We examined the functional description of the ETCS (SUBSET-26) with more than 33.000 requirements. We had to reduce the number of requirements which had to be formalized to handle the case study with the available manpower. We restricted us to ETCS Level 1, shown in Fig. 2 as the rejection of Euroloop and Radio Communication. From this, over 4.200 requirements had been identified as relevant for the case study.

2.2 B: Semi-Formal System Analysis

The *Semi-Formal System Analysis* represents typical system modeling tasks. It aims at modeling architectural and behavioral requirements in UML [17]. These modeling tasks are described in more detail in Sect. 3.

The overall idea is to determine a static functional architecture from the SRS. This is based on the observation that the SRS typically covers a basic structural definition of the system. Additionally, the SRS also typically covers a description of the intended behavior. Sequence diagrams are extracted from the behavioral requirements with the help of the functional architecture to represent the intended behavior. We focus on sequence diagrams because the SRS does not cover a complete behavioral definition. This is justified by the fact that a SRS is written in natural language.

We apply state-of-the-art requirements traceability: we use requirement diagrams to clarify the lifeline of requirements. Every element, derived from a requirement, shall be linked it. We use trace relations to link semi-formal elements and requirements. An example is depicted in Fig. 4b. Tool support is available in the form of Sparx Enterprise Architect with an IBM Rational DOORS connector.

2.3 C: Formal Verification

The goal of this phase is to verify safety claims. These are typically part of the SRS: we call them safety requirements. In order the verify these safety requirements with the help of model checking, we firstly need to build a formal model. We propose to develop the formal model using the semi-formal model. To do so, we reuse the semi-formal architecture: we automatically formalize the semi-formal architecture, by translating architectural elements to the specific formal language. The formal behavior has to be implemented manually. Further, we propose to use semi-formal sequences as an acceptance test for the formal model: we use them to generate acceptor automata in order to demonstrate that the behavior is implemented correctly in the formal model.

The formal model's architecture is automatically generated from the previous defined semi-formal architecture using the methods described in [11]. The basic idea is to translate every semi-formal architectural element into its formal equivalent, such that the transformation is bijective. We automatically derive requirement links to formal elements in order to provide traceability. The automatic transformation ensures the correctness of the mapping from the static architecture to the formal model.

When the architecture of the formal model is generated, the formal behavior has to be implemented as different automata. The modeler implements every automaton of the formal model with the help of a subset of requirements. The modeler has to preserve traceability manually by linking the requirements to the automata elements.

Since the automata are modeled by hand, it is important to demonstrate that they describe the intended system behavior. We use the previously defined sequences to automatically generate acceptance tests in the form of observer automata. By checking if the formal model fulfills the specified sequence we demonstrate the correct implementation of the expected behavior. Traceability is preserved by automatically linking the requirements linked to a sequence and a sequence ID to the generated observer.

Finally, given safety requirements are manually translated into temporal logic statements. We use these statements and formal model to verify the safety properties with the help of model checking [4]. The results are composed to a requirement verification report. We explain the complete phase in Sect. 4 in more detail.

2.4   D: System Development

Parallel to the phase C, "normal" system development activities are performed. We summarize these activities as *System Development* (cf. Fig. 1). These activities contain, e.g., the refinement of the functional architecture, the definition of the system design, the implementation of the system, and the verification and validation of the resulting implementation.

Phase D is not in the scope of this paper, as the process is meant to be an extension, at most to the specification phase of the safety lifecycle. However, we see the formal model as a possibility to aid in the verification and validation of the implementation. For example, different authors proposed approaches to utilize a model checker as a test oracle for the resulting implementation [3].

2.5   E: Assessment

Finally, the *Assessment* is performed - the overall functional safety is evaluated according to the relevant safety norm. Typical assessment documents like the validation report or safety cases are issued. Additionally, we issued a requirement verification report in phase C (cf. Sect. 2.3). It contains results, calculated by a model checker, which prove the safety requirements with mathematical rigor. The proves are used by an assessor to evaluate the functional safety of the system. However, the results generated from the model checker rely on the correct implementation of the formal model. If the formal model is faulty one has to question the result's value for the assessment. This, in our opinion, demonstrates the importance of the proposed process: we have to ensure the correct implementation of the formal model. We introduced a set of semi-automatic checks to verify that the formal model implements the expected behavior (cf. Sect. 2.2). We also introduced a set of manually traceability reports, to validate that the automata rely on specific requirements (cf. Sect. 4). Further, if additional verification needs are identified in this phase, we could easily expand the verification report in an iteration.

Beside the pure verification of the safety requirements, the formal model can be used for a variety of other methods to aid in the assessment, e.g., Failure Analysis [12], Fault Tree Analysis [7,18] or Deductive Cause Consequence Analysis [13].

3   B: Semi-formal System Analysis

During this phase, the functional system architecture and representative system behavior descriptions are created from a subset of categorized requirements. The activities of this phase are depicted in Fig. 3.

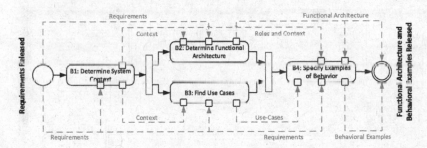

Fig. 3. The *Semi-Formal System Analysis* consists of five different phases. The goal of this phase is to derive a functional architecture and examples of the expected behavior of the system from the requirements.

3.1   B1: Determine System Context

In this phase, we determine the border of the system. We define the system-to-be-developed, other external systems, and their roles that directly or indirectly interact with the system-to-be-developed. This determines the context of the specified system. Several external systems may be classified as the same role while other components directly represent their role. The goal is to achieve a consent with the involved stakeholders about the difference and similarities of external systems. This reassembles a typical engineering task - thus, we do not describe it in further detail. The context definition is used by the system architect to model the functional architecture of the system.

In the case study, we identified the border of the system as follows: The system-to-be-developed is the *European Vital Computer*. We identified different surrounding systems and roles, e.g., trackside subsystem, balise transmission unit, train interface unit, train components, and the driver.

3.2   B2: Determine Functional Architecture

In this phase, we design the functional architecture by modeling system modules and their relations and interfaces. We will use the architecture to design a formal model and to implement the system in later phases.

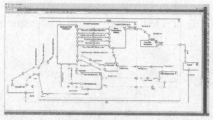
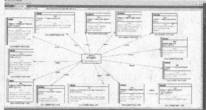

(a) The architecture of our case study. Different components are assembled via ports, which implement interfaces.

(b) Requirement diagram for the interface *BaliseUplink*. Multiple requirements have been linked to the interface.

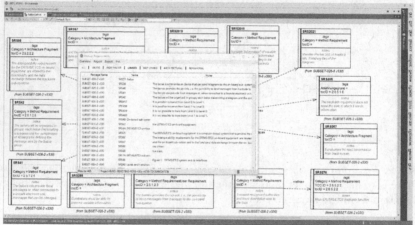

(c) Requirement validation report view: different reports have been implemented. Based on the requirement categorization we can identify requirements correctly linked to semi-formal elements.

Fig. 4. An excerpt of the functional architecture. Figure 4a depicts an excerpt of the architecture of our case study. Figure 4b depicts a requirement diagram, demonstrating the traceability approach for a single interface. Figure 4c depicts the requirement validation view implemented as a plugin in Enterprise Architect.

We identify components, ports, and interfaces from the SRS, in specific from the subset of architecture, method and glossary requirements. We use the requirements according to their categorization: Glossary fragments, architecture and method requirements represent architectural statements in the requirement pattern [10] used in this paper. Components are derived from Glossary fragments. Relations of components (e. g., ports or assemblies) are identified via architecture requirements, whereas method requirements are used to derive method definitions for interfaces. A more detailed look on this is given in our previous work in [11].

The functional architecture of the ETCS model has been derived from 363 Requirements and consists of 31 components with 135 Ports as well as 23 interfaces with 161 methods and 136 corresponding call parameters. An excerpt is shown in Fig. 4a. We directly linked (via «trace» relations) the requirements and the semi-formal elements during this phase. This ensures traceability. Further, we set ourselves the following goal: Every semi-formal element shall be linked to at least one requirement.

During this phase, it is vital to monitor the traceability. Thus, we designed traceability reports: a straight forward report to identify the elements linked to requirements and those who are not. However, due to the usage of a requirement pattern, other reports are of more value: We design a report to identify the architectural elements, which have been linked to requirements. Further, we can identify the requirements, that *should* have been linked to some architectural element - but are not. We also designed these reports for other requirement categories, e. g., behavioral requirements.

These reports have been proven their value during the development: They enable us to detect which requirements still have to be processed and to evaluate the progress of the current phase. They also enable us to identify misscategorized requirements or identify incorrect and inconsistent requirements due to the elements introduced during the modeling and then start a requirement change request (See Fig. 1). They further help to increase the acceptance of the model of others, who are not directly involved in the development, e. g., assessors, since the reports enable others to judge the requirement linkage.

3.3 B3: Find Use Cases

Besides the definition of the semi-formal architecture, we require a definition of behavior. Based on the context definition, the system analyst needs to define use cases. These use cases enable us to derive a top-level behavioral description of the SRS. Further, we require the analyst to link the use cases and requirements. After this phase, we refine the behavioral descriptions with the help of sequence diagrams.

Based on the previously established context definition, the use cases and the traceability reports for a subset of behavioral requirements (in specific user requirements) we can enhance the quality of our semi-formal model. If we identify use cases that are not traced to a requirement, we either identified creativity in the semi-formal model or identified an inconsistency in the requirements. Further, if we identify behavioral requirements that are not used to derive a use case, we identified a blind spot of the semi-formal model.

These use cases and our traceability reports help us to enforce a consistent, complete and correct semi-formal behavioral description. However, these use cases describe an overview of the behavior - we refine these descriptions with the help sequence diagrams in phase B4.

3.4   B4: Specify Expected Behavior

Use cases describe the basic behavior of the system. However, they are to imprecise to derive internal system behavior. Further, the behavioral description within the SRS is often incomplete: The SRS typically specifies the expected behavior. However, it does not describe the (mathematically) complete behavior. Hence, we use sequence diagrams to model the system's behavior: A set of sequence diagrams is modeled by domain experts from the set of behavioral requirements until the necessary behavior is described. The set of modeled sequences is used in later phases to demonstrate that the formal model contains the expected behavior of the semi-formal system model (*cf.* Sect. 4). We chose sequence diagrams instead of activity charts because they allow each to model one exemplary behavior trace of the system, whereas an activity diagram would imply that it defines the only paths the system model is allowed to represent. Every sequence diagram must be linked to a requirement. An example is depicted in Fig. 5. The traceability reports in combination with the requirement pattern enable us to detect incomplete elements and missing requirements.

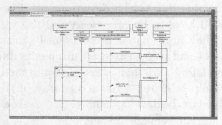 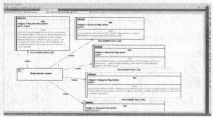

(a) Example sequence from the case study: it describes the update of the position information via a balise.

(b) Requirement diagram to demonstrate the requirement linkage of the sequences depicted in Fig. 5a.

Fig. 5. Exemplary sequence diagram taken from the case study. Every sequence has to be traced to at least a single requirement as shown in Fig. 5b.

4   C: Formal Requirements Verification

This phase, the *Formal Requirements Verification*, covers the implementation of the formal model and the verification of the SRS with the help of model checking. It consists of five different phases (*cf.* Fig. 6).

4.1   C1: Design Formal Model

From the functional architecture, the formal model's architecture is generated: semi-formal elements are automatically translated into their formal representation. The basic idea is that every UML element translates into some formal element, such that the translated formal element maps to a specific semi-formal

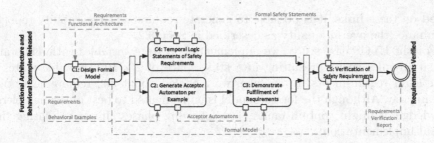

Fig. 6. The *Formal Requirements Verification* consists of five phases. The goal is to derive a formal model and verify safety requirements.

element. For example, the semi-formal architecture (e. g., a set of hierarchical components) is translated into a set of formal, hierarchical components. We refer the reader for further details on the transformation to our work in [11].

Given the formal representation, we can automatically preserve traceability: Every formal element is annotated with the unique ID of the semi-formal element which it represents. Further, we automatically translate the requirements linked to the specific semi-formal element. An example of the formal model is depicted in Fig. 7.

The task of the modeler is to implement the formal behavior according to the requirements. To do so, he has to formalize the behavior specified in the SRS. He has to rely on the architecture while implementing the automata. Further, he has to add a requirement link manually to the formal model, to preserve traceability.

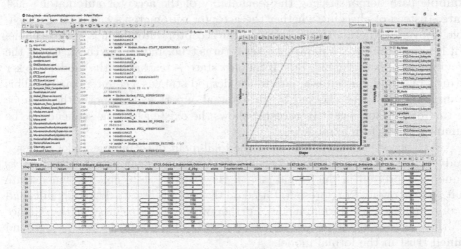

Fig. 7. A screenshot of the VECS debugger with the ETCS case study model. Here, the fulfilling of a sequence has been analyzed. As a result, a representative model path is given that can be used to check the validity of the sequence and for documenting the validity of the formal model for the assessment.

Based on these links, it is possible to generate requirement traceability reports to enhance the overall quality as described in Sect. 3.2.

For the ETCS case study, we implemented 53 state variables with 444 state transition rules so far (resulting in a state space of 2×10^{25} possible states[3]) from 1.511 requirements. In average, we modeled about 300 requirements per working day. Although the formal model is implemented to best of the modelers' knowledge, it might contain faults. The following phases aim at validating the formal implementation.

4.2   C2: Generate Acceptor Automaton per Example and C3: Demonstrate Fulfillment of Requirements

The goal of these phases is to show that the intended behavior is implemented in the formal model. We make use of sequence diagrams (cf. Sect. 3.4) to demonstrate the complete behavior implementation.

The formal model is an automaton. Thus its semantic is the set of all independent traces which are generated by executing it. A sequence diagram represents a single execution trace [17]. We say that the formal model covers a sequence if we can show that it is a sub-trace of at least one trace within the semantics of the formal model. To verify this, the sequence is translated into an acceptor automaton relying on the same architecture as the UML model, such that it moves to the next state every time a message occurred as described in the sequence.

We verify that the last state is reachable with the help of model checking [4]. To verify the reachability retractable, we provoke a witness. A witness is an example path demonstrating the reachability of the acceptor automaton's last state. Instead of checking whether the acceptor automaton's last state is reachable, we verify whether the last state of the acceptor automaton is not reachable. If it is not reachable, the model checker returns true, and we can check, e.g., if the previous state is reachable. But, if the last state is reachable, the model checker returns false and generates a path to the desired state as a counterexample. This example path can be checked by an external expert and supports the reliance on the formal model as it retraceable shows the existence of the sequence in the semantic of the formal model.

Up to now, the demonstration of the fulfillment of requirements for our case study is not 100% completed, because we have not demonstrated that *every* sequence is present in the formal model. However, we were able to demonstrate that *some* sequences are present. Based on the first results, we detected faults and inconsistencies in the formal model. Further, we were able to increase the reliance of others on our model: especially others without a strong formal background gained trust in the formal model.

---

[3] Worst case approximation by multiplying all possible state variable values.

4.3 C4: Temporal Logic Statements of Safety Requirements and C5: Verification of Safety Requirements

The safety requirements can be verified as soon as they are implemented. To do so, the formal modeler translates the natural language safety requirements into the used formal language (cf. Fig. 6). The formal language corresponds to preferred verification engine, i.e., the model checker. In most cases, this is either Computation Tree Logic or Linear-time Temporal Logic [4].

The output the model checker generated during the verification contains the result (cf. Fig. 6 *Verification of Safety Requirements*). These results demonstrate whether the specification fulfills the safety requirements. If the formal model fulfills the safety requirements, the system requirement specification covers the desired safety specifications. This holds if we applied the proposed process and demonstrated completeness and consistency.

5 Related Work

Hallerstede et al. [14] transformed requirements directly into a formal model. They offer tool support through Rodin and ProR to trace requirements. However, the direct transformation, in contrast to our approach, seems much more difficult to perform as it requires extensive expert knowledge in the domain of the system and the used formal verification technique.

Aceituna and Do propose an approach to find errors in specifications [1]. Our goals differ slightly, as the authors try to expose possible, unintended, off-nominal behavior. In contrast to that, our approach has a broader scope: verifying safety specifications, whereas off-nominal behavior can be detected as a side product during the verification if it opposes the safety goals. Aceituna et al. translate natural language requirements into causal components [1,2]. The authors propose to expand the transition rules of the system by modeling explicit rules for the entire state space. Although the authors display the feasibility of the proposed approach, their case studies are rather small. For large system requirement specifications, this approach seems to unfeasible, because of the need to expand the transition rules. In a previous work [2], the authors demonstrated how causal components can directly be mapped into SMV. However, the approach lacks some behavior validation mechanism to ensure wanted behavior to be present in the model.

An approach enforcing a correct behavior translation through automatic validation as been proposed by Soliman et al. [19]. A test case generator is used to perform the automatic validation of the transformation process based on scenarios. The generated test cases are integrated into the safety application timed-automata network and simulated automatically with UPPAAL. Finally, the output variables have to be compared. The authors did not specify if the comparison can be done automatically and did not ensure traceability.

The COMPASS toolset [6] is quite similar to our approach: A formal model is used for a variety of model-based verifications. However, the toolset requires a formal model; it does not address its derivation from a SRS. Recently, the toolset was extended with a specific requirement pattern, originated in the aerospace domain, to structure the derivation [5]. However, the approach lacks a semi-formal phase which increases the understandability of the resulting formal model.

6   Conclusions and Future Work

In this paper, we presented our approach for integrating formal verification techniques into the safety lifecycle of critical systems. This includes a well-defined and structured process which supports the creation of a formal model from a given set of system requirements. For increasing the acceptance, in particular, during the assessment, of the verification artifacts and the applicability of the process, we integrated structural UML models in a semi-formal step. This supports the comprehension of the model and reliability of all involved in the correctness of the formal model.

Together with our project partners, we demonstrated the applicability of our approach on an industrial-size case study of the European Train Control System. In this context, we processed about 4.200 requirements from functional description (SUBSET-026) of the ETCS, containing more than 33.000 requirements in total.

From this, we built a verifiable formal model, which were also accepted by the project partner as a reliable representation of the system specification. In particular, this resulted from the rigorous implementation of the traceability and the use of UML sequence charts as a measure of the model's validity. Further, this was supported by the implementation of the semi-formal UML phase introducing the representation of the formal model's structure in a widely accepted and known representation.

Also, another important step towards the integration of the process is its implementation within our formal modeling and verification tool chain VECS, offering an interface to the widely used requirement tool Rational Doors and the UML modeling tool Enterprise Architect. Whereby, the traceability and, moreover, the comprehensibility of the modeling and verification results got improved.

Raising the quality of the specification on a trustworthy level should always be one central demand. However, if the formal model has been build once it should also be used for further safety measurements. Therefore, we plan to integrate several further model-based analysis methods, e.g., Fault Tree Analysis in the next step. Besides this, we are also working on the enabling correlation and trace refinement measures between the formal model and the implemented program code, to open the process integration not only for new developments but also for extensions of already existing systems.

Acknowledgments. The work presented in this paper is funded by the German Ministry of Education and Science (BMBF) in the VIP-MoBaSA project (project-Nr. 16V0360).

References

1. Aceituna, D., Do, H.: Exposing the susceptibility of off-nominal behaviors in reactive system requirements. In: RE, pp. 136–145 (2015). doi:10.1109/RE.2015.7320416
2. Aceituna, D., Do, H., Srinivasan, S.: A systematic approach to transforming system requirements into model checking specifications. In: ICSE, pp. 165–174 (2014). doi:10.1145/2591062.2591183
3. Ammann, P.E., Black, P.E., Majurski, W.: Using model checking to generate tests from specifications. In: Proceedings of the Second International Conference on Formal Engineering Methods, pp. 46–54. IEEE (1998). doi:10.1007/3-540-48166-4_10
4. Baier, C., Katoen, J.P., Larsen, K.G.: Principles of Model Checking. MIT Press, Cambridge (2008). ISBN: 9780262026499
5. Bos, V., Bruintjes, H., Tonetta, S.: Catalogue of system and software properties. In: Skavhaug, A., Guiochet, J., Bitsch, F. (eds.) SAFECOMP 2016. LNCS, vol. 9922, pp. 88–101. Springer, Cham (2016). doi:10.1007/978-3-319-45477-1_8
6. Bozzano, M., Cimatti, A., Katoen, J.P., Nguyen, V.Y., Noll, T., Roveri, M.: The COMPASS approach: correctness, modelling and performability of aerospace systems. In: Buth, B., Rabe, G., Seyfarth, T. (eds.) SAFECOMP 2009. LNCS, vol. 5775, pp. 173–186. Springer, Heidelberg (2009). doi:10.1007/978-3-642-04468-7_15
7. Bozzano, M., Cimatti, A., Tapparo, F.: Symbolic fault tree analysis for reactive systems. In: Namjoshi, K.S., Yoneda, T., Higashino, T., Okamura, Y. (eds.) ATVA 2007. LNCS, vol. 4762, pp. 162–176. Springer, Heidelberg (2007). doi:10.1007/978-3-540-75596-8_13
8. Cimatti, A., Roveri, M., Susi, A., Tonetta, S.: From informal requirements to property-driven formal validation. In: Cofer, D., Fantechi, A. (eds.) FMICS 2008. LNCS, vol. 5596, pp. 166–181. Springer, Heidelberg (2009). doi:10.1007/978-3-642-03240-0_15
9. EN 50128: Railway applications-communication, signaling and processing systems-software for railway control and protection systems (2011)
10. Filax, M., Gonschorek, T., Lipaczewski, M., Ortmeier, F.: On traceability of informal specifications for model-based verification. In: IMBSA: Short & Tutorial Proceedings, pp. 11–18. OvGU Magdeburg (2014)
11. Filax, M., Gonschorek, T., Ortmeier, F.: Correct formalization of requirement specifications: a v-model for building formal models. In: Lecomte, T., Pinger, R., Romanovsky, A. (eds.) RSSR 2016. LNCS, vol. 9707, pp. 106–122. Springer, Cham (2016). doi:10.1007/978-3-319-33951-1_8
12. Ge, X., Paige, R.F., McDermid, J.A.: Analysing system failure behaviours with PRISM. In: SSIRI-C, pp. 130–136 (2010). doi:10.1109/SSIRI-C.2010.32
13. Güdemann, M., Ortmeier, F., Reif, W.: Using deductive cause-consequence analysis (DCCA) with SCADE. In: Saglietti, F., Oster, N. (eds.) SAFECOMP 2007. LNCS, vol. 4680, pp. 465–478. Springer, Heidelberg (2007). doi:10.1007/978-3-540-75101-4_44
14. Hallerstede, S., Jastram, M., Ladenberger, L.: A method and tool for tracing requirements into specifications. Sci. Comput. Program. **82**, 2–21 (2014). doi:10.1016/j.scico.2013.03.008
15. IEC 61508: Functional safety of electrical/electronic/programmable electronic safety-related systems (2005)
16. ISO 26262: Road Vehicles-Functional Safety (2009)
17. OMG UML: Unified modeling language, superstructure (2011)

18. Ortmeier, F., Schellhorn, G.: Formal fault tree analysis-practical experiences. Electron. Not. Theoret. Comput. Sci. **185**, 139–151 (2007). doi:10.1016/j.entcs.2007.05.034
19. Soliman, D., Frey, G., Thramboulidis, K.: On formal verification of function block applications in safety-related software development. IFAC **46**(22), 109–114 (2013). doi:10.3182/20130904-3-UK-4041.00015
20. Withall, S.: Software Requirement Patterns (Developer Best Practices). Microsoft Press (2007). ISBN: 9780735623989

Handling Consistency Between Safety and System Models

Tatiana Prosvirnova[1(✉)], Estelle Saez[1], Christel Seguin[2],
and Pierre Virelizier[1]

[1] IRT Saint-Exupéry, 118 Route de Narbonne, 31432 Toulouse, France
tatiana.prosvirnova@irt-saintexupery.com,
estelle.saez@liebherr.com,
pierre.virelizier@safrangroup.com
[2] ONERA, 2 avenue Edouard Belin, 31055 Toulouse, France
christel.seguin@onera.fr

Abstract. Safety analyses are of paramount importance for the development of embedded systems. In order to perform these analyses, safety engineers use different modeling techniques, such as, for instance, Fault Trees or Reliability Block Diagrams. One of the industrial development process challenges today is to ensure the consistency between safety models and system architectures.

Model Based Safety Analysis (MBSA) is one of the newest modeling methods, which promises to ease the exchange of information between safety engineers and system designers. The aim of this article is to discuss an approach to manage the consistency between MBSA models and system architectures.

Our study is based on the experimentation of the co-design of an RPAS (Remotely Piloted Aircraft System) involving system design and safety teams during the early conception phases of an industrial development process. We simulate the process of exchange between the system design and the safety assessment with the constraint of creating safety models close to system architecture. We identify significant exchange points between these two activities. We also discuss the encountered problems and perspectives on the possibility to ensure the consistency between safety and system models.

Keywords: MBSA · AltaRica · FHA · Development process · System architecture · Safety assessment · RPAS · ARP4761 · ARP4754A

1 Introduction

One of the industrial challenges to improve the current development process is to ensure consistency between safety analyses and system design, which currently requires a very costly effort.

In the industrial practice, the use of models is often limited to a particular engineering domain, e.g. safety, mechanics, thermic. There is no pivot model shared by the different engineering teams and information is most of the time available in textual or informal graphical form. Safety engineers use models (e.g. Fault Trees) to support the validation of system architectures. These models are created from system architecture descriptions provided by system design teams and validated by reviews involving

© Springer International Publishing AG 2017
M. Bozzano and Y. Papadopoulos (Eds.): IMBSA 2017, LNCS 10437, pp. 19–34, 2017.
DOI: 10.1007/978-3-319-64119-5_2

system and safety engineers. Classical safety models (e.g. Fault Trees) are structurally far from system architecture descriptions. This makes them difficult to maintain, to update and to share with other stakeholders.

We are convinced that the generalization of models use for system architecture description on one hand and the adaptation of Model-Based Safety Analysis approach on the other hand, will bring a solution to this problem.

In this article we study the co-design of the architecture of AIDA (Aircraft Inspection by Drone Assistant) system during early conception phases and following the aeronautical development process standards. We simulate the process of exchange between system designers and safety engineers with the constraint of creating safety models as close as possible to system architecture in order to ease the common understanding of models and speeds up their validation.

The contribution of this article is twofold. First, we identify significant exchange points between the system design and safety assessment activities and show how the use of models contributes to coordinate them. Second, our experiment highlights the possibility of automating the review and exchange processes through the synchronization of architecture and safety models in order to ensure their consistency.

The remainder of this article is organized as follows: Sect. 2 presents the related work, Sect. 3 introduces the experimental framework of this study, Sect. 4 describes the activities of the architecture design team, Sect. 5 is dedicated to safety modeling, Sect. 6 discusses the coordination between safety and system design activities, Sect. 7 concludes this article and gives an overview of the foreseen perspectives.

2   Related Work

Model Based Safety Analysis (MBSA) is one of the newest modeling methods that promises to make easier the exchange of information between safety engineers and system designers. The idea is to write models in high level modeling formalism so to keep them close to the functional and physical architecture of the system under study. Several modeling languages and tools support the MBSA approach, for instance, AltaRica [3, 4, 10], Figaro [5], SAML [7], HiP-HOPS [6], AADL EMV2 [8], SOPHIA [9].

Basically, two approaches to integrate safety models with system architectures can be found in literature. The first one consists in creating a common single model, which describes the system architecture and also encompasses the safety data. To do this, the formalisms used in other system engineering domains are extended. The system model is expressed in a dedicated modeling language; and is annotated with safety data and converted into a low level formalism to perform safety analyses (e.g. Fault Tree). This approach is used in AADL, where the system architecture is described in AADL and is then extended with error model using the EMV2 annex [8]. A similar approach is proposed by the CEA-LIST, where SysML is used to define the system architecture, and SOPHIA for safety modeling and annotation [9].

The second approach consists in using two different domains specific modeling languages: the first one dedicated to the architecture description, the second one to safety analyses. The co-evolution of software architecture and Fault Tree models is studied in [17]. An interesting approach to synchronize system and safety models is proposed in [16].

In this study we focus on the synchronization of system development and safety assessment processes from an industrial perspective.

3 Experimental Framework

3.1 Studied System: The AIDA (Aircraft Inspection by Drone Assistant) System

The studied system is a Remotely Piloted Aircraft System (RPAS). The system is composed of a quadcopter drone, a control computer and a remote control. The mission of this system is to help the pilot to inspect the aircraft before flight. The quadcopter drone can be piloted in automated or manual mode. In manual mode, the pilot guides the inspection of the aircraft by the drone. In automated mode, the drone follows a flight plan and records the video of the inspected zone.

RPAS has been chosen for this study because it is representative of a safety critical embedded system.

3.2 Industrial Development Framework

Our work purpose is to provide methodologies that are applicable to industrial developments. To do so, we position our development activities within the development processes described in the ARP4754A and ARP4761 standards [1, 2] for transport airplanes. They are unquestionable guidelines to show compliance with regulations.

Our experiment implements some of the system development processes that occur during the concept main stage, defined by the ISO 15288 [14] and ISO 24748 [15], during the architecture framing stage. This stage is dedicated to the system preliminary definition. Several architectures can be defined, assessed and compared upon several criteria such as safety, availability, system performance, price, or risk level.

Given the numerous design iterations performed during this stage, the proposed safety assessment process has to remain lightweight.

3.3 Collaborative Experiment Plan

Our study focuses on the co-design activities involving system and safety teams during the early concept stage. In practice, industrial developments require bringing together a large set of skills which are brought to projects by dedicated specialists usually organized in separated teams. That is why, in addition to MBSA specialists, our analysis also involves a system architect and a safety specialist, both of them with an industrial background.

The experiment plan of the co-design (Fig. 1) includes the following activities: Architecture definition, presented in Sect. 4.2; Functional Hazard Assessment, discussed in Sect. 5.2; Safety modeling, described in Sect. 5.3; Safety model review, presented in Sect. 6.1; Safety Analysis, given in Sect. 6.2.

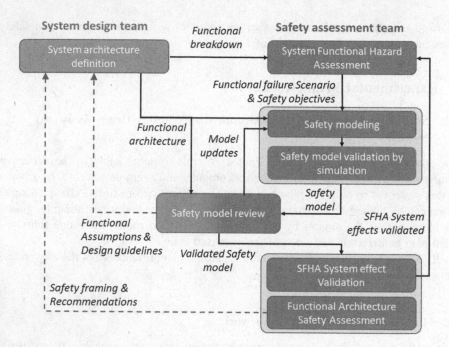

Fig. 1. Co-design of the AIDA system

Table 1. Link between AIDA activities and ARP4761 activities or guidelines

Co-design activities	System development activities from ARP 4754A
System architecture definition	Aircraft Function Development; Allocation of Aircraft Functions to systems; Development of System Architecture (Functional breakdown)
System Functional Hazard Assessment	System Functional Hazard Assessment (SFHA); Functional failure scenario and definition of safety objectives qualitative and quantitative
Co-design activities	Development process guidelines from ARP4761
Safety modeling	Provide a systematic examination of the proposed architecture to determine how failures could cause the Failure Conditions identified by the SFHA
Safety model validation by simulation, and Safety model review	Provide the necessary assurance that all relevant failure conditions have been identified and that all significant combinations of failures which could cause those failure conditions have been considered
SFHA System effects validation	Provide understanding of possible failure modes and effect of failure conditions on the aircraft, crew and occupants
Functional safety assessment	We focus on recommendation directly related with ARP guidelines: FDAL allocation constraints, potential Independence between functions, potential monitors, fail safe criteria and Common failure/faults cause failure

Fundamental interactions, including input and output synchronization between system early development processes and functional hazard safety assessments, described in ARP 4761 [2], are respected in our experiment (Fig. 1). In addition activities in the proposed experiment plan, can be directly related to ARP early development process and guidelines as shown Table 1.

4 Architecture Description

4.1 The Current Practices and Needs

System engineering challenges are numerous and very well detailed by INCOSE [12]. From an industrial perspective, System Engineering promises to solve the problems arising when developing complex systems. But, on the other hand, it is also a costly activity that requires rethinking well-established processes and organization.

Industrials cannot only rely on technical excellence in order to face the new challenges brought by the development of systems with high level of complexity and innovation. System engineering promises to assist and to coordinate development teams, to answer the customer needs and to continuously monitor and mitigate the technical risks.

To do so, system engineers and architects rely on high level abstract representations of the system of interest also named views. Those views are the material that improves the communication with all the stakeholders of the project and carries a common reference vision of the system for the development team. It is the system architect responsibility to insure the views consistency and to define the right piece of information to share with the stakeholders, including the safety analyst. This right amount of information is critical to avoid oversizing architecture description that is costly to manage.

The system team builds its architecture proposal progressively: view by view, and from abstract to detailed systemic levels. System engineers try to secure each incremental conceptual step, by validating the consistency of the whole proposal, by checking the compliance with system key requirements and by seeking feedback from other design teams. In particular, it is of main interest to assess the safety of proposed architectures as soon as possible. Safety assessment provides design safety requirements and recommendations. By taking into account this early feedback, system team expects to make wise design choices and to prevent further heavy reworks.

4.2 Architecture Modeling Activity

The proposed system model is produced by following an industrial method, which proposes to describe the system with views grouped into three main domains: operational, functional and physical.

Our experiment represents the architecture framing stage, and only a limited number of views are available: the system team has chosen to model approximately 80% of the operational architecture and 50% of the functional architecture. Detailed mission scenarios, functional behavior and functional control flow, as well as functional scenarios are not modelled. The physical architecture is not addressed, which is a recommended practice in order to leave the field of investigation opened.

The main kinds of views used for the safety assessment are the functional breakdown and the functional interaction views. The functional breakdown lists all the system functions, in a three levels hierarchy. The AIDA system contains 6 functions of level 1, 23 functions of level 2 and 59 functions of level 3.

The functional interaction views describe all the functional flows between all the functions and the system stakeholders. Several views represent each systemic level. For instance, Fig. 2 describes the functional flows between the first level functions

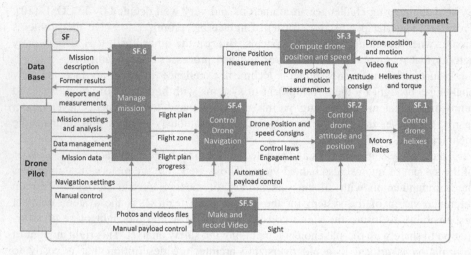

Fig. 2. AIDA upper level functional interactions view

5   Safety Modeling

5.1   The Current Practices and Needs

During early conception phases, safety analyses provide system design teams with a safety frame. This safety frame ensures that safety aspects in architecture design are identified and handled. Safety teams identify the safety critical functions and provide recommendations to ensure the architecture complies with safety objectives. This activity leads, for instance, to the addition of function segregation constraints, failure detection and isolation, recovery functions as well as safety requirements on functional behavior.

Safety assessments rely on a systematic examination of how functional failures cause the failure conditions identified in the System Functional Hazard Assessment (SFHA). The assessment quality requires a good understanding and representativeness of: the system definition, the interfaced systems, the environment, and the operations and operators actions with regards to their impact on safety. Note that handling efficiently design modifications and evolution tracking is a major challenge for large industrial systems. Eventually, safety analysis validation is part of the development process. During this validation, consistency with system design is usually checked by reviews. That is why safety models need to facilitate these reviews and to contain sufficient level of details and information.

In current practices, Fault Tree Analysis, which provide a graphical representation, are widely used. They fulfill all the needs previously enumerated, but at a heavy cost. For instance, modeling rework workload is an issue, as well as design evolution tracking. The chosen MBSA approach proposes an alternative, closer to the functional architecture representation. Our expectations regarding MBSA is to respond to safety current practices and needs in an economical and modular way. Moreover, MBSA guidelines are about to be introduced and detailed in the next revision of ARP4761 standard. This will allow a larger application of this modeling method in industrial developments, in particular for certification.

5.2 Functional Hazard Assessment Activity

In our experiment the SFHA is performed based on the system functional breakdown, following ARP4761 safety guidelines: functional system failure modes, also called functional failure scenarios, are identified for each function of level 2 in order to determine and classify the effects of the failure conditions on users and environment. Each functional failure scenario details the functional failure conditions effects and repercussions, the operator actions, the detection means, the high level reconfiguration and the allocated criticality. In a second time, functional failure scenarios with the same repercussions are regrouped in order to identify higher level failure conditions and related safety objectives (see Table 2).

Table 2. SFHA Failure Conditions of the AIDA system

Function failure conditions	S/R repercussion immediate effect of failure on drone, operator, people around	Detection means	Classification	FDAL
FC01: Uncontrolled drone, crash in an unauthorized area	Potentially flight in unauthorized zone leading at worst to fatalities	Visually detected by operator	CAT	B fail safe criteria
FC02: Uncontrolled drone, crash in an authorized area	Loss of drone uncontrolled in authorized area. Potentially crash on inspected aircraft	Visually detected by operator	HAZ	C
FC03: Controlled loss of drone	Loss of the capability to control drone position. Increased workload with small reduction of safety margins. End of mission	Visually detected by operator	MAJ	D
FC04: Degradation of drone control	Aircraft inspection fails. No workload increase	None	Min	E

Note: Classification and corresponding FDAL allocation, provided in Table 2, are defined following CS25.1309 [11] transport aircraft approach adapted to RPAS. For instance, catastrophic classification is allocated in case of "Multiple serious or fatal injury", "Material destruction with major impact on safety", or "critical reduction of safety margins".

5.3   Safety Modeling Activity

The entry points of safety modeling activity are system functional architecture pro-vided by the system design team and functional failure scenarios and failure conditions provided by the SFHA activity. This activity consists in two steps: the safety model creation, and the safety model validation by simulation. The result of this activity is the safety model that will be validated by the system design team.

One of the constraints for creating the safety model is to be as close as possible to the functional architecture of the AIDA system, and to represent system reconfigurations. To satisfy these constraints, we use AltaRica Data-Flow modeling language [4] and Cecilia OCAS workbench in order to create convenient graphical models.

The AltaRica model of the AIDA system is made of three parts: the functional architecture view, the reconfigurations managed by the pilot, and the observers on failure conditions and high level functions.

The first part of the model (see Fig. 3) is made by connecting components such that the model topology reflects as much as possible the functional architecture of the AIDA system, given Fig. 2. It is structured in the same way: high level functions SF1, SF2, SF3, SF4, SF5 and SF6 defined in the functional architecture and connections between them are represented in the AltaRica model.

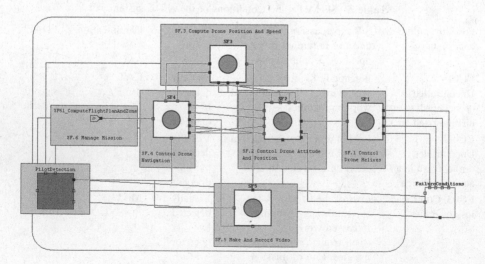

Fig. 3. AltaRica model: functional architecture view

Each basic component models a basic function with interfaces that can propagate or contain failures. The local function behavior is described by a state machine given Fig. 4. The state of the function is represented by a state variable which can take three values: OK, LOST or ERRONEOUS to account with the SFHA failure modes. The transitions between states are caused by stochastic events: `fail_loss` and `fail_error`.

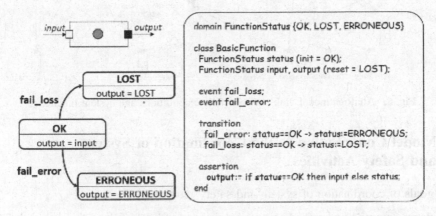

Fig. 4. AltaRica model of a basic function

The second part of the model describes the detection and reconfiguration functions performed by the pilot. For this analysis step human errors are not expected to be considered and consequently we do not introduced failure modes in the model of the pilot.

The third part makes the connection between the failure conditions, high level functions (RPAS functions) and the system functions described in the functional architecture of the AIDA system. This view, given Fig. 5, is closed to a Fault Tree. The top events of the Fault Tree represent the failure conditions FC01, FC02 and FC03 defined in the SFHA (see Table 2). The leaves of the Fault Tree are observers on variables from the functional architecture view. Intermediate events describe failures of high level functions.

The second step of the activity is the validation of the safety model by simulation. It works as follows: sequences of failure events are triggered, their propagations paths to the failure conditions are analyzed and compared by the safety engineer to the SFHA. Functional failure scenarios of the SFHA are represented by sequences of events in the AltaRica model. All of them are simulated. On one hand, it confirms that all the functional failure scenarios have been taken into account in the AltaRica model. On the other hand, it allows the verification of system effects and their severity.

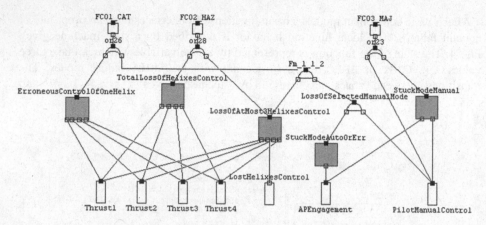

Fig. 5. AltaRica model: link between failure conditions and system functions

6   Model Contribution to the Coordination of System and Safety Activities

The goals of coordination of system and safety activities are to:

- Ensure common understanding and consistency of working hypotheses: validation of the safety model by a system designer and conversely;
- Support design with safety considerations: identification of acceptable design choices from the safety analysis.

6.1   Safety Model Review Activity

The safety model review activity is an important exchange point between system designer and safety assessment teams. The entry points of this activity are the system functional architecture and the corresponding safety model. This activity is the safety model review by the system designer. It consists in reviewing the safety model with the support of the safety engineer and in comparing it to the functional architecture. The results of this activity are multiple. First, it provides the safety model updates, i.e. remarks to take into account in order to better comply with the functional architecture of the system. The process is iterative (see Fig. 1): the safety model is updated according to the remarks of the design team, it is then validated by simulation and reviewed again by the system designer. Second, it provides missing elements and assumptions on functional and stakeholders behavior to be integrated into the next version of system architecture. Finally, at the end of iterations it provides a validated safety model to be assessed by the safety team.

AIDA system safety model review. In order to perform efficiently the safety model review, we establish a set of comparison criteria. For each function of the functional architecture the following criteria are verified:

- Representation of the function in the safety model,
- Representation of the function input and output ports in the safety model,
- The function internal failure events and their propagations to the outputs and to the other functions.

Our analysis justifies the differences found between models. The safety model has the same structure as the functional architecture. It contains: the 6 level 1 functions, 19 out of 23 level 2 functions and only 3 out of 59 level 3 functions. Only two levels of functional breakdown are considered (the same levels as in the SFHA). This abstraction level is sufficient to perform preliminary analysis of the proposed architecture. In addition, it is possible to refine the model in the next iterations. Few functions of level 2 are not represented in the safety model. Basically, functions with failure modes leading only to failure conditions of Minor severity and/or having no impact on other functions (e.g. functions used only on ground with no dependency on the flight). Three functions of level 3 are introduced to clarify dependencies between functions of level 2; all of them manage RPAS control mode.

However, to create the safety mode, assumptions are done about functional flow dependencies via connections (not provided by the functional architecture definition). The safety modeling of a function should characterize the quality of each function output depending on the quality of the functional input and the function state. Based on our experiment, functions with multiple inputs and outputs raises the following questions:

- *How to combine several inputs in function to calculate the output?* A certain number of assumptions are made by the safety assessment team to create the model. The minimal quality is propagated when several inputs are used to calculate the output.
- *How are calculated the function outputs when there are several?* Functions of level 3 are analyzed to find out the possible paths for failure propagation. In some cases it is possible to assemble together several outputs to simplify the model.
- *How are calculated the flows in case of loops between functions?* Temporal loops are not specified in the functional architecture. However, causality hypotheses are needed to analyze the failure propagation. They should be discussed with the system designer.

Compared to the system model, the safety model also contains some additional components and connections. Main information to build the pilot safety model is taken from the SFHA. For example, the safety model of the pilot represents the corrective actions following the visual detection of system failures. This detection requires some observations modeled by additional connections with system functions. The safety model also contains the view on the failure conditions and high level functions as explained earlier in Sect. 5.3.

The review activity produces a document which lists all the differences between the models, their justifications and actions to be done by safety and system design teams. The safety model may need to be updated in order to take into account the remarks of system designers. This process is iterative: the safety model is updated by the safety team, then it is reviewed by the system design team and so on, until the validation of the safety model.

Benefits of using models for the safety model review. Our experiment shows that the use of new modeling techniques for both system architecture description and safety assessment makes the review activity easier. First, it improves a common understanding. As we have seen earlier, our models are structured in the same way, the functions have the same names. To some extent both disciplines are manipulating the same objects. Second, it allows the definition of the stopping criterion for the review activity. The review is considered finished when all the functions from the functional architecture have been analyzed. Finally, it enables to establish a clear set of criteria to compare and to validate the models.

The use of MBSA models also speeds up the safety model updates. Indeed, differences between models are localized to functions. So, the safety model updates are also very local. Also, the next model review only focuses on the modified part which increases the efficiency.

Benefits of the safety model review activity. Doing the review of the safety model at this stage of the development process brings the following gains:

- It enables to identify some missing elements in the system functional architecture. In the proposed exercise, we identify the list of functions used and not used in the automated control mode and in the manual control mode and the list of functions used and not used in flight or on ground, to be able to take them into account in the analysis of failure conditions. They will be integrated into the next version of the functional architecture.
- It highlights ways to improve the functional architecture. For example, the modeling of failure propagations from the payload to the control laws function, outlines a possible design drawback.
- Several target assumptions on functional and stakeholders behavior are produced, for example, formalization of pilot actions in case of visual detection of the AIDA system loss of control.
- The review activity also allows to identify the elements of the functional architecture having critical impact on system safety in order to take them into account efficiently in the next iteration.
- Finally, it enables the safety engineers to have a feedback and an early validation of the model very soon in the development process.

Towards automation of model review. On the basis of the established comparison criteria presented earlier, it is possible to define an algorithm to automatically compare the models structure. The main constraint is to use in the AltaRica model with the same names (or prefix) of functions and input/output ports as in the functional architecture.

Let denote by $FA = (F, C)$ one hierarchical level of system functional architecture, where F is a set of functions and C is a set of connections. A function $f \in F$ is defined by its name and two sets: the set of input ports $I(f)$ and the set of output ports $O(f)$. Each input or output port is defined by its name. A connection $c \in C$ between two functions f and g is a relation between two ports of functions f and g. Let denote it by $c(i(f), o(g))$.

Let denote by $ASM = (F', C')$ one hierarchical level of the abstracted safety model, where F'' and C' are sets of functions and connections represented in the safety model.

In the AltaRica model, class instances (also called nodes) are abstracted to functions, flow variables are abstracted to input or output ports, and assertions representing the failure propagation paths between functions are abstracted to connections of the form $c'(i(f'), o(g')) \in C'$.

For each hierarchical level of system functional architecture the algorithm starts with the comparison of function sets F and F'. For each function f from F, it searches if the function with the same name (or prefix) exists in F'. If it does not exist, it reports that the function f is missing in the safety model. Otherwise, the algorithm compares the input and output ports of the functions f and f' and reports if there are missing or additional ports in the abstracted safety function f'. This comparison is done by port names. Additional functions of the safety model are also reported.

The next step of the algorithm compares the sets of connections C and C'. For each connection $c(i(f), o(g))$ from C, it searches if there is a corresponding connection $c'(i (f'), o(g'))$ in C', i.e. a connection which makes a relation between two ports with the same names. If it does not exist it reports that the connection c is missing in the safety model. It also reports if there are additional connections in the safety model.

At the end, the algorithm produces a report on missing and additional elements which would help to perform the review activity.

In fact, to be able to compare structures of models efficiently, it is of interest, to first abstract them into a pivot language. The candidate of such a pivot modeling language could be S2ML (System Structure Modeling Language) [13], which provides a small but sufficient set of constructs to structure models.

6.2 Safety Analysis Activity

The entry point of the Safety Analysis activity is the safety model validated by the system designer. The activity is performed in two steps. First, functional failure scenarios described in the SFHA are simulated in order to check their resulting failure conditions. The safety model allows to validate SFHA system effects or correct them in case of discrepancy. It also allows to identify safety impacts of functional dependences. As an example consider the following functional failure scenario: *"Loss of the capability to make and record video"*, which is related to the function SF5: Make and Record Video. The system safety effect in the SFHA is minor (FC04 (MIN)), but in the chosen design, video flux is used to calculate the speed in automated pilot mode. The simulation allows to detect that the *"Loss of the capability to make and record video"* leads to a MAJOR effect because it forces the pilot to switch to manual mode with additional safety constraints.

The second step of the activity is the functional architecture safety assessment. It consists in generating Minimal Cut Sets (MCS) leading to the failure conditions of severity CAT and HAZ. The MCS of order 1 and 2 are analyzed in order to provide safety framework and recommendations to the design team. An example is given in Table 3 for an order one MCS.

Table 3. Example of safety recommendations

MCS leading to FC01 (CAT)	Regulatory safety requirements	Recommendations
SF1. ControlHelix4.fail_error *"Erroneous control of helix 4"*	Single functional failure leading to FC01 => FDALA	No hardware single failure
	Two independent functions leading to FC01 => FDAL A + FDAL C, or FDAL B + FDAL B	System robust to erroneous control of one helix, or new monitoring function

The safety model provides the expected feedback to the system designer. The safety recommendations will be integrated to the system design and its justification.

One of the main contributions of doing safety analysis at this stage of development process is also to avoid "over-design". The idea is to start with a minimal architecture and then to add necessary monitorings, reconfigurations and redundancies, according to the recommendations of the safety assessment team. In that way, all the safety related mechanisms are clearly justified and "over-design" driven by previous experiences or habits, can be avoided. This methodology relies on the capacity of system design and safety teams to iterate quickly and efficiently through models.

7 Conclusion and Perspectives

According to the experiment plan given Fig. 1, we have identified four important exchange points between system design and safety assessment teams. The first one corresponds to the providing of system functional breakdown by the system design team to the safety assessment team in order to perform Functional Hazard Assessment. The second exchange point consists in providing the functional architecture by the system design team to the safety assessment team. The safety assessment team uses this information to create the corresponding safety model. It is an entry point of the safety modeling activity. The third exchange point is the safety model review activity. It produces useful feedback for both safety and system design teams: safety model updates and functional assumptions and design guidelines. The fourth exchange point is the safety recommendations provided to the system design team after the model analysis.

Our experiment has shown that the use of new modeling techniques from an industrial perspective for safety and system design supports efficiently exchange between safety and design teams in early design phases because the perimeter of the exchange data is clearly identified. It makes the safety model review easier, improves the common understanding and speeds up the safety model update. It is worth to note that used safety and functional models have both commonalities and differences. Commonalities speed up understanding exchange between safety and design teams that is a must in early design phases. Differences are also necessary to avoid the overload of system model, whilst keeping an efficient safety model that provides useful feedback.

Our experiment has proved that the functional architecture view provided by the system team is necessary to frame most of the safety model. It has also shown that a view describing the system functional modes would greatly improve the system understanding by the safety engineer.

Moreover, our experiment highlights the possibility for automating the review and exchange process. Further work will consider the synchronization of architecture and safety models to ensure the consistency between them.

The experiment has been carried out for one architecture version. It is also interesting to study how the proposed process will support an incremental design.

Finally, we intend to continue our work and to propose another process for the safety assessment of a physical architecture based on the updated and extended architecture views, supported by a safety model. One of our main challenges will be to increase the efficiency of this new process by benefitting from the models and results that we have obtained at functional level.

This study is based on aerospace development and safety assessment processes. As a future work, it would be also interesting to study a mapping of the identified synchronization points to other engineering domains.

Acknowledgements. The authors thank all people and industrial partners involved in the MOISE project. This work is supported by the French Research Agency (ANR) and by the industrial partners of IRT Saint-Exupery Scientific Cooperation Foundation (FCS).

References

1. SAE, ARP4754A: Guidelines for development of civil aircraft and systems (2010)
2. SAE, ARP4761: Guidelines and methods for conducting the safety assessment process on civil airborne system and equipment (1996)
3. Point, G., Rauzy, A.: AltaRica: constraint automata as a description language. J. Européen des Systèmes Automatisés **33**(8–9), 1033–1052 (1999)
4. Rauzy, A.: Modes automata and their compilation into fault trees. Rcliab. Eng. Syst. Saf. **78**, 1–12 (2002)
5. Bouissou, M., Bouhadana, H., Bannelier, M., Villatte, N.: Knowledge modelling and reliability processing: presentation of the FIGARO language and associated tools. In: Proceedings of SAFECOMP 1991, Trondheim, Norway (1991)
6. Adachi, M., Papadopoulos, Y., Sharvia, S., Parker, D., Tohdo, T.: An approach to optimization of fault tolerant architectures using HiP-HOPS. Softw. Pract. Exper. **41**(11), 1303–1327 (2011)
7. Güdemann, M., Ortmeier, F.: A framework for qualitative and quantitative model-based safety analysis. In: Proceedings of HASE (2010)
8. Delange, J., Feiler, P., Gluch, D., Hudak, J.: AADL Fault Modeling and Analysis Within an ARP4761 Safety Assessment. Carnegie Mellon University, Pittsburgh (2014)
9. Cancila, D., Terrier, F., Belmonte, F., Dubois, H., Espinoza, H., Gerard, S., Cuccuru, A.: SOPHIA: a modeling language for model-based safety engineering. In: MoDELS 2009 ACES-MB Workshop Proceedings, Denver, CO, USA (2009)
10. Prosvirnova, T., Batteux, M., Brameret, P.-A., Cherfi, A., Friedlhuber, T., Roussel, J.-M., Rauzy, A.: The AltaRica 3.0 project for model-based safety assessment. In: Proceedings of IFAC Workshop on Dependable Control of Discrete Systems, York (Great Britain) (2013)

11. EASA, CS-25: Certification Specifications and Acceptable Means of Compliance for Large Aeroplanes, Amendment 12 (2012)
12. INCOSE website. http://www.incose.org/AboutSE/WhatIsSE
13. Batteux, M., Prosvirnova, T., Rauzy, A.: System Structure Modeling Language (S2ML) specification (2015)
14. ISO 15288: Systems Engineering – System Life-Cycle Processes (2015)
15. ISO 24748-2: Systems and software engineering - Life cycle management - Part 2: Guide to the application of ISO/IEC 15288 (System life cycle processes) (2011)
16. Zeller, M., Höfig, K.: INSiDER: incorporation of system and safety analysis models using a dedicated reference mode. In: Proceedings of RAMS, Tucson, AZ, pp. 1–6 (2016)
17. Getir, S., Tichy, M., van Horn, A., Grunske, L.: Co-evolution of software architecture and fault tree models: an explorative case study on a pick and place factory automation system. In: Proceedings of the 5th International Workshop on Non-functional Properties in Modeling, Miami, USA, 29 September 2013

Toward Model Synchronization Between Safety Analysis and System Architecture Design in Industrial Contexts

Anthony Legendre[1]([✉]), Agnes Lanusse[1]([✉]), and Antoine Rauzy[2]([✉])

[1] CEA, LIST, Laboratory of Model Driven Engineering for Embedded Systems,
91191 Gif-sur-Yvette, France
{anthony.legendre,agnes.lanusse}@cea.fr
[2] NTNU, S.P. Andersens veg 5, 7491 Trondheim, Norway
antoine.rauzy@ntnu.no

Abstract. Classical organization in disciplinary silos in the industry reaches its limits to manage complexity: problems are discovered too late and the lack of communication between experts prevents the early emergence of solutions. This is why it is urgent to provide new collaborative methods and ways to integrate various engineering fields, early in and all along the development cycle. In this context, we are particularly interested in the possible exchanges between two engineering fields: system architecture design and safety analysis. The questions are: how can one ensure that the parties involved are speaking about the same system? And which concepts can synchronize several engineering fields? First we present a use case: a system embedded in a helicopter. Second we present the concepts that we define to implement synchronization of models. Finally we give our feedbacks, limits and related works.

Keywords: Model based safety analysis · Models synchronization · Integration in interdisciplinary processes · Model-driven engineering · System design · Safe complex systems

1 Introduction

Engineers solicitation to assess new proposal of critical systems (particularly new architectures) in terms of safety performances is increasingly important. They are more and more asked for a fast feedback on the design choices coming from upstream stages of the development cycle, without providing them reliable or accurate sources of information. In this context, we are particularly interested in system architecture design and safety analysis that play major roles in a critical system development.

Mathematical framework are the core of risk and safety assessments since the beginning of the discipline with dedicated artifacts such as fault tree, event tree, markov chain and the like. However, such models are still poorly connected with design models. Indeed, analysis started from paper documentation

© Springer International Publishing AG 2017
M. Bozzano and Y. Papadopoulos (Eds.): IMBSA 2017, LNCS 10437, pp. 35–49, 2017.
DOI: 10.1007/978-3-319-64119-5_3

(issued by others disciplines). Information was captured manually into dedicated safety analysis tools and/or spreadsheets. This era of document based safety assessment is now leaving the way to MBSA (Model-Based Safety Assessment) where information on the architectures and behaviors of the system come from various models and contexts, especially from system design models. This observation could be generalized on major disciplines of engineering. They virtualize their contents to a large extent, i.e. they are designing models. This is the era of model-based. Currently, the design/production/operation/decommissioning involves the design of dozens if not hundreds of models. Models are designed by different teams in different languages at different levels of abstraction, for different purposes. They are strongly linked to various activities implied by processes. Complexity impacts not only these products but also the processes involved in modeling tasks.

Today, relations between models and activities are not clearly formalized. Often done manually, interactions are time consuming and error prone. It may introduce mistakes by misinterpretation of models produced by different disciplines. This can bias the becoming system. This way of proceeding is risky and more and more difficult to deal with as complexity increases. No effective means are deployed to ensure consistency between these engineering fields. Indeed, although there is a great expertise in the Model Driven Engineering (MDE) community, its generalization to the whole industry is still a huge challenge.

The purpose of this paper is to present the results of a reflexion on the concepts, practices and recommendations that are useful to implement synchronization of models in an actual industrial context. This work is focused on Safety Analysis and Assessment issues and their synchronization with Architecture Design. In this paper, we present an industrial case study: a fire detection system embedded in a fighting helicopter in Sect. 3. Then, we present the concepts that we use to support our methodology: environment of synchronization, the configuration and applications of models synchronization in Sect. 4. In particular, we introduce the notion of need of exchange and point of synchronization that permit to identify and specify relations between models. Finally, we give our results, feedbacks and limits on this approach and quote some related works in Sect. 5.

2   Related Work

The context of this work is intended to support systems engineering where global views of systems is required and where interplay of different fields is important to capture and order requirements corresponding to multi-objective concerns. It also targets the elaboration of consistent solution in an incremental and cooperative way.

To carry MBSA approaches in accordance with MBSE, researchers explored several clues. Some are trying to incorporate safety properties on system architecture viewpoints [13]. Others attempt to add safety properties on the architecture models to drive safety analysis [7,22]. Technologies are based on properties annotations (profile for SysML [15], Error annex for AADL [8] or EAST-ADL [3,5]). These approaches may be criticized because they consider only oriented relations from system architecture design to safety analysis. Most of the works are strongly tool oriented, and not enough cooperative.

Finally, some propose cooperative techniques (also called federative approaches) [9], that attempt to establish relationships between elements of models with different concerns. They conceptualize way to ensure consistency between heterogeneous viewpoints. They permit to build cross-concerns views, while maintaining traceability relations in order to ensure global consistency. In [21] a framework to implement synchronization links between model elements is proposed. They don't consider the needs of semantic synchronization between activities, but in the future their results could be used to support synchronization. Concerning semantic mappings we found that model weaving, as seen by [6], is an interesting approach to define dependencies between models. Many works related to ontology [2] could be profitable to support mappings and traceability as well as conflicts resolution. However, few contributions were found on both engineering fields.

In this paper, the position of the approach is a cooperative application that tries to manage models between MBSE and MBSA approaches. It supports dialog between engineering teams. It manages interfaces from several modeling contexts on different concerns to get a global cohesion. It is an iterative application that builds consistency of models used by different fields.

3 Case Study

The studied system is a fire detection system onboard a fighting helicopter. The system's mission is to detect fire events in three specific areas in the helicopter. The areas concerned are: the main engine, the secondary engine and the main rotor. This automatic fire alarm system is designed to detect the unwanted occurrence of fire by monitoring environmental changes associated with combustion. The system is intended to notify the helicopter crew and airport on ground.

This system is composed of four interconnected equipments, as shown in the Fig. 1: a set of sensors, an alert device, a power supply and fire-fighting equipment.

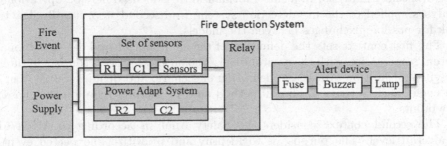

Fig. 1. Composite view of fire detection system

The case study has been considered in system architecture design and safety analysis concerns [11]. We consider the recommendation of following avionics standards: ARP 4761 [19] and ARP4754 [20] for the development and the safety assessment. In the article the fire detection system will permit to illustrate our argumentation by showing case studies focused on specific activities (illustrated by viewpoints) or sequence of activities.

4   Principles of Synchronization

Models used during an application's life-cycle are multiple and quite heterogeneous. They are strongly connected to the processes and activities achieved all along the development. Their nature depends largely on levels of abstraction, and purposes. To be able to compare them, we have chosen to rely on architectural concepts reflecting their structure. The principles proposed for synchronization are organized according to three activities:

- definition of the context and identification of the needs of exchanges,
- configuration of the synchronization,
- application of synchronization mechanisms based on: abstractions, comparison, concretization.

4.1   Definition of Context

To build a model synchronization, we first try to define the contexts that characterize the models involved according to processes and activities used in the application domain (and generally required by standards). In this section, we define concepts of business contexts modeling and apply them on the case study.

One context definition is considered for each domain. It describes processes, activities, methods and viewpoints used. In a second step, it will allow to look for possible exchanges between models according to the activities concerned in the processes.

The Fig. 2 illustrates the contexts definition stage applied on the case study. It brings out concepts allowing the structuration of processes, activities and viewpoints. In this case it represents two engineering processes (system architecture and safety analysis) in a single formalism. It is focused here on operational analyses applied to the fire detection system. In a second step, it will allow to look for possible exchanges between the models.

The first context sets the definition of the environment and the operational system's interaction with the environment. The business process consists in three activities: definition of usecase, definition of scenario and definition of system's life cycle. Each activity applies a method and the method relies on the chosen viewpoints.

The second context considers the Safety Analysis according to ARP4761 at aircraft level. The purpose is to identify and prioritize unexpected events at aircraft level. The business process consists in three activities: Preliminary

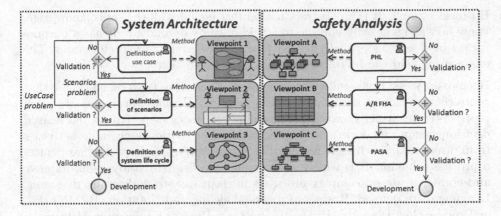

Fig. 2. Application of the definition of the context

Hazard List (PHL), Aircraft (FHA) and Preliminary Aircraft Safety Analysis (PASA). Each activity applies a method and the method relies on the chosen viewpoints.

Concepts. In this section we present definitions to describe the context of study or analysis of engineering fields. We define which engineering fields, purposes of analysis, models and elements will be able to interact with the synchronization and when ? We chose concepts as generic and as close as possible to industry terms. The definition of the context will allow, during the synchronization, to consider and manage multiple levels of abstraction, several interleaving between models used at different activities. The Fig. 3 spells out the link between each main concept and concepts from ISO42010.

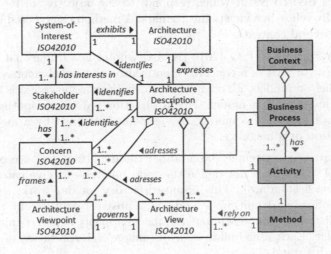

Fig. 3. Definition of the context

Business context: It is an abstract notion that includes all the skills: knowledge, know-how and soft skills specific to a field of study or analysis. It has a purpose (or set of objectives), usually to deliver a service, product or specific result. The engineering field can be considered as a business context.

Business process: It is a collection of structured activities (also called tasks), that produce a service in a specific business context. Business processes are often represented by using flowcharts containing sequences of activities, interleaved decision points and fork/join. The sequence of activities is chaining activities from directional flow line. A flowchart is a mathematical framework that depicts a process behavior. It is widely used in multiple fields to study, plan, improve and communicate on complex processes in clear, easy-to-understand diagrams. Languages are defined: Business Process Modeling and Notation (BPMN) [14], or Process Flow Diagram (PFD) [10], Software Process Engineering Metamodel (SPEM). Some are related to other diagrams, such as Data Flow Diagrams (DFDs) [18] and Activity Diagrams of UML [16]. In the case study, the chosen representation was BPMN, it supports business context, business process, activities, method and viewpoint concepts. Other formalisms have not been tested. The decision point and fork-join allows to represent a division or to group several sequences of activities according to alternative or parallel sequences (temporally or logically).

Activity: It is the application of an accurate method at a given moment in a business process. It clearly defines input and output models whose added value are measurable. Interim models may exist to represent intermediate results. Thus an activity serves a clearly defined objective (sub-purpose of business context). It is possible to consider a condition (guard) on the feasibility of the activity according to the maturity of the input and/or the accomplishment of the upstream activities.

Method: It is a logically ordered set of principles, rules, steps, which is a means of achieving a desired result which responds to the objective of its activity. A method usually relies on a viewpoint. Remark: A method can be used by different activities in several contexts.

Viewpoint: According to ISO 42010 [1], a viewpoint is a frame that shall spotlight a concern (or part of a concern) identified by the stakeholders. To do so, a viewpoint relies on models. To complete the definition, a viewpoint is an abstraction of data included in a model. This abstraction is built to spotlight specific concerns into a model. As "model", a viewpoint is defined by a metamodel, a formal definition or a language.

Model: Literature is extremely large about the definition and use of the term "model". ISO 42010 does not define the term but tries to give cases of use in the international standards. This is unsatisfactory for our work; therefore we propose the following definition: a model is an abstract capture of a practical or intended reality. Like the viewpoint, the model appeals to the cognitive faculty of the modeller. Each user builds its own (unique) interpretation of the reality and model in his mind.

In the context of system engineering, the model is an artefact. It could be characterized by two major criteria: the nature and the purpose.

The nature of a model can be defined by conceptual, mathematical, informatical (language, algorithm) or graphical (representations, structure, behavior) frameworks. The purpose of a model relies on the business context or a subset of this one. A model is defined for a specific purpose and highlights results or problems according to this purpose. We distinguish three kinds of model purposes: model to communicate, model to calculate, model to generate.

The defined concepts have been identified on the case study. It has been considered in system architecture design and safety analysis concerns. The following table lists activities conducted by the two engineering fields (Generic process for System architecture and ARP4761 for Safety program).

	System Architecture	Safety Program Plan	
Operational analysis	System environment and use case definition	Safety Analysis Level Aircraft / Helicopter	Aircraft FHA
	Definition of scenarios		PASA
Functional Architecture Design	System life cycle definition	Safety Analysis System Level	System FHA
	Functional decomposition system		PSSA
	Internal functional architecture	Safety Analysis Equipment Level	System FTA
	Functional behavior		System FMEA
Physical Architecture Design	Physical decomposition system	Commun causes analyses	Aircraft CCA
	Internal Physical architecture		System CCA
	Physical behavior of components		PRA & CMA & ZSA

Fig. 4. Activities led by both expertises for the fire detection system

From Figs. 2 or 4, we can define relationships between points of view. We call these relationships: needs of exchange because they will involve discussions on the meaning of models.

Identification of the Need of Exchanges. The identification of relations between viewpoints open four questions: What are the needs of the engineering field vis-à-vis another field? Why do they need these exchanges? When, in the business processes, do we need exchanges? What do we want to exchange (what model elements, properties)?

We define a need of exchange as a clear selection of activities in both business processes where there is a need to establish a consistency between the models. This corresponds to a formalized need to share a model by two business context which handle elements of dependent models. The needs of exchange can refine studies through the decisions taken when pooling business context across viewpoints. The need of exchanges consists in three attributes:

- The main need and personal interest of each engineering field,
- The processes, activities, methods and viewpoints involved in the exchange,
- The elements and properties which depend on this exchange.

The identified need of exchanges shall necessarily comply with the definition of the context, i.e. to answer the previous questions, engineers should use defined business processes, activities, methods and viewpoints. This step needs an important maturation of "what it really needed to exchange?".

In the case study, we tried to identify a need of exchange [12]. Around 50 needs of exchange have been identified.

4.2   Configuration of the Synchronization

The configuration consists in identifying and formalizing possible exchanges between engineering fields. This configuration will define the implementation of the synchronization using interactive methods presented in Sect. 4.3. The need of exchanges is subjective. However, it is interesting to formalize needs of exchanges into a more formal concept: the point of synchronization. This concept is consistent with the definition of context and the application of the synchronization. It considers three sub-concepts (cf. Fig. 5).

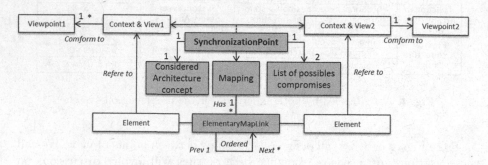

Fig. 5. Formalization of the point of synchronization

The considered architecture concepts capture part of system architecture that we want a consistency establishment. Indeed, we cannot build consistency of anything in only one try. That's why we promote the use of iterative cycles for synchronization. The points of synchronization shall respect the order of concepts in a structuring paradigm of each model. The considered architecture concepts will provide a pivot metamodel that encompasses structuring paradigms from models in each business context.

The mappings between metamodels describe the ways of transformation between each viewpoint and pivot metamodel. This spells out the dependency between elements, properties or relations of the models. We assume that the notion of "mapping" is highly bound to the principles of model to model transformation. There are as many mappings as viewpoint involved in this point of synchronization (minimum two).

The list of possible operations or compromises capitalizes a set of trade-offs that each business context could apply in case of inconsistency between elements. The operations (compromises) shall respect the purposes and rules of each business context. Generic operations can be considered as: add, modify, delete element, rename property, move element, etc.). It can also be more developed as application of pattern for example. Redundancy is probably the most popular class of patterns. In case of an application of pattern, it should consider at least one concretization by business context and selected viewpoint.

The illustration, Fig. 6, is an application of the configuration of synchronization on functional architecture of the case study. The point of synchronization intends to establish a consistency of the composition of functions at system level. This considers a composition as: considered Architecture concept, a mapping and, a set of generic operations for the both engineering fields as lists of possible compromises.

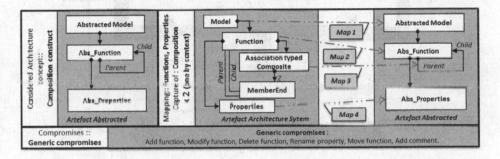

Fig. 6. Fire detection system application on point of synchronization of functional composition

4.3 Application of the Synchronization

The target synchronization must satisfy constraints which will frame the methodology (to be applied). It must maintain a separation of concerns between system architecture and safety analysis. We consider synchronization as follows:

$$\textbf{Synchronization} = \textbf{Abstraction} + \textbf{Comparison} + \textbf{Concretization}$$

Abstraction. Here we consider a pragmatic definition of abstraction. It allows to read a source model, select the information carried by this viewpoint and rewrite the information in a target viewpoint (provided a target metamodel is defined). We assume that the abstraction applies to model-to-model transformation. The notion of abstraction highlights important concepts: the information encapsulated in the target viewpoint is a subpart of the information included in the source viewpoint. Abstraction could be generalized by formal definition.

Comparison. It identifies the differences between two abstract viewpoints defined by the same metamodel. Model objects are compared two by two. An algorithm must be developed to order comparisons according to dependencies of metamodel elements. Two types of results can be obtained as outputs of the comparison: a set of consistencies and a set of inconsistencies associated with chosen operation that users decide to apply or not in their own viewpoint.

Concretization. It allows, from an existing source model, to refine it by using a more abstract model. This latter has to provide consistent properties of metamodel used by source artifact.

The Fig. 7 resumes the relation of Abstraction, Comparison and Concretization with models, viewpoint:

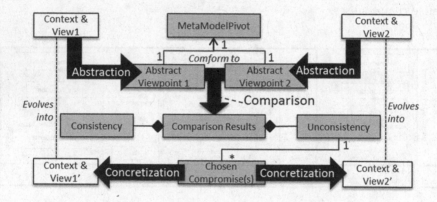

Fig. 7. Application of the synchronization

The application of the defined synchronization is an iterative and collaborative method. The method is a succession of 5 steps: verification of the consistencies from the previous synchronisation point, abstraction of the views, comparison of the abstract views, if one observes at least one inconsistency then concretization of the compromises and evolution of the views, or else validation of the consistencies of views [12].

We present in Fig. 8 an application of this synchronization method on the case study. The method is applied on two structural descriptions using dedicated modeling formalism for both business contexts.

The source views in Fig. 8 concerns the assembly of components. We consider that a previous point of synchronization has established consistency in the (hierarchical) description of the system architecture composition. The viewpoints are represented by SysML, Internal block diagram for the system architect and by S2ML [4,17] for the safety engineer. Both viewpoints capture the internal interconnection of the fire detection system but the level of refinement is different and declaration data have different level of abstraction. The application in Fig. 8 shows the viewpoints of each engineering field, the abstraction of

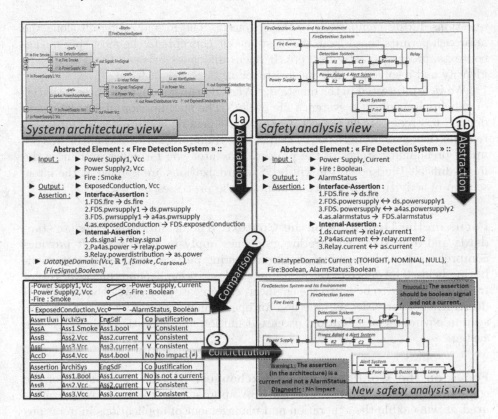

Fig. 8. Fire detection system application of synchronization on physical architecture considering assertion.

each viewpoint, the result of comparison and the concretization of operations (compromises) on the safety viewpoint. The result of the concretization step results in proposing two possible operations ("The assertion should be boolean signal and not a current" and "The assertion (in the architecture) is a current and not an AlarmStatus") to Safety engineers.

5   Lessons Learned

We present our results from the application of these concepts and propose approach on the fire detection case study. Frequent asked questions are: What is the gain in applying this approach? How are points of synchronization bound? What are the dependencies between configurations of synchronizations? Which structural concepts should bear the pivot language?

General Lessons. A main benefit of the approach is to formalize exchanges. Indeed, a clear formalization permit, in second time, to addresses precise questions during comparison to the engineers. The formalization all along the approach permits to set from the most generic concepts to the most specific, i.e. contexts, processes, activities, etc. It opens dialogues between the activities to identify and resolve possible inconsistencies.

We were interested in the question: "When do you conduct the three activities of synchronization in a system's life cycle?" The specification of contexts were defined upstream of the project. Concepts are generic and are needed for larger reasons than synchronization concerns. The configuration of exchanges was set up at preliminary stages of the project. The later you formalize exchanges the more difficult (and costly) it will be. Synchronizations are applied at the intersection of activities during deployments of the processes.

Focus on the Definition of the Context. The definitions are close to standards and from some engineering guidelines apply by enterprises. It provides comprehensive understanding of the engineering purposes and interest of neighboring fields. The depth of the environment description depends on the degree of freedom we want to be let to the engineer, e.g. on case study, we define high level description of activities and method for operational analyses by three activities: system environment definition, usecase definition and operation behavior of the system.

Focus on the Configuration of Exchanges. This is the keystone of the collaboration between MBSE and MBSA approaches. If it is correctly configured, it will enable the generation and management of applications in iterations ways. We observe two main benefits of configuration: synchronization has the best benefits when points of synchronization are very specific with appropriate scheduling.

Difficulties of collaboration rely on exchanges dependencies, according to the scheduling of iterations and architecture considerations. Constraints shall be formalized and respected to avoid missing inconsistencies. We had tried to identify content of libraries mappings, considered Architectures and lists of possible compromises to assist configuration and avoid forget concepts.

The impact of applying such synchronization at early stages brings several advantages. On the fire detection system, we noticed larger need of exchanges on precise architecture concepts at the beginning of the process. Because of their impacts on solutions, it provides huge benefits in terms of project costs and time. The point of synchronization allows the generation of the iterative applications. Relations between configuration and application are shown in Fig. 9.

The application of this stage on the case study helped us consolidate structuring constructs and operators: composition of the system, assembly of components seems to be quite appropriate to operate on system architecture description. It seems that the scheduling of exchanges is directly linked to dependencies between architecture concepts.

Application Configuration	Abstraction	Pivot Metamodel	Comparison	Concretization
Considered architecture concept	Determine the target model (pivot metamodel) of transformations	Define metamodel that capture considered architecture concept	Ordering the comparison	
Mapping	Establish abstraction transformations			Establish concretization transformation
List of possible operation			Set operations for identified inconsistency	Apply proposal in viewpoint

Fig. 9. Relation between configuration concepts and application concepts

This opens the following question: Which candidate languages are appropriate to represent pivot models? We have not tested a global pivot metamodel (or language) but only local and simple models that capture a part of the structure. This perspective shall take care of model semantics and engineering practices. It also needs more experience and feedback from industry.

Focus on the Applications of Exchanges. On fire detection system, the application steps show abilities of interaction between several concerns at adapted abstraction levels. We were able to provide the definition and internal descriptions of fire detection system from system architect to safety engineer by iterate three points of synchronization. Step by step, safety engineer has selected then enriched elements and properties. The Probabilistic safety assessment [12] has allowed to identify weakness of architecture. The applications of the synchronization had permit addressing to architect the gap and propose redundancy on specific branch of the system.

6 Conclusions

The methodology has been defined, formalized then applied manually to an industrial case. An experimental framework is under construction. It already contains possibilities of abstraction and concretization, a profile dedicated to context definitions and identifications of needs of exchange. We partially implement a first point of synchronization at operational level. This has allowed to test the feasibility and the efforts required to support the approach. A second implementation of a point of synchronization at architecture design level is underway. It encompasses system modeling with block diagrams (by SysML) and safety analyzes using AltaRica 3.0 [17] within Sophia framework [22] as an experimental test bench.

We address questions on model synchronization: "How can one ensure that the parties involved are speaking about the same system?". We propose a case study to support our argumentation. Three stages have been presented to implement synchronization: context definition, configuration and application of synchronization. This work has allowed to give feedbacks on contributions. Finally we quickly introduce the state of implement of synchronization and relate it with other contributions.

Acknowledgments. This work is part of a PhD thesis contribution funded by CEA LIST and the DGA (the French Defense Procurement Agency). This thesis is co-supervised by Agnes LANUSSE at CEA LIST (Laboratory of Model Driven Engineering for Embedded systems), and Antoine RAUZY (Supervisor). I would also like to thank APSYS for allowing the dissemination of case studies.

References

1. ISO-42010 Systems and Software Engineering - Architecture Description, December 2011
2. Arnold, P., Rahm, E.: Semantic enrichment of ontology mappings: a linguistic-based approach. In: Catania, B., Guerrini, G., Pokorný, J. (eds.) ADBIS 2013. LNCS, vol. 8133, pp. 42–55. Springer, Heidelberg (2013). doi:10.1007/978-3-642-40683-6_4
3. ATESST, Project: EAST-ADL Domain Model Specification, June 2010
4. Batteux, M., Prosvirnova, T., Rauzy, A.: System Structure Modeling Language (S2ML), hal-01234903, December 2015
5. Bozzano, M., Cimatti, A., Griggio, A., Mattarei, C.: Efficient anytime techniques for model-based safety analysis. In: Kroening, D., Păsăreanu, C.S. (eds.) CAV 2015. LNCS, vol. 9206, pp. 603–621. Springer, Cham (2015). doi:10.1007/978-3-319-21690-4_41
6. Didonet, D., Fabro, M., Bézivin, J., Jouault, F., Breton, E.: AMW: a generic model weaver. 1ère Journées sur l'Ingènierie Dirigée par les Modèles (IDM 2005), hal-00448112, pp. 105–114 (2005)
7. Fada, M., Nga, N., Choley, J.Y.: SafeSysE: a safety analysis integration in systems engineering approach. IEEE Syst. J. **10**, 1–12 (2016)
8. Feiler, P.H., Gluch, D.P., John, J.H.: The Architecture Analysis & Design Language (AADL). Software Engineering Institute, February 2006. http://resources.sei.cmu.edu/library/asset-view.cfm?AssetID=7879
9. Guychard, C., Guerin, S., Koudri, A., Beugnard, A., Dagnat, F.: Conceptual interoperability through models federation. In: Semantic Information Federation Community Workshop, Miami, United States, hal-00905036, October 2013
10. KLM: PFD process flow diagrams (project standards and specifications). http://kolmetz.com/pdf/ess/PROJECT_STANDARDS_AND_SPECIFICATIONS_process_flow_diagram_Rev1.2.pdf
11. Legendre, A., Lanusse, A., Rauzy, A.: Directions towards supporting synergies between design and probabilistic safety assessment activities: illustration on a fire detection system embedded in a helicopter. In: PSAM 2013. Korean Nuclear Society, Séoul, hal-01425309, October 2016
12. Legendre, A., Lanusse, A., Rauzy, A.: Model synchronisation between architecture system and risk analysis: which gain, how and why? In: CNRS (ed.) Conference: Congrès Lambda Mu 20 de Maîtrise des Risques et de Sûreté de Fonctionnement, Lambda Mu 20, IMdR, Saint Malo, France, hal-01425284, October 2016
13. Mauborgne, P., Deniaud, S., Levrat, E., Micaëlli, J.P., Bonjour, E., Lamothe, P., Loise, D.: Towards a safe systems engineering. INSIGHT **16**, 21–23 (2013)
14. OMG: Business Process Model and Notation (BPMN) V2.0, January 2011

15. OMG: Systems Modeling Language (OMG SysML), September 2015
16. OMG: Unified Modeling Language (OMG UML), March 2015
17. Prosvirnova, T.: AltaRica 3.0: a model-based approach for safety analyses. Thesis, Ecole Polytechnique, tel-01119730, November 2014
18. Rosziati, I., Siow Yen, Y.: Formalization of the data flow diagram rules for consistency check. Int. J. Softw. Eng. Appl. (IJSEA) **1**, 95–111 (2010)
19. SAEAerospace: ARP4761 Guidelines and Methods for Conducting the Safety Assessment Process on Civil Airborne Systems and Equipment, December 1996
20. SAEAerospace: ARP4754 Certification Considerations for Highly-Integrated or Complex Aircraft Systems, December 2010
21. Wouters, L., Kaeri, Y., Sugawara, K.: Multi-domain multi-lingual collaborative design. In: Proceedings of the 2013 IEEE 17th International Conference on Computer Supported Cooperative Work in Design (CSCWD), pp. 269–274, June 2013
22. Yakymets, N., Perin, M., Lanusse, A.: Model-driven multi-level safety analysis of critical systems. In: SysCon (ed.) 2015 9th Annual IEEE International Systems Conference, pp. 570–577. IEEE, April 2015

Model-Connected Safety Cases

Athanasios Retouniotis[✉], Yiannis Papadopoulos, Ioannis Sorokos, David Parker, Nicholas Matragkas, and Septavera Sharvia

Department of Computer Science, University of Hull, Hull HU67RX, UK
A.Retouniotis@2014.hull.ac.uk, I.Sorokos@2012.hull.ac.uk,
{Y.I.Papadopoulos,D.J.Parker,N.Matragkas,S.Sharvia}@hull.ac.uk

Abstract. We propose the concept of a model-connected safety case that could simplify certification of complex systems. System design models support the synthesis of both the structure of the safety case and the evidence that supports this structure. The resultant safety case argues that all hazards are adequately addressed through meeting the system safety requirements. This overarching claim is demonstrated via satisfaction of the integrity requirements that are assigned to subsystems and components of the system through a sound process of model-based allocation that respects the system design and follows industry standards. The safety evidence that substantiates claims is supported by evidence which is also auto-constructed from the system model. As the system model evolves during design, the corresponding model-connected safety case can be auto-updated. The approach is underpinned by a data model that connects safety argumentation and safety analysis artefacts, and is facilitated by a software tool.

Keywords: Safety case · Automation · Safety assessment · ARP4754-A

1 Introduction

Regulatory authorities have established different means to certify safety critical systems. Currently, the most common practice is a 'safety case', a document which aims to provide clear, convincing and comprehensive arguments that a system will operate acceptably safe in a given context supported by appropriate evidence [1]. The structure of the arguments is as critical as the evidence, as it illustrates the relationship between safety evidence and safety requirements as they have been set by regulators and developers [2]. To facilitate this effort, graphical notations have been developed to help improve the representation of arguments and better express compliance claims. These are the Goal Structuring Notation (GSN) [3] and the Claims-Arguments-Evidence (CAE) [4] notation. Moreover, the concept of patterns is now well-established for supporting best practice when constructing and reviewing safety cases [5].

Despite these advances, the production and maintenance of safety cases remains mostly a manual process, and safety cases are unconnected to models of the system which they represent. Additionally, the considerable size of the documents, the heavy usage of cross-referencing and the complexity of evidence required to satisfy modern standards represent a great challenge for safety case developers. As underlying systems become complex, relevant safety cases grow larger and more convoluted. Further, the

© Springer International Publishing AG 2017
M. Bozzano and Y. Papadopoulos (Eds.): IMBSA 2017, LNCS 10437, pp. 50–63, 2017.
DOI: 10.1007/978-3-319-64119-5_4

safety case should be considered a 'living document', requiring maintenance across a system's entire life span. Such maintenance requires significant effort and time reassessing the system for safety as well as validating arguments. The combined challenges mentioned above suggest automation as a potential solution. Prior research has focused on automating only fragments of the safety case, such as safety analysis techniques that provide the necessary evidence or the automatic generation of abstract arguments. Moreover, lack of tool support renders evaluation of newly introduced methodologies difficult.

This paper highlights our effort in supporting the safety case generation process via live connection to system models and automation. This approach integrates the model-based design paradigm with safety analysis methods and integrity levels allocation. The generated model-based safety cases are connected to design models and can be automatically updated in accordance with system changes as these happen during design phase and beyond. The key contributions of the paper are:

- The novel concept of integrating model-based safety analysis with safety integrity levels and user-defined safety argument patterns to automatically construct and maintain safety argument structures which are compliant with contemporary standards.
- The metamodel that underpins the operationalisation of the proposed method.

Alongside these concepts, a supporting software tool is being developed, to enable evaluation of the method through case studies. The paper focuses on the civil aviation industry, under the guidelines of ARP4754-A safety standard, though the approach is generally applicable to other safety-critical industries that centralise safety around the concept of safety integrity levels (SILs). To safeguard against hazards that arise from the development of software and electronic hardware components, which are challenging to address with traditional methods, the ARP4754-A safety standard has introduced the Development Assurance Process. This entails the notion of Development Assurance Levels (DALs), which encapsulate the level of rigour of safety assurance tasks across the system architecture. DALs are derived from the concept of SILs introduced in earlier safety standards, but are specialized for the aerospace industry. A method to optimally allocate DALs was proposed in [6], based on the decomposition rules established by the standard and a cost estimation for implementing an element of the system with a particular DAL. The method was developed as an extension to the reliability analysis method Hierarchically Performed Hazard and Origins Propagation Studies (HiP-HOPS) [7]. Earlier work illustrates how to generate preliminary safety argument structures using GSN's argument patterns [8].

The paper is organised as follows: Sect. 2 introduces the safety argument notations and the safety assessment processes under the guidelines of the ARP4754-A standard. This section also provides the essential background in safety analysis methods and related work. In Sect. 3, we describe our method for automatically constructing safety arguments with an example and provide our metamodel. In Sect. 4 we conclude and discuss benefits and limitations.

2   Background

2.1   Safety Argument Notations

There is a substantial body of work that aims to provide a structured way of constructing and representing safety arguments. The Goal Structuring Notation (GSN) originated from the University of York in the early '90s [9]. GSN aims to provide a systematic process for construction, maintenance and representation of GSN-structured arguments. Another approach is the Claims Arguments Evidence (CAE) notation, which was developed in the late '90s by Adelard, an independent specialist consultancy in the UK [4].

To represent safety arguments, GSN uses goal, strategy and solution nodes amongst other elements. CAE uses claims, arguments and evidence as its core elements. Goals or claims represent requirements, objectives, or other properties the system is argued to fulfil or intermediate inferential steps within the argument. Strategies or arguments describe the rationale that links goals or sub-goals with the corresponding evidence. Solutions or evidence are references to information usually deduced from analyses in order to support claims. These elements are rendered in the form of standardized graphical shapes (e.g. goals are represented as rectangles). The popularisation of software design patterns, most notably through [10], were adapted for use within safety cases. Specifically, GSN's argument patterns were introduced by Tim Kelly in [3] as a means to support the reuse of successful safety arguments between safety cases. Argument patterns capture and promote best practice in safety case design by dissociating the details of an argument from the context of a particular system.

2.2   Safety Assessment in Civil Aircraft

The foundation for safety assessment and the procedures for generating the appropriate evidence are provided by one or more safety standards and differ from industry to industry. Aerospace Recommended Practice (ARP) is a set of standards developed by regulatory bodies and engineers to provide generic guidelines towards the development of civil aircraft and corresponding systems. The ARP4754-A provides general guidance for the development of aircraft functions and systems. ARP4754-A has adopted the concept of Safety Integrity Levels (SILs), known as Development Assurance Levels (DALs) in the aerospace industry. DALs describe the level of rigour necessary for the safety assessment activities applied to corresponding parts of the aircraft architecture. The standard defines 5 DALs: from E (least stringent) to A (most stringent). Regulatory authorities and the standard encourage applying safety assessment in a top-down sequence to better synchronize with system development.

The standard focuses on two major architectural concepts; functions and items. Functions describe an intended high-level behaviour, such as navigation or flight control. Items define the hardware or software components that are responsible for performing said functions. Aircraft functions are typically identified at the early stages of development, during a process known as functional analysis. Failures or errors associated with functions might relate to system hazards and can be identified via a classic analysis technique known as Functional Hazard Analysis (FHA). The standard defines those associated hazards as Failure Conditions (FCs). Each FC is associated with a severity classification, ranging from No Safety Effect to Catastrophic based on the FC's effect on the aircraft and its occupants. It is important to note that the FHA is revised as soon as new functions or FCs emerge over the course of development. Following the FHA, candidate system architectures supporting functions are evaluated via the Preliminary System Safety Assessment (PSSA) and Common Cause Analysis (CCA) processes. During PSSA, aircraft or system requirements are established and appropriate DALs are assigned based on the FC severity classification from the FHA. Additionally, preliminary evidence that these architectures can meet safety requirements is provided. In CCA, physical and functional requirements are distributed across systems and validate that these have been met. Once a preliminary architecture has been established, a structured failure analysis, such as Fault Tree Analysis (FTA) [11], is conducted to determine if and how failures that can trigger FCs propagate within the architecture. Through FTA, the minimal cut sets are determined, which in the ARP4754-A are stated as Functional Failure Sets (FFSs). The FFSs contain the minimal combinations of basic failure events that are necessary and sufficient to cause a system failure (top event). In general, FFSs highlight vulnerabilities in the system design, such as single points of failure [12]. They are particularly useful for determining the appropriate DALs for systems and items during the PSSA [13]. DAL allocation is applied recursively, from higher to lower levels of the system architecture, and iteratively, following architectural changes. The process completes when the system design is determined and development proceeds with the implementation of components [14].

2.3 DAL Decomposition Rules

During the FHA process, DALs are assigned to top-level aircraft functions based on their highest FC severity classification. The allocation of DALs to systems and items is performed during the PSSA in a top-down approach across the aircraft architecture. The main concern involves cases where a combination of failures of systems, sub-systems or items leads to top-level failure conditions. Thus, to systematically assign DALs to the lower levels of architecture, the ARP4754-A supports the idea of utilizing the FFSs for DAL allocation and is referred to as DAL 'decomposition'. System safety assessment techniques, such as FTA or Markov Analysis [15], are conducted to identify the FFSs for each failure condition and the member of each FFS. Once the FFSs have been identified the ARP4754-A provides the following two rules for allocating DALs to the sub-systems.

- One of the members of the FFS that contributes to the top-level FC is assigned the same DAL with the parent system, whereas the rest of the members are assigned an equal or up to two levels lower than the top system. If the FFS of the system has only one member, then the first rule is obligatory.
- Two of the members of the FFS that contribute to the top-level FC are assigned one lower level DAL, whereas the remaining members are assigned an equal or up to two levels lower than the top system.

Even though only two options are provided for a single combination of members that lead to a system failure, the overall number of alternatives is subject to combinatorial explosion as FFS members increase and members participate across multiple FFSs.

2.4 Related Work on Automatic Construction of Safety Cases

Previous work towards automating the construction of safety cases in [16] focused on generating safety cases for automatically generated code based on formal software safety verification. The basic argument structure is generated via formal analysis of automatically generated code and is adjusted based on the set of formal requirements and assumptions. The contextual elements and other supportive information within the safety argument are derived from other verification activities. In [17], the method presented achieves safety argument construction from 'safety contracts'. These contracts encapsulate arguments of safety properties for commercial off-the-shelf (COTS) software components. The authors generate such contracts from the model of a given COTS component following failure analysis via Fault Propagation and Transformation Calculus (FPTC).

The method proposed in this paper shares some similarities with the methods above; however, there are substantial differences. First, our approach can be applied from the early stages of design and requires less rigorous annotation of the system model compared to formal methods for software components. Second, our approach incorporates the widely-employed concept of SILs (DALs in this case). Last, our approach is a top-down method and our notion of reuse applies on the level of systems and components instead of exclusively to COTS software components.

Another approach that shares similarities with our method is presented in [18]. Specifically, the author integrates compositional safety analysis, allocation of safety integrity requirements, assurance case techniques and variability management into software product line engineering (SPLE) processes. Software Product Line (SPL) is a development method that enables a set of software-intensive systems, which share similar characteristics and fulfil identical purposes, to be developed from a set of core assets in a prescribed way [19]. The approach in [18] focused on providing a systematic way to reuse safety analysis and assurance case safety artefacts for SPL, whereas our method applies to a general range of products from hardware to avionics.

Earlier work in [20] has established a model, known as the 'Weaving model', supporting model-based assurance case development. The Weaving model captures dependencies and reference information across the assurance case and information models, enabling automatic argument instantiations and supporting traceability. In our approach, the model of the system is extended instead to contain all the appropriate information in the form of containers and/or properties, which are exploited for the argument structure generation.

3 Model-Based Safety Argument Construction

The reason that we believe that model-based safety cases can be auto-constructed is that modern standards seem to converge to a common pattern for arguing safety. This pattern can be found in one form or another in the automotive ISO26262, the aerospace APR 4754-A and the generic IEC61508 standard. In all these standards safety is defined as a property that is controlled from the early stages of design and is not left to emerge at the end. At the early stages of design, a process of risk analysis is recommended to establish the system safety requirements by examining the system in its environment. Once an architecture for the system is developed, then designers are asked to determine the integrity requirements of system elements that will fulfill the safety requirements of a system. The allocation should respect dependencies in the model which propagate failures and the overall procedure can be iterated as the system is refined from subsystem to component levels. With a sound process in place, it is possible to argue that a system is adequately safe because all hazards identified in the systematic risk analysis can be shown to be addressed through meeting the appropriately allocated subsystem and component integrity requirements. This means that conceptually the structure of a safety case will always have the same logical form. This above is illustrated in Fig. 1.

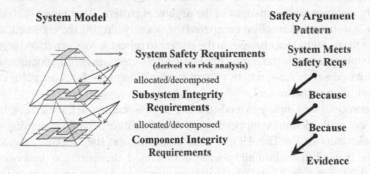

System Model

Safety Argument Pattern

System Safety Requirements
(derived via risk analysis)

allocated/decomposed

Subsystem Integrity
Requirements

allocated/decomposed

Component Integrity
Requirements

System Meets
Safety Reqs

Because

Because

Evidence

Fig. 1. Diagrammatic overview of the approach

The process illustrated in Fig. 1 is the conceptual basis for the proposed approach. The approach is operationalised by exploiting capabilities of the HiP-HOPS tool. For the aerospace sector, we build on the DAL allocation approach presented in [6].

The results of a risk analysis performed at system level can be inserted as identified hazards and safety requirements in the HiP-HOPS tool. Hazards are linked to logic that connects functional failures at the outputs of a system and requirements for avoidance are specified as DALs. A safety engineer then develops a model of the system architecture in a modeling tool (e.g. MATLAB Simulink or equivalent) and annotates systems and components with local failure behaviour information. The model is parsed by HiP-HOPS, which automatically analyses the model, produces fault trees and then calculates FFSs. This analysis helps to determine the contribution of components to system failures and provides a basis for automatically and cost-optimally allocating DALs across the system architecture. We extend this approach by automatically instantiating a safety argument pattern that corresponds to the reasoning of the standard. This enables the automatic construction of a safety argument structure.

To improve upon the benefits of HiP-HOPS methodology and its extensions, we are developing an integrated development environment (IDE). Currently, to address model changes, the user is required to introduce them and repeat file parsing across the toolchain involved to obtain the revised safety argument. Considering the vast amount of changes that can occur during a development lifecycle, significant time is spent repeating this arduous task. Additionally, version control of the model and relevant information is currently manual, exacerbating the aforementioned issues. The IDE currently being developed aims to address these inefficiencies and integrates a graphical editor with HiP-HOPS and its various extensions. For example, based on the corresponding FFSs produced by the HiP-HOPS engine, the systems and components will be automatically allocated with the appropriate DALs. With the information about the target system, the engineer is able to manually develop a suitable argument pattern to define the desired argument structure and proceed to the argument generation. As such, if a change to the system occurs, the engineer will only have to update the system model and failure behaviour, assuming the argument pattern remains suitable, the argument will be generated without further effort. On the other hand, if changes occur to the safety assurance process (i.e. an assumption becomes invalidated due to testing) the engineer will have to manually incorporate the changes in the argument pattern. That being said, the latter can require significantly less effort compared to manually altering the argument structure itself, given the potential for changes in the pattern to repeat across generated arguments. This methodology extends the notion of classic safety cases, presently document-based, to a model-based safety case, where system certification procedures are achieved automatically within a software tool.

The metamodel we employ extends the HiP-HOPS metamodel, which combines the system model with elements supporting FTA and failure behaviour annotation. Key structural elements of the HiP-HOPS metamodel are; (a) the "model", the top-level element that is used to contain all other system-related elements, (b) the systems/sub-systems, (c) the components and (d) (fault tree) events, including basic events and inter-mediate nodes. Basic events are base sources of failure, e.g. component's lack of output. Intermediate nodes propagate combined failure from other basic events, usually via Boolean logic gates. For simplicity, we present only a subset of the core elements. We extend the metamodel to support automatic generation and maintenance of safety arguments with elements similar to GSN and OMG's ARM metamodels [21]. Our metamodel is featured in Fig. 2, which illustrates inter-element relationships. On the right side of the figure, we find the system model and related elements. Integrity requirement support is found through the model, system and component elements on the right side of the figure. The center of the figure is populated by elements related to safety assessment artefacts that HiP-HOPS generates such as fault trees. On the left of the figure, safety argumentation elements such as goals and solutions are included. Both FTA and FMEA outputs are usable as safety artefacts, part of the evidence supporting the safety argument in the form of GSN solutions.

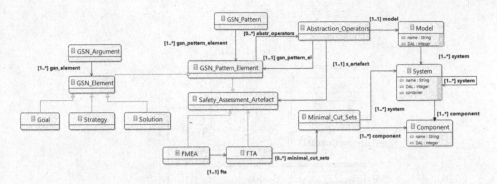

Fig. 2. Prototype of tool's metamodel

Finally, the abstraction operators suggest GSN's structural abstractions of multiplicity and optionality. The former enable sub-graphs of the argument to be applied iteratively across sets of contextual elements, whereas the latter enables the inclusion of optional strands of argumentation. Our metamodel aims to support referencing of reusable safety artefacts generated automatically by HiP-HOPS in safety cases. Towards this aim, argument patterns are linked to the system model and refer abstractly to model and safety assessment elements.

3.1 Automatic DAL Decomposition

The choice of DAL dictates the safety arguments associated with particular functions, systems or items. A brief example is provided to demonstrate how DALs are assigned onto an abstract system. In Fig. 3, the architectural model of an abstract system is presented. The system has a single output and comprises two sub-systems, which in turn include two elements each; A, B, C and D. The element in dotted lines (component E) will be added later when design changes emerge to showcase the maintainability of our approach. Logical gates define how the failure of the elements may lead to the system's functional failure. Assuming the system function has been assigned DAL A from the PSSA, following the ARP4754-A guidelines the following options for the components are available in Table 1. In this example, two FFSs occur; in FFS 1 the system function will fail if components A, C and D fail. In FFS 2, the system will fail if components B, C and D fail. The corresponding options are identical across the two FFSs. The total range of options for allocation can be formed by combining the possibilities from each FFS.

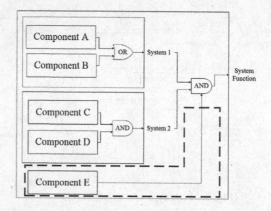

Fig. 3. Example model of an abstract System

Table 1. DAL decomposition options for components.

FFS	FFS 1		
Components	Component A	Component C	Component D
Option 1	A	C	C
Option 2	C	A	C
Option 3	C	C	A
Option 4	B	B	C
Option 5	B	C	B
Option 6	C	B	B

Furthermore, ARP4754-A explicitly states that regardless of the number of functional decompositions, it is important to apply the options that correspond to the DAL allocation of the given top-level FC (i.e. DAL A).

At this stage, we can determine the most cost-effective option by evaluating the cost of implementing each element of the architecture with the given DAL. Table 2 provides cost values for each DAL for illustrative purposes.

Table 2. Cost of DALs for the abstract system.

DAL	A	B	C	D	E
Cost	100	80	40	20	0

Adding the costs of the component DALs, we identified three groups of allocations with identical costs. For example, allocating DALs C, C, A, C to components A, B, C, D yields one optimal solution of cost 220. The simplicity of this example translates into a rather trivial solution. If we examine a system with twice as many components, then the solution would not be so apparent. The more complex a system is, the more extensive the design space of available options becomes. This renders the exhaustive search for optimal solutions into an intractable problem for systems of non-trivial scale or complexity.

The combinatorial nature of the problem rendered exhaustive techniques in [22] inadequate for large scale systems. The authors focused instead on metaheuristic techniques. Metaheuristic techniques do not guarantee optimal results, but are known to reliably achieve nearly optimal solutions. Specifically, in [6, 22] the metaheuristic method Tabu Search was adopted for its superior performance when allocating ASILs and DALs respectively. The method initiates with a random, yet feasible, solution of allocated DALs across the system architecture. Then, it iterates through the neighbouring solutions for lower cost allocations. The approach features a memory structure known as a 'Tabu Tenure'. This memory structure registers the recent allocations investigated. The recently registered states are avoided and search moves towards different areas in the design space that might hold better solutions. Finally, the use of an Aspiration Criterion allows the search to select candidate solutions that are better than Tenure's current best solution, ignoring the Tabu Tenure.

3.2 Argument Pattern Instantiation

Figure 4 features a part of the model (i.e. in Fig. 3 Sub-system 1 and its components) and the part of the argument pattern that corresponds to the derived argument structure for these elements in XML (i.e. Fig. 5 G5 and its children nodes). We instantiate the argument pattern from the bottom part of Fig. 4 using the model information from the top part of Fig. 4. The pattern is able to retrieve the information through the use of the text elements in brackets. For instance, in {S} a system is referenced defined earlier in the pattern. Properties of {S} are accessed via the "dot" operator; for instance, the

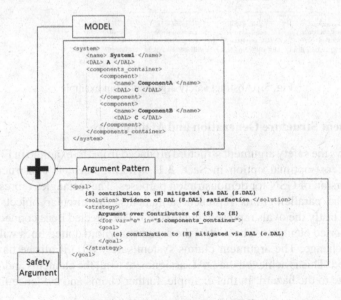

Fig. 4. Model and pattern in XML

system's DAL can be accessed this way. The "for" element pattern enables iteration over the contained elements of the system (i.e. the components). Each component is referenced through the "var" declaration in the pattern. The system's components container acts as the source of each component variable. The approach shown here can be repeated throughout the entire pattern to synthesize argument structures, which can span the entire system architecture.

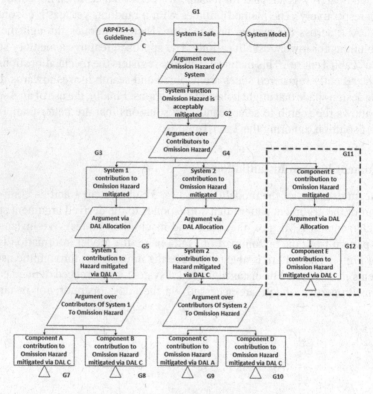

Fig. 5. Abstract safety argument from example

3.3 Argument Structure Generation and Maintenance

Figure 5 shows the safety argument structure produced from the example in Fig. 3 (based on the most cost-optimal option in Sect. 3.1). The argument is constructed with a simplified version of GSN for demonstration purposes. The rectangles represent claims (G1–G10), the parallelograms represent arguments, the circular objects represent evidence and lastly the ovals represent context (C). The directed lines connect and indicate the supported elements. The part of the argument within dotted lines will be added after design change. The argument claims system safety (G1) if all the hazards have been mitigated. This is achieved via DAL assignment to all the elements and/or systems that contribute to the hazard. In this example, further claims and evidence that support how the components satisfy the assigned DAL are left 'undeveloped' for simplicity and a triangle is placed to indicate that purpose.

Following system evaluation, the engineers may decide to change the design and add the component within the dotted lines to the system. Subsequently, a new safety argument can be constructed to claim system safety. The introduction of the new component changes the results in Table 1 by providing new allocation options.

The argument is updated based on the new most cost-effective option and claims that in addition to the sub-systems, the new component E also contributes to the mitigation of the hazard via its DAL. This option is similar to the allocation governed the argument structure initially, but now has also assigned a DAL C to the new component. Similar to the previous argument, further claims for component E (in this case, undeveloped) would normally follow. In our example, the generated argument structures are only partial and in practice would require appropriate evidence. The type of evidence is defined by the corresponding standards and aims to show that any component requirements, assumptions as well as component independence, fault propagation and fault mitigation have been met in practice. Part of the evidence comprises failure analysis, such as FTA and Failure Mode and Effects Analysis (FMEA), which are susceptible to system changes and frequent reapplication is required. Performing those analyses manually for every design change of the system during the development cycle is a time-consuming and error-prone task. However, model-based techniques such as HiP-HOPS can alleviate this burden by automating the safety assessment.

4 Conclusion

We have demonstrated construction of a safety argument structure from a system model by addressing the decomposition of integrity requirements under the ARP4754-A guidelines. The method connects the safety cases to the design model. Hence safety argument maintenance is more efficient following design changes, as demonstrated in Sect. 3. The progressive use of SILs/DALs throughout the various safety-critical domains means that our approach can be adopted and with little effort expand in those domains. To the best of our knowledge, there is not a similar approach on safety argument generation via the automatic allocations of SILs that applies on a generic array of systems and not only in software-intensive systems as presented in [18].

Currently, the tool is still under refinement while larger case studies are being developed. It is clear that the proposed method cannot create a complete safety case. The latter requires the inclusion of all the supplementary documents such as the DO-178C for software components, DO-254 for hardware components and DO-297 for integrated avionics. Additionally, it requires the incorporation of process-based arguments that provide support for justifying the confidence of the processes utilized to generate the evidence. However, our method does capture and realise a general syllogism of how to argue safety, which is compatible with many contemporary standards. The produced structure argues that the system examined is adequately safe because all hazards identified in a systematic risk analysis are addressed through meeting the appropriately determined safety requirements. This overarching claim is then demonstrated via satisfaction of the integrity requirements that are assigned to subsystems and components of the system through a sound process of model-based allocation that respects system design, dependencies, and follows industry standards. The argument patterns are one of the key elements in the model-connected safety cases that can be produced by this method. While the user-defined argument pattern stays the same, its instantiation changes every time a new system is considered or the model of the system under examination changes. The benefit of the approach is that changes in the structure of the safety case or the evidence supporting it can be effected in a largely automatic fashion by exploiting the connection of the safety case to the design model.

The evaluation of the method relies on case studies and well-defined criteria. Scalability is one of our main concerns which is implicitly supported by the use of argument modules, the algorithm responsible for the automatic instantiation of the argument pattern and other elements that will enable iteration and recursion. Naturally, the evaluation is being supported by quantitative results, obtained by examining larger case studies with our tool.

Given that the proposed approach can only generate part of the structure and evidence one can expect to find in a typical safety case, it is envisioned that the method will be part of a safety case approach in which some parts of the safety case are manually defined while other parts are connected to design models and are auto-updated as these models evolve.

Acknowledgments. This work was partly funded by the DEIS H2020 project (Grant Agreement 732242).

References

1. Kelly, T.P.: A Systematic Approach to Safety Case Management. SAE International (2003)
2. Kelly, T.P., Weaver, R.: The goal structuring notation – a safety argument notation. In: Proceedings of Dependable Systems and Networks, Workshop on Assurance Cases (2004)
3. Kelly, T.P.: Arguing safety – a systematic approach to managing safety cases. Thesis, University of York (1998
4. Bishop, P., Bloomfield, R.: A methodology for safety case development. In: Proceedings of the Sixth Safety-Critical Systems Symposium on Industrial Perspectives of Safety-Critical Systems, Birmingham, UK (1998)
5. Hawkins, R., Clegg, K., Alexander, R., Kelly, T.: Using a software safety argument pattern catalogue: two case studies. In: Flammini, F., Bologna, S., Vittorini, V. (eds.) SAFECOMP 2011. LNCS, vol. 6894, pp. 185–198. Springer, Heidelberg (2011). doi: 10.1007/978-3-642-24270-0_14
6. Sorokos, I., Papadopoulos, Y., Azevedo, L., Parker, D., Walker, M.: Automating allocation of development assurance levels an extension to HiP-HOPS. In: Lopez-Mellado, E., Ramirez-Trevino, A., Lefebvre, D., Ortmeier, F. (eds.) 5th IFAC International Workshop on Dependable Control of Discrete Systems – DCDS (2015). IFAC-PapersOnLine 48(7), 9–14
7. Papadopoulos, Y., Walker, M., Parker, D., Rude, E., Rainer, H., Uhlig, A., Lien, R.: Engineering failure analysis and design optimisation with HiP-HOPS. In: Gagg, C., Clegg, R. (eds.) The Fourth International Conference on Engineering Failure Analysis, Part 1 (2011). Eng. Fail. Anal. 18(2), 590–608

8. Sorokos, I., Papadopoulos, Y., Bottaci, L.: Maintaining safety arguments via automatic allocation of safety requirements. In: Emmanouilidis, C., Iung, B., Macchi, M., Peres, F. (eds.) 3rd IFAC Workshop on Advanced Maintenance Engineering, Services and Technology, AMEST, Biarritz, France (2016). IFAC-PapersOnLine **49**(28), 25–30
9. Origin Consulting (York) Limited: GSN Community Standard Version 1 (2011)
10. Gamma, E., Helm, R., Johnson, R., Vlissides, J.: Design Patterns: Elements of Reusable Object-Oriented Software. Addison-Wesley Professional, Boston (1994)
11. Vesely, W., Goldberg, F., Roberts, N.: Fault Tree Handbook. Nuclear Regulatory Commision, Washington, DC (1981)
12. Vesely, W., Dugan, J., Fragola, J., Minarick, J., Railsback, J., Stamatelatos, M.: Fault Tree Handbook with Aerospace Applications. NASA Office of Safety and Mission Assurance, Washington, DC (2002)
13. ARP4754-A: Guidelines for Development of Civil Aircraft and Systems. SAE Aerospace (2010)
14. Joshi, A., Heimdahl, M., Miller, S., Whalen, M.: Model-Based Safety Analysis. NASA Langley Research Center, Hampton (2006)
15. Fuqua, N.: The applicability of markov analysis methods to reliability, maintainability, and safety. In: Start, vol 10, no. 2 (2003)
16. Basir, N., Denney, E., Fischer, B.: Building heterogeneous safety cases for automatically generated code. In: AIAA Infotech@Aerospace Conference (2011)
17. Sljivo, I., Gallina, B., Carlson, J., Hansson, H., Puri, S.: A method to generate reusable safety case fragments from compositional safety analysis. In: Schaefer, I., Stamelos, I. (eds.) ICSR 2015. LNCS, vol. 8919, pp. 253–268. Springer, Cham (2014). doi:10.1007/978-3-319-14130-5_18
18. Oliveira, A.: A model-based approach to support the systematic reuse and generation of safety artefacts in safety-critical software product line engineering. Thesis, Instituto de Ciencias Matematicas e de Computacao (2016)
19. Clements, P., Northrop, L.: Software Product Lines: Practices and Patterns. Addison-Wesley, Boston (2001)
20. Hawkins, R., Habli, I., Kolovos, D., Paige, R., Kelly, T.: Weaving an assurance case from design: a model-based approach. In: 16th IEEE International Symposium on High Assurance Systems Engineering, pp. 110–117 (2015)
21. Object Management Group (OMG): Structured Assurance Case Metamodel (SACM), Version 2.0 (2016)
22. Azevedo, L., Parker, D., Walker, M., Esteves, A.: Assisted Assignment of Automotive Safety Requirements. IEEE Softw. **31**(1), 62–68 (2014)

Safety Models and Languages

Performing Safety Analyses with AADL and AltaRica

Julien Brunel[1], Peter Feiler[4], Jérôme Hugues[3], Bruce Lewis[5],
Tatiana Prosvirnova[2(✉)], Christel Seguin[1], and Lutz Wrage[4]

[1] ONERA, 2 Avenue Edouard Belin, 31055 Toulouse, France
{julien.brunel,christel.seguin}@onera.fr
[2] IRT Saint-Exupéry, 118 Route de Narbonne, 31432 Toulouse, France
tatiana.prosvirnova@irt-saintexupery.com
[3] ISAE SUPAERO, 10 Avenue Edouard Belin, 31055 Toulouse, France
jerome.hugues@isae-supaero.fr
[4] Software Engineering Institute, Carnegie Mellon University, 4500 Fifth Ave,
Pittsburgh, PA 15213, USA
{phf,lwrage}@sei.cmu.edu
[5] US Army, AMRDEC, Huntsville, AL 35898, USA
bruce.a.lewis.civ@mail.mil

Abstract. AADL and AltaRica languages can be used to support the
safety assessments of system architectures. These languages were defined
with different concerns and this paper aims at presenting their principles
and how they can be related. A translator from AADL to AltaRica is
proposed and its prototype is applied to a simplified flight control system
of a UAV. The resulting AltaRica model has been analyzed with the
AltaRica safety tools and the experimental results are discussed.

Keywords: AADL · AltaRica · MBSA · Safety patterns

1 Introduction

The interest of industrial community in Model-Based System Engineering
(MBSE) and Model-Based Safety Assessment (MBSA) is gradually increasing.
In this paper we consider two modeling languages: AADL and AltaRica.

AADL (Architecture Analysis and Design Language) is a multi-concerns
modeling language dedicated to distributed real-time embedded systems [11].
It proposes several annexes to describe embedded systems behavior. The AADL
Error Model V2 (EMV2) [6] is an error annex focused on Safety Analyses. It
offers a terminology and an ontology to capture key features of failure/error
propagations.

AltaRica [2,8] is a high level modeling language dedicated to Safety Analyses.
Its formal semantics allowed the development of a set of efficient assessment
tools, such as compilers to Fault Trees [9,10] and Markov chains, stochastic
and stepwise simulators. It is in the core of several commercially distributed

© Springer International Publishing AG 2017
M. Bozzano and Y. Papadopoulos (Eds.): IMBSA 2017, LNCS 10437, pp. 67–81, 2017.
DOI: 10.1007/978-3-319-64119-5_5

integrated modeling and simulation environments and has been successfully used to perform industrial scale experiments [1].

In this article we study the mapping between AADL EMV2 and AltaRica concepts. To illustrate our purpose, we use as a study case a simplified flight control system of a small UAV quadcopter with a particular focus on safety mitigation architectures, also called safety patterns. The transformation of AADL EMV2 models to AltaRica is interesting because it enables us to enlarge the set of safety assessment tools for AADL and to perform cross check verifications. Indeed, to implement the transformation we use the standardized version of AltaRica Data-Flow, which is a subset of AltaRica 3.0 [8]. AltaRica 3.0 is supported by the OpenAltaRica platform, which is free of use for research and education purposes. This platform already includes a Fault Tree compiler and a stepwise simulator. A stochastic simulator and a sequence generator are currently under development.

The remainder of this article is organized as follows. Section 2 describes a simplified flight control system of a small UAV quadcopter which is used as a running example of this article. Section 3 gives an overview of AADL EMV2 concepts. Section 4 introduces the AltaRica modeling language. Section 5 explains AADL to AltaRica translation principles. Section 6 presents some analysis results of this study. Section 7 summarizes related works. Section 8 concludes this article.

2   Running Example

The case study is inspired by the flight control system of a small UAV quadcopter. We address a simplified software architecture that encompasses different significant safety patterns (Fig. 1).

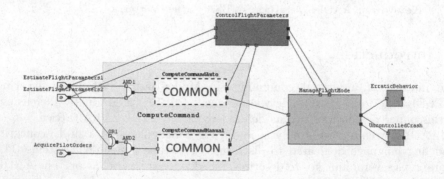

Fig. 1. Overview of the flight control software architecture

High level functional architecture. The control is achieved by three main functions. The *ComputeCommand* function aims at computing the commands to control the helixes in automated or manual mode. The function needs two different flight parameters to be performed correctly in the automated mode whereas it needs at least one flight parameter and the pilot order in the manual mode. The quality of the inputs and outputs of this function is checked by the function *ControlFlightParameters*. The function *ManageFlightMode* adapts the piloting mode and the applicable order according to the checked status.

Failure modes and failure conditions. Each function may fail and its computation may be *erroneous* or *lost*. The loss of control is not catastrophic as long as the crash is controlled in an acceptable area. The erroneous control is a worse case because the UAV may fly away and lose the separation with other aircraft or it may crash over populated area. So the system safety assessment is needed to compute the causes and probability of occurrences of such failure conditions.

In this study we consider two failure conditions:

- FC01: "Quadcopter fly away, i.e. erratic behavior, potentially fly and crash in an unauthorized area, leading at worst to fatalities".
- FC02: "Uncontrolled crash, i.e. loss of the quadcopter control".

Safety patterns. Several safety patterns are introduced to reduce the failure occurrences or their effects. A COMMON (COMmand and MONitoring) architecture is proposed to detect and mitigate the effect of potential erroneous computations.

The pattern, shown Fig. 2, works as follows. We assume that the computation is achieved in parallel by two different channels so that a computation error of one channel may be detected by comparison with the other channel. If no alarm is raised, the order computed by the command lane is applied. Otherwise, the computed order is no more selected and the order is lost.

The mode manager is proposed to adapt as long as possible the control architecture according to the integrity and availability of its basic functions. Initially, the engaged mode is the automated mode. When the check of the flight parameters detects that the automated flight is no longer safe, the manual mode is engaged. A crash mode is engaged when the manual mode is also estimated unsafe.

Modeling and Safety assessment needs. This case study is modeled using the AADL notation and the AltaRica formal language to better understand each notation and the principles of the translation of the AADL model into an AltaRica one. Then the translation is applied to produce an AltaRica model from the AADL one. AltaRica fault tree generator [9] is used for both the hand made

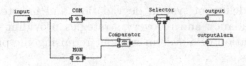

Fig. 2. Command and Monitoring pattern

AltaRica model and the generated one. The comparison of the Minimal Cut Sets for FC01 and FC02 contributes to the validation of our translation process.

3 AADL EMV2 Presentation

The SAE "Architecture Analysis and Design Language" (AADL) [11] is a language for model-based engineering of embedded real-time systems. The AADL allows for the description of both software and hardware parts of a system. It focuses on the definition of clear block interfaces, and separates the implementations from these interfaces. From the separate description of these blocks, one can build an assembly of blocks that represents the full system. To take into account the multiple ways to connect components, the AADL defines different connection patterns: subcomponent, connection, binding.

An AADL description is made of *components*. Each component category describes well-identified elements of the actual architecture, using the same vocabulary of system or software engineering. The AADL standard defines software components (`data`, `thread`, `subprogram`, `process`), execution platform components (`memory`, `bus`, `processor`, `device`, ...) and composite components (`system`, `abstract`). Besides, the language defines precise legality rules for component assemblies, and both its static and execution semantics.

The AADL defines the notion of *properties*. They model non-functional properties that can be attached to model elements (components, connections, features, instances, etc.). Properties are typed attributes that specify constraints or characteristics that apply to the elements of the architecture such as clock frequency of a processor, execution time of a thread, bandwidth of a bus, implementation of the functional part.

From this core of elements, AADL allows the designer to attach annex elements that further refine one dimension of the system. The Error Modeling Annex V2 (EMV2) addresses safety modeling concerns. See [6] for more details.

EMV2 supports architecture fault modeling at three levels of abstraction:

- Focus on error propagation between system components and with the environment: modeling of fault sources, along with their impact through propagation. It allows for safety analysis in the form of hazard identification, fault impact analysis, and stochastic fault analysis.
- Focus on component faults, failure modes, and fault handling: fault occurrences within a component, resulting fault behavior in terms of failure modes, effects on other components, the effect of incoming propagations on the component, and the ability of the component to recover or be repaired.
  It allows for modeling of system degradation and fail-stop behavior, specification of redundancy and recovery strategies providing an abstract error behavior specification of a system without requiring the presence of subsystem specifications.
- Focus on compositional abstraction of system error behavior in terms of its subsystems.

In addition, EMV2 introduces the concept of error type to characterize faults, failures and propagations. It includes a set of predefined error types as starting point for systematic identification of different types of error propagations providing an error propagation ontology. Users can adapt and extend this ontology to specific domains.

As an illustration consider an AADL EMV2 model given below. It represents a function with an input and an output. It may be in three states: *s_Ok*, *s_Erroneous* and *s_Lost*, representing respectively the nominal behavior, the erroneous behavior and the loss of the function. If the function is in the state *s_Ok* and it receives an error on its input, it propagates it on the output. If the function is in the state *s_Erroneous* it propagates an error on its output and so on.

```
abstract BasicInOutFunction
  features
    input : in feature;
    output : out feature;
  annex EMV2 {**
    use types FunctionFailureModesLib;
    use behavior FunctionFailureModesLib::ErroneousLostBehavior;
    error propagations
      input  : in  propagation{BasicFunctionFailures};
      output : out propagation{BasicFunctionFailures};
    end propagations;
    component error behavior
      propagations
        s_Ok -[input]-> output;
        s_Erroneous -[]-> output{ERRONEOUS};
        s_Lost -[]-> output{LOST};
      end component;
  **};
end BasicInOutFunction;
```

EMV2 follows regular convention for the description of state transition and error propagation, $\langle initial\_state \rangle - [trigger] \rightarrow \langle error\_event \rangle$, that reads as follows: when the system is in state $\langle initial\_state \rangle$, it propagates the corresponding $\langle error\_event \rangle$. This propagation may be controlled by the *trigger*.

4   AltaRica Presentation

AltaRica is a high level formal modeling language dedicated to Safety Analyses [2]. Its Data-Flow version has been created to handle industrial scale models [4]. A number of assessment tools have been developed ([10,12]). AltaRica Data-Flow is at the core of several Modeling and Simulation tools and has been successfully used for industrial applications [1]. In 2011, an initiative was launched to standardize the syntax of AltaRica Data-Flow.

To implement the transformation of AADL to AltaRica we use the standardized version of AltaRica Data-Flow – a subset of AltaRica 3.0 [8], supported by the OpenAltaRica platform. This platform is developed by IRT SystemX and is free of use for research and education purposes. It already includes a Fault Tree compiler [9] and a stepwise simulator. Other tools are under development.

In this article we only focus on concepts of AltaRica Data-Flow illustrated using the running example. The interested reader can refer to [3] to know more about AltaRica 3.0.

Basic blocks. The following AltaRica code represents the behavior of a basic function.

```
domain BasicFunctionStatus {OK, LOST, ERRONEOUS}
class BasicFunction
  BasicFunctionStatus status (init = OK);
  event fail_loss (delay = exponential(0.001));
  event fail_error (delay = exponential(0.0005));
  transition
    fail_loss: status == OK -> status := LOST;
    fail_error: status == OK -> status := ERRONEOUS;
end
```

States: The internal state of the function is represented by means of the state variable *status*, which takes its value in the domain *BasicFunctionStatus*. So, the function can be in three states: *OK* representing the nominal behavior, *LOST* (loss of the function), and *ERRONEOUS* (erroneous behavior). The initial value of the state variable is specified by the attribute *init*.

Events: The state of the function changes under the occurrence of an event, introduced with the keyword *event*. In our example, the function has two failure events: *fail_error* (erroneous behavior), and *fail_loss* (loss of the function). A delay is associated with each event by means of the attribute *delay*. Delays of the events *fail_loss* and *fail_error* are random exponentially distributed variables.

Transitions: A transition is a triple $e : G \rightarrow P$, where e is an event, G is a Boolean expression, the so-called guard of the transition, P is an instruction, the so-called action of the transition. In the example above if the state of the function is *OK*, then two transitions are fireable: the transition labeled with the event *fail_loss* and the transition labeled with the event *fail_error*. If the delay drawn for the transition *fail_loss* is the shortest, then this transition is fired and the variable *status* is switched to *LOST*.

Flow propagations: In AltaRica the propagation of errors/failures and nominal values is done in the same way: via flow variables and assertions. The value of flow variables are recalculated after each transition firing by means of assertions. Assertions are instructions as are actions of transitions. The difference is that actions of transitions assign only state variables, while assertions assign only flow variables. Consider, for example, the following AltaRica code:

```
class BasicInOutFunction
  extends BasicFunction;
  BasicFunctionStatus input, output (reset = LOST);
  assertion
    output := if (status==OK) then input else status;
end
```

There are two flow variables: *input* and *output*, taking their values in the domain *BasicFunctionStatus*. They represent respectively the quality of the data received and sent by the function. The assertion states that if the state of the function is *OK*, then its output is equal to its input, if its state is *LOST* then its output is also *LOST*, otherwise it is *ERRONEOUS*.

Hierarchical models. In AltaRica Data-Flow components are represented by classes. Classes can be instantiated in other classes in order to create hierarchical models. Their inputs and outputs can be connected via assertions.

The Fig. 2 is a graphical view of the class *COMMONPattern*. This class contains two instances of the class *BasicInOutFunction*, named *COM* and *MON*, one instance of the class *Selector* named *selector* and one instance of the class *Comparator* named *comparator*. The *Comparator* (cf code below) and *Selector* are considered as component connectors that are free of failure modes in our case study. Other direct connections between components are represented by plane lines in the figure and by equality assertions linking input and output of connected components in the class *COMMONPattern*.

```
class Comparator
  BasicFunctionStatus input1 (reset=LOST);
  BasicFunctionStatus input2 (reset=LOST);
  Boolean alarm (reset=false);
  assertion
    alarm:= if (input1==input2) then false else true;
end
```

Flight modes and reconfigurations. Flight modes can be represented by a state variable *mode* which takes its value in the domain *FlightModeDomain*. The reconfigurations are represented by immediate transitions, introduced by the attribute delay equal to Dirac(0). They are fireable as soon as their guards are true. As an illustration consider a part of the AltaRica model representing the function *ManageFlightMode* of the running example.

```
domain FlightModeDomain{AUTO, MANUAL, CRASH, DANGER}
class ManageFlightModeFunction
  Boolean inputAlarm, inputCrashAlarm (reset = false);
  FlightModeDomain mode(init = AUTO);
  event GoToManualMode (delay = Dirac(0));
  ...
  transition
    GoToManualMode:
```

```
    (mode == AUTO) and inputAlarm and not inputCrashAlarm ->
    mode := MANUAL;
  ...
end
```

In this model, we define an immediate event *GoToManualMode* and the associated transition, which represents the reconfiguration: while in the automated mode, if the alarm is received (*inputAlarm* is true), then the transition is fired immediately and the mode is switched to manual.

5   AADL EMV2 to AltaRica Translation

Models in AADL with EMV2 and AltaRica are structurally similar so that it is possible to translate one notation into the other. On the structural side AADL components correspond to AltaRica classes. AADL subcomponents correspond to AltaRica variables whose type is an AltaRica class. Thus, given an AADL model it is possible to create an AltaRica model that exhibits the same hierarchical containment structure.

For safety analysis we are interested in the occurrence and propagation of faults throughout the analyzed system. The interface of an AADL component with regard to fault propagation is given by its error propagations as defined in the component's EMV2 annex subclause. Each of these EMV2 error propagations corresponds to an AltaRica flow variable whose domain can be derived from the set of faults that are associated with the error propagation.

Several AADL model constructs are involved in the propagation of faults from one AADL component to another. (a) Connections modeling data and control flow can propagate faults related to, for example, data validity and timing. (b) Faults that occur in an execution platform component, e.g. power loss, propagate to software components that are bound to, i.e. propagation via binding properties. (c) Additional propagations without an explicit path in the architectural model are defined in an EMV2 annex subclause, e.g. fault propagation due to heat transfer between hardware components located in close proximity. All these constructs are translated into "external" AltaRica assertions, i.e. assertions connecting flow variables from different classes.

The internal fault behavior of an AADL component is given using the AADL EMV2 *error behavior* and *component error behavior* constructs. The translation of these constructs to AltaRica proceeds as follows:

- An EMV2 *error event* describes the occurrence of an internal fault that happens in the component. Each such event is translated into an AltaRica event. The occurrence probability of an error event is given by the value of property *EMV2::OccurrenceDistribution* which is translated into a delay attribute for the AltaRica event.
- EMV2 *error states* are defined as an identifier, i.e. the state's name. All error states of an AADL component are translated into a single state variable in AltaRica. The domain of this variable is the set of symbols created from the EMV2 error state names.

– EMV2 *state transitions* are translated to AltaRica transitions. If the transition is caused by an internal fault, i.e., an error event, it is translated into an AltaRica transition that is enabled by the corresponding AltaRica event and uses the source state as the guard. The action assigns the target state to the state variable. If, on the other hand, the transition is caused by incoming fault propagations, we create an AltaRica transition that is always enabled and translate the EMV2 error condition into the guard condition. To enable this kind of transition we add an event with the attribute delay equal to $Dirac(0.0)$ (immediate event) to each AltaRica class.

EMV2 *out propagation conditions* determine the error type produced at an out propagation based on the state and an error condition involved in propagations. Each out propagation condition is translated to an *internal* AltaRica assertion that sets the value of an outgoing flow variable to the symbol representing the propagated error type.

The following two listings show a simple example in AADL, the comparator component used in the COMMON pattern, and the AltaRica code generated by the translator. It is easy to see the correspondence between the two models.

```
abstract Comparator
  features
      in1: in data port;        -- ports defined in AADL core
      in2: in data port;        -- language
      out0: out data port;
  annex EMV2 {**
    use types FailMode;
    error propagations        -- propagated errors defined in
                              -- EMV2 annex
      in1: in propagation {lost, err};
      in2: in propagation {lost, err};
      out0: out propagation {lost, err};
    end propagations;
    component error behavior   -- no error states needed
      propagations
                                -- propagated error if in1 = in2
        all -[in1{lost} and in2{lost}]-> out0{lost};
        all -[in1{err} and in2{err}]-> out0{err};
                                -- propagated error if in1 != in2
        all -[in1{noerror} and in2]-> out0{lost};
        all -[in1 and in2{noerror}]-> out0{lost};
        all -[in1{lost} and in2{err}]-> out0{lost};
        all -[in1{err} and in2{lost}]-> out0{lost};
                                -- default: no error is propagated
      end component;
  **};
end Comparator;
```

Note that in EMV2 it is not possible to compare error types with each other. For example, the Comparator class as shown in the code in Sect. 4 uses the expression *input1 == input2*. Such comparisons must be modeled in EMV2 by using several out propagations that enumerate all possible combinations of error types occurring at the two propagation points.

```
domain domain_4 {        // domain names are generated
  noerror, lost, err     // constants generated from error types
}
domain domain_5 {
  noerror, lost, err
}
class Comparator_6
  event error_propagation (delay = Dirac (0.0)); // not used
  domain_4 out0 (reset = noerror);       // initially no error
  domain_5 in2_3;
  domain_5 in1_4;
  assertion
    out0 := switch {   // all out propagation conditions
                       // aggregated into one switch statement
      case in1_4 == err and in2_3 == lost: lost
      case in1_4 == lost and in2_3 == lost: lost
      case in1_4 == lost and in2_3 == err: lost
      case in1_4 == noerror and in2_3 != noerror: lost
      case in1_4 != noerror and in2_3 == noerror: lost
      case in1_4 == err and in2_3 == err: err
      default: noerror // noerror is the default
    };
end
```

Modeling the comparison of error types as several out propagation conditions results in a somewhat unwieldy AltaRica assertion since the translator does not perform any simplification of the generated code. The assertion is equivalent to

```
out0 := if (in1_4 == in2_3) then in1_4 else lost;
```

Resolution of mismatches between AADL EMV2 and AltaRica. There are a couple of differences between AADL EMV2 and AltaRica which must be taken into account when translating between the two formalisms.

One difference concerns the way error types are defined in EMV2. In general error types can be thought of as typed tokens that propagate through an architecture. However, EMV2 error types are organized in a generalization hierarchy, and all EMV2 allows use of generalized error types wherever an error type can occur. For example, *AboveRange* is a subtype of *OutOfRange*, which is a subtype of *DetectableValueError*. The most general error in this generalization chain is the *ItemValueError*. AltaRica does not support a notion of generalization in the definition of constants used to create domains. We solve this mismatch by always replacing generalized error types with the most specific error types. For example, a *DetectableValueError* in an error propagation or condition is replaced with the most specific error types of which *DetectableValueError* is a generalization, namely *OutOfBounds*, *BelowRange*, and *AboveRange*.

Another difference is that EMV2 uses sets of error types to define error propagations and conditions, whereas AltaRica does not support a built-in notion of sets. This leads to difficulties when assigning a domain to an incoming flow variable if the flow is generated based on an AADL feature that has multiple incoming connections (fan-in). Such an AADL model is valid if the set of error types F_i at each of the connected out propagations o_i are contained in the type set at the in propagation: $\forall i \in \{1, ..., n\} F_i \subseteq E$. In general all type sets F_i may be different. To resolve this mismatch we generate multiple flow variables from an EMV2 in propagation, one per incoming connection. As the domain we use the domain generated from the error of the corresponding out propagation at the other end of the connection. This way both flow variables have the same domain as their type and can be connected using an AltaRica assertion.

Unfortunately, the 1 to n translation of in propagations to flow variables complicates the translation of error conditions on transitions and out propagation conditions. The error conditions contain atomic terms of the form $ip(C)$, with $C = \{t_1, t_2, ..., t_k\}$ a set of error types. Such a term is true if and only if one of the error types is propagated in via the in propagation ip. In the simplest case this term is translated into the following Boolean expression in AltaRica: $ip = t_1 \lor ip = t_2 \lor ... \lor ip = t_k$. When the in propagation is split into several flow variables, the resulting AltaRica expression is the disjunction of the expressions generated for each of the new flow variables, which can become long and difficult to read.

Another consequence of the 1 to n relationship between in propagations and flow variables is that the number of generated flow variables is not the same for all instances of an AADL classifier. It depends on the context in which the component is used, in particular, how it is connected to other components in the model. Therefore, it is not possible to generate the AltaRica classes based on the declarative AADL model alone. Instead, we translate each AADL component instance into an AltaRica class, potentially resulting in an AltaRica model with several classes that are identical except for identifiers. This increases the size of the AltaRica model but has not much influence on analyses of the models. As an AltaRica model is "flattened" to transform it into a guarded transition system, it is necessary to insert a full copy of a class for each class instance. This is similar to what happens during the generation of an AADL instance model, thus resulting in essentially the same guarded transition system.

AADL EMV2 also has the concept of a typed error state. This is an error state that has an error type associated with it. The error types allowed for a state are enumerated in a type set given with the error state declaration. Even though we have not included typed error states in the translation, it could be extended to generate multiple AltaRica domain constants for each typed EMV2 error state, one per declared type token.

Implementation of the translator. We have implemented the AADL EMV2 to AltaRica translator as a plugin to OSATE, the open source AADL tool environment. The translation is implemented using the Atlas Transformation Language. The source code for our translator is available on github[1], and the plugin can be installed into OSATE from our p2 repository.[2]

The current version supports a subset of AADL EMV2 sufficient for the analysis of the UAV system used in our case study. We are planning to extend that translation to include more EMV2 concepts as needed, e.g. error detections and stochastic state transitions.

6   Experiments

The automatically generated AltaRica model can be analyzed with the various tools which are provided within the OpenAltaRica platform. In particular, we can simulate the model in order to observe the effect of different failure scenarios on the overall system. We can also analyze the potential causes of the failure conditions by generating Fault Trees and Minimal Cut Sets (MCS).

Let us consider the failure condition FC02 (uncontrolled crash). The analysis returns 12 MCS presented in Fig. 3.

AcquirePilOrder.loss	CommandAuto.COMMON.COM.error
AcquirePilOrder.loss	CommandAuto.COMMON.COM.loss
AcquirePilOrder.loss	CommandAuto.COMMON.MON.error
AcquirePilOrder.loss	CommandAuto.COMMON.MON.loss
AcquirePilOrder.loss	EstimFlightParam1.loss
AcquirePilOrder.loss	EstimFlightParam2.loss
ContrlFlightParam.Alarm.loss	EstimFlightParam1.loss
ContrlFlightParam.Alarm.loss	EstimFlightParam2.loss
ContrlFlightParam.Alarm.loss	CommandAuto.COMMON.COM.error
ContrlFlightParam.Alarm.loss	CommandAuto.COMMON.COM.loss
ContrlFlightParam.Alarm.loss	CommandAuto.COMMON.MON.error
ContrlFlightParam.Alarm.loss	CommandAuto.COMMON.MON.loss

Fig. 3. Minimal cut sets for FC2: uncontrolled crash

This result fully complies with the result that we obtained with the handwritten AltaRica model of the quadcopter. As a first remark, all the MCS are of order 2. So, we can deduce that no single failure can lead to FC02. As we can see, the pilot order is of prime importance. This is not surprising since one of the main ideas behind this system is to switch from automatic mode to manual mode in case of a problem (loss of a source for the estimation of flight parameters, loss of the automatic command, ...). Once the system switches

---

[1] At http://github.com/osate/aadl2altarica.
[2] At http://aadl.info/aadl/osate/experimental.

to manual mode, if the function that acquires the pilot order also fails, then an uncontrolled crash occurs. A similar argument holds for the alarm of the function *ControlFlightParameters*, which is responsible for detecting a problem and switching to manual mode.

The same analysis has been performed for the failure condition FC01. Again, the result is similar to the result obtained from the hand-written model. For this failure condition, there are 2 MCS of order 1, which correspond to the erroneous behavior of each of the sources for the estimation of the flight parameters. This was expected since the system does not implement any mitigation for this specific failure (contrary to the loss of one source, or the erroneous behavior of the command computation).

We have obtained the same results for the handwritten and the automatically generated AltaRica models. It is a first validation step for our translator.

7   Related Work

Another translation of AADL to AltaRica, based on the definition of ontologies, has been proposed in [7].

Translations of AADL models into classical safety models exist (see e.g. [6]). It is worth noting that each type of translation takes advantage of different features of the AADL model according to the targeted safety models. For instance, the translation into a Fault Tree requires the features *composite error behavior* and *error events*. Such features describe static dependencies between failure modes of components and are well suited for the compilation into Boolean formulas. *Component error behavior* gives a more dynamic view of the failure propagation and is useful for the computation of probability of occurrences of states of Markov chains or stochastic processes. AltaRica has been designed to integrate in one formalism both static and dynamic features of the failure propagation; it supports not only the computation of the probability of occurrences of states but also the computation of sets/sequences of events leading to undesired states. So, the proposed translation should ease the analysis of reconfigurable systems with multiple modes as our flight control system.

A translation of an AADL subset into NuSMV formal language is a pioneer work to achieve more powerful safety analysis in the framework of the COMPASS project [5]. NuSMV language is close to AltaRica Data-Flow: they have similar expressive power. Several safety tools have been developed for NuSMV. However, AltaRica was designed to support safety analysis whereas NuSMV is a more general language. Specific annotations are introduced in a native NuSMV model to distinguish error concepts that should appear in a safety report. The available tools are effective [1], but the annotation process raises practical questions when mixed with AADL view. First versions of COMPASS built the annotations by asking end users to extend AADL nominal models in the COMPASS framework. It could be clearer for end users to perform the model extension in an AADL framework compliant both with the principle of the AADL Error Annex and the level of rigor requested by NuSMV as experimented in our work.

8   Conclusions

The AADL is a language that is used to describe the software and hardware architectures of system. The AADL EMV2 enables the extension of the architecture models with artefacts that are relevant to generate safety related models. For instance, Fault Trees can be generated from models extended according the principle of the EMV2. AltaRica is a formal language specifically defined to support advanced safety analysis of complex systems that integrate modes and dynamic reconfiguration on specific conditions.

We have presented an example of a simplified version of such a kind of dynamic systems and we have modeled it both in AltaRica and in the AADL as starting point. This first activity has enabled a better understanding of the philosophy of both approaches. Both languages have to deal with failure propagations inside a system architecture. In the AADL, the failure extension of a component is flexible and it enables the connexion of components that are subject to heterogeneous failure modes. As a counterpart, end users need to be quite explicit on the various cases of composition of the failure modes. In AltaRica, the connexion of component shall be compliant with stronger typing rules. So end users can less easily propagate heterogeneous failure modes. As a counterpart, the connexion is straight forward and the propagation between connected components results directly from the language semantics.

Then we have developed a translator from the AADL EMV2 into AltaRica and we have generated an AltaRica model for our case study. The manual AltaRica model and the generated one have been simulated and analyzed. They have produced the same results. This is a first encouraging validation step for our translator. Moreover, the analysis exhibits relevant sequences of causes of the undesired events for a multi-mode system. Thus the AADL model can be analyzed with latest generation of safety assessment tools.

Further works will aim at short term to more widely validate the translator and the benefit of the coupled approach. At longer term, the AADL EMV2 could be updated to ease modeling in the spirit of some interesting AltaRica features. Conversely, the flexibility of the failure type definition in AltaRica could be extended to better account for extension approach like in the AADL EMV2.

Acknowledgements. This material is based upon work funded and supported by the Department of Defense under Contract No. FA8721-05-C-0003 with Carnegie Mellon University for the operation of the Software Engineering Institute, a federally funded research and development center. [Distribution Statement A] This material has been approved for public release and unlimited distribution. Please see Copyright notice for non-US Government use and distribution. DM-0004294.

References

1. Akerlund, O., Bieber, P., Boede, E., Bozzano, M., Bretschneider, M., Castel, C., Cavallo, A., Cifaldi, M., Gauthier, J., Griffault, A., Lisagor, O., Luedtke, A., Metge, S., Papadopoulos, C., Peikenkamp, T., Sagaspe, L., Seguin, C., Trivedi, H., Valacca, L.: ISAAC, a framework for integrated safety analysis of functional, geometrical and human aspects. In: Proceedings of 3rd European Congress Embedded Real Time Software, ERTS 2006, Toulouse, France (2006)
2. Arnold, A., Griffault, A., Point, G., Rauzy, A.: The AltaRica language and its semantics. Fundamenta Informaticae **34**, 109–124 (2000)
3. Batteux, M., Prosvirnova, T., Rauzy, A.: AltaRica 3.0 specification. Technical report, AltaRica Association (2015). http://openaltarica.fr/docs/AltaRica3. 0LanguageSpecification.pdf
4. Boiteau, M., Dutuit, Y., Rauzy, A., Signoret, J.P.: The AltaRica data-flow language in use: assessment of production availability of a multistates system. Reliab. Eng. Syst. Saf. **91**, 747–755 (2006)
5. Bozzano, M., Cimatti, A., Katoen, J.P., Nguyen, V.Y., Noll, T., Roveri, M.: Safety, dependability and performance analysis of extended AADL models. Comput. J. **54**(5), 754–775 (2011). http://dx.doi.org/10.1093/comjnl/bxq024
6. Delange, J., Feiler, P.: Architecture fault modeling with the AADL error-model annex. In: 40th Euromicro Conference on Software Engineering and Advanced Applications. IEEE (2014)
7. Mokos, K., Katsaros, P., Bassiliades, N., Vassiliadis, V., Perrotin, M.: Towards compositional safety analysis via semantic representation of component failure behaviour. In: Proceedings of the 2008 Conference on Knowledge-Based Software Engineering, pp. 405–414. Amsterdam, The Netherlands (2008)
8. Prosvirnova, T., Batteux, M., Brameret, P.A., Cherfi, A., Friedlhuber, T., Roussel, J.M., Rauzy, A.: The AltaRica 3.0 project for model-based safety assessment. In: Proceedings of 4th IFAC Workshop on Dependable Control of Discrete Systems, DCDS 2013. IFAC, York, Great Britain, September 2013
9. Prosvirnova, T., Rauzy, A.: Automated generation of minimal cut sets from AltaRica 3.0 models. IJCCBS **6**(1), 50–80 (2015)
10. Rauzy, A.: Mode automata and their compilation into fault trees. Reliab. Eng. Syst. Saf. **78**, 1–12 (2002)
11. SAE: Architecture Analysis and Design Language (AADL) AS-5506B. Technical report, The Engineering Society For Advancing Mobility Land Sea Air and Space, Aerospace Information Report, Version 2.1, September 2012
12. Teichteil-Königsbuch, F., Infantes, G., Seguin, C.: Lazy forward-chaining methods for probabilistic model-checking. In: Advances in Safety, Reliability and Risk Management, pp. 318–326. Informa UK Limited, August 2011. http://dx.doi.org/10. 1201/b11433-47

Safety Analysis of a Data Center's Electrical System Using Production Trees

Walid Mokhtar Bennaceur[1]([⊠]), Leïla Kloul[1], and Antoine Rauzy[2]

[1] Laboratoire DAVID, Université de Versailles,
45, Avenue des Etats Unis, Versailles, France
{walid-mokhtar.bennaceur2,leila.kloul}@uvsq.fr
[2] Department of Production and Quality Engineering,
Nowegian University of Science and Technology, Trondheim, Norway
antoine.rauzy@ntnu.no

Abstract. In this paper, we investigate the production availability of a data center's power system using Production Trees, a new modeling methodology for availability analysis of production systems. Production Trees (PT) allow modeling the relationship between the units of a production system with a particular attention to the production levels of the units located upstream and downstream a production line. For that new modeling operators have been introduced allowing to gather or to split the flows upstream or downstream a PT. Our results include the reliability level of the power system configuration in terms of load interruption, load loss probability and related frequency indices, and the importance factor of components to identify the critical parts of the system.

1 Introduction

In information technology (IT), the emergence of social networking services, e-commerce and cloud computing has led to a rapid increase in computing and communication capabilities provided by data centers [20]. Over the last years, there has been a significant concern about the availability of services in general. For instance, in companies that heavily depend on the Internet for their operations, service outages can be very expensive, easily running into millions of dollars per hour [13]. An essential component of the data center infrastructure is the electrical power system which is responsible for providing energy to cooling and IT devices.

An electrical power system is designed to deliver power to customer loads [2]. It is a complex system consisting of components such as generators, switches, transformers and load points. A failure of one or multiple of these components can cause the failure of all the system. An enhancement of the electrical power system reliability improves the safe and reliable operation of delivering power.

Reliability studies are conducted for two purposes. First, long-term evaluations are performed to assist in system planning. Secondly, short-term evaluations assist in day to day operating decisions. Typical reliability indices used in power systems evaluation are the load interruption indices, the loss of load probability and frequency and duration indices.

© Springer International Publishing AG 2017
M. Bozzano and Y. Papadopoulos (Eds.): IMBSA 2017, LNCS 10437, pp. 82–96, 2017.
DOI: 10.1007/978-3-319-64119-5_6

In order to perform safety analysis of an electrical system, several techniques are used. They are classified in two categories: Boolean formalisms and States/Transitions formalisms [5]. Boolean techniques are the most popular, they look at the system components, critical events, and system characteristics. These techniques include Fault Tree Analysis (FTA) and Reliability Block Diagrams (RBD). They provide convenient graphical representations which is important for industrial models. However, Boolean formalisms put very strong constraints on events (failures) to be considered. All events are supposed to be statistically independent. Among other consequences, it is not possible to take into account the order in which events occur and events can occur any time, no matter the current state of the system. This problem is solved by using Dynamic Fault Trees (DFT). However, these techniques don't allow to estimate the production availability.

States/Transitions techniques are able to represent dependencies between failures. Many techniques have been proposed in the literature such as Markov Chains (MC) and Generalized Stochastic Petri Nets (GSPN) [10]. These techniques are very used to represent dynamic models. They have a convenient graphical representation but this representation becomes unreadable for large scale models and it is difficult to represent the propagation of flows. Another major limitation is the state space explosion due to the large size of the system.

These techniques take into account only the internal state of each component. However, the state of a component in an electrical system may depend also on the electrical flows (production) circulating between components. Indeed, an electrical power system is a complex system with dependence relationships. Each component's failure can affect another component or all the system. In addition, the electrical power system is a reconfigurable system. It changes its state dynamically due to redundant components. Furthermore, to satisfy load demands in the electrical power system, it is necessary to generate sufficient energy (production) and transport it to the load points, taking into account the maximum power capacity of each component in the system. This can be seen like a flow network model. One of the difficulties of these models is that the actual production level of a component depends on the production levels of components located downstream and upstream the network (production line).

In this paper, in order to analyze the electrical system reliability and production availability, we consider a new modeling methodology called Production Trees proposed in [11]. It allows modeling the relationship between the components of a system with a particular attention to the flows circulating between these components. Production Trees look like (Dynamic) Fault Trees with nodes representing components and gates that represent behaviors. A capacity flow moving from source to target component is also represented to provide a sound semantics to classical Fault Trees.

So far, Production Trees models are not tool supported. Therefore to analyze the safety of the data center's electrical power system we model using Production Trees, we implement this model using the AltaRica 3.0 modeling language [14] and use its dedicated stochastic simulator to estimate the reliability indices of the system.

This paper is structured as follows. In Sect. 2, we discuss related works. Section 3 presents the electrical power system we are interested in. Section 4 presents an overview of Production Trees. Section 5 is dedicated to modeling the electrical power system using Production Trees methodology. In Sect. 6 we discuss the Production Tree model implementation. Section 7 summarizes the obtained results. Finally, Sect. 8 concludes this article.

2   Related Works

In the last decade several model-based safety analysis of electrical systems have been carried out, however few were carried out in the context of data centers.

In [16] the Dynamic Reliability Block Diagram (DRBD) model is proposed, an extension of RBD with new blocks, which supports the reliability analysis of systems with dependence relationships. These additional blocks for modeling dependencies made the DRBD model complex. The DRBD model is automatically converted to a colored Petri net (CPN) model in order to perform behavior properties analysis, which may certify the correctness of the model [17]. But the most serious problem is that it does not take into account the maximum power capacity to evaluate adequacy.

A methodology which combines the advantages of both Stochastic Petri nets (SPN) and RBD to assess dependability in power systems is adopted in [18]. This technique is event based, and describes interactions between components, but it is impossible to take into account the order in which events occur any time. Considering RBDs as a strong mathematical modeling techniques, Failure Modes, effects, and Critically analysis (FMECA) is employed with RBD to evaluate the reliability of data center's electrical power system and provide high system availability [21]. But it is difficult to use this technique since the failure rates are particularly difficult to estimate when human performance is involved.

An approach to calculate the reliability of different topologies using SPN is presented in [12]. Continuous-time Markov chain (CTMC) models are adopted to compute the availability of data center's electrical topology in [6]. Finally a tooled approach to estimate reliability and availability of data center's power system called Mercury is presented in [7]. This tool supports RBD, SPN, CTMC and Energy Flow Model (EFM). The EFM verifies the energy flow model on the electrical power system, taking into account the power capacity that each component can provide. However, all techniques based on Petri nets in general may partly be categorized as simulation, since simulation methods often are necessary to solve the model.

One of the examples of application of graph theory in reliability is network flow reliability. The most related work is the research in [8]. The basic disadvantage of their approach is that it generates a large number of flow combinations, that is, all possible flows that satisfy the demands for all specified components simultaneously. The method thus becomes extravagant even for the small sized network.

Currently, rare are the techniques which provide an integrated approach to estimate reliability and availability of data center's power system. Production

Trees are a simple technique that describes the interactions between components of the system taking into account the maximum capacity flow. It is useful to represent dynamic model and compute different performance and safety indicators.

3   Data Center's Electrical Topology

We consider the electrical topology depicted in Fig. 1. This topology consists of two flow paths from the electric power sources to the load point, namely the server. In a normal operating mode, the server is powered by both paths.

Each path is supplied by two different power sources PS_1 and PS_2. However, if one of these power supplies fails, the power is supplied by a backup power generator (PG). Thus, initially, the generator is on standby and is only brought online after PS_1 or PS_2 becomes unavailable. Power sources provide a medium voltage, typically less than $50\,kV$. This voltage is used for distribution to two transformers Tr_1 and Tr_2, one on each flow path [9]. Transformers are used to decrease the voltage of electricity. Then, the power enters the building with low-voltage lines going to FDP_1 and FDP_2, the front low-voltage master distribution panels, to supply four uninterruptible power supply systems noted UPS_i, $i = 1, \ldots, 4$, two per path.

Typically, an UPS combines three functions in one system. First, it contains a transfer switch that chooses the active power input (either power source or generator power). After a power source failure, the transfer switch senses when the generator has started and is ready to provide power. Typically, a generator takes 10 to 15 s to start and complete the full rated load [9]. Second, the UPS contains some form of energy storage (battery) to bridge the time between the utility failure and the availability of power generator. Third, the UPS conditions the incoming power feed, removing voltage spikes in the alternating current. This conditioning is accomplished via the two components included in the UPS system (inverter and converter).

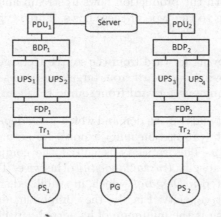

Fig. 1. A typical electrical power system of a datacenter

The output lines from the two UPS systems on each flow path are finally routed to a back low-voltage master distribution panel (BDP) installed in the datacenter floor. We note BDP_i the panel on i^{th} flow path, $i = 1, 2$. Finally, each BDP_i is connected to a power distribution unit, noted PDU_i.

The power distribution units are like the breaker panels in residential houses but can also incorporate transformers for final voltage adjustments. They take a larger input feed and break it up into many smaller circuits that distribute power to the servers. A typical PDU handles 75 to 225 kW of load [9]. PDUs are the last layer in the distribution architecture to route the power to the server or the load point.

The Uptime Institute [19] has created a classification standard of data center's power system to evaluate various facilities, in terms of performance, site infrastructure or availability. The system under study is an example of tier IV classification, since there are two redundant paths, and in each path, electrical components are redundant (in our system, only the UPSs in each path are redundant).

In the following section, we give an overview of *Production Trees*, the formalism we use to model the electrical power system in Fig. 1.

4   Production Trees

Production Trees (PT) are a new modeling methodology for production availability analysis [11]. They allow modeling the relationship between basic components of a system with a particular attention to the flows circulating between these components.

Production Trees provide two types of components to model a production system: basic components and gates. Basic components represent the production or treatment units of the system whereas the gates model the behavior of the system. Basic components are similar to basic events in Fault Trees. However, unlike the gates of Fault Trees, the gates of Production Trees are not logical. They allow dealing with the production flows upstream and downstream a production line, according to the type of these flows. Three types of flows circulate in a PT:

- A *capacity flow* moving forward from the source to target units.
- A *demand flow* moving backward from target units to source units.
- A *production flow* moving forward from source to target units.

The production depends on the demand which itself depends on the capacity. First, each component (production unit) exports its actual production capacity, noted $outCapacity$. This capacity is null if the component is failed and equal to its intrinsic capacity ($intraCapacity$) otherwise. Then, the component receives a demand, noted $inDemand$, which, in stabilized situations, should not exceed the component capacity. Finally, the component exports a production ($outProduction$), which is the minimum of its actual capacity and the demand. If the demand is null, the component is considered in standby mode. Figure 2

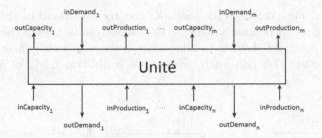

Fig. 2. Flows circulating in and out a component

shows the flows circulating in and out a component having m parents and n children.

In PT, the gates serve to permit, inhibit or modify the passage of flows. There are three types of gates: the *PLUS-gate*, the *MIN-gate* and the *SPLITTER-gate*.

1. The *MIN-gate*: This gate is a direct extension of the AND gate of FTs. The *MIN-gate* has one parent and two or more children. Its output capacity is the minimum of the output capacities of its children and of its intrinsic capacity (Eq. 1). The input demand of the gate (coming from its parent) is propagated unchanged to its children. Finally, the output production of the gate is the minimum of the output production of its children. Figure 3(a) shows the graphical representation of the *MIN-gate* with two children (n = 2).

$$outCapacity = min(outCapacity_1, \ldots, outCapacity_n, intraCapacity) \quad (1)$$

2. The *PLUS-gate*: It extends the OR gate of Fault Trees, but in a less obvious way than does the *MIN-gate* to the AND gate. The *PLUS-gate* has one parent and several children. Its output capacity is the minimum of its intrinsic capacity and the sum of the output capacities of its children as specified in Eq. 2. The input demand of the gate is propagated unchanged to its children. Finally, the output production of the gate is the sum of the output productions of its children. In the case where the output capacity of the gate is not equal to the output capacity of its children, the input demand of the gate is propagated to its children according to an allocation strategy. For example, the demand can be allocated according to a pro-rata of their capacities. Another strategy consists to allocate the maximum production to the first child, the maximum of the rest to the second child, etc. (priority). Figure 3(b) illustrates the gate with two children (n = 2).

$$outCapacity = min(\sum_{i=1}^{n} outCapacity_i, intraCapacity) \quad (2)$$

3. The *SPLITTER-gate*: Unlike the other gates, this gate has only one child and several parents. The output capacity of the *SPLITTER-gate* is the minimum of its intrinsic capacity and the output capacity of its unique child. It is

transmitted unchanged to its parents. The input demand of the gate is the sum of its parents demands. Finally, the output production of the gate is split among its parents following an allocation strategy (priority, pro-rata, ...), as for *PLUS-gate*. This gate with two parents is illustrated in Fig. 3(c).

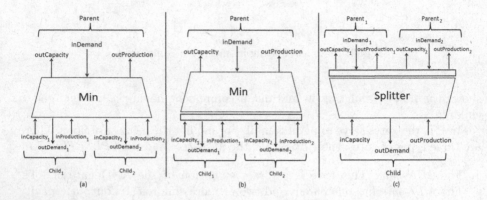

Fig. 3. Gates of Production Trees

5   Modeling the Electrical Power System Using PT

The production tree modeling the electrical power system has to catch the different interactions between the production and treatment units. Building the model goes through different steps.

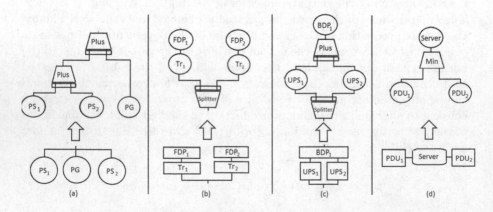

Fig. 4. Production tree of different parts of the system

Step 1: the first step is the transmission of production capacity of the power sources in the system. It starts with the treatment units just ahead in the production line, that is transformers Tr_1 and Tr_2. Thus power sources PS_1, PS_2 and power generator PG export their production capacity $outCapacity_{PS_1}$, $outCapacity_{PS_2}$ and $outCapacity_{PG}$, respectively. Since the production capacity of the electrical power system is the sum of all power supplies production capacities, these are combined using $PLUS$-$gate$ as depicted in Fig. 4(a).

Since transformers Tr_1 and Tr_2 are on two redundant paths, the second step consists in dividing the system production capacity between them. Each transformer will receive a percentage of the total capacity according to the maximum capacity it can treat (pro-rata strategy). In the PT, this is modeled using a $SPLITTER$-$gate$ as illustrated in Fig. 4(b).

In each path, the transformer is directly connected, in series, to the front low-voltage master distribution panel. Therefore there is no need for any gate between Tr_1 and FDP_1 or between Tr_2 and FDP_2.

As FDP_1 has to supply UPS_1 and UPS_2, a $SPLITTER$-$gate$ is used to dispatch the production capacity $outCapacity_{FDP_1}$ coming from FDP_1. Then both UPSs have to supply power distribution unit PDU_1 through BDP_1, the back master distribution panel in series with PDU_1. Therefore production capacities $outCapacity_{UPS_1}$ and $outCapacity_{UPS_2}$ are routed to a $PLUS$-$gate$ as illustrated in Fig. 4(c). A similar PT is used to model the second path of the system involving FDP_2, UPS_3, UPS_4 and BDP_2.

Finally, the server is supplied by two PDUs in parallel. In this case, we consider a MIN-$gate$ to model the flow from both $PDUs$ to the server since only the minimum capacity of $outCapacity_{PDU_1}$ and $outCapacity_{PDU_2}$ must be routed to the server. This is illustrated in Fig. 4(d).

Step 2: once the server has been informed about the production capacity of the power sources, it sends its power demand $outDemand_{server}$, according its needs. This demand is propagated first to all the children of the MIN-$gate$ (PDU_1, PDU_2) and then to BDP_1 and BDP_2. From each BDP, it goes through the corresponding $PLUS$-$gate$ based on priority strategy to its children (UPSs). The server demand continues its tree traversal until it reaches the power sources.

As initially, PS_1 and PS_2 are working and PG is in standby mode, if this one receives a demand, it is activated and starts working. This is modeled by $PLUS$-$gate$ based on priority strategy (gives priority to PSs).

Step 3: the third and final step is the transmission of the power production from the sources to the server. According to the demand received by each power source, the required quantity is sent to the server (bottom-up) through the gates. The complete model is presented in Fig. 5.

6 Production Tree Model Analysis

Production trees are a new modeling methodology for which there is no dedicated analysis tool yet. Therefore to analyze the production tree in Fig. 5, we

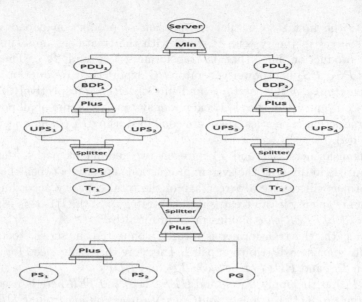

Fig. 5. PT of the electrical power system

implement it using the AltaRica 3.0 modeling language [14] and use its dedicated stochastic simulator. Using the high level language AltaRica 3.0, it is possible to design the model with a structure that is close to the functional and the physical architecture of the system under study. AltaRica 3.0 implements the prototype-oriented paradigm [14]. This paradigm fits well with the level of abstraction reliability and safety analysis standards. As for mathematical foundations, AltaRica 3.0 is based on Guarded Transition Systems (GTS) [15].

A GTS is an automaton where states are represented by variables. Changes of states are represented by transitions triggered by events. Each event is associated with a cumulative probability distribution of its delay. Variables are separated into two groups: states variables whose values are modified only in the actions of transitions and flow variables that represent flows circulating through the network. It is also possible to synchronize events in order to describe remote interactions between components of the system under study. The semantics of GTS is similar to the one of GSPN [4]. Basic components are represented by means of classes. Classes are GTSs that contain variables, events, transitions, and everything necessary to describe their behavior.

In this paper, the idea is to design a library of modeling patterns to represent basic event and gates. As all the components in the electrical power system may fail and then be repaired, the class we implement represents a repairable component that can be either working, failed or in standby. Using the hierarchical decomposition shown in Fig. 2, this class contains a Boolean state variable WORKING and three flow variables: *outCapacity*, *inDemand* and *outProduction*. The graphical representation of the GTS is presented in Fig. 6.

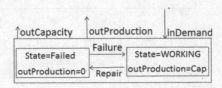

Fig. 6. GTS for a repairable component

```
class Min_gate                                  class Splitter_gate
  Line l1;                                        Line l1;
  Line l2;                                        Line l2;
  Real outCapacity (reset=0.0);                   Real inCapacity (reset=0.0);
  parameter Real Intra Capacity = 0.0;            parameter Real Intra Capacity = 0.0;
  Real outProduction (reset =0.0);                Real inProduction (reset =0.0);
  Real inDemand (reset =0.0);                     Real outDemand (reset =0.0);
  assertion                                       Real sommeCap (reset=0.0);
   outCapacity := if(l1.outFlowCap<=l2.outFlowCap  assertion
                and                                 l1.inFlowCap := if(inCapacity<=Intra Capacity)
                 l1.outFlowCap<Intra Capacity)             then inCapacity else CapacityIntra;
           then l1.outFlowCap else                  l2.inFlowCap := if(inCapacity<Intra Capacity)
   if (l2.outFlowCap<=l1.outFlowCap                          then inCapacity else Intra Capacity;
  and                                              outDemand := l1.inFlowDem + l2.inFlowDem;
 l2.outFlowCap<= Intra Capacity)                   sommeCap := l1.outFlowCap + l2.outFlowCap;
   then l2.outFlowCap else Intra Capacity;         l1.inFlowPro:=if(inProduction >= l1.outFlowDem)
     l1.inFlowDem := inDemand;                              then l1.outFlowDem else 0.0;
     l2.inFlowDem := inDemand;                     l2.inFlowPro:=if(inProduction-l1.outFlowDem>=
     outProduction:= if(l1.outFlowPro<=l2.outFlowPro                        l2.outFlowDem)
                and                                        then l2.outFlowDem else 0.0;
                 l1.outFlowPro<Intra Capacity)   end
           then l1.outFlowPro
else if(l2.outFlowPro<=l1.outFlowPro

              (a)                                                  (b)
```

Fig. 7. AltaRica class for (a) *MIN-gate* and (b) *SPLITTER_gate*

Table 1. Reliability data (per hour)

Components	Failure rate	Repair rate
PS	3.8e−8	2.35e−3
PG	3.0e−3	3.70e−3
Tr	1.8e−5	2.35e−3
BDP	3.8e−7	3.90e−3
FDP	3.8e−7	3.90e−3
PDU	1.6e−7	6.13e−3
Server	2.8e−6	1.00e−3

Table 2. Components numbering

Number	Component	Number	Component
1	PS_1	9	UPS_2
2	PS_2	10	UPS_3
3	PG	11	UPS_4
4	Tr_1	12	BDP_1
5	Tr_2	13	BDP_2
6	FDP_1	14	PDU_1
7	FDP_2	15	PDU_2
8	UPS_1	16	$Server$

Figure 8(a) provides the corresponding AltaRica class of the GTS in Fig. 6. It is assumed that the failure and repair delays of a repairable component are exponentially distributed with rates *lambda* and *mu*, respectively.

AltaRica code for the *PLUS-gate* implementing the priority allocation strategy is provided in Fig. 8(b), whereas the AltaRica code implementing the *MIN-gate* and *SPLITTER_gate* is given in Fig. 7(a) and (b), respectively. The reliability data for components are given in Table 1. The data we use are taken from [1,3]. All components extend the class *RepairableComponent*, and add to it the flow variables representing the input and output streams and the corresponding assertion.

```
domain ComponentState{WORKING,FAILED,SHORTAGE}      class PLUS_gate
class RepairableComponent                            Line 11;
ComponentState s (init = WORKING);                    Line 12;
parameter Real Intra Capacity = 0.0;                 Real outCapacity (reset=0.0);
Real outCapacity (reset=0.0);                         parameter Real Intra Capacity = 0.0;
Real inDemand (reset=0.0);                            Real outProduction (reset =0.0);
Real outProduction (reset =0.0);                      Real inDemand (reset =0.0);
Real inProduction (reset =0.0);                       Real sommeCap (reset=0.0);
Real outDemand (reset =0.0);                          Real sommePro (reset=0.0);
Real inCapacity (reset =0.0);
parameter Real lambda = 0.0005;                       assertion
parameter Real mu = 0.02;                              sommeCap:=11.outFlowCap+12.outFlowCap;
event failure (delay = exponential(lambda));           outCapacity :=if(sommeCap<=Intra Capacity)
event repair (delay = exponential(mu));                     then sommeCap else Intra Capacity;
event inadequacy (delay = 0.0);                        11.inFlowDem :=if((inDemand - 11.outFlowCap)<=0)
event adequacy (delay = 0.0);                               then inDemand else 11.outFlowCap;
transition                                             12.inFlowDem :=if(inDemand - 11.outFlowCap<=0)
  failure: s==WORKING -> s:=FAILED;                          then 0.0 else inDemand-11.outFlowCap;
  inadequacy: s==WORKING and                           sommePro:=11.outFlowPro + 12.outFlowPro;
          (inProduction<outDemand)->s:=SHORTAGE;       outProduction :=if (sommePro<=Intra Capacity)
  adequacy: s==SHORTAGE and                                  then sommePro else Intra Capacity;
          (inProduction>=outDemand)->s:=WORKING;      end
  repair: s==FAILED -> s:=WORKING;
assertion
  outDemand := inDemand;
  outCapacity:=if(s==WORKING)and
          (inCapacity<=Intra Capacity)
        then inCapacity else Intra Capacity;
  outProduction := if(s==WORKING)and
                (inDemand<=inProduction)
              then inDemand else 0.0;
end
```

(a)   (b)

Fig. 8. AltaRica class for (a) repairable components and (b) the *PLUS-gate*

7   Reliability Analysis of the System

There is a variety of assessment tools in AltaRica 3.0. The stochastic simulation is one of them [15]. This Monte Carlo based assessment tool estimates the reliability indicators by simulating the actual behavior of the system in order to create a realistic life time scenario of the system. A set of 1000 histories and a time limit of 36000 h were performed.

Three reliability indicators are estimated: the reliability of the system (R), the Mean Frequency of Interruptions (MFI) at the load point (Server) and the Mean Duration of Interruptions (MDI).

$$MFI = \frac{1}{MTBF} = 0,0031 \qquad MDI = \frac{MTTF}{NbreO} = 22,5649\,h$$

Where the Mean Time between Failure $MTBF = 322.484$, the Mean Time To Failure $MTTF = 116.244$, and the total number of failures $NbreO = 5.15$. The probability that system will perform its requested function which is based on the load point operation is:

$$R = 1 - \frac{MTTF}{Mission\ time} = 0,996771$$

In order to validate these results, we consider a second model of the electrical power system, which is built directly in AltaRica without considering any production tree. Because of the page number constraint, this model is not provided in this paper. The simulation results of the second AltaRica model match those obtained using the production tree model.

The simulator works by defining observers which statistics are made. In this article, three observers are defined: the total production of the system, the production of the generator and the production of power supplies PS1 and PS2.

The installed capacity of the system is 40 KW, provided by both PS_1 and PS_2 (20 KW each). Figure 9(a) shows the probability distribution of the total production in the system, knowing that the server needs 20 KW to operate properly. Figures 9(b) and 10(a) show the generator's production probability distribution and the combined production (PS_1 and PS_2), respectively.

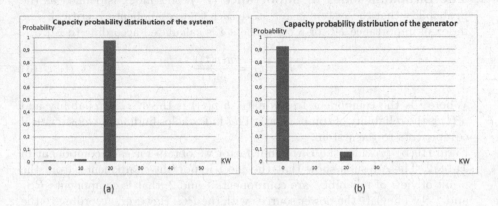

(a)   (b)

Fig. 9. Probability distribution of the production capacity

According to these figures, it is clear that the total production capacity is provided by PS_1 and PS_2. The probability of having 0 KW of generator's production is greater than 0.9. This means that the generator provides only the missing capacity caused by the failure of one of the power suppliers.

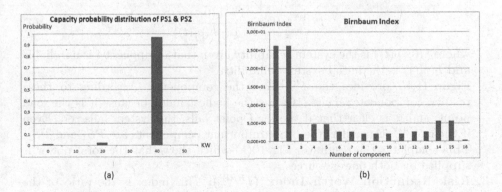

(a)   (b)

Fig. 10. Probability distribution (a) — The Birnbaum index of importance (b)

The reliability of the global system is used to obtain the importance factor of components in order to identify which parts of the system must be improved.

There are different indexes for assessing the importance of the components in the system. The following indexes are calculated:

- The Birnbaum index of importance I^B.
- Risk Reduction Worth Index I^{RRW}.
- Risk Achievement Worth Index I^{RAW}.

For that, we number all the components in the system under study (see Table 2).

1. **The Birnbaum index of importance** (I^B): this index is defined as the probability that the system is in a state such that component i is critical. The index of importance I^B for a component i is calculated according to Eq. 3.

$$I^B(i|t) = \frac{h(p(t))}{p_i(t)} \tag{3}$$

Where i is the component to evaluate, $h(p(t))$ is the system reliability and $p_i(t)$ is the reliability of component i. This index helps finding the most critical components to the system.

Figure 10(b) provides the Birnbaum factor we obtain for each component in Table 2. These results show that the most important components, from the point of view of reliability, are components 1 and 2, that is components PS_1 and PS_2. They are the power sources with the PG. However, according to the data of the system under study, the PG alone cannot satisfy the load demand if PS_1 or PS_2 fails. Thus, each failure of these components will cause a system failure and a supply interruption to the load point (server).

2. **Risk Achievement Worth Index** (I^{RAW}): this index indicates the importance of maintaining the current level of component reliability for system reliability. It is interesting in a design stage to think to duplicate some components in order to improve the total reliability. It is defined as follows:

$$I^{RAW}(i|t) = \frac{1 - h(0_i, p(t))}{1 - h(p_i(t))} \tag{4}$$

where $h(0_i, p(t))$ is the system reliability given that component i is unreliable and $h(p(t))$ is the initial system reliability.

Figure 11(b) provides the I^{RAW} of the components. According to these results, component $Server$ (16) has the highest index because it is the load point, and it is clear that if the load point fails, the system fails too. Even if their I^{RAW} is smaller, the other important components are PS_1 and PS_2. This completes the results in Fig. 10(a) which show that the total power is supplied by both power sources.

3. **Risk Reduction Worth Index** (I^{RRW}): This index is the ratio of the current system unreliability if component i is always failed with the failure rate of current system.

$$I^{RRW}(i|t) = \frac{1 - h(p(t))}{1 - h(1_i, p_i(t))} \tag{5}$$

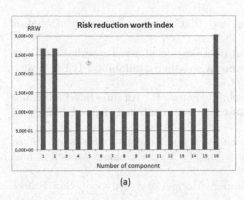
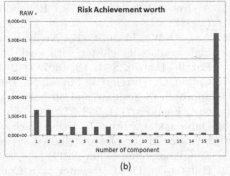

(a)   (b)

Fig. 11. Importance indices I^{RRW} (a) and I^{RAW} (b)

Where $h(p(t))$ is the initial system reliability and $h(1_i, p(t))$ is the system reliability knowing that component i is unreliable.

Figure 11(a) confirms the previous results as PS_1 and PS_2 are the most important components with the server, according to this figure. The other components are less important since they are distributed in two supply paths.

8 Conclusion

In this paper we showed how easily Production Trees allow modeling the flows in an electrical power system and help analysing the safety of this system. The simulation results show a promising effectiveness of this integrated methodology to estimate reliability. The calculated importance factors indicate the importance of each component according to different interests. For example, to identify potential components to improve safety, a combination of indices I^{RRW} and I^{RAW} is often used. However, this is not enough for other operations such as maintenance and optimization. In the future, it is important to introduce other importance factors for dynamic systems and different types of maintenance. Another future direction is to develop an approach which allows analyzing directly production trees models.

References

1. Component Reliability Data for use in Probabilistic Safety Assessment. IEEE Gold Book 473 (2013)
2. Design of Reliable Industrial and Commercial Power Systems. IEEE Gold Book 473 (2013)
3. Service level agreement for data center services (2013). http://www.earthlinkbusiness.com/static/files/pdfs/legal/DataCenterServiceSLA.pdf
4. Ajmone-Marsan, M., Balbo, G., Conte, G., Donatelli, S., Franceschinis, G.: Modeling with Generalized Stochastic Petri Nets: Application to Two Test Cases. Parallel Computing. Wiley, Hoboken (1994)

5. Andrews, J.D., Moss, T.R.: Reliability and Risk Assessment. Wiley, Hoboken (1993)
6. Ang, C.-W., Tham, C.-K.: Analysis and optimization of service availability in a high availability cluster with load-dependent machine availability. IEEE Trans. Parallel Distrib. Syst. **18**, 1307–1319 (2007)
7. Callou, G., Ferreira, J., Maciel, P., Tutsch, D., Souza, R.: An integrated modeling approach to evaluate and optimize data center sustainability, dependability and cost. Energies **7**(1), 238–277 (2014)
8. Dabrowski, C., Hunt, F.: Using Markov chain and graph theory concepts to analyze behavior in complex distributed systems. In: The 23rd European Modeling and Simulation Symposium (2011)
9. Hill, M.D.: The Datacenter as a Computer. Morgan and Calypool, San Rafael (2009)
10. Kehren, C.: Motifs formels d'architectures de systemes pour la surete de fonctionnement. These de Doctorat, Ecole Nationale Superieure de l'Aeronotique et de l'Espace (SUPAERO) (2005)
11. Kloul, L., Rauzy, A.: Production trees: a new modeling methodology for production availability analyses (2017, Submitted)
12. Marwah, M., Maciel, P., Shah, A., Sharma, R., Christian, T.: Quantifying the sustainability impact of data center availability. ACM SIGMETRICS Perform. Eval. Rev. **37**(4), 64–68 (2010)
13. Microsoft: Creating a greener data center (2013). http://www.microsoft.com/presspass/features/2009/apr09/04-02Greendatacenters.mspx
14. Noble, J., Taivalsaari, A., Moore, I.: Prototype-Based Programming: Concepts, Languages and Applications. Springer, Heidelberg (1999)
15. Rauzy, A.: Guarded transition systems: a new states/events formalism for reliability studies. J. Risk Reliab. **222**, 495–505 (2008)
16. Robidoux, R.: Automated modeling of dynamic reliability block diagrams using colored petri nets. IEEE Trans. Syst. Man Cybern. Part A Syst. Hum. **40**(2), 337–351 (2010)
17. Robidoux, R., Xu, H., Zhou, M., Xing, L.: Automated modeling of dynamic reliability block diagrams using colored petri net. IEEE Trans. Syst. Man Cybern. Part A Syst. **40**, 337–351 (2010)
18. Silvaa, S., Silvaa, B., Romero, P., Maciela, M., Zimmermannb, A.: Dependability evaluation of data center power infrastructures considering substation switching operations. In: Probabilistic Safety Assessment and Management conference, June 2014
19. Turner, W.P., Seader, J.H., Brill, K.: Tier classifications define site infrastructure performance. Uptime Institute White Paper (2013)
20. Weihl, B., Teetzel, E., Clidaras, J., Malone, C., Kava, J., Ryan, M.: Sustainable data centers. XRDS **17**, 8–12 (2011)
21. Wiboonrat, M.: An empirical study on data center system failure diagnosis. In: Internet Monitoring and Protection, July 2008

Architectural Modeling and Analysis for Safety Engineering

Danielle Stewart[1]([✉]), Michael W. Whalen[1], Darren Cofer[2],
and Mats P.E. Heimdahl[1]

[1] Department of Computer Science and Engineering,
University of Minnesota, 200 Union Street, Minneapolis, MN 55455, USA
{dkstewar,whalen,heimdahl}@cs.umn.edu
[2] Advanced Technology Center, Rockwell Collins,
400 Collins Rd. NE, Cedar Rapids, IA 52498, USA
darren.cofer@rockwellcollins.com

Abstract. Architecture description languages such as AADL allow systems engineers to specify the structure of system architectures and perform several analyses over them, including schedulability, resource analysis, and information flow. In addition, they permit system-level requirements to be specified and analyzed early in the development process of airborne and ground-based systems. These tools can also be used to perform safety analysis based on the system architecture and initial functional decomposition.

Using AADL-based system architecture modeling and analysis tools as an exemplar, we extend existing analysis methods to support system safety objectives of ARP4754A and ARP4761. This includes extensions to existing modeling languages to better describe failure conditions, interactions, and mitigations, and improvements to compositional reasoning approaches focused on the specific needs of system safety analysis. We develop example systems based on the Wheel Braking System in SAE AIR6110 to evaluate the effectiveness and practicality of our approach.

Keywords: Model-based systems engineering · Fault analysis · Safety engineering

1 Introduction

System safety analysis techniques are well established and are a required activity in the development of commercial aircraft and safety-critical ground systems. However, these techniques are based on informal system descriptions that are separate from the actual system design artifacts, and are highly dependent on the skill and intuition of a safety analyst. The lack of precise models of the system architecture and its failure modes often forces safety analysts to devote significant effort to gathering architectural details about the system behavior from multiple sources and embedding this information in safety artifacts, such as fault trees.

© Springer International Publishing AG 2017
M. Bozzano and Y. Papadopoulos (Eds.): IMBSA 2017, LNCS 10437, pp. 97–111, 2017.
DOI: 10.1007/978-3-319-64119-5_7

While model-based development (MBD) methods are widely used in the aerospace industry, they are generally disconnected from the safety analysis process itself. Formal model-based systems engineering (MBSE) methods and tools now permit system-level requirements to be specified and analyzed early in the development process [3,7,8,21,22,26]. These tools can also be used to perform safety analysis based on the system architecture and initial functional decomposition. Design models from which aircraft systems are developed can be integrated into the safety analysis process to help guarantee accurate and consistent results. This integration is especially important as the amount of safety-critical hardware and software in domains such as aerospace, automotive, and medical devices has dramatically increased due to desire for greater autonomy, capability, and connectedness.

Architecture description languages, such as SysML [10] and the Architecture Analysis and Design Language (AADL) [1] are appropriate for capturing system safety information. There are several tools that currently support reasoning about faults in architecture description languages, such as the AADL error annex [18] and HiP-HOPS for EAST-ADL [6]. However, these approaches primarily use *qualitative* reasoning, in which faults are enumerated and their propagations through system components must be explicitly described. Given many possible faults, these propagation relationships become complex and it is also difficult to describe temporal properties of faults that evolve over time (e.g., leaky valve or slow divergence of sensor values). This is likewise the case with tools like SAML that incorporate both *qualitative* and *quantitative* reasoning [11]. Due to the complexity of propagation relationships, interactions may also be overlooked by the analyst and thus may not be explicitly described within the fault model.

In earlier work, University of Minnesota and Rockwell Collins developed and demonstrated an approach to model-based safety analysis (MBSA) [14,16,17] using the Simulink notation [20]. In this approach, a behavioral model of (sometimes simplified) system dynamics was used to reason about the effect of faults. We believe that this approach allows a natural and implicit notion of fault propagation through the changes in pressure, mode, etc. that describe the system's behavior. Unlike qualitative approaches, this approach allows uniform reasoning about system functionality and failure behavior, and can describe complex temporal fault behaviors. On the other hand, Simulink is not an architecture description language, and several system engineering aspects, such as hardware devices and non-functional aspects cannot be easily captured in models.

This paper describes our initial work towards a behavioral approach to MBSA using AADL. Using assume-guarantee compositional reasoning techniques, we hope to support system safety objectives of ARP4754A and ARP4761. To make these capabilities accessible to practicing safety engineers, it is necessary to extend modeling notations to better describe failure conditions, interactions, and mitigations, and provide improvements to compositional reasoning approaches focused on the specific needs of system safety analysis. These extensions involve creating models of fault effects and weaving them into the analysis process.

To a large extent, our work has been an adaptation of the work of Joshi et al. in [14,16,17] to the AADL modeling language.

To evaluate the effectiveness and practicality of our approach, we developed an architectural model of the Wheel Braking System model in SAE AIR6110. Starting from a reference AADL model constructed by the SEI instrumented with qualitative safety analysis information [9], we added behavioral contracts to the model. In so doing, we determine that there are errors related to (manually constructed) propagations across components, and also an architecture that contains single points of failure. We use our analyses to find these errors.

2   Example: Wheel Brake System

As a preliminary case study, we utilized the Wheel Brake System (WBS) described in [2] (previously found in ARP4761 Appendix L). This ficticious aircraft system was developed to illustrate the design and safety analysis principles of ARP4754A and ARP4761. The WBS is installed on the two main aircraft landing gears and is used during taxi, landing, and rejected take off. Braking is either commanded manually using brake pedals or automatically by a digital control system with no need for the pedals (autobrake). When the wheels have traction, the autobrake function will provide a constant smooth deceleration.

Each wheel has a brake assembly that can be operated by two independent hydraulic systems (designated green and blue). In normal braking mode, the green hydraulic system operates the brake assembly. If there is a failure in the green hydraulics, the system switches to alternate mode which uses the blue hydraulic system. The blue system is also supplied by an accumulator which is a device that stores hydraulic pressure that can be released if both of the primary hydraulic pumps (blue and green) fail. The accumulator supplies hydraulic pressure in Emergency braking mode.

Switching between the hydraulic pistons and pressure sources can be commanded automatically or manually. If the hydraulic pressure in the green supply is below a certain threshold, there is an automatic switchover to the blue hydraulic supply. If the blue hydraulic pump fails, then the accumulator is used to supply hydraulic pressure.

In both normal and alternate modes, an anti-skid capability is available. In the normal mode, the brake pedal position is electronically fed to a computer called the Braking System Control Unit (BSCU). The BSCU monitors signals that denote critical aircraft and system states to provide correct braking function, detect anomalies, broadcast warnings, and sent maintenance information to other systems.

2.1   Nominal System Model

The WBS AADL model of the nominal system behavior consists of mechanical and digital components and their interconnections, as shown in Fig. 1. The following section describes this nominal model from which the fault model was generated.

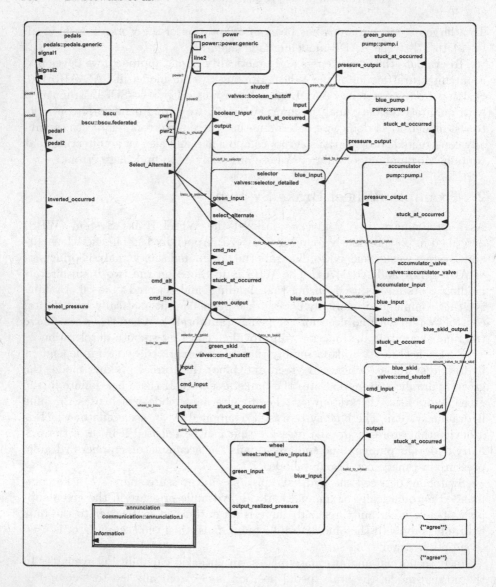

Fig. 1. AADL simple model of the wheel brake system

Wheel Braking System (WBS). The highest level model component is the WBS. It consists of the BSCU, green and blue hydraulic pressure lines (supplied by the green pump and blue pump/accumulator respectively), a Selector which selects between normal and alternate modes of hydraulic pressure, and the wheel system. The WBS takes inputs from the environment including PedalPos1, AutoBrake, DecRate, AC_Speed, and Skid. All of these inputs are forwarded to the BSCU to compute the brake commands.

Braking System Control Unit (BSCU). The BSCU is the digital component in the system that receives inputs from the WBS. It also receives feedback from the green and blue hydraulic lines and two power inputs from two separate power sources. The BSCU is composed of two command and monitor subsystems each powered independently from separate power sources. The pedal position is provided to these units and when skidding occurs, the command and monitor units will decrease the pressure to the brakes. The command unit regulates the pressure to the brakes in the green hydraulic line through the command cmd_nor. Computing this command requires both the brake requested power and the skid information. The command unit also regulates the pressure in the blue hydraulic line in order to prevent skidding which it does through the cmd_alt command. The monitor unit checks the validity of the command unit output.

The BSCU switches from normal to alternate mode (blue hydraulic system) when the output from either one of its command units is not valid or the green hydraulic pump is below its pressure threshold. Once the system has switched into alternate mode, it will not switch back into normal mode again.

Hydraulic Pumps. There are three hydraulic pumps in the system, green pump (normal mode), blue pump (alternate mode), and accumulator pump (emergency mode). Each pump provides pressure to the system and is modeled in AADL as a floating point value.

Shutoff Valve. The shutoff valve is situated between the green pump and the selector. It receives an input from the BSCU regarding valve position and regulates the pressure coming through the green pipe accordingly.

Selector Valve. The selector receives inputs from the pumps regarding pressure output and the BSCU regarding which mode the system is in. It will output the appropriate pressure from green, blue, or accumulator pump. An added requirement of the selector system is that it will only output pressure from one of these sources. Thus, the case of having pressure supplied to the wheels from more than one pump is avoided. The Selector takes the two pipe pressures (green and blue) as input, selects the system with adequate pressure and blocks the system with inadequate pressure. If both systems have pressure greater than the threshold, the AADL selects normal mode as the default.

Skid Valves. The blue_skid and green_skid valves receive input from the selector as pressure coming through the respective pipes as well as input from the BSCU that commands normal or alternate mode. The skid valves will use these inputs to choose between the green or the blue pressure to send to the wheel.

2.2 Modeling Nominal System Behavior

In order to reason about behaviors of complex system architectures, we have developed a compositional verification tool for AADL models. Our tool, the

```
annex AGREE {**

eq nominal_Select_Alternate : bool;

eq pedals_pressed: bool = (pedal1.val > 0.0) and (pedal2.val > 0.0);

eq skid_active: bool = (cmd_nor.activate_antiskid) or (cmd_alt.activate_antiskid);

eq commanded_pressure: bool = (cmd_nor.val > 0.0) or (cmd_alt.val > 0.0);

guarantee "If pedals pressed, no skid, and wheel pressure is nonexistant, then
          select alternate should be true" :
    (nominal_Select_Alternate =
    faults.historically(false -> not (pre(pedals_pressed and not(skid_active)) =>
        wheel_pressure.val > 0.0)));

guarantee "Pedals pressed and no skid and normal implies pressure commanded" :
    pedals_pressed and (not skid_active) => commanded_pressure;

guarantee "Alternate pressure and normal pressure don't occur simultaneously." :
    not(cmd_alt.val > 0.0 and cmd_nor.val > 0.0);

**};
```

Fig. 2. AGREE contract for BSCU

Assume-Guarantee Reasoning Environment (AGREE) [8] is based on *assume-guarantee* contracts that can be added to AADL components. The language used for contract specification is based on the LUSTRE dataflow language [12]. The tool allows scaling of formal verification to large systems by splitting the analysis of a complex system architecture into a collection of verification tasks that correspond to the structure of the architecture.

We use AGREE to specify behavioral contracts corresponding to the behaviors expected of each of the WBS components. An example of a contract is shown in Fig. 2.

3 Model-Based Safety Analysis

A model-based approach for safety analysis was proposed by Joshi et. al in [14–16]. In this approach, a safety analysis system model (SASM) is the central artifact in the safety analysis process, and traditional safety analysis artifacts, such as fault trees, are automatically generated by tools that analyze the SASM.

The contents and structure of the SASM differ significantly across different conceptions of MBSA. We can draw distinctions between approaches along several different axes. The first is whether models and notations are purpose-built for safety analysis (such as AltaRica [23], smartIflow [13] and xSAP [4]) vs. those that extend existing system models (ESM) (HiP-HOPS [6], the AADL error annex [25]). A second dimension involves the richness of the modeling languages used to represent failures. Most existing safety analysis languages only support model variables types drawn from small discrete domains (which we call *discrete*); the xSAP platform is a notable exception that allows *rich types*. Another dimension whether *causal* or *non-causal* models are allowed. Non-causal models allow simultaneous (in time) bi-directional failure propagations; currently only AltaRica [23] and smartIflow [13] allow this. Yet another dimension involves whether analysis is *compositional* across layers of hierarchically-composed systems or *whole-system.*

In this section, we will focus on the dimension of failure propagation, and contrast failure logic modeling (FLM) vs. failure effect modeling (FEM) [19]. In FLM, *failures* are propagated between components explicitly and the analysis proceeds by determining the likelihood of failures reaching system boundaries. In FEM, failures propagate by changing the system dynamics, which may cause the system behavior to visibly change. Our approach is an extension of AADL (FSM), richly-typed, causal, compositional, mixed FLM/FEM approach. We believe this is in a unique area of the trade space compared to other state-of-the-art MBSA approaches.

3.1 Failure Logic Modeling (FLM) Approaches

The FLM approach focuses on faults rather than constructing a model of system dynamics. We illustrate this approach with the AADL error model annex [25] that can be used to describe system behaviors in the presence of faults. This annex has facilities for defining *error types* which can be used to describe *error events* that indicate faults, errors, and failures in the system (the term *error* is used generically in the annex to describe faults, errors, and failures). The behavior of system components in the presence of errors is determined by state machines that are attached to system components; these state machines can determine error propagations and error composition for systems created from various subcomponents.

Error types in this framework are a set of enumeration values such as NoData, BadData, LateDelivery, EarlyDelivery, TimingError, and NoService. These errors can be arranged in a hierarchy. For example, LateDelivery and EarlyDelivery are subtypes of TimingError. The errors do not have any information (other than their type) associated with them. AADL includes information on the bindings of logical components (processes, threads, systems) and their communication mechanisms onto physical resources (memories, processors, busses), and the error annex uses this information to describe how physical failures can manifest in logical components.

An example is shown in Fig. 3 Errors are labeled with error types: 1-BadData, 2-NoData, 3-NoSvc. Failure events that can cause a component to fail are labeled with the corresponding error number. The error behavior of components is described by their state machines. Note that while all state machines in Fig. 2 have two states, they can be much more complex. The dashed arrows indicate propagations describing how failures in one component can cause other components to fail. For example, failures in the physical layer propagate to failures in the associated logical components.

Although the error model annex is very capable, it is not closely tied to the behavioral model of components or their requirements. For example, in the wheel braking system (WBS) example [24], it is possible that hydraulic system valves can fail open or fail closed. In fail closed, downstream components receive no flow and upstream pipes may become highly pressurized as a natural consequence of

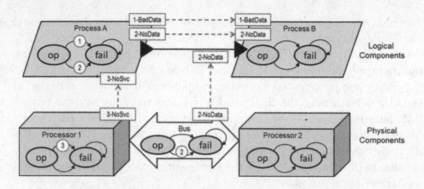

Fig. 3. Example of error model information and propagation

the failure. Physical models of these behavioral relationships often exist that can propagate failures in terms of the behavioral relationships between components. However, with the AADL error model annex, the propagations must be (re)specified and defined for each component. This re-specification can lead to inconsistencies between physical models and error annex models. In addition, the physical relationships between failures can be complex and may not be describable using enumeration values, leading to additional inconsistencies between the behavior of the physical phenomena and the behavior of the error model.

3.2   Failure Effect Modeling (FEM) Approaches

In a failure effect modeling approach, the analysis starts from a *nominal* model of the system that describes the system behavior when no faults are present. To perform safety analysis, we then also formalize the fault model. The fault model, in addition to common failure modes such as *non-deterministic, inverted, stuck_at* etc., could encode information regarding fault propagation, simultaneous dependent faults and fault hierarchies, etc. After specifying the fault model and composing it with the original system model, the safety analysis involves verifying whether the safety requirements hold in presence of the faults defined in the fault model.

In this approach, a safety engineer can model different kinds of fault behavior: e.g., stuck-at, ramp-up, ramp-down, and nondeterministic, and then *weave* these fault models into the nominal model. The language for describing faults is extensible, allowing engineers to define a catalog of faults appropriate for their domain. In addition, the weaving process allows error propagation between unconnected components within a system model [15]. This allows consideration of physical aspects (e.g., proximity of components, shared resources such as power) that may not be present in a logical system model but can lead to dependent failures. In addition, it allows propagation of faults in the reverse direction of the model data flow. This can occur when physical components have coupling such as back-pressure in fluid systems or power surges in the opposite direction of communication through connected components. Finally, it is possible to create fault mediations to describe the output in the presence of multiple simultaneous faults.

A safety analysis system model can be used for a variety of simulations and analyses. Modeling allows trivial exploration of *what-if* scenarios involving combinations of faults through simulations. The current AADL tool suite contains a graphical symbolic simulator that allows for forward and back-stepping through different failure scenarios. In addition it contains a test-case generator that can automatically generate such scenarios. For more rigorous analyses, we can use model checking tools to automatically prove (or disprove) whether the system meets specific safety requirements. As we will demonstrate on the WBS, an engineer first verifies that safety properties hold on the nominal system, an idealized model of the digital controller and the mechanical system containing no faults. Once the nominal model is shown to satisfy the safety property, the behavior of the fault-extended model can be examined to examine its resilience to faults.

4 Architectural Failure Effect Modeling for the WBS

We illustrate our FEM approach on the Wheel Braking System. Starting from the nominal model described in Sect. 2.1, we first determine whether a given safety property of interest holds on a fault-free instance of the model. We then extend the model with faults and determine whether the property continues to hold under reasonable fault scenarios.

The initial safety property to be proven determines whether the system will apply pressure to the wheels when commanded to do so:

If pedals are pressed and no skid occurs, then the brakes will receive pressure.

Using the reference AADL model constructed by the SEI [9] extended with AGREE contracts describing system behaviors, this property proves immediately. From this point, we focus our attention on component failures and how this will affect the top level property of the system.

We would like to specify different component failure modes. These failure modes can be triggered by some internal or propagated fault. In order to trigger these faults, additional input was added to the AADL model for each fault that can occur within a nominal model component. This consists of two types:

– *fail_to* fault: This type of fault accounts for both nondeterministic failures and stuck-at failures. The components that are affected by this fault include meter valves and pumps. This fault can be used to describe both digital and mechanical errors. Examples of digital failures include a *stuck_at* failure for the command subsystem in the BSCU component, which causes the command unit to become stuck at a previous value. An example of a mechanical failure would be a valve stuck open (or closed).

– *inverted_fail* fault: This type of fault will be used on components which contain boolean output. It will simply take boolean input, negate it, and output the negated value. An example of this is the selector. In the nominal model, input to the selector consists of a boolean value *select_alternate* value from the BSCU.

These faults can be easily encoded in AGREE as shown in Fig. 4. The failures simply return an alternate value (for *fail_to*) or invert the input value (for *inverted_failure*) when a failure occurs.

```
node fail_to(val_in: real, alt_val: real, fail_occurred: bool) returns (val_out: real);
let
   val_out = if (fail_occurred) then alt_val else val_in;
tel;


node inverted_fail(val_in: bool, fail_occurred: bool) returns (val_out:bool);
let
  val_out = if fail_occurred then not(val_in) else val_in;
tel;
```

Fig. 4. AGREE definition of a *fail_to* and *inverted_failure* faults

While modeling faults, the duration of the fault must also be taken into account. The AGREE tools allow a great deal of flexibility in terms of how faults are defined and their duration. For the purposes of this model, we currently consider only *transient* and *permanent* faults, where transient faults occur for an instant in time (e.g., a single-event upset) and a permanent fault persists for the remainder of the system execution.

4.1   Analysis of Faulty Models

The following is a short summary of the failures defined in the fault model.

– Valves and Pumps: All valves and pumps have the possibility of a *fail_to* fault. This includes green pump, blue pump, accumulator, and the shutoff valves.
– The selector can also have a digital *fail_to* fault regarding the inputs from BSCU commanding to use normal or alternate means of pressure along with an *inverted_fail* fault which would change the boolean value that commands antiskid to activate.

Given our understanding of the WBS, our assumption was that any single permanent fault could be introduced into the system and the pilot would still be able to command brake pressure. However, our analysis tools returned a counterexample to the property, and upon examination, the structure of the reference model was insufficient to guarantee the property.

The first issue was *feedback*; the reference model did not have a sensor to determine pressure after the selector valve. This means that a single failure of (for example) the blue or green antiskid valve cannot be detected by the BSCU (see Fig. 1), and it cannot route around the failure. In order to address this, we added a pressure sensor to the wheel that communicates with the BSCU to detect lack of pressure at the wheel.

After adding a sensing apparatus to the wheel, the analysis generated another counterexample due to a single failure of the selector valve. In the reference model, there is a single selector component that takes as inputs the green pump, the blue pump, and the accumulator. A single failure in this component can lead to no pressure along either of the two outgoing pressure lines. To solve this issue, we removed the accumulator from the selector and added an accumulator valve. This component takes in the blue pressure from the selector and the accumulator pressure. It also takes in a *select_alternate* flag from the BSCU. The output of the accumulator_valve goes directly to the blue_skid component and is either the blue or the accumulator pressure.

Finally, our BSCU is currently structured to always fail-over from the green system to the blue system but never the reverse. Because of this choice (which matches the AIR6110 document), it is also necessary to guarantee that *select_alternate* is false until a failure occurs in the system; otherwise, a single failure in the blue anti-skid valve can cause the system to fail to provide pressure. This asymmetry is something that could be revisited in future work.

Even after making these three changes to the model, the original property still does not prove. At issue is that the sensing of a no-pressure situation is not instantaneous; there is a delay for this information to reach the BSCU and be acted upon to switch to the alternate braking system. In our current timing model for the system, the feedback to the BSCU involves a delay, but the BSCU and valves can react. Thus, we weaken our top-level property to state that if the brakes are pressed for two consecutive time instants, then pressure will be provided to the wheels:

If pedals are pressed in the previous state and pressed in the current state and no skid occurs, then the brakes will receive pressure.

The nominal WBS model extended with the faults described in this section can be found at https://github.com/loonwerks/AMASE.

5   Discussion

We have used the WBS model as a vehicle to experiment with different modeling and fault representation ideas, and to get a feel for the scalability of our approach. We started from the reference AADL model [9] to attempt to contrast our FEM approach using AGREE contracts vs. the FLM-based approach that was already part of this model. Part of this was driven by curiosity as to whether important faults might be caught by one approach and missed by the other, and to contrast the two styles of analysis.

During the process of defining and injecting faults, subtle issues of the system structure and behavioral interactions became much clearer. The idea that the system must use the green side until a failure occurs was unexpected. In addition, the extensions to the model were driven by the counterexamples returned by the tools. The approach quickly and precisely provided feedback towards aspects of the system that were not robust to failure. The researcher who produced the model (Stewart) was not involved in earlier MBSA work and had no prior exposure to the WBS model and yet was able to relatively quickly construct a fault-tolerant model. The fact that these holes in the reference model perhaps means that the behavioral approach can be better at drawing attention to certain kinds of failures.

On the other hand, the utility of the safety analysis is driven by the "goodness" of the properties. Our one example property is clearly insufficient: for example, it is not possible to detect faults related to over-pressurization or mis-application of the brakes when no braking is commanded. Of course, any complete analysis should have properties related to each hazardous condition. The approach is foundationally a top-down analysis (like fault trees) rather than a bottom up approach (like a FMEA/FMECA). In addition, if properties are mis-specified, or the system dynamics are incorrectly modeled, then properties may verify even when systems are unsafe. The explicit propagation approach of the FLM techniques force the analyst to consider each fault interaction. This too is a double-edged sword: when examining some of the fault propagations in the reference model, we disagreed with some of the choices made, particularly with respect to the selector valve. For example, if no select alternate commands are received from the BSCU, then both the green and blue lines emit a *No_Service* failure.

In terms of scalability, the analysis time for counterexamples was on the order of 1–2 s, and the time for proofs was around 4 s, even after annotating the model with several different failures. From earlier experience applying compositional verification with the AGREE tools (e.g., [3, 21]), we believe that the analysis will scale well to reasonably large models with many component failures, but this will be determined in future work.

The analysis in this paper involved hand-annotating the models with failure nodes. This process is both schematic and straightforward: we define the AGREE contracts over internal *nominal output variables* and then define the actual outputs using the nominal output variables as inputs to the fault nodes like those in Fig. 4. We are currently in the process of defining a fault integration language which will eliminate the need for hand-annotation. Some aspects of the Error Annex could be directly relevant: the state machines describing leaf-level faults could easily be compiled into behavioral state machines that determine when faults occur. On the other hand, in a behavioral approach we need to be able to bring in additional quantities (inputs, parameters) to instantiate behavioral faults, and the two approaches have very different notions of propagation.

The xSAP tool [4] has an elegant extension language that allows for fault definition, selection between multiple faults for a component, and "global" dependent faults that can affect multiple components. The authors have used this support to construct a sophisticated analysis model for the WBS [5]. However, some useful aspects of fault modeling, such as global faults that are driven by the state of the model, appear to be hard to construct. For example, a pipe-burst failure can be seen as a global failure because it may cause unconnected components within the model to fail, so can be represented as having a certain probability. On the other hand, the likelihood of failure in the real system is driven by the number of currently pressurized pipes in the system, which appears to be hard to define. We hope to allow for such conditional and model-driven failures in our fault definition language.

6   Conclusions and Future Work

In this paper, we describe our initial work towards performing MBSA using the AADL architecture description language using a failure effect modeling approach. Our goal is to be able to perform safety analysis on common models used by systems and safety engineers for functional and non-functional analyses, schedulability, and perhaps system image generation. To perform this analysis, we use existing capabilities within AADL to describe the structure of the system, and build on the existing AGREE framework for compositional analysis of components.

As part of our exploration, we are interested in examining the strengths and weaknesses of our FEM and the AADL Error Annex FLM-based approach. We believe that the FEM approach has advantages both in terms of brevity of specifications and accuracy of results, and can build on existing analyses performed for systems engineering. However, there are also risks in the FEM approach involving incomplete or mis-specified properties.

We illustrated the ideas using architecture models based on the Wheel Braking System model in SAE AIR 6110 [2] and use this in the evaluation of our approach. Using assume-guarantee compositional reasoning techniques, we prove a top level property of the wheel brake system that states when the brake pedals are pressed in the absence of skidding, there will be hydraulic pressure supplied to the brakes.

Starting from the error model notions of error types, two main faults were defined: *fail_to* which will describe failures of valves and pressure regulators and *inverted_fail* which describes the failures occurring to components that output boolean values. Using the AADL behavioral model of the WBS, these permanent faults were tied into the nominal model in order to reason about how this model behaves in the presence of specific kinds of faults.

In order to demonstrate that the system was resilient to single faults, we modified the model to allow feedback from the wheel pressure to the BSCU. This changed the way the system responded to faults that were further downstream of the BSCU or Selector and created a chance for the system to switch to alternate forms of hydraulic pressure. We also reasoned about the initialization values of the system in regards to which mode is the starting mode. It is crucial for the system to begin in Normal mode in order to function successfully in the presence of faults. After model modification and a small weakening of our original property to account for feedback delay, the model does fulfill the top level contract even when a permanent fault of one of the high level components is introduced.

The current capabilities of AGREE are well-suited to specifying faults. Our approach allows for scalar types of unbounded integers and reals, as well as composite types such as tuples and structures. It is possible to model systems and reason about them in either discrete time or real-time. However, adding faults to existing components is cumbersome and can obscure the nominal behaviors of the model. We are currently examining several fault specification languages, giving special consideration to the xSAP modeling language.

Future research work will involve the continuation of development of the methods and tools needed to perform model-based safety analysis at the system architecture level. By introducing a common set of models for both nominal system design and safety analysis, we hope to reduce the cost of development and improve safety. Our hope is to demonstrate the practicality of formal analysis for early detection of safety issues that would be prohibitively expensive to find through testing and inspection. We will base this research on industry standard notations that are being used in airborne and ground-based avionics in order to ensure transition of this technology.

Acknowledgements. This research was funded by NASA AMASE NNL16AB07T and University of Minnesota College of Science and Engineering Graduate Fellowship.

References

1. AADL: Predictable Model-Based Engineering
2. AIR 6110: Contiguous Aircraft/System Development Process Example (2011)
3. Backes, J., Cofer, D., Miller, S., Whalen, M.W.: Requirements analysis of a quad-redundant flight control system. In: Havelund, K., Holzmann, G., Joshi, R. (eds.) NFM 2015. LNCS, vol. 9058, pp. 82–96. Springer, Cham (2015). doi:10.1007/978-3-319-17524-9_7
4. Bittner, B., Bozzano, M., Cavada, R., Cimatti, A., Gario, M., Griggio, A., Mattarei, C., Micheli, A., Zampedri, G.: The xSAP Safety Analysis Platform. In: Proceedings of 22nd International Conference on Tools and Algorithms for the Construction and Analysis of Systems (TACAS 2016), Held as Part of the European Joint Conferences on Theory and Practice of Software (ETAPS 2016), Eindhoven, The Netherlands, 2–8 April 2016, pp. 533–539 (2016)
5. Bozzano, M., Cimatti, A., Pires, A.F., Jones, D., Kimberly, G., Petri, T., Robinson, R., Tonetta, S.: Formal design and safety analysis of AIR6110 wheel brake system. In: Proceedings of 27th International Conference on Computer Aided Verification (CAV 2015), Part I, San Francisco, CA, USA, 18–24 July 2015, pp. 518–535 (2015)
6. Chen, D., Mahmud, N., Walker, M., Feng, L., Lnn, H., Papadopoulos, Y.: Systems modeling with EAST-ADL for fault tree analysis through HiP-HOPS*. IFAC Proc. Vol. **46**(22), 91–96 (2013)
7. Cimatti, A., Tonetta, S.: Contracts-refinement proof system for component-based embedded system. Sci. Comput. Program. **97**, 333–348 (2015)
8. Cofer, D., Gacek, A., Miller, S., Whalen, M.W., LaValley, B., Sha, L.: Compositional verification of architectural models. In: Goodloe, A.E., Person, S. (eds.) NFM 2012. LNCS, vol. 7226, pp. 126–140. Springer, Heidelberg (2012). doi:10.1007/978-3-642-28891-3_13

9. Delange, J., Feiler, P., Gluch, D.P., Hudak, J.: AADL Fault Modeling, Analysis Within an ARP4761 Safety Assessment. Technical report CMU/SEI-2014-TR-020, Software Engineering Institute
10. Friedenthal, S., Moore, A., Steiner, R.: A Practical Guide to SysML. Morgan Kaufman Publisher, San Francisco (2008)
11. Gudemann, M., Ortmeier, F.: A framework for qualitative and quantitative formal model-based safety analysis. In: Proceedings of the 2010 IEEE 12th International Symposium on High-Assurance Systems Engineering, HASE 2010, pp. 132–141. IEEE Computer Society, Washington, D.C. (2010)
12. Halbwachs, N., Caspi, P., Raymond, P., Pilaud, D.: The synchronous dataflow programming language lustre. Proc. IEEE 79(9), 1305–1320 (1991)
13. Hnig, P., Lunde, R., Holzapfel, F.: Model based safety analysis with smartIflow. Information 8(1), 7 (2017)
14. Joshi, A., Heimdahl, M.P.E.: Model-based safety analysis of simulink models using SCADE design verifier. In: Winther, R., Gran, B.A., Dahll, G. (eds.) SAFECOMP 2005. LNCS, vol. 3688, pp. 122–135. Springer, Heidelberg (2005). doi:10.1007/11563228_10
15. Joshi, A., Heimdahl, M.P.: Behavioral fault modeling for model-based safety analysis. In: Proceedings of the 10th IEEE High Assurance Systems Engineering Symposium (HASE) (2007)
16. Joshi, A., Miller, S.P., Whalen, M., Heimdahl, M.P.: A proposal for model-based safety analysis. In: Proceedings of 24th Digital Avionics Systems Conference (Awarded Best Paper of Track) (2005)
17. Joshi, A., Whalen, M., Heimdahl, M.P.: Automated Safety Analysis Draft Final Report. Report for NASA Contract NCC-01001 (2005)
18. Larson, B., Hatcliff, J., Fowler, K., Delange, J.: Illustrating the AADL error modeling annex (v.2) using a simple safety-critical medical device. In: Proceedings of the 2013 ACM SIGAda Annual Conference on High Integrity Language Technology (HILT 2013), pp. 65–84. ACM, New York (2013)
19. Lisagor, O., Kelly, T., Niu, R.: Model-based safety assessment: Review of the discipline and its challenges. In: Proceedings of 2011 9th International Conference on Reliability, Maintainability and Safety, pp. 625–632 (2011)
20. MathWorks: The MathWorks Inc., Simulink Product Web Site (2004). http://www.mathworks.com/products/simulink
21. Murugesan, A., Whalen, M.W., Rayadurgam, S., Heimdahl, M.P.: Compositional verification of a medical device system. In: ACM International Conference on High Integrity Language Technology (HILT 2013), ACM (2013)
22. Pajic, M., Mangharam, R., Sokolsky, O., Arney, D., Goldman, J., Lee, I.: Model-driven safety analysis of closed-loop medical systems. IEEE Trans. Industr. Inf. pp. 1–12 (2012)
23. Prosvirnova, T., Batteux, M., Brameret, P.-A., Cherfi, A., Friedlhuber, T., Roussel, J.-M., Rauzy, A.: The AltaRica 3.0 project for model-based safety assessment. IFAC Proc. Volum. 46(22), 127–132 (2013)
24. SAE ARP 4761: Guidelines and Methods for Conducting the Safety Assessment Process on Civil Airborne Systems and Equipment (1996)
25. SAE AS 5506B-3: Aadl annex volume 1 (2015)
26. Sokolsky, O., Lee, I., Clarke, D.: Process-algebraic interpretation of AADL models. In: Proceedings of 14th Ada-Europe International Conference on Reliable Software Technologies (Ada-Europe 2009), Brest, France, 8–12 June 2009, pp. 222–236 (2009)

Invariant Management in the Presence of Failures

Richard Banach[✉]

School of Computer Science, University of Manchester,
Oxford Road, Manchester M13 9PL, UK
banach@cs.man.ac.uk

Abstract. In the effort to develop critical systems, taking account of failure modes is of vital importance. However, when systems fail (even in a manner previously determined as acceptable), a lot of the invariants that hold in the case of nominal behaviour also fail. A technique is proposed that permits the inclusion of the strong invariants of nominal behaviour alongside the provisions for degraded behaviour in an inclusive formal system model. The faulty system model is derived from the nominal one via fault injection, and the nominal and faulty system models are related via a formal retrenchment step. Manipulation of the retrenchment data permits the inclusion of the stronger invariants, which remain provable when faults are disabled in a generic manner in the faulty model, thus increasing confidence in the overall system design. The details are developed in Event-B, and the concept is illustrated using a toy switching example.

1 Introduction

When developing critical systems, it is rarely (in fact never) possible to assume all components will work perfectly all the time. Provision for the judicious handling of degraded operation is a vital concern in the design of all categories of critical system. This creates a dilemma of the following kind. When all components are working normally (nominal behaviour), very many specific invariants will hold about the detailed working of each of the components and about their interworking. The verification of these in the nominal system can provide a useful measure of confidence in the correctness of the model of the desired system. But the system cannot be viewed as being always nominal, so all these detailed invariants cannot be assumed to hold in the real system, when degraded operation in the presence of failure modes is contemplated. So the purported invariants are not in fact invariants, and the confidence in the correctness of the model of the desired system that their verification can provide, is lost. Only fewer, and inevitably weaker invariants will hold in the full system, these capturing the perforce weaker requirements that are demanded of the full system when all foreseen failure modes are taken into account.

In this paper, we present an approach that can straddle these two extremes. Briefly, a suitable formal model of the nominal system is first developed. Since

M. Bozzano and Y. Papadopoulos (Eds.): IMBSA 2017, LNCS 10437, pp. 112–128, 2017.
DOI: 10.1007/978-3-319-64119-5_8

faults are not contemplated at this stage,[1] a suite of incisive invariants is developed accompanying the model. These tightly police the detailed inner workings of the early nominal model, and their verification gives a lot of confidence in the correctness of its design. In the next stage, faults are introduced into the nominal model via fault injection. Of course, this destroys the validity of the strong invariants developed earlier. So the modified model removes those, and contains only invariants sustainable in both nominal and faulty regimes, i.e. weaker ones capturing the requirements of the full system. This process is formalised within a retrenchment development step [11–13]. But, equally evidently, provided no fault occurs during a run of the system, the earlier stronger invariants will hold true. So, in the next stage, the stronger invariants are reinstated, and the non-occurrence of faults is axiomatised (typically by setting all fault variables permanently to false, or by disabling fault occurrence in some other way) — the formality of the retrenchment step helps to do this in a structured way that is intended to be non-invasive, as regards the pivotal features of the system model. In this model, modified from the faulty system model in a stylised manner, despite the presence of all the fault machinery (except for the actual invocation of faults), the stronger invariants are provable, and their verification gives added confidence in the design, even when the fault machinery is present. That, in a nutshell, is the proposal of this paper.

The rest of this paper is as follows. Section 2 recalls the small set of Event-B [1] and its refinement and retrenchment theory to enable us to handle the concepts of this paper and of our illustrative example. Section 3 introduces a toy switching example in nominal form. Section 4 considers injecting faults into the nominal model, and structures the process using the retrenchment machinery. Section 5 discuses how the stronger invariants of the nominal model can be retained within the failing model using the formal machinery introduced earlier. Section 6 covers related work. Section 7 concludes.

2   Event-B Essentials, Refinement, Retrenchment

In this section we recall a few essential features of Event-B, omitting a large number of facts not needed for our exposition. See [1–3,17,24–26] for a fuller exposition.

Event-B is a formalism for defining, refining and reasoning about discrete event systems. Its relatively uncluttered design makes it useful in many kinds of application. The syntactic unit that expresses self-contained behaviour is the MACHINE. This declares the VARIABLES of the machine, and crucially, the INVARIANTS that all runs of the machine must conform to. Runs are specified implicitly via successions of EVENTS, each being of the form:

$EvName \mathrel{\hat{=}} \text{WHEN } grd \text{ THEN } xs := es \text{ END}$

---

[1] Of course, in reality, the fault portfolio is contemplated from the earliest stages of development, but we do not include any failure modes in the early stages of formal modelling.

In this, *grd* is a guard, a boolean expression in the variables and constants, the truth of which enables the event to execute (otherwise the event cannot run), and the THEN clause defines a set of parallel updates $xs := es$ to the variables, executed atomically. Of course, there are many additional forms of event syntax in the more definitive [1]. Some of these we will meet below.

For machine M to be *correct*, the following PO schemas must be provable:

$$Init(u') \Rightarrow Inv(u')$$
$$Inv(u) \wedge grd_{Ev}(u) \Rightarrow \exists u' \bullet BApred_{Ev}(u, u')$$
$$Inv(u) \wedge grd_{Ev}(u) \wedge BApred_{Ev}(u, u') \Rightarrow Inv(u')$$

In this, *Init*ialisation is treated as an event so its after-value must establish the machine invariants *Inv*; grd_{Ev} is the guard of event Ev, and $BApred_{Ev}$ is the before-after predicate of event Ev, specifying in a logical form the update to variables that it defines, with primes referring to after-values. Thus the first PO ensures that *Init* establishes the invariants, the second PO gives event feasibility (i.e. there is some after-state for an enabled event), and the third PO ensures all event executions maintain the invariants.

Event-B refinement is based on the action refinement model [4–7]. Suppose a machine MR, with variables v refines machine M with variables u. Suppose the u and v state spaces are related by a refinement invariant $R(u, v)$ (also referred to as the joint invariant). Suppose abstract Ev_A is refined to concrete Ev_C. Then the principal refinement PO schemas are:

$$Init_C(v') \Rightarrow \exists u' \bullet Init_A(u') \wedge R(u', v')$$
$$R(u, v) \wedge grd_{Ev_C}(v) \Rightarrow grd_{Ev_A}(u)$$
$$R(u, v) \wedge grd_{Ev_C}(v) \wedge BApred_{Ev_C}(v, v') \Rightarrow \exists u' \bullet BApred_{Ev_A}(u, u') \wedge R(u', v')$$

In this, the first PO establishes refinement of initialisation, the second is guard strengthening, and the third establishes the simulation property of any concrete step by some abstract step. In addition to refinements of abstract events, the concrete machine may contain new events. These satisfy a PO in which there is no change of the abstract state:

$$R(u, v) \wedge grd_{NewEv_C}(v) \wedge BApred_{NewEv_C}(v, v') \Rightarrow R(u, v')$$

If all of the above are provable for a pair of machines M and MR, then an inductive proof of simulation of any concrete execution by some abstract execution follows relatively readily.

Retrenchment is a looser variant of the refinement relationship between machines. If machine MR with variables v is retrenched to machine MRF with variables w, then firstly, either machine may contain events unrelated by retrenchment to events in the other machine. Secondly, for a pair of corresponding events Ev_A and Ev_C which *are* related by retrenchment, the retrenchment relationship is given by (in addition to the preceding data for refinement), an OUTput clause O_{Ev} and a CONCedes clause C_{Ev}.

The concrete syntax will be exemplified below in our example, but the PO that expresses the retrenchment relationship between Ev_A and Ev_C is:

$$R(v, w) \wedge grd_{Ev}(v, w) \wedge BApred_{Ev_C}(w, w') \Rightarrow \exists v' \bullet BApred_{Ev_A}(v, v') \wedge$$
$$((R(v', w') \wedge O_{Ev}(v, v', w, w')) \vee C_{Ev}(v, v', w, w'))$$

In this, notice that the grd_{Ev}, O_{Ev} and C_{Ev} clauses have no A/C subscripts; they specify arbitrary joint properties. So the PO says that either O_{Ev} is established, strengthening the joint invariant R, or the concedes relation C_{Ev} is established, useful for exceptional cases. For this to be useful, it is often the case that R is trivialised to true, with the grd_{Ev} and O_{Ev} relations expressing any needed non-trivial relationship between the state spaces, as needed by various retrenchment-related event pairs.

3   A Simple Switching Example

Our case study considers a simplified switching application. We model the switching in or out of some high consequence apparatus. This might concern high voltage equipment, or bulk gas transportation, or heavy duty water management switching machinery, etc. Indeed, any situation in which the energetics of the physical elements of the system requires management of large quantities of energy, whereas the switching commands —computer mediated as is invariably the case these days— are energetically negligible by comparison, is a potential application. Figure 1 shows our system. There is a button, pressed by the operator, to switch the apparatus on (and to switch it off again).

The button command is sent to the computer that controls the functioning of the various electro-mechanical components of the switching apparatus. The computer does this via a number of sensor inputs and actuator outputs, most of which we ignore here. Once the operations of the switching have completed, the computer sends a signal telling the lamp to light, confirming success to the operator.

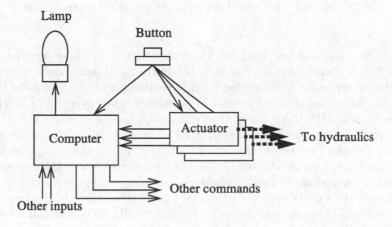

Fig. 1. A simplified switching mechanism.

The button command is also sent to a triplicated hydraulic actuator to power up the hydraulics that will cause the movement of the electromechanical components needed for the actual switching of the apparatus. Successful powerup of the hydraulics is signalled to the computer from a sensor in each hydraulic actuator. This signal acts as a safety interlock that helps prevent malfunction of the system (which could result in costly damage to the equipment). Thus, if the hydraulics fails, the absence of the sensor signal prevents the computer from issuing further commands, avoiding damage. Likewise, if the computer fails, the mere powerup of the hydraulics does not cause anything to move, and again, damage is avoided. Such mutual confirmation is a common feature of high criticality systems. To permit discussion of degraded behaviour, we assume the hydraulic actuators (alone among all the components) are triplicated. This is not very convincing from a critical systems perspective but helps keep our example small.

```
MACHINE Switch
VARIABLES btn, lamp
INVARIANTS
  btn ∈ { UP, DN }
  lamp ∈ { OFF, ON }
EVENTS
  INITIALISATION
    BEGIN
      btn, lamp := UP, OFF
    END
  ButtonDown
    WHEN bth = UP ∧ lamp = OFF
    THEN btn := DN
    END
...   ...
```

```
...   ...
  ButtonUp
    WHEN btn = DN ∧ lamp = ON
    THEN btn := UP
    END
  LampOn
    WHEN btn = DN
    THEN lamp := ON
    END
  LampOff
    WHEN btn = UP
    THEN lamp := OFF
    END
END
```

Fig. 2. Top level (operator's) model of the power switching system.

Figure 2 contains a top level model of the system, machine *Switch*. There are variables *btn* and *lamp* representing the button and lamp. Both are binary. The *ButtonDown* event is permitted when everything is off, and puts the button *DowN*. Likewise, the *ButtonUp* event is permitted when everything is on, and puts the button *UP*. With the button down, the lamp can come *ON* whereas if the button is up, the lamp can go *OFF*. The guards on *ButtonDown* and *ButtonUp* prevent race conditions when switching on has not completed before switching off is commanded, etc. This is the operator's view of the system.

Note the invariants of machine *Switch*. They are just typing invariants. Brief inspection of the events convinces that all four combinations of the two values for the two variables are possible, so there are actually *no* non-trivial invariants at this level with the events as we have defined them.

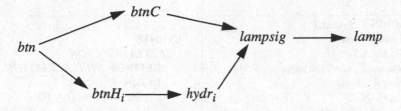

Fig. 3. Variable dependencies in the refined model.

In Figs. 4 and 5, the *Switch* machine is refined to *SwitchR* to include the additional detail described above. Consequently, there are many events to propagate the operator's commands into the system. Figure 3 shows the intended aspects of this by showing the dependencies among the various variables. Thus, a *ButtonDown* command to the *btn* variable enables corresponding commands to the *btnC* (computer) variable, and to the replicated $btnH_i$ (actuator) variables ($i \in \{1, 2, 3\}$). The latter enable commands to $hydr_i$. Both *btnC* and $hydr_i$ are needed to enable the *lampsig* command, which is in turn needed to enable the *lamp* itself. The sequence for *ButtonUp* is similar.

We comment on the invariants of *SwitchR*. When a switching on or switching off process is in progress, little can be said about the relationships between the values of variables. A particular value of a given variable in Fig. 3 does not imply anything non-trivial about the value of any other variable. However, if we have a set of values for variables across a *cut* of Fig. 3 consistent with a *ButtonDown* command, and a set of values for variables across a *later cut* of Fig. 3 also consistent with a *ButtonDown* command, then we can know that all the variables between the two cuts must also have values consistent with a *ButtonDown* command, because a *ButtonDown* command must complete fully, before a *ButtonUp* command can start (this is clear from the guards on *ButtonDown* and *ButtonUp*). This allows us to write down a whole collection of invariants.

In the left box of Fig. 4 typing invariants occur above the first horizontal line. Beneath are some invariants based on the above observations. So the first one is based on a cut through *btn* and another through *lamp* (defining the hypothesis of the implication) and the conclusion claims values for all the other variables, these all being values consistent with a *ButtonDown* process. The next invariant moves the second cut to *lampsig*. And so on, until the cuts meet in the middle leaving no variable in between whose value is to be claimed in the conclusion. Note that we have not even exhausted the possibilities for generating invariants according to the scheme described, since all our invariants either include (or exclude) values for all three $btnH_i$ variables together. There will be additional invariants in which some *btnH* variable(s) is/are hypothesised and the other(s) is/are concluded, and vice versa. Likewise for the $hydr_i$ variables. Between the second and third horizontal lines are analogous invariants for the *ButtonUp* process, given by inverting all the variable values.

MACHINE *SwitchR*
REFINES *Switch*
VARIABLES
  $btn, btnC, btnH_i, hydr_i,$
  $lampsig, lamp$
INVARIANTS
  $btn \in \{UP, DN\}$
  $btnC \in \{UP, DN\}$
  $\bigwedge_i btnH_i \in \{UP, DN\}$
  $lampsig \in \{OFF, ON\}$
  $lamp \in \{OFF, ON\}$
  $\bigwedge_i hydr_i \in \{OFF, ON\}$

  $btn = DN \wedge lamp = ON \Rightarrow$
    $btnC = DN \wedge \bigwedge_i btnH_i = DN \wedge$
    $\bigwedge_i hyrd_i = ON \wedge lampsig = ON$
  $btn = DN \wedge lampsig = ON \Rightarrow$
    $btnC = DN \wedge \bigwedge_i btnH_i = DN \wedge$
    $\bigwedge_i hyrd_i = ON$
  $btn = DN \wedge btnC = DN \wedge$
    $\bigwedge_i hyrd_i = ON \Rightarrow \bigwedge_i btnH_i = DN$
  $btnC = DN \wedge \bigwedge_i btnH_i = DN \wedge$
    $lamp = ON \Rightarrow$
    $\bigwedge_i hyrd_i = ON \wedge lampsig = ON$
  $btnC = DN \wedge \bigwedge_i btnH_i = DN \wedge$
    $lampsig = ON \Rightarrow \bigwedge_i hyrd_i = ON$
  $btnC = DN \wedge \bigwedge_i hyrd_i = ON \wedge$
    $lamp = ON \Rightarrow lampsig = ON$

  $btn = UP \wedge lamp = OFF \Rightarrow$
    $btnC = UP \wedge \bigwedge_i btnH_i = UP \wedge$
    $\bigwedge_i hyrd_i = OFF \wedge lampsig = OFF$
  $btn = UP \wedge lampsig = OFF \Rightarrow$
    $btnC = UP \wedge \bigwedge_i btnH_i = UP \wedge$
    $\bigwedge_i hyrd_i = OFF$
  $btn = UP \wedge btnC = UP \wedge$
    $\bigwedge_i hyrd_i = OFF \Rightarrow \bigwedge_i btnH_i = UP$
  $btnC = UP \wedge \bigwedge_i btnH_i = UP \wedge$
    $lamp = OFF \Rightarrow$
    $\bigwedge_i hyrd_i = OFF \wedge lampsig = OFF$
  $btnC = UP \wedge \bigwedge_i btnH_i = UP \wedge$
    $lampsig = OFF \Rightarrow \bigwedge_i hyrd_i = OFF$
  $btnC = UP \wedge \bigwedge_i hyrd_i = OFF \wedge$
    $lamp = OFF \Rightarrow lampsig = OFF$

... ...
EVENTS
  INITIALISATION
    REFINES *INITIALISATION*
    BEGIN
      $btn, btnC := UP, UP$
      $\|_i btnH_i, hydr_i := UP, OFF$
      $lampsig, lamp := OFF, OFF$
    END
  ButtonDown
    REFINES *ButtonDown*
    WHEN $btn = UP \wedge lamp = OFF$
    THEN $btn := DN$
    END
  ButtonDownC
    WHEN $btn = DN$
    THEN $btnC := DN$
    END
  ButtonDownH_i
    WHEN $btn = DN$
    THEN $btnH_i := DN$
    END
  ButtonUp
    REFINES *ButtonUp*
    WHEN $btn = DN \wedge lamp = ON$
    THEN $btn := UP$
    END
  ButtonUpC
    WHEN $btn = UP$
    THEN $btnC := UP$
    END
  ButtonUpH_i
    WHEN $btn = UP$
    THEN $btnH_i := UP$
    END
  HydraulicsOn_i
    WHEN $btnH_i = DN$
    THEN $hydr_i := ON$
    END
  HydraulicsOff_i
    WHEN $btnH_i = UP$
    THEN $hydr_i := OFF$
    END
... ...

Fig. 4. The *SwitchR* machine, a refinement of *Switch* to include additional modelling detail.

```
...   ...                          ...   ...
    LampSignalOn                       LampOn
      WHEN  btnC = DN ∧                  REFINES  LampOn
        ⋀ᵢ hydrᵢ = ON                    WHEN  lampsig = ON
      THEN  lampsig := ON                THEN  lamp := ON
      END                                END
    LampSignalOff                      LampOff
      WHEN  btnC = UP ∧                  REFINES  LampOff
        ⋀ᵢ hydrᵢ = OFF                   WHEN  lampsig = OFF
      THEN  lampsig := OFF               THEN  lamp := OFF
      END                                END
...   ...                            END
```

Fig. 5. The *SwitchR* machine, continued.

Whether or not a genuine engineering process would choose to assert all these invariants is open to discussion. Provided they are true, their proof lends some additional assurance to, and confidence in, the correctness of the model. But that is not the only issue. The proofs may come at some cost in labour to establish their truth, so the effort that must be invested in doing such verification must be weighed against the additional assurance to be gained, in a cost-benefit analysis.

In any event, overwhelmingly often, the invariants that one chooses to include in a development are precisely that: i.e. a matter of choice and judgment. The choice might be influenced by many things, not the least of these being the ease with which one or other system property is capable of being expressed in the formalism being used for the system model. In the vast majority of cases, the invariants express only a safe approximation to the reachable set of the state space, so *which* safe approximation is chosen to be represented via the invariants is not an absolute and immutable attribute of the problem. (Despite the obvious truth of this, it is surprising how often we speak of *the* invariants, as though there were no choice in the matter.)

4 Switching Under Degraded Operation

We now develop our switching application to include some failure modes. We permit failures in the actuators, but these are the only components in our development that we permit to fail. Although this is not very convincing in an engineering sense, it helps keep the development to a size we can accommodate in this paper, thus illustrating the brief remarks about our general technique made in the Introduction. Although we introduce and tolerate some faults, we do not go so far as to recover from them, or to model faults beyond the tolerable regime we define.

Figures 6 and 7 show the faulty machine *SwitchRF*. It retrenches *SwitchR* since the difference in behaviour compared with *SwitchR* is too great to reconcile via refinement. There are three new boolean variables $ffAct_i$ to model the presence of a fault in one of the actuators.

MACHINE *SwitchRF*
RETRENCHES *SwitchR*
VARIABLES
  $btn, btnC, btnH_i, hydr_i,$
  $lampsig, lamp,$
  $ffAct_i$
INVARIANTS
  $btn \in \{UP, DN\}$
  $btnC \in \{UP, DN\}$
  $\bigwedge_i btnH_i \in \{UP, DN\}$
  $lampsig \in \{OFF, ON\}$
  $lamp \in \{OFF, ON\}$
  $\bigwedge_i hydr_i \in \{OFF, ON\}$
  $\bigwedge_i ffAct_i \in BOOL$
  $\overline{\overline{}}$

  $btn^R = btn$
  $btnC^R = btnC$
  $lampsig^R = lampsig$
  $lamp^R = lamp$
  $\overline{}$

  $\bigvee_{i \neq j} btnH_i = btnH_j$
  $\bigvee_{i \neq j} hydr_i = hydr_j$
EVENTS
  INITIALISATION
    REFINES *INITIALISATION*
    BEGIN
      $btn, btnC := UP, UP$
      $\|_i btnH_i, hydr_i := UP, OFF$
      $lampsig, lamp := OFF, OFF$
      $\|_i ffAct_i := \mathsf{false}$
    END
  InjectFault
    WHEN $\bigwedge_i \neg ffAct_i$
    THEN $\|_i ffAct_i, btnH_i, hydr_i \mid:$
    $\neg \bigwedge_i ffAct'_i \wedge \bigoplus_i ffAct'_i \wedge$
    $\bigwedge_i [\, \neg ffAct'_i \Rightarrow$
      $(btnH'_i = btnH_i \wedge$
      $hydr'_i = hydr_i) \,]$
    END
  ButtonDown
    REFINES *ButtonDown*
    WHEN $btn = UP \wedge lamp = OFF$
    THEN $btn := DN$
    END
  ButtonDownC
    REFINES *ButtonDownC*
    WHEN $btn = DN$
    THEN $btnC := DN$
    END
  ... ...

... ...
  ButtonDownH_i
    REFINES *ButtonDownH_i*
    WHEN $\neg ffAct_i \wedge btn = DN$
    THEN $btnH_i := DN$
    END
  ButtonUp
    REFINES *ButtonUp*
    WHEN $btn = DN \wedge lamp = ON$
    THEN $btn := UP$
    END
  ButtonUpC
    REFINES *ButtonUpC*
    WHEN $btn = UP$
    THEN $btnC := UP$
    END
  ButtonUpH_i
    REFINES *ButtonUpH_i*
    WHEN $\neg ffAct_i \wedge btn = UP$
    THEN $btnH_i := UP$
    END
  HydraulicsOn_i
    REFINES *HydraulicsOn_i*
    WHEN $\neg ffAct_i \wedge btnH_i = DN$
    THEN $hydr_i := ON$
    END
  HydraulicsOff_i
    REFINES *HydraulicsOff_i*
    WHEN $\neg ffAct_i \wedge btnH_i = UP$
    THEN $hydr_i := OFF$
    END
  LampSignalOn
    RETRENCHES *LampSignalOn*
    WHEN $btnC^R = btnC = DN \wedge$
    $\bigwedge_i hydr_i^R = ON \wedge$
    $[\, \bigwedge_i \neg ffAct_i \wedge hydr_i = ON \vee$
    $\bigvee_{i \neq j} (\neg ffAct_i \wedge hydr_i = ON \wedge$
    $\neg ffAct_j \wedge hydr_j = ON) \,]$
    OUT $\bigvee_{i \neq j} [\, \neg ffAct_i \wedge \neg ffAct_j \wedge$
    $btnH_i = btnH'_i = btnH_i^R = btnH_i^{R'} \wedge$
    $hydr_i^R = hydr_i = hydr_i^{R'} = hydr'_i \wedge$
    $btnH_j = btnH'_j = btnH_j^R = btnH_j^{R'} \wedge$
    $hydr_j^R = hydr_j = hydr_j^{R'} = hydr'_j \,]$
    CONC false
    THEN $lampsig := ON$
    END
... ...

Fig. 6. The *SwitchRF* machine, a retrenchment of *SwitchR* to include failure modes.

```
...   ...
   LampSignalOff
     RETRENCHES LampSignalOff
     WHEN btnC^R = btnC = UP ∧
     ⋀_i hydr_i^R = OFF ∧
     [ ⋀_i ¬ ffAct_i ∧ hydr_i = OFF ∨
       ⋁_{i≠j} (¬ ffAct_i ∧ hydr_i = OFF ∧
               ¬ ffAct_j ∧ hydr_j = OFF) ]
     OUT ⋁_{i≠j} [ ¬ ffAct_i ∧ ¬ ffAct_j ∧
     btnH_i = btnH'_i = btnH_i^R = btnH_i^{R'} ∧
     hydr_i^R = hydr_i = hydr_i^{R'} = hydr'_i ∧
     btnH_j = btnH'_j = btnH_j^R = btnH_j^{R'} ∧
     hydr_j^R = hydr_j = hydr_j^{R'} = hydr'_j ]
     CONC false
     THEN lampsig := OFF
     END
...   ...
```

```
...   ...
   LampOn
     REFINES LampOn
     WHEN lampsig = ON
     THEN lamp := ON
     END
   LampOff
     REFINES LampOff
     WHEN lampsig = OFF
     THEN lamp := OFF
     END
END
```

Fig. 7. The *SwitchRF* machine, continued.

The invariants of *SwitchRF* start with the usual typing invariants. The three horizontal lines suggest the two large blocks of 'two cuts' invariants that we have removed from the *SwitchR* version of the machine. We discuss these a little later.

Next come the joint invariants. In situations where we deal with behaviours as different as nominal vs. faulty, and use retrenchment, it is very important to maintain the distinction between the two models. The easiest way is to ensure all variable names are disjoint between the two models. So we have renamed the *SwitchR* variables by attaching an 'R' superscript, and have kept the *SwitchRF* variables undecorated. So $btn^R = btn$ declares that the *SwitchR* and *SwitchRF* versions of the button variable always have the same value, etc. Evidently, since the actuators can fail, the $btnH_i$ and $hydr_i$ variables do not figure among the non-trivial joint invariants.

Below the horizontal line come two examples of the kind of weaker invariants that express the maximum that may be sustainable in the presence of faults. They say that for at least one two-out-of-three combination of actuator variables, the $btnH$ variables will agree, and the $hydr$ variables will agree. When both kinds of variable are two-valued, and there are three of each to compare to each other, this cannot help but be true.

Among the events, after initialisation, there is the fault injection event *InjectFault*, which features some unfamiliar syntax. It is only enabled when there have been no faults hitherto ($⋀_i ¬ ffAct_i$), and it specifies its update using Event-B's 'arbitrary assignment satisfying a predicate' operator '$|:$'. Thus, the after-values (primed) of all the $ffAct_i$, $btnH_i$, $hydr_i$ variables are assigned to satisfy the clauses that follow. Firstly, exactly one of the $ffAct'_i$ variables is set to true via the negated overall and combined with the exclusive or over the three variables (thus disabling *InjectFault* in future). Secondly, whenever a fault variable $ffAct'_i$ is unset, then the after-values of the corresponding $btnH_i$ and $hydr_i$ variables do not change from their before-values. Saying nothing about the after-values of the $btnH_i$ and $hydr_i$ variables for the $ffAct'_i$ variable that *is* set, allows them to be assigned arbitrarily within their type.

Turning to the other events, the $ButtonDown/Up(C)$ events are unaffected. Moreover, the $ButtonDown/UpH_i$ and $HydraulicsOn/Off_i$ events are enabled only when there is no fault in the corresponding actuator. Since, for these events, the only change is this strengthening of the enabledness condition, these events refine their $SwitchR$ versions according to Event-B rules. The $LampOn/Off$ events are also unchanged.

The fact that the actuator events are disabled by faults, and once a fault has arisen, no further change in the faulty actuator can take place, makes our model a reasonable depiction of a '$stuck\_at$' type of fault at our level of abstraction.

This leaves the $LampSignalOn/Off$ events. Here we need to relate the $SwitchR$ behaviours to the $SwitchRF$ behaviours. The guards demand agreement between the $btnC^{(R)}$ clauses, since the computer does not fail. Beyond this, the $SwitchR$ behaviours demand all three $hydr_i^R$ variables fix on the same value before enabling the event, whereas in the $SwitchRF$ behaviours, either there is no fault, and the behaviour is as for $SwitchR$, or there is a fault, and fault tolerance requires that two non-failing actuators agree on a value to enable the event.

All this is recorded in the WHEN clauses.[2] Thus, the WHEN clauses contain the conjunctions of the three $hydr^R$ conditions from $SwitchR$, alongside a disjunction between, either firstly: the conjunction of the corresponding three fault-free $\neg ffAct \wedge hydr$ conditions from $SwitchRF$, or secondly: of any two-out-of-three combination of fault-free $SwitchRF$ conditions. The enabled events then set $lampsig$ appropriately.

The OUT clauses of the two events declare some facts about the state of affairs upon event completion. It is claimed that the before- and after- values, in both the $SwitchR$ and $SwitchRF$ machines, of the $hydr$ variables, are all equal, for both the i'th and j'th non-failing actuators. This is evidently true from the definitions of the events (i.e. it follows from the assumed WHEN clause and the $lampsig$ update).

The same is claimed for the $btnH$ variables. This is also true for our system, since we could only arrive at a situation in which the $SwitchRF$ event is enabled, when two non-failing actuators in the $SwitchR$ and $SwitchRF$ systems have followed the same trajectory. The proof would depend on the fact that the only way to set the enabling $btnC$ variables, is via the $HydraulicsOn/Off$ events and these can only execute with the $btnH$ variables at the right values. Actually establishing this mechanically would invariably entail the creation of additional invariants to express this fact, which could then be used in the proof of the OUT properties. (This reinforces what was said about invariants at the end of Sect. 3.)

---

[2] The generalised kind of guard used in retrenchment is typically referred to as the WITHIN clause in work on retrenchment.

There is no non-trivial CONCession clause in these events. The overall updates are refining, even if 'non-refining' behaviour is seen in the events themselves — our approach was to merely define behaviour for the *HydraulicsOn/Off* events that could sidestep the faults that are permitted in the system. Non-trivial concessions clauses would most likely be needed if we had defined additional behaviour to react to and recover from detected faults.[3]

It is relatively self-evident that the retrenchment PO quoted at the end of Sect. 2 is provable for the *HydraulicsOn/Off* events, and that it defaults to the refinement PO for the other, refining events of the *SwitchRF* machine.

5   Strong Invariants in Degraded Operation

Suppose we now took the *SwitchRF* machine and removed the *InjectFault* event. Let us call the resulting machine $SwitchRF_{\overline{IF}}$. In $SwitchRF_{\overline{IF}}$, since no fault can arise, the faulty states catered for in the various events become unreachable. So all the invariants of the nominal *SwitchR* machine become true again in $SwitchRF_{\overline{IF}}$. So, suppose we now took the $SwitchRF_{\overline{IF}}$ machine and added to it the blocks of strong invariants between the horizontal lines of Fig. 4. Let us call the resulting machine $SwitchRF_{\overline{IF}}INV$. Then $SwitchRF_{\overline{IF}}INV$ is a correct machine. Thus, we have shown that by performing a relatively superficial syntactic transformation on the faulty system model, we have been able to reintroduce strong invariants that held only in the nominal model. We are done!

It is important to note that the procedure just outlined affects only the syntactic periphery of the *SwitchRF* machine. We took out the *InjectFault* event, which is isolated from the other events in the sense that it is always enabled (until it disables itself), and does not interact with any of the complex functional interdependencies that the internal parts of a complicated design would display. A lot of work would have gone into the creation of the faulty model in a realistic engineering problem, and we do not wish to interfere with that for the sake of some additional assurance, especially if that would involve the risk of inadvertently introducing some inconsistency with the true model. Aside from the *InjectFault* removal, we added invariants, which again does not interfere with the internal structure of the true faulty model. Any useful variation of the process we are describing needs to be non-invasive in the manner we have suggested.

Still, before we get too elated about this outcome, we underline that we said that the invariants added to the $SwitchRF_{\overline{IF}}$ machine to get the $SwitchRF_{\overline{IF}}INV$ machine were true, not that they were provable (at least not necessarily provable relatively easily). This is related to the invariants being a safe approximation to the reachable set, in a kind of converse.

Normally, all the events we write in a system model, and all of their capabilities, represent what we desire our system model to actually be capable of. In the case of a faulty model like the *SwitchRF* machine, we purposely added

---

[3] We write 'non-refining' in quotes because we have carefully defined the joint invariants to be oblivious to the faulty behaviour.

faulty capabilities to the events because we wished to be able to handle that kind of behaviour in a real world implementation. But when we disable fault activation, the parts of events' behaviours relevant to the faulty aspects can never be reached, because the relevant part of the events' enabled sets are outside the reachable set of the modified system. Thus, though events are still defined as being capable of faulty behaviour, that behaviour can never arise in a run of the model. Thereby the stronger invariants of the nominal model become true, even in the context of the faulty capability.

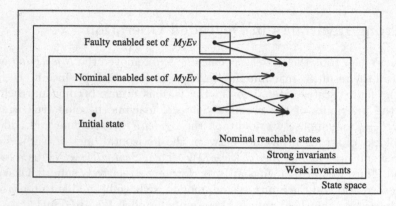

Fig. 8. State space, weak and strong invariants, and enabled sets for a faulty event $MyEv$.

Figure 8 gives a picture of the situation. It shows the total state space, the states described by the weak invariants relevant to faulty behaviour, the states described by the strong invariants relevant to nominal-only behaviour, and the nominal reachable states. Once faults have been deactivated, only states in the nominal reachable set can arise in any run of the system. So for a putative potentially faulty event like $MyEv$, having an enabled set containing faulty as well as nominal states, only the nominal enabled states need to be checked to preserve the invariants, and it is the strong invariants that will hold. That the nominal enabled states can be neatly partitioned from the faulty enabled states follows from the fact that all variables are discrete valued.

The above discussion relies heavily on observations concerning global reachability. This always makes event-by-event reasoning, which is the paradigm in formalisms like Event-B, more difficult. In the context of our toy case study, the remedy is not hard to find. In $SwitchRF_{\overline{IF}}INV$, since the initialisation sets all fault variables to false, and no event changes any fault variable, the falseness of the fault variables becomes an invariant, which is immediately provable, and which may therefore be added to the machine invariants. Since all unruly behaviour by any event involves fault variables that have the value true in a non-trivial manner, unruly behaviour is immediately ruled out during the proof of the simulation PO by the assumed invariants in the PO hypothesis. So only nominal cases need to preserve the invariants, which *should* follow from the properties of the nominal behaviour inside the faulty event. The '*should*' crystalises the additional assurance in the design that our process is intended to provide.

Still, before we get too elated about the preceding conclusion, we should note that it relies on the explicit presence of the fault variables inside the details of the events of the faulty model. The trouble is that the fault variables are really a fiction that abstracts from more detailed model behaviour at lower levels of description. Although a fault injection technique will always require some kind of external event, such as *InjectFault* to initiate the faulty behaviour, at lower levels of description, the ensuing activity will normally involve the variables that describe how the system is constructed, using sensor data values and similar quantities. Moreover, the system will infer some approximation to the value of the fault variables indirectly, by correlating these sensor and other internal values, to determine the best guess at the actual system state.

In a situation as just described, it may be a lot harder to infer the effective values of fault variables, than when fault variable values are available directly. Thus, a proof that only nominal cases can execute and that they preserve the stronger invariants of the nominal model becomes much harder to carry through. Inevitably, more complicated cases will require reasoning about larger or smaller fragments of system runs, and this makes life much more taxing for an approach that strives to divide and conquer the problem of whole system verification by breaking it down into a *per event* proof activity. In such cases, per-event reasoning entails the creation of a host of additional invariants, which capture the properties of the progress through the required fragment of a system run in a relatively finegrained way. Discovering the needed additional invariants can become very non-trivial. Observations such as these lead us to alternatively advocate approaches based around *k*-induction [18,27] as potentially offering reasonable possibilities for outflanking maneuvres, if a direct 1-inductive proof of the desired invariants becomes sufficiently challenging.

With the above caveat on board, we can summarise our approach to the gaining of additional assurance in the design of faulty system models in the following way.

- Develop the nominal model first. Populate it with as many strong invariants as desirable or useful.
- Develop the faulty model via a set of functional departures from the nominal model, and by removal of invariants that only hold in the nominal model. Retrenchment provides a useful vehicle for this.
- Ensure faults are activated in the faulty model in a way that is easy to disable non-invasively, e.g by using fault injection.
- Disable the activation of faults and reintroduce the removed strong invariants.
- Reprove the model.

6   Related Work

Overtly formal techniques, based on confirming that invariants attributed to a system model hold, and fault engineering, based on considering behaviours that violate such invariants, are like oil and water. Overwhelmingly, formal techniques, even when not proving that invariants hold, are concerned with issues involving consistency of invariants and behaviour, such as the process of synthesising invariants from behaviour. In this vein we can mention [14,19,20,23], among many others.

The formal treatment of safety (including fault tolerance) throws up issues similar to ones treated in this paper. See for example [15,16]. The connection with the retrenchment approach can be seen in [9,10].

Also close to the approach of this paper is the work on the KAOS requirements methodology [21,22]. Although focused on requirements, behind the scenes it is highly formalised, and the kinds of departures from ideal behaviour that are unavoidable when debating a family of requirements and that are comparable to our failure modes are, in KAOS, termed *obstacles*. The parallels between the KAOS approach and what is done in retrenchment are described in [8].

7   Conclusions

In the preceding sections we summarised Event-B, and in particular, its refinement and retrenchment POs. Discharging these forms the crux of the Event-B development method. We then introduced a simple switching example to exemplify the subsequent discussion. It was intended to be small enough that we could accommodate it within this paper, yet was complex enough that it admitted the kind of non-trivial invariants that we wanted to consider.

We started with a controller's view and refined it to a more detailed internal model, though still only exhibiting nominal behaviour. We argued for the validity of a large number of strong invariants in this nominal model. We then introduced faults into the model via fault injection, using the retrenchment technique. The latter offers some POs to help control the process of relatively arbitrary system model change. With faults included, we had to remove the strong invariants, which would fail any attempt to verify them. This gave us the springboard for discussing the controlled reintroduction of the strong invariants when faults were deactivated. Provided the deactivation can be done in a suitably non-invasive manner, the resulting model ought to be correct.

We pointed out that establishing the correctness of the resulting model may be easy if the model involves fault variables explicitly, but may be more difficult if all behaviour is exclusively expressed in terms of real system quantities. Thus the tractability of our proposed technique can vary greatly depending on the level of abstraction at which it is applied. That said, in all developments it should be possible to identify a level of abstraction which is high enough so that a system model pitched at that level will prove tractable as regards the applicability of the technique, and thus, to apply the technique there. Refinement may then be sufficient to propagate the guarantess obtained to lower levels of abstraction, if needed.

References

1. Abrial, J.R.: Modeling in Event-B: System and Software Engineering. Cambridge University Press, Cambridge (2010)
2. Abrial, J.R., Butler, M., Hallerstede, S., Hoang, T., Mehta, F., Voisin, L.: Rodin: an open toolset for modelling and reasoning in event-b. Int. J. Soft. Tools Tech. Trans. **12**(6), 447–466 (2010)
3. ADVANCE: European Project ADVANCE. IST-287563. http://www.advance-ict.eu/
4. Back, R.J.R., Sere, K.: Stepwise refinement of action systems. In: Snepscheut, J.L.A. (ed.) MPC 1989. LNCS, vol. 375, pp. 115–138. Springer, Heidelberg (1989). doi:10.1007/3-540-51305-1_7
5. Back, R.J.R., Wright, J.: Trace refinement of action systems. In: Jonsson, B., Parrow, J. (eds.) CONCUR 1994. LNCS, vol. 836, pp. 367–384. Springer, Heidelberg (1994). doi:10.1007/978-3-540-48654-1_28
6. Back, R., Kurki-Suonio, R.: Decentralisation of process nets with centralised control. In: 2nd ACM SIGACT-SIGOPS Symposium on PODC, pp. 131–142. ACM (1983)
7. Back, R., Sere, K.: Superposition refinement of reactive systems. Form. Asp. Comp. **8**(3), 324–346 (1996)
8. Banach, R.: A deidealisation semantics for KAOS. In: Lencastre, M. (ed.) Proceedings of the ACM SAC 2010 (RE track), pp. 267–274. ACM (2010)
9. Banach, R., Bozzano, M.: The mechanical generation of fault trees for reactive systems via retrenchment I: combinational circuits. Form. Asp. Comp. **25**, 573–607 (2013)
10. Banach, R., Bozzano, M.: The mechanical generation of fault trees for reactive systems via retrenchment II: clocked and feedback circuits. Form. Asp. Comp. **25**, 609–657 (2013)
11. Banach, R., Jeske, C.: Retrenchment and refinement interworking: the tower theorems. Math. Struct. Comput. Sci. **25**, 135–202 (2015)
12. Banach, R., Jeske, C., Poppleton, M.: Composition mechanisms for retrenchment. J. Log. Alg. Program. **75**, 209–229 (2008)
13. Banach, R., Poppleton, M., Jeske, C., Stepney, S.: Engineering and theoretical underpinnings of retrenchment. Sci. Comput. Program. **67**, 301–329 (2007)
14. Beyer, D., Henzinger, T.A., Majumdar, R., Rybalchenko, A.: Invariant synthesis for combined theories. In: Cook, B., Podelski, A. (eds.) VMCAI 2007. LNCS, vol. 4349, pp. 378–394. Springer, Heidelberg (2007). doi:10.1007/978-3-540-69738-1_27
15. Bittner, B., Bozzano, M., Cavada, R., Cimatti, A., Gario, M., Griggio, A., Mattarei, C., Micheli, A., Zampedri, G.: The xSAP safety analysis platform. In: Chechik, M., Raskin, J.-F. (eds.) TACAS 2016. LNCS, vol. 9636, pp. 533–539. Springer, Heidelberg (2016). doi:10.1007/978-3-662-49674-9_31
16. Bozzano, M., Villafiorita, A.: Design and Safety Assessment of Critical Systems. CRC Press (Taylor and Francis), an Auerbach Book, Boca Raton (2010)
17. DEPLOY: European Project DEPLOY. IST-511599. http://www.deploy-project.eu/
18. Donaldson, A.F., Haller, L., Kroening, D., Rümmer, P.: Software verification using k-induction. In: Yahav, E. (ed.) SAS 2011. LNCS, vol. 6887, pp. 351–368. Springer, Heidelberg (2011). doi:10.1007/978-3-642-23702-7_26
19. Furia, C.A., Meyer, B.: Inferring loop invariants using postconditions. In: Blass, A., Dershowitz, N., Reisig, W. (eds.) Fields of Logic and Computation. LNCS, vol. 6300, pp. 277–300. Springer, Heidelberg (2010). doi:10.1007/978-3-642-15025-8_15

20. Ghilardi, S., Ranise, S.: Goal-directed invariant synthesis for model checking modulo theories. In: Giese, M., Waaler, A. (eds.) TABLEAUX 2009. LNCS, vol. 5607, pp. 173–188. Springer, Heidelberg (2009). doi:10.1007/978-3-642-02716-1_14

21. van Lamsweerde, A.: Requirements Engineering: From System Goals to UML Models to Software Specifications. Wiley, Chichester (2009)

22. Letier, E.: Reasoning about Agents in Goal-Oriented Requirements Engineering. Ph.D. thesis, Dépt. Ingénierie Informatique, Université Catholique de Louvain (2001)

23. Qin, S., He, G., Luo, C., Chin, W.N.: Loop invariant synthesis in a combined domain. In: Dong, J.S., Zhu, H. (eds.) ICFEM 2010. LNCS, vol. 6447, pp. 468–484. Springer, Heidelberg (2010). doi:10.1007/978-3-642-16901-4_31

24. RODIN: European Project RODIN (Rigorous Open Development for Complex Systems) IST-511599. http://rodin.cs.ncl.ac.uk/

25. Sekerinski, E., Sere, K.: Program Development by Refinement: Case Studies Using the B-Method. Springer, London (1998)

26. Voisin, L., Abrial, J.R.: The rodin platform has turned ten. In: Ait Ameur, Y., Schewe, K.D. (eds.) ABZ 2014. LNCS, vol. 8847, pp. 1–8. Springer, Heidelberg (2014). doi:10.1007/978-3-662-43652-3_1

27. Wahl, T.: The k-induction principle. http://www.ccs.neu.edu/home/wahl/Publications/k-induction.pdf

SafeConcert: A Metamodel for a Concerted Safety Modeling of Socio-Technical Systems

Leonardo Montecchi[1,2(✉)] and Barbara Gallina[3]

[1] University of Florence, Florence, Italy
[2] University of Campinas, Campinas, Brazil
leonardo@ic.unicamp.br
[3] Mälardalen University, Västerås, Sweden
barbara.gallina@mdh.se

Abstract. Socio-technical systems are characterized by the interplay of heterogeneous entities i.e., humans, organizations, and technologies. Application
domains such as petroleum, e-health, and many others rely on solutions based on
safety-critical socio-technical systems. To ensure a safe operation of these interacting heterogeneous entities, multifaceted and integrated modeling and analysis
capabilities are needed. Currently, such capabilities are not at disposal. To
contribute to the provision of such capabilities, in this paper we propose Safe-
Concert, a metamodel that offers constructs to model socio-technical entities and
their safety-related properties. SafeConcert also represents a unified and harmonized language that supports the integrated application of qualitative as well as
quantitative safety analyses techniques. To support our claims we briefly report
about the evaluation that was conducted and documented in the context of the EU
CONCERTO project.

Keywords: Safety-critical · Socio-technical systems · Modeling · Safety analysis

1 Introduction

In application domains such as petroleum, e-health, etc., safety-critical socio-technical
systems play a crucial role. Offshore installations as well as telenursing, for instance,
are characterized by the interplay of heterogeneous entities: humans (e.g., workers,
caregivers and patients), organizations (e.g., regulatory bodies) and technology (e.g.,
decision support systems, databases, etc.). To prevent accidents, the interplay between
such heterogeneous entities must be acceptably safe. To perform safety analysis, both
qualitative and quantitative compositional techniques are available. Currently, automated techniques are at disposal, addressing different aspects of the safety analysis of
a complex safety-critical socio-technical system. However, the current gap resides in
the integration: such kind of systems require the integrated application of different techniques, and currently no satisfying means is at disposal for multifaceted, integrated, and
tool-supported safety modeling and analysis of socio-technical systems.

One of the objectives of the CONCERTO project [2], was to contribute to the provision of such means. In this paper, we propose a novel metamodel developed within the

© Springer International Publishing AG 2017
M. Bozzano and Y. Papadopoulos (Eds.): IMBSA 2017, LNCS 10437, pp. 129–144, 2017.
DOI: 10.1007/978-3-319-64119-5_9

project, called SafeConcert, which permits architects to interpret human, organizational, and technological entities in terms of components, and model their behavior with respect to safety. SafeConcert supports, as in a concert, multiple voices: not only technological components but also human and organizational components; not only a single safety analysis technique but the interplay of safety analyses techniques; not only a single safety standard but a family of standards.

To summarize, the contribution of this paper is a novel metamodel that targets the design of safety-critical socio-technical systems by: (i) offering constructs for modeling both socio (i.e., human and organizational), and technical entities in a common model, thus facilitating the unified analysis of their interdependencies; (ii) offering constructs for modeling the nominal, erroneous, and fault-tolerant behavior of both socio and technical components; (iii) offering constructs for classifying entities with respect to their criticality, supporting both cross-domain and domain-specific annotations; and (iv) facilitating the interplay of qualitative quantitative safety analyses, by using a common harmonized conceptual model.

Two widely adopted techniques for safety analysis are those based on failure propagation logic, typically for qualitative analysis, and those based on stochastic Petri nets, when quantitative analysis is needed. After introducing the SafeConcert metamodel, we discuss its ability to support both techniques, and the benefits in such cross-fertilizing interplay. Finally, we briefly discuss about the implementation and the different ways in which the metamodel has been evaluated.

The rest of the paper is organized as follows. In Sect. 2, we provide essential background information. In Sect. 3, we present our metamodel, SafeConcert. In Sect. 4, we discuss how the metamodel supports safety analysis, and we summarize on its evaluation. In Sect. 5, we discuss related work. Finally, in Sect. 6, we present some concluding remarks and future work.

2   Context and Background

2.1   Safety-Critical Socio-Technical Systems

Safety is defined as the "absence of catastrophic consequences on the user(s) and the environment" [13], and it is an attribute of dependability. Safety-critical systems are those systems whose failure may have impact on the safety, i.e., can lead to catastrophic consequences on users and the environment. Many systems on which we rely every day fall in this category: transportations, medical devices, power plants.

Socio-technical refers to the interrelatedness of "social" (of people and society) and "technical" (of machines and technology) aspects [3, 9]. Successful (or unsuccessful) system performance depends on this interrelatedness, which comprises linear 'cause and effect' relationships, and 'non-linear', complex, even unpredictable relationships. A wide range of safety-critical systems exhibit socio-technical aspects as well. Proper safety practices should try to investigate the cause-effect relations that play a role in reduced human performance, and put the blame on such relations rather than on humans mistakes alone [30].

Such systems must ensure harm-free operation, even in the event of components' failure or incorrect interactions between components. This is typically assessed through a structured development process that includes the execution of safety analysis, whose objective is to define safety-related requirements, and assess whether the system fulfills them. The metamodel in this paper aims to support such process.

Manufacturers as well as suppliers have to comply with safety standards e.g., ISO 26262 [16] in the automotive domain. These standards tend to be conservative, so new practices typically are not incorporated due to the impossibility to measure their confidence. In fact, in the industry, prevalently manual techniques like Fault Tree Analysis (FTA) and Failure Modes and Effects Analysis (FMEA) are still the main instrument to analyze the propagation of threats (faults/errors/failures [13]), and produce evidence that the system fulfills its safety requirements.

Model-based approaches (e.g., [14]), by improving the formalization and consistency of concepts, have the potential to support a better documentation of safety aspects, and semi-automated support to safety analysis. Nevertheless, the gap between industrial state of practice and academic state of the art is still evident, for different reasons, including the lack of supporting tools. Only recently, in the avionics domain, model-based development has been included as a DO-178C supplement, known as DO-331 [22]. Guidance is now available for applying model-based development.

2.2 Safety Analysis in the CHESS Framework

The "CHESS Framework" is a framework for the design, development, and analysis of safety-critical systems, with a strong focus on the specification and analysis of non-functional properties. The framework defines a UML-based modeling language, called CHESS ML [23], and includes a set of plugins to perform code generation, constraints checking, and different kinds of analyses. The framework was originally developed within the CHESS project [1], later extended within CONCERTO [2], and then released as open source under the Polarsys initiative [5]. Two safety analysis techniques are supported: CHESS-FLA and CHESS-SBA.

CHESS-FLA [31] allows users (system architects and safety engineers) to decorate component-based architectural models (specified using CHESS-ML) with dependability related information, execute Failure Logic Analysis (FLA) techniques, and get the results back-propagated onto the original model. Different FLA techniques are available in the literature [14], and can be used at the early stages of the design phase to achieve a robust architecture with respect to linear relationships. CHESS-FLA supports FPTC [4] and FI^{4}FA [26]; the reason behind this choice in relation to other existing techniques was discussed in [31]. FPTC is a compositional technique to qualitatively assess the dependability/safety of component-based systems, and partially combines and automatize traditional safety analysis techniques (i.e., FMEA and FTA). FPTC allows users to calculate the behavior at system-level, based on the specification of the behavior of individual components. The behavior of the individual components, established by studying the components in isolation, is expressed by a set of logical expressions (FPTC rules) that relate output failures (occurring on output ports) to combinations of input failures (occurring on input ports). FI^{4}FA extends FPTC for reasoning about failures related to faulty design of concurrency control or fault tolerance within transaction-based systems.

The CHESS "State-based analysis" plugin (CHESS-SBA) [10] allows users to perform quantitative dependability analysis on models specified using CHESS-ML and enriched with quantitative (i.e., probabilistic/stochastic) dependability information, including failure and repair distribution of components, propagations delays and probabilities, and some fault-tolerance and maintenance concepts. Such information is added to the functional model in two main ways: (i) with a set of stereotypes that allow simple attributes to be attached to software and hardware components [19], or (ii) with an "error model", i.e., a particular kind of StateMachine diagram in which a more detailed failure behavior of a component can be specified.

Such enriched model is transformed to a stochastic state-based model, which is then analyzed to evaluate the degree of satisfaction of system-level dependability attributes, in the form of probabilistic metrics. As opposed to combinatorial models like Fault-Trees, state-based methods like Stochastic Petri Nets (SPNs) [29] are able to take into account complex dependencies between events.

One of the limitations that we faced in the previous versions of the framework was the lack of integration between the different analysis techniques. While they could be applied starting from the same system architecture specified in CHESS ML, those analyses were using different portions of the language, being de-facto impossible to use them in an integrated way. In general, in safety analysis some aspects are more conveniently analyzed with a certain technique with respect to another, and different levels of detail are required at different stages. Also, results obtained with a technique are useful inputs for subsequent analysis steps. Being able to apply both techniques on the same model is a contribution towards integrated model-based safety analysis.

3   SafeConcert

In CONCERTO we improve the integration of safety analyses by defining a common underlying metamodel, called SafeConcert, which solves inconsistencies and redundancies. Besides adding new modeling features, SafeConcert serves as a common abstract syntax for both FLA and SBA. From this common metamodel, different concrete syntaxes, suitable to the specificities of each technique, are then derived.

The harmonization is based on a set of principles, which are discussed in the following. The modeling philosophy follows the *component-based* approach, meaning that components, ports, and connectors are the main entities. Failure modes will be specified with respect to the services that a component provides, i.e., its output ports. We describe the failure behavior of system elements as *state machines*, which are flexible while being relatively simple to describe and understand. This also adheres to the classical literature on dependability, which defines key concepts like errors and failures as states and events, respectively [13].

The presentation of the SafeConcert metamodel is organized by topics: *structure, organizational components, human components, failure modes and criticality, behaviors, input and output events, internal events,* and *fault tolerance events.* A complete view of the metamodel is available at [21].

3.1 Structure

The central element of SafeConcert is the *SystemElement* abstract metaclass, which is the common supertype for all the entities that may have dependability information attached to them. A *SystemElement* can be either a *Component* or a *Connector.* We distinguish three kinds of components: *SoftwareComponents, HardwareComponents* (including mechanical ones), and *SocioComponents.* Software and hardware components can be described in a hierarchical fashion, i.e., they can contain sub-components of the same type. Software components can be allocated on hardware components (*isAllocatedOn* relation). Socio components are partitioned into two distinct kinds of components: *Organization* and *Human.*

A Connector represents anything via which two elements may interact including, but not only, hardware and software connections, which are modeled with the *HardwareConnector* and *SoftwareConnector* elements, respectively. Software connectors may be allocated on hardware connectors, by means of the *isAllocatedOn* relation. Other links that do not fit in that category (e.g., voice communication for human entities) are modeled as a generic *Connector* element.

A *SystemElement* may own a certain number of *Ports,* which allow it to interact with other system elements. Since also connectors can fail (e.g., a network cable), differently than in functional modeling, we adopt ports also for *Connector* elements. We assume here that component instances inherit the failure behavior of the component type, and we thus do not introduce the concept of component instance.

3.2 Organizational Components

For social components, as initially explored in [3], we base our model on the SERA (Systematic Error and Risk Analysis)-related classification [18]. An organization can be decomposed in a certain number of different "units", modeling different aspects of how the organization gathers and processes information, and interacts with the other entities of the socio-technical system.

The abstract class *OrganizationUnit* is specialized to reflect different kinds of units, which are identified by the prefix "OU". Following [18], we include units devoted to mission management (*OUMissionManagement*), to the management of rules and regulations (*OURules&RegulationManagement*), climate (*OUClimateManagement*), oversight (*OUOversightManagement*), process (*OUProcessManagement*), and resources (*OUResourceManagement*).

3.3 Human Components

Following what initially devised in [3], human components are represented as composite components; the motivation stems from the SERA-related classification. By inspecting thoroughly the twelve categories of human failures (e.g. attention failure), it has been recognized that these failures were related to two types of human functionalities: internal functionalities responsible of sensing, perceiving, deciding, etc., and functionalities responsible of acting. Thus, a *Human* component consists of a set of *HumanSensorUnit* and a set of *HumanActuatorUnit* elements (Fig. 1).

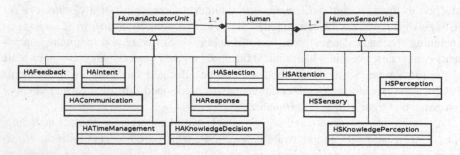

Fig. 1. SafeConcert model elements to model human components.

A sensor-like capability (*HumanSensorUnit*) can be one of the following kinds. *HSAttention*, responsible of attending to relevant information that is present or accessible; *HSPerception*, responsible of assessing a situation; *HSKnowledgePerception*, responsible of interpreting a situation, based on pre-existing baseline knowledge; and *HSSensory*, responsible of sensing the incoming visual, auditory, tactile and olfactory information.

An actuator-like capability (*HumanActuatorUnit*) can be one of the following kinds. *HAFeedback*, responsible of maintaining error-correcting feedbacks, aimed at adjusting the imprecision of the internal models; *HAIntent*, responsible of exercising a goal in compliance with rules and regulations; *HACommunication*, responsible of passing/receiving correct information; *HASelection*, responsible of formulating the right plan to achieve the goal; *HAResponse*, responsible of actuating the physical response required to perform the task; *HAKnowledgeDecision*, responsible of forming an appropriate or correct response to the situation; and *HATimeManagement*, responsible of using appropriate and effective time management strategies.

There may be different reasons for including human behavior in safety models. In the automotive domain, for example, it would help in characterizing the aspect of controllability [16] of the driver.

3.4 Failure Modes and Criticality

In our metamodel, a *Port* is the point where failures are propagated from/to other entities of the socio-technical system, i.e., its *service interface* as meant by [13]. In this perspective, also a *SocioComponent* can own ports.

As shown in Fig. 2, *Ports* are the model elements to which failure modes (*Failure-Mode* entity) are associated. More precisely, failure modes are grouped into *Failure-ModeGroups*, which are then associated to ports. The motivation of this choice is well explained in [11]: in this way failure modes can be organized by domain or context. For example, distinguishing failure modes related to mechanical failures from those related to electrical failures.

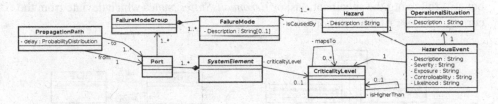

Fig. 2. SafeConcert model elements to represent failure modes and criticality.

Propagation between two *Ports* is established by the *PropagationPath* entity, which has essentially the role of the classical "connector", i.e., it connects two *Port* entities. The *delay* attribute may specify a propagation delay between the two ports.

SafeConcert also includes a set of constructs especially devoted to safety aspects. As defined in safety standards (e.g., [16]), a hazardous event occurs as a combination of a hazard and an "operational situation", e.g., parking vs. driving for the automotive domain, takeoff vs. landing for avionics. As such, the *HazardousEvent* element relates itself to an *OperationalSituation* and a *Hazard*. A *Hazard* is in relation with one or more *FailureModes* that are its causes. Besides having a textual description, a *HazardousEvent* has also additional attributes that characterize the event. Controllability, severity and exposure, for instance, are attributes used to establish the criticality level of hazardous events in the automotive domain. Such attributes allow analysts to derive a criticality level to be assigned to the hazardous event.

Due to the different existing classification of criticality levels in different domains (e.g., SILs, ASILs, DALs [15]), the metamodel allows hierarchies of criticality levels to be specified and put in relation with each other. A *CriticalityLevel* may then be related to a lower-level one through the *isHigherThan* relation; for example, "SIL-4" would be in such relation with "SIL-3". Criticality levels from different domains can be put in relation through the *mapsTo* relation; for example, "ASIL-D" could be in such relation with "SIL-3" [15]. Using this approach permits to: (i) reuse (at least partially) safety models from different domains, and (ii) have both domain-specific and cross-domain criticality levels defined in the same model.

A criticality level can be associated to both *SystemElement* and to *HazardousEvent*. In principle, the criticality level assigned to a system element should be equal or higher than the highest criticality level associated with hazards caused by its failure modes. Ensuring such consistency is beyond the scope of this paper: actually such consistency should be reached as a result of the safety analysis process.

3.5 Behaviors

The failure behavior of system elements is defined as a state machine, i.e., states and transitions between them. Note that we want to model the behavior from the perspective of safety analysis only. Accordingly, each *SystemElement* owns one or more *States* (Fig. 3), either *NormalStates*, states that belong to the nominal behavior of the component; *DegradedStates*, states in which the service provided by the component is degraded but still following the specifications; or *ErroneousStates*, states which deviate from the correct behavior of the component.

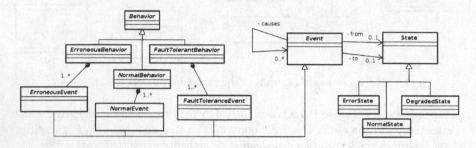

Fig. 3. Modeling of behaviors, events, and states in SafeConcert.

An *Event* is something that occurs either internally or externally to the component, and that is deemed atomic with respect to the adopted level of detail. An event may (but not necessarily), cause the component to transition from one state to another. We classify events according to two dimensions: (i) location, i.e., whether they are *InputEvents, InternalEvents*, or *OutputEvents*, and (ii) type, i.e., whether they are *NormalEvents, ErroneousEvents,* or *FaultToleranceEvents*.

A *SystemElement* may own a set of *Behaviors*, i.e., collections of events related to that component, organized according to different views. We separate different aspects of a component's behavior into three views: *NormalBehavior*, which contains transitions related to the nominal behavior of the component (*NormalEvents*), *ErroneousBehavior*, which contains transitions related to the erronoeus behavior of the component (*ErroneousEvents*), and *FaultTolerantBehavior*, which contains fault-tolerant behavior, in terms of *FaultToleranceEvents*. This approach adheres to the concept of "idealized fault-tolerant component" [17], in which different aspects of a component's behavior are kept separated.

3.6 Input and Output Events

External events occur on the ports of a system element, and are either *InputEvents* or *OutputEvents*. In both cases, they are in relation with a *Port* element (Fig. 4). Two kinds of events may occur as an input event: a *NormalInput* event, or an *ExternalFault*, meaning that the component has received an input that deviates from the specification, i.e., the service it receives from another entity is not correct [13].

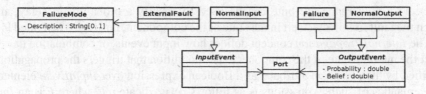

Fig. 4. Input events and output events in SafeConcert.

Output events can be *NormalOutput*, i.e., the component provides a correct service, or *Failure*, meaning that the service provided by the component on the involved port has become incorrect [13]. A *Failure* event has a relation to a *FailureMode* entity, which specifies the kind of failure that has occurred.

It is often difficult to precisely know the failure behavior of a component. In Safe-Concert such uncertainty can be expressed according to two dimensions: (i) in terms of the *probability* of occurrence of one failure mode with respect to others, or (ii) in terms of the *belief* on which failure mode will occur. In the first dimension, it is assumed that different failure modes can be clearly distinguished, and they occur with known probabilities. The second dimension reflects the condition in which the actual nature of failure modes is known only with a certain *belief*, as intended in the fuzzy logic domain. Belief supports the integration of F^2I^4FA [33].

3.7 Internal Events

We distinguish between two macro-categories of internal events: *NormalInternalEvent*, and *InternalThreat* (Fig. 5). An internal event may have a *delay*, expressed by a probability distribution, and a *probability* of occurrence.

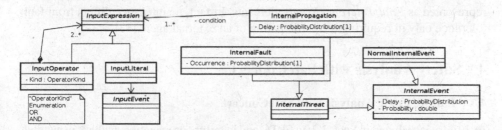

Fig. 5. Internal events in SafeConcert.

A *NormalInternalEvent* is an event foreseen by the specification, e.g., a switch to a power saving mode due to a low battery level. For the purpose of safety analysis it is important to take into account such aspects of a component's behavior: the occurrence of failures, as well as their effects and criticality, may depend, for example, on the current system operational mode (e.g., take off, cruise, and landing for an aircraft).

An *InternalThreat* is essentially an *InternalFault*, or an *InternalPropagation*. An *InternalFault* represents a fault that occurs spontaneously within the component (e.g., an electrical fault) or that is pre-existing and dormant [13] (e.g., a software fault). The *occurrence* attribute can be used to specify a probabilistic delay, after which the fault manifests itself in the state of the component, i.e., it gets activated [13].

The *InternalPropagation* concept defines how input events, or combination thereof, affect the internal state of the component. The condition that triggers the propagation is specified by the *condition* attribute, as a Boolean expression over *InputEvent* elements. The semantics of such expressions is as follows. A predicate *p.E*, where *E* is an *InputEvent* element occurring on port *p*, is *true* iff the most recent event occurred on *p* is *E*, and *false* otherwise. The effects of an *InternalPropagation* are specified by: (i) specifying a state-transition for it, or (ii) specifying a set of events that are triggered by it (e.g., *Failure* events), through the *causes* relation.

3.8 Fault-Tolerance Events

The classical taxonomy of dependable computing [13] classifies fault tolerance techniques in three main groups: error detection, error handling, and fault handling. In SafeConcert we follow such classification.

The *ErrorDetection* event represents the detection of an error in the state of the component, to which different actions may follow. Those actions can be defined by associating a state transition with the event (e.g., to a safe state), or by specifying that additional events are triggered by the error detection event (e.g., reconfiguration events). The *ErrorHandling* event represents the elimination of an existing error in the state of the component, thus bringing the component to an error-free state (e.g., rollback or rollforward [13]). The *FaultHandling* event represents the application of a technique that prevents existing faults from being reactivated, e.g., fault isolation (faulty components are excluded from the service delivery) or reconfiguration.

We note that maintenance concepts are not explicitly addressed in our metamodel. Events like physical repairs, replacement of failed components, restart of software are represented as *FaultToleranceEvents* elements. In fact, maintenance differs from fault tolerance only in requiring the participation of an external agent [13].

4   Safety Analysis with SafeConcert

4.1 Failure Logic Analysis with SafeConcert

As briefly introduced in Sect. 2.2, in FPTC and in failure propagation analysis in general, a specification for a component contains a set of expressions that relate the failures occurring on its input ports with failures occurring on its output ports.

In SafeConcert, the behavior corresponding to an FPTC specification is described by a collection of *Events*, grouped in one or more *Behavior* elements. Each failure received as input, and thus referenced in the left part of a FPTC rule in the specification, is described by an *ExternalFault* event, referencing the involved *FailureMode* and *Port* elements. Similarly, each failure that can be produced by the component, i.e., those referenced in the right part of a FPTC rule, is described by a *Failure* event, with the appropriate *FailureMode* and *Port* elements as references. Such events are grouped into the *ErroneousBehavior* of the involved component.

A set of *NormalInput* events, one for each of the input ports of the component, expresses the occurrence of a "normal" input on the ports of the component (i.e., the "nofailure" of [3]); similarly, a set of *NormalOutput* events, one for each output port of the component, express the "normal" output emitted on those ports. Those are collectively grouped into the *NormalBehavior* of the involved component.

For each rule, the causation link between the input events (left part of the rule), and output events (right part of the rule) is represented through an *InternalPropagation* model element for which (i) the *condition* attribute is set based on the left hand side of the FPTC rule, referring the corresponding *NormalInput* and/or *ExternalFault* events; and (ii) the *causes* attribute is instead set based on the right hand part of the rule, adding all the corresponding *NormalOutput* and/or *Failure* events.

Concerning states, the adopted level of detail implies a single *State* for each component, which is not modified by the occurrence of events. This is consistent with the interpretation of failure propagation specifications: cause-effect relations between input events (external faults) and output events (failures), that are abstraction of the internal behavior of the component, and do not change over time.

4.2 State-Based Analysis with SafeConcert

We first consider the "template" stereotypes that are used in CHESS-SBA to compactly describe the failure and repair behavior of component [19]. For stateless components («StatelessSoftware» or «StatelessHardware»), and components annotated with «SimpleStochasticBehavior» , it is assumed that they immediately become failed as result of fault activation. In SafeConcert, this is represented by defining two states for the component, "healthy" and "failed", and an *InternalFault* event causing a transition between them. The event causes (through the *cause* relation) one or more *Failure* events, one for each output port of the component.

For stateful components instead («StatefulSoftware» and «StatefulHardware»), time elapses between fault activation and the subsequent component failure. In SafeConcert this is modeled with an additional "erroneous" state of the component. The *InternalFault* event makes the component transition from "healthy" to "erroneous"; an additional *InternalPropagation* event, representing error latency, triggers the transition from "erroneous" to "failed", and causes the *Failure* events for the component. Concerning repairs, in both cases, they are modeled with a *FaultHandling* event, which makes the component transition from the "failed" state back to the "healthy" one. The *FaultHandling* event also causes one or more *NormalOutput* events (one for each output port of the component), meaning that normal service is restored.

Mapping elements of the CHESS ML "ErrorModel" is even simpler, since it is defined using a UML StateMachine diagram. The initial healthy state, as well as «Error» and «FailureMode» states defined in the CHESS ML error model are mapped to states of the SafeConcert metamodel. Similarly, «InternalFault» elements and «InternalPropagation» elements have an almost direct correspondence with elements in SafeConcert. The main difference resides in how failures are described. In the CHESS ML ErrorModel the ports that are affected by a failure are specified on «FailureMode» states. In SafeConcert they are specified using the *causes* attribute of *InternalPropagation* events. This way provides greater flexibility and it allows users to model a wider range of failure behaviors with respect to what it was possible in CHESS.

How the modeled information will actually be translated into a Stochastic Petri Nets model is beyond the scope of this paper. The CHESS-SBA implementation is based on an intermediate model [5, 10] that bridges the distance between the CHESS ML profile and the Stochastic Petri Nets formalism. The plugin architecture and implementation is described in [10].

4.3   Approach Evaluation

Latest releases of the CHESS Framework [5] incorporate SafeConcert, as well as the new plugins for performing safety analyses based on it [25]. The evaluation has adopted an incremental and iterative approach. An initial evaluation is reported in [3], where concepts for socio-technical systems are applied to a case study in the petroleum domain. A further evaluation has been performed by industrial partners of the CONCERTO project and it is reported in [24]. Representatives of the petroleum domain have applied the implemented profile to a case study of a gas detection system, providing useful feedback for the refinement of concepts. The evaluation has then been extended to the telecare domain in [25], in which a use case is modeled with the profile derived from SafeConcert, and availability of the system analyzed.

At the end of the project, industrial partners have provided further feedback, judging their satisfaction in using the features of the CONCERTO framework. Figure 6 reports the evaluation of petroleum and telecare partners; "component modeling" and "fault propagation and analysis", which are features related to SafeConcert, received a positive judgment. Afterwards, this positive experience has led to the definition of a systematic way to integrate CHESS-SBA in the safety procedures within the petroleum domain [27].

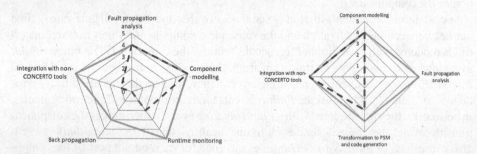

Fig. 6. Evaluation of CONCERTO features by petroleum (left) and telecare (right) users [24].

Finally, as part of the project's self-assessment, a questionnaire about CONCERTO features has been prepared and submitted to 9 external experts in the field of safety assessment. Concerning dependability modeling, 80% of the responses are positive [24]. Concerning analyses, while still no negative answers were received, we noticed that experts were more cautious (almost half of the answers were blank or "neutral"). This might reflect the lack of confidence with a specific analysis technique, and the difficulty in judging it without extensive first-hand usage.

5 Related Work

To offer dependability modeling capabilities, many works (including ours) have proposed UML extensions that are then implemented as UML profiles. EAST-ADL2 [8], for instance, is a modeling language for electronics system engineering within the automotive domain, which extends UML and SysML. While safety properties and error propagation can be specified to some extent, EAST-ADL2 is very tied to the automotive domain. For example, integrity levels can be defined only by means of ASILs (*Automotive* Safety Integrity Levels).

The SAE "Architecture Analysis and Design Language" standard defines the AADL language. Its Error Model Annex [6] is of particular relevance, since it allows users to add information on erroneous behavior to functional models. AADL models extended with the Error Model Annex have been shown to be analyzable using Generalized Stochastic Petri Nets [12]. While using a similar approach for modeling the failure behavior, SafeConcert also includes elements for socio-technical systems, and for modeling of the criticality associated with components and failure modes.

The work in [7] defined the Dependability Analysis Modeling (DAM) profile, a MARTE-based UML profile for dependability modeling. The same work includes an interesting survey on UML profiles for dependability analysis. While DAM is an important step forward in the introduction of dependability attributes at UML level, it was not suitable for ours and project's objectives. The DAM profile offers too much freedom to the modeler, and it is very coupled with MARTE: this is against the "correctness-by-construction" and "separation of concerns" pillars behind CONCERTO.

The authors of [32] define SafeML, a SysML profile for modeling safety-related information. Their focus is on information presentation and traceability, and they assume that all the safety analyses have been already performed [32]. Thus, SafeML does not support the application of safety analyses, but only the documentation of results. To a certain extent, SafeML is complementary to our work, which has instead a stronger focus on the analysis dimension.

As the above works do, we also aim at supporting safety annotations via an UML profile. However, in this paper we do not focus on the UML representation of our language (i.e., its concrete syntax, available at [23]), but only on the underlying metamodel, i.e., we define which are the concepts and the relationships between them. Furthermore, our work goes beyond the objectives of the previous mentioned works: (i) it provides support for modeling both "socio" and "technical" entities, as well as their interactions; and (ii) it provides support for both failure logic analysis and stochastic state-based analysis in a common metamodel.

Other works in the literature focused on the conceptual level, introducing metamodels that provide the foundation for more concrete and user-oriented languages. Lisagor [11] defined a metamodel to support the application of different existing failure propagation analysis techniques. This is perhaps the work which is most closely related to the one presented in this paper. With respect to Lisagor's work, our metamodel covers a wider range of aspects: (i) quantitative analysis, (ii) the modeling of socio-technical systems, and (iii) criticality levels.

6   Conclusion and Future Work

In this paper we introduced a novel metamodel, SafeConcert, which aims at supporting architects in the iterative and incremental modeling and analysis of safety-critical socio-technical systems. Safe concertation of human, organizational and technological entities is enabled thanks to the promising interplay of qualitative and quantitative safety analyses.

Currently, work is devoted at further evaluating SafeConcert within industrial settings beyond the research project's border. Several directions are open for long-term activities. Based on what done by Sljivo et al. [20], we aim to enable the generation of fragments of safety case arguments from analysis results. Based on the extensive taxonomy work in [28], we aim to extend the metamodel to integrate concepts from the Systems-of-Systems approach, thus further expanding the range of systems addressed by SafeConcert.

Acknowledgement.   This work has been partially supported by the EU ARTEMIS project CONCERTO [2], and by the ECSEL Joint Undertaking project AMASS (No 692474).

References

1. ARTEMIS-JU-100022 CHESS: Composition with Guarantees for High-Integrity Embedded Software Components Assembly. http://www.chess-project.org
2. ARTEMIS-JU-333053 CONCERTO: Guaranteed Component Assembly with Round Trip Analysis for Energy Efficient High-integrity Multicore Systems. http://www.concerto-project.org/
3. Gallina, B., Sefer, E., Refsdal, A.: Towards safety risk assessment of socio-technical systems via failure logic analysis. In: 2014 IEEE International Symposium on Software Reliability Engineering Workshops (ISSREW), 3–6 November 2014, pp. 287–292 (2014)
4. Wallace, M.: Modular architectural representation and analysis of fault propagation and transformation. Electron. Notes Theor. Comput. Sci. **141**(3), 53–71 (2005)
5. PolarSys CHESS. https://www.polarsys.org/chess/. Accessed 01 June 2017
6. Society of Automotive Engineers: SAE Standards: AS5506/1, Architecture Analysis & Design Language (AADL) Annex Volume 1, June 2006
7. Bernardi, S., Merseguer, J., Petriu, D.C.: A dependability profile within MARTE. Softw. Syst. Model. **10**(3), 313–336 (2011)
8. ATESST consortium: EAST-ADL2 UML2 Profile Specification, January 2008
9. Walker, G., Stanton, N., Salmon, P., Jenkins, D.: A Review of Sociotechnical Systems Theory: A Classic Concept for New Command and Control Paradigms, Human Factors Integration Defence Technology Centre, U.K. Ministry of Defence Scientific Research Programme, HFIDTC/2/WP1.1.1/2 (2007)
10. Montecchi, L., Lollini, P., Bondavalli, A.: A reusable modular toolchain for automated dependability evaluation. In: VALUETOOLS 2013, Torino, Italy, pp. 298–303, December 2013
11. Lisagor, O.: Failure logic modelling: a pragmatic approach. Ph.D. thesis, Department of Computer Science, University of York, March 2010

12. Rugina, A.-E., Kanoun, K., Kaâniche, M.: A system dependability modeling framework using AADL and GSPNs. In: Lemos, R., Gacek, C., Romanovsky, A. (eds.) WADS 2006. LNCS, vol. 4615, pp. 14–38. Springer, Heidelberg (2007). doi:10.1007/978-3-540-74035-3_2

13. Avižienis, A., Laprie, J.-C., Randell, B., Landwehr, C.: Basic concepts and taxonomy of dependable and secure computing. IEEE Trans. Dependable Secure Comput. 1, 11–33 (2004)

14. Grunske, L., Han, J.: A comparative study into architecture-based safety evaluation methodologies using AADL's error annex and failure propagation models. In: 11th IEEE High Assurance Systems Engineering Symposium, Nanjing, China, pp. 283–292, 3–5 December 2008

15. Verhulst, E., de la Vara, J.L., Sputh, B.H., de Florio, V.: ARRL: a criterion for composable safety and systems engineering. In: SAFECOMP 2013 Workshops – SASSUR 2013 (2013)

16. ISO26262: Road vehicles – Functional safety. International Standard, November 2011

17. de C. Guerra, P.A., Rubira, C.M.F., Romanovsky, A., Lemos, R.: A fault-tolerant software architecture for COTS-based software systems. In: Proceedings of the 9th European Software Engineering Conference, pp. 375–378. ACM (2003)

18. Hendy, K.C.: A tool for Human Factors Accident Investigation, Classification and Risk Management. Defence R&D Canada, Toronto, DRDC Toronto TR 2002–057, March 2003

19. Montecchi, L., Lollini, P., Bondavalli, A.: Towards a MDE transformation workflow for dependability analysis. In: IEEE International Conference on Engineering of Complex Computer Systems, Las Vegas, USA, pp. 157–166 (2011)

20. Sljivo, I., Gallina, B., Carlson, J., Hansson, H., Puri, S.: A method to generate reusable safety case argument-fragments from compositional safety analysis. J. Syst. Softw. (2016). https://doi.org/10.1016/j.jss.2016.07.034. Special Issue on Software Reuse

21. Montecchi, L., Gallina, B.: Complete diagram of the SafeConcert metamodel. http://rcl.dsi.unifi.it/~leonardo/safeconcert.png. Accessed 01 June 2017

22. DO-331, Model-Based Development and Verification Supplement to DO-178C and DO-278A. RTCA, December 2011

23. CONCERTO Deliverable D2.7: Analysis and back-propagation of properties for multicore systems – Final Version, November 2015

24. CONCERTO Deliverable D5.6: Use Case Evaluations – Final Version, April 2016

25. CONCERTO Deliverable D3.3: Design and implementation of analysis methods for nonfunctional properties – Final version, November 2015

26. Gallina, B., Punnekkat, S.: FI4FA: a formalism for incompletion, inconsistency, interference and impermanence failures' analysis. In: 37th EUROMICRO Conference on Software Engineering and Advanced Applications (SEAA 2011), pp. 493–500, 30 August–2 September 2011

27. Montecchi, L., Refsdal, A., Lollini, P., Bondavalli, A.: A model-based approach to support safety-related decisions in the petroleum domain. In: 46th IEEE/IFIP International Conference on Dependable Systems and Networks (DSN 2016), Toulouse, France, pp. 275–286, 28 June–1 July 2016

28. Bondavalli, A., Bouchenak, S., Kopetz, H. (eds.): Cyber-Physical Systems of Systems – Foundations – A Conceptual Model and Some Derivations: The AMADEOS Legacy. LNCS, vol. 10099. (2016)

29. Ciardo, G., German, R., Lindemann, C.: A characterization of the stochastic process underlying a stochastic petri net. IEEE Trans. Softw. Eng. 20, 506–515 (1994)

30. Holden, R.J.: People or systems? To blame is human. The fix is to engineer. Prof. Saf. 54(12), 34–41 (2009)

31. Gallina, B., Javed, M.A., Ul Muram, F., Punnekkat, S.: Model-driven Dependability Analysis Method for Component-based Architectures. In: Proceedings of the Euromicro-SEAA Conference, Cesme, Izmir, Turkey, September 2012
32. Biggs, G., Sakamoto, T., Kotoku, T.: A profile and tool for modelling safety information with design information in SysML. Softw. Syst. Model. **15**(1), 147–178 (2016)
33. Gallina, B., Dimov, A., Punnekkat, S.: Fuzzy-enabled failure behaviour analysis for dependability assessment of networked systems. In: IEEE International Workshop on Measurement and Networking (M&N), Anacapri, Italy, p. 6, August 2011

Fault Detection and Propagation

A Model-Checking Approach to Analyse Temporal Failure Propagation with AltaRica

Alexandre Albore[1,2,3]([✉]), Silvano Dal Zilio[2], Guillaume Infantes[3],
Christel Seguin[3], and Pierre Virelizier[1,4]

[1] Institute of Research and Technology (IRT) Saint Exupéry, Toulouse, France
alexandre.albore@irt-saintexupery.com
[2] LAAS-CNRS, Université de Toulouse, CNRS, Toulouse, France
[3] ONERA, 2 Avenue Edouard Belin, 31055 Toulouse, France
[4] SAFRAN Tech, Rue des Jeunes Bois, 78772 Magny-Les-Hameaux, France

Abstract. The design of complex safety critical systems raises new technical challenges for the industry. As systems become more complex—and include more and more interacting functions—it becomes harder to evaluate the safety implications of local failures and their possible propagation through a whole system. That is all the more true when we add time to the problem, that is when we consider the impact of computation times and delays on the propagation of failures.

We describe an approach that extends models developed for Safety Analysis with timing information and provide tools to reason on the correctness of temporal safety conditions. Our approach is based on an extension of the AltaRica language where we can associate timing constraints with events and relies on a translation into a realtime model-checking toolset. We illustrate our method with an example that is representative of safety architectures found in critical systems.

1 Introduction

The increasing complexity of interactions between functions in modern industrial systems poses new technical challenges. In fact, developing complex systems often raise integration problems during the product final testing and verification phase. Besides, correcting these issues often generates a heavy rework and is a well-known cause for cost overruns and project delays. Therefore, finding solutions that contribute to anticipate and resolve integration problems as early as possible in the design process has become a prior concern for the industry.

New modelling techniques, such as MBSE or MBSA, propose to master the combinatorial complexity at early concept phases by using abstract high level representations of a system. These views constitute a promising ground to implement early validation techniques of the architectures. But, in order to be profitable and implemented by the industry, those validation techniques must remain lightweight and well integrated in the system design process. That is to say, the modelling workload must be limited, and the analysis results (even preliminary) must be available at the same time as designers evaluate the possible architecture choices.

© Springer International Publishing AG 2017
M. Bozzano and Y. Papadopoulos (Eds.): IMBSA 2017, LNCS 10437, pp. 147–162, 2017.
DOI: 10.1007/978-3-319-64119-5_10

In this paper, we describe an approach that allows us to extend models developed for safety analysis in order to reason about the correctness of temporal conditions. We intend to offer the capability to study a new range of system requirements that can be of main interest for functions such as failure detection, isolation and recovery. We advocate that timing properties are critical when assessing the safety of embedded and real-time systems. Indeed, temporal aspects—like network delays or computation times—can be the cause of missed failure detections or undesired reactions to (delayed) failure propagation. It is therefore necessary to be able to analyse the temporal properties of a model in order to build systems that will operate as intended in a real-world environment.

We define a model-based process to check simultaneously safety and temporal conditions on systems. Our approach is based on an extension of the AltaRica language [1] where timing constraints can be associated with events. This extension can then be translated into the intermediate language Fiacre [6], a formal specification language that can be used to represent both the behavioural and timing aspects of systems. This Fiacre model can be analysed with the realtime model-checker Tina [5]. The results of model-checking shed light on the dysfunctional behaviour of the original model, including how the cascading effects due to failure propagation delay reveal transitory failure modes.

Our contribution is as follows. We define a lightweight extension of AltaRica, meaning that timing constraints are declared separately from the behaviour of a system. Therefore it is easy to reuse a prior safety model and to define its temporal behaviour afterwards. We illustrate our method with an example inspired by safety architectures found in avionic systems. This example illustrate the impact of time when reasoning about failure propagation. We use this example to show that taking into accounts timing constraints—in particular propagation delays—can help finding new failure modes that cannot be detected in the untimed model currently in use. In the process, we define two safety properties: *loss detection*; and its temporal version, *loss detection convergence*, meaning that a system applies an appropriate and timely response to the occurrence of a fault before the failure is propagated and produces unwanted system behaviours. We show that these two properties, which are of interest in a much broader context, can be reduced to effective model-checking problems.

The paper is organised as follows. We start by defining the AltaRica language and the time model in Sect. 2. In Sect. 3, we introduce the Fiacre language by taking as example the encoding of an AltaRica node. This example gives an overview of how to encode AltaRica in Fiacre. We discuss the problem associated with time failure propagation in Sect. 4. Finally, before concluding with a discussion on related works, we give some experimental results in Sect. 5.

2   Model-Based Safety Analysis with AltaRica

Failure propagation models are defined by safety engineers and are usually obtained through manual assessment of the safety of the system. This is a complicated task since failures can depend on more than one element of the system; be the result of the interaction between many faults; be the consequence of the missed detection of another fault (e.g. a fault inside an element tasked with detecting faults); etc. To cope with the complexity of the systems and the scenarios that need to be analysed, several model-based approaches have been proposed such as AltaRica, Figaro [10], etc. each with their associated tooling.

AltaRica is a high level modelling language dedicated to Safety Analysis. It has been defined to ease the modelling and analysis of failure propagation in systems. The goal is to identify the possible failure modes of the system and, for each mode, the chain of events that lead to an unwanted situation.

In AltaRica, a system is expressed in terms of variables constrained by formulas and transitions. Several versions of the language have been defined (see for instance [1,15]). In this work, we use the AltaRica 2.0 Dataflow language which is a fragment of other versions and which is sufficient to analyse the behaviour of computer based systems. (The approach discussed here could be applied on other AltaRica dialects.) The models used in this work have been edited and analysed using Cecilia OCAS, a graphical interactive simulator developed by Dassault Aviation [7].

An AltaRica model is made of interconnected *nodes*. A node can be essentially viewed as a mode automaton [2] extended with guards and actions on data variables. A node comprises three parts: a declaration of variables and events, the definition of transitions, and the definition of assertions. We illustrate these concepts with the example of a simple node called Function. We give the code (textual definition) of Function in Listing 1.1 and a schematic representation in Fig. 1. The node Function has one input, I, and one output, O.

```
domain FState = {NOMINAL, LOST, ERROR} ;
domain FailureType = {Err, Loss, Ok} ;

node Function
    flow   I : FailureType : in ; O : FailureType : out ;
    state  S : FState ;
    event  fail_loss, fail_err ;
    init   S := NOMINAL ;
    trans  S != LOST   ⊢ fail_loss → S := LOST ;
           S =  NOMINAL ⊢ fail_err  → S := ERROR ;
    assert O = case { S = NOMINAL : I, S = LOST : Loss, else Err } ;
edon
```

Listing 1.1. Example of AltaRica code for the node Function.

Nodes can have an internal state stored in a set of *state variables*, declared in a heading called state. In its nominal state (when S = NOMINAL), the Function node acts as a perfect relay: it copies on its output the value provided by its input (we have O = I); this is expressed in the assert block. On the opposite, its output is set to Loss or Err when S equals LOST or ERROR, respectively. The assert directive is used to express constraints on the values of the input and output variables of a node, also called *flow variables*, establishing a link between the node and its environment, i.e. the other interconnected nodes. It distinguishes between input (in) and output (out) variables. An assertion defines a rule to

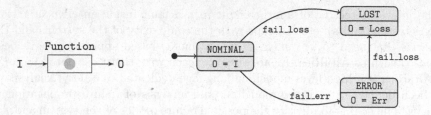

Fig. 1. Graphical representation of node `Function` (left) and its associated failure mode automaton (right).

update the value of output flows according to the state of the component and the value of input flows.

The state variables of a node can only change when an event is triggered. The code of `Function` declares two events: `fail_err`, that changes the state from `NOMINAL` to `ERROR`, and `fail_loss`, that can transition from any state to `LOST`. This behaviour is the one displayed on the mode automaton of Fig. 1. Transitions are listed in the `trans` block of the node. Each transition has an (event) name and a definition of the form g ⊢evt→ e, where the guard g is a Boolean condition that can refer to state and flow variables. The event `evt` can be triggered when the guard is satisfied. In this case we apply the effect, e, that is an expression that modifies the values of state variables.

Events are useful to model the occurrence of failures or the reaction to conditions on the flow variables. We can assign a law of probability on the occurrence of the failure using the heading `extern`. For instance we could assert that event `fail_loss` follows an exponential distribution with the declaration: `extern law (<event fail_loss>)="exp 1e-4";` In the next section, we propose a way to enrich this syntax to express timing constraints on events instead of probability distributions. At the moment, it is not possible to use stochastic events in addition to time events.

In the general case, an AltaRica model is composed of several interconnected node instances, following a component-based approach. Global assertions relate the input flows of a component to the output flows of other components. For the sake of brevity, we do not describe component synchronisation here and we refer the reader to [16] for further details. More importantly, a hierarchical AltaRica model can always be "flattened", i.e. represented by a single node containing all the variables, events, assertions, and transitions from the composite system. We use this property in our interpretation of AltaRica in Fiacre.

Adding Timing Constraints to Events. There already is a limited mechanism for declaring timing constraints in AltaRica. It relies on the use of external law associated with a *Dirac distribution*. An event with Dirac(0) law denotes an instantaneous transition, that should be triggered with the highest priority. Likewise, an event with Dirac(d) (where d is a positive constant) models a transition that should be triggered with a delay of d units of time. In practice, Dirac laws are rather a way to encode priorities between events than an actual mean to express duration. Moreover, while Dirac laws are used during simulation, they are not taken into account by the other analysis tools. Finally, the use of Dirac laws is not expressive enough to capture non-deterministic transitions that can occur within time intervals of the form $[a, b]$, where $a \neq b$. These constraints are useful to reason about failure propagation delays with different best and worst case traversal time. For this reason, we propose to extend event properties with *temporal laws* of the form: `extern law (evt) = "[a,b]"`; It is also possible to use open and/or unbounded time intervals, such as $]a, \infty[$.

With such a declaration, the transition $g \vdash evt \rightarrow e$ can be triggered only if the guard g is satisfied for a duration (or *waiting time*) δ, with $\delta \in [a, b]$. A main difference with the original semantics of AltaRica is that the timing constraint of an event is not reinitialised unless its guard becomes false. Moreover, our semantics naturally entails a notion of *urgency*, meaning that it is not possible to miss a deadline: when δ equals b, then either `evt` is triggered or another transition should (instantaneously) change the value of the guard g to false.

```
domain BType = {Empty, Full} ;
node Pre
   flow I : FailureType : in; O: FailureType : out;
   state Stored, Delayed : FailureType, S : BType;
   event pre_read, pre_wait;
   init  Stored := Ok, Delayed := Ok, S := Empty;
   trans
      (Stored != I) & (S = Empty) ⊢ pre_read → Stored := I, S = Full;
      (S = Full) ⊢ pre_wait → Delayed := Stored, S = Empty;
   assert  O = Delayed;
   extern law (pre_read) = "[0,0]"; law (pre_wait) = "[a,b]";
edon
```

Listing 1.2. Example of Time AltaRica code: the basic delay.

We can illustrate the use of temporal laws with the following example of a new node, `Pre`; see Listing 1.2. This node encodes a buffer that delays the propagation of its input. When the input changes, event `pre_read` has to be triggered instantaneously. Then, only after a duration $\delta \in [a, b]$, the value stored by `Pre` (in the state variable `Stored`) is propagated to its output.

3   A Definition of Fiacre Using Examples

Fiacre [6] is a high-level, formal specification language designed to represent both the behavioural and timing aspects of reactive systems. Fiacre programs are stratified in two main notions: *processes*, which are well-suited for modelling structured activities (like for example simple state machines), and *components*, which describes a system as a composition of processes. In the following, we base our presentation of Fiacre on code examples used in our interpretation of Time AltaRica. We give a simple example of Fiacre specification in Listing 1.3.

This code defines a process, `Function`, that simulates the behaviour of the AltaR-ica node given in Listing 1.1.

```
type FState      is union NOMINAL | LOST | ERROR end
type FailureType is union Err | Loss | Ok end
type Flows       is record I:FailureType, O:FailureType end

function update(S : FState, env : Flows) : Flows is
   var  f : Flows := {I=env.I, O=env.O}
   begin
      f.O := (S = NOMINAL ? f.I : (S = LOST ? Loss : Err));
      return f
   end
process Function(&S : FState, &env : Flows) is
   states s0
   from s0 select
      on (S != LOST); S := LOST; env := update(S, env); loop
   [] on (S = NOMINAL); S := ERROR; env := update(S, env); loop
   end
```

Listing 1.3. Example of Fiacre code: type, functions and processes

Fiacre is a strongly typed language, meaning that type annotations are exploited in order to avoid unchecked run-time errors. Our example defines two enumeration types, `FState` and `FailureType`, that are the equivalent of the namesake AltaRica domains. We also define a record type, `Flows`, that models the environment of the node `Function`, that is an association from flow variables to values. Fiacre also supports native *functions* that provide a simple way to compute on values. In our example, function `update` is used to compute the state of the environment after an event is triggered; that is to model the effect of assertions in AltaRica. It uses two ternary (conditional) operators to mimic the `case`-expression found in the `assert` heading of Listing 1.1.

A Fiacre *process* is defined by a set of parameters and control states, each associated with a set of *complex transitions* (introduced by the keyword `from`). Our example defines a process with two shared variables—symbol & denotes variables passed by reference—that can be updated concurrently by other processes. In our case, variable `S` models the (unique) state variable of node `Function`.

Complex transitions are expressions that declares how variables are updated and which transitions may fire. They are built from constructs available in imperative programming languages (assignments, conditionals, sequential composition, ...), non-deterministic constructs (such as external choice, with the `select` operator), communication on ports, and jump to a state (with the `to` or `loop` operators). In Listing 1.3, the `select` statement defines two possible transitions, separated by the symbol [], that loop back to s0. Each transition maps exactly to one of the AltaRica events, `fail_loss` and `fail_err`, that we want to translate. Transitions are triggered non-deterministically and their effects are atomic (they have an "all or nothing" semantics). A transition can also be guarded by a Boolean condition, using the operator `on` or another conditional construct.

It is possible to associate a time constraint to a transition using the operator wait. Actually, the ability to express directly timing constraints in programs is a distinguishing feature of Fiacre. We illustrate this mechanism in Listing 1.4, that corresponds to the interpretation of the node Pre of Listing 1.2. Basically, a transition constrained by a (time) interval I can be triggered after a time δ, with $\delta \in I$, only if its guard stayed continuously valid during this time. It is this behaviour that inspired our choice of semantics for the temporal law.

A Fiacre *component* defines a parallel composition of components and/or processes using statements of the form par $P_0 \parallel \cdots \parallel P_n$ end (or par * when all the process are in parallel). It can also be used to restrict the visibility of variables and ports and to define priorities between communication events. We give an example of Fiacre component in Listing 1.4.

A possible issue with the implementation of Pre is that at most one failure mode can be delayed at a time. Indeed, if the input I of Pre changes while the state is Full, then the updated value is not taken into account until after event pre_wait triggers. It is not possible to implement a version that can delay an unbounded number of events in a bounded time as it would require an unbounded amount of memory to store the intermediate values. More fundamentally, this would give rise to undecidable verification problems (see e.g. [11]). To fix this issue, we can define a family of operators, Pre_k, that can delay up-to k simultaneous different inputs. Our implementation relies on a component that uses three process instances: one instance of front, that reads messages from the input (variable I), and two instances of delay, that act as buffers for the values

```
process Pre(&Stored, &Delayed : FailureType, S : BType, &env : Flows) is
   states s0
   from s0 select
      on (Stored != env.I and S = Empty); wait [0,0]; Stored :=
env.I; ...
   [] on (S = Full); wait [a,b]; Delayed := Stored; S := Empty; ...
   end

process delay[go : in FailureType](&O : FailureType) is
   states sEmpty, sFull
   var delayed : FailureType := Ok
   from sEmpty go?delayed; to sFull
   from sFull  wait [a,b]; O := delayed; to sEmpty

process front[p,q : out FailureType](&I : FailureType) is
   states s
   var stored : FailureType := Ok
   from s on (I != stored); stored := I; select p!I [] q!I end; loop

component Pre_2(&I, &O: FailureType) is
   port go1, go2 : FailureType in [0,0]
   priority go1 > go2
   par * in front[go1,go2](&I) || delay[go1](&O) || delay[go2](&O) end
```

Listing 1.4. An upgraded version of the delay operator Pre, with wait statement, components and synchronisation on ports.

that need to be delayed. Process `front` uses the local ports `go1` and `go2` to dispatch values to the buffers, managing a priority on the port usage. Indeed, any element in the system may propagate at most two different status, one from `Ok` to `Err` and then from `Err` to `Loss`.

4   Example of a Failure Detection and Isolation System

We study the example of a safety critical function that illustrates standard failure propagation problems. We use this example to show the adverse effects of temporal failure propagation even in the presence of Failure Detection and Isolation (FDI) capabilities. This example is inspired by the avionic functions that provide parameters for Primary Flight Display (PFD), which is located in the aircraft cockpit. The system of interest is the computer that acquires sensors measurements and computes the aircraft *calibrated airspeed* (CAS) parameter. Airspeed is crucial for pilots: it is taken into account to adjust aircraft engines thrust and it plays a main role in the prevention of over speed and stall.

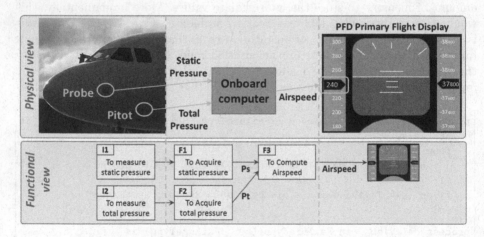

Fig. 2. Functional and physical views of the airspeed computation function.

CAS is not directly measured by a dedicated sensor, but is computed as a function of two auxiliary pressure measurements, the static pressure (Ps) and total pressure (Pt); that is $CAS = f(Pt, Ps)$. These two measurements come from sensors located on the aircraft nose, a pressure probe and a pitot tube.

Our proposed functional view is given in Fig. 2. It consists in two external input functions I1 and I2 that measure static and total pressure; and three inner functions of the system, F1 and F2 for sensor measurements acquisition by the on-board computer and F3 for airspeed computation. For simplification purposes, the PFD functions have not been modelled.

Next, we propose a first failure propagation view aiming at identifying the scenarios leading to an erroneous airspeed computation and display to the pilot (denoted `Err`). Such failure can only be detected if a failure detector is implemented, for instance by comparing the outputs of different functions. Undetected, it could mislead the pilot and, consequently, lead to an inappropriate engine thrust setting. We also want to identify the scenarios leading to the loss of the measure (denoted `Loss`). In such a case, the pilot can easily assess that the measure is missing or false and consequently rely upon another measure to control the aircraft (note that such redundancy is not modelled). For example, airspeed out of bound—indicating that an airliner has crossed the sonic barrier—is considered to be of kind `Loss`. It can be understood that scenarios leading to the loss of the airspeed are less critical than the ones leading to erroneous values.

Safety Model of the Architecture Without FDI. We provide an AltaRica model corresponding to the functional view of the CAS function in Fig. 3. This model, tailored to study failure propagation, is comprised of: two external functions, `I1` and `I2`, with no input (in their nominal state, the output is set to `Ok`); two inner functions, `F1` and `F2`, which are instances of the node `Function` described in Sect. 2; and a function, `F3`, that is the composition of two basic elements: a multiplexer `F3Mux`, representing the dependence of the output of `F3` from its two inputs, and a computing element `F3Processing` that represents the computation of the airspeed. `F3Processing` is also an instance of node `Function`.

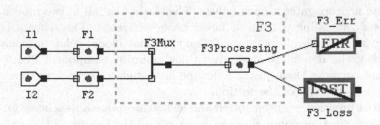

Fig. 3. A simple example of failure propagation.

In case of single failure scenario, `F3Mux` propagates the failure coming either from one input or the other. In case of multiple failures, when different failures propagate, one being `Loss` and the other being `Err`, and without appropriate FDI—the system outcome is uncertain. Solving this uncertainty would require a detailed behavioural model of the on-board computer and a model for all the possible failure modes, which is rarely feasible with a sufficient level of confidence, except for time-tested technology. Given this uncertainty, it is usual to retain the state with the most critical effect, that is to say: the output of `F3` is `Err`.

Our goal is to prevent the computation of an erroneous airspeed while one of `F3` input signals is lost. The rationale is that the system should be able to passivate automatically the airspeed when it detects that one of its input signals is not reliable. This behaviour can be expressed with the following property:

Safety Property 1 (Loss Detection and Instantaneous Propagation).
A function is *loss detection safe* if, when in nominal mode, it propagates a Loss
whenever one of its input nodes propagates a Loss.

We can show that our example of Fig. 3 does not meet this property using the
Sequence Generation tool available in Cecilia OCAS. To this end, we compute the
minimal cuts for the target equation $((\text{F1.0.Loss} \vee \text{F2.0.Loss}) \wedge \neg\text{F3.0.Loss})$,
meaning the scenario where F3 does not propagates Loss when one of F1 or F2
does. Hence function F3 is loss detection safe if and only if the set is empty.

In our example, once we eliminate the cases where F3 is not nominal (that
is when F3Processing is in an spontaneous error state), we find eight minimal
cuts, all of order 2, corresponding to the cases when the outputs of F1 and F2 are
(for various reasons) in state Loss and Err. In the following section, we correct
the behaviour of F3 by considering a new architecture based on detectors and a
switch to isolate the output of F3 when faulty.

Safety Model of the Architecture with FDI. The updated implementation
of F3 (see Fig. 4) uses two perfect detectors, F1Loss and F2Loss, that can detect
a loss failure event on the inputs of the function. The (Boolean) outputs of
these detectors are linked to an OR gate (AtLeastOneLoss) which triggers an
Alarm when at least one of the detectors outputs true. The alarm commands a
Switch; the output of Switch is the same as F3Mux, unless Alarm is activated, in
which case it propagates a Loss failure. The alarm can fail in two modes, either
continuously signaling a Loss or never being activated. The schema in Fig. 4
also includes two delays operators, D1 and D2, that model delay propagation at
the input of the detectors, similarly to how done by component Pre_2 above;
we will not consider them in the following lines, but come back to these timing
constraints at the end of the section.

The FDI function—with a switch and an alarm—is a stable scheme for failure
propagation: when in nominal mode, it detects all the failures of the system and
it is able to disambiguate the case where its inputs contains both Err and Loss.
Once again, this can be confirmed using the Sequence Generation tool. If we
repeat the same analysis as before—and if we abstract away the delay nodes—
we find 56 minimal cuts, all involving a failure of either Alarm or F3Processing,

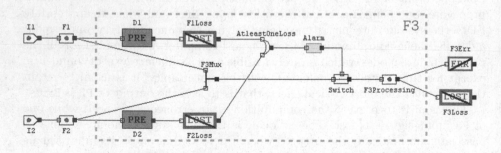

Fig. 4. Model of a FDI function with a switch and an alarm.

i.e. a non-nominal mode. This means that, in an untimed model, our new implementation of F3 satisfies the loss detection property, as desired. Even so, it is easy to find a timed scenario where the safety property is violated.

Assume now that F1 and F2 propagate respectively the status Loss and Err, at the same date. In such a case and considering possible latencies, while Err reaches F3Mux instantaneously, the output of F1 might reach F1Loss at successive date. This leads to a transient state where the alarm is not activated whereas the output of F3Mux is set to Err. This brings us back to the same dreaded scenario than in our initial model.

This example suggests that we need a more powerful method to compute the set of cuts in the presence of temporal constraints. On the other hand, we may also advocate that our safety property is too limiting in this context, where perfect synchronicity of events is rare. Actually, it can be proven that the output of F3 will eventually converge to a loss detection and isolation mode (assuming that F3 stays nominal and that its inputs stay stable). To reflect this situation, we propose an improved safety property that takes into account temporal properties of the system:

Safety Property 2 (Loss Detection Convergent). A function is *loss detection convergent* if (when in nominal mode) there exists a duration Δ such that it continuously outputs a Loss after the date $\delta_0 + \Delta$ if at least one of its input nodes continuously propagates a Loss starting from δ_0 onward. The smallest possible value for Δ is called the *convergence latency* of the function.

Hence, if the latency needed to detect the loss failure can be bound, and if the bound is sufficiently small safety-wise, we can still deem our system as safe. In the example in Fig. 2, this property can indicate for how long an erroneous airspeed is shown on the PFD to the pilot, before the failure is isolated.

In the next section, we use our approach to generate a list of "timed cuts" (as model-checking counterexamples) that would have exposed the aforedescribed problems. We also use model-checking to compute the convergence latency for the node F3. In this simple example, we can show that the latency is equal to the maximal propagation delay at the input of the detectors. The value of the latency could be much harder to compute in a more sophisticated scenario, where delays can be chained and/or depends on the internal state of a component.

5 Compilation of AltaRica and Experimental Evaluation

We have implemented the transformation outlined in Sect. 3; the result is a compiler that automatically generates Fiacre code from an AltaRica model. The compilation process relies on the fact that it is possible to "flatten" a composition of interconnected nodes into an intermediate representation, called a *Guarded Transition System* (GTS) [3]. A GTS is very similar to a (single) AltaRica node and can therefore be encoded in a similar way. Our tool is built using the code-base of the model-checker EPOCH [17], which provides the functionalities for the syntactic analysis and the linking of AltaRica code. After compilation, the

Fiacre code can be checked using Tina [5]. The core of the Tina toolset is an exploration engine that can be exploited by dedicated model-checking and transition analyser tools. Tina offers several abstract state space constructions that preserve specific classes of properties like absence of deadlocks, reachability of markings, or linear and branching time temporal properties. These state space abstractions are vital when dealing with timed systems that generally have an infinite state space (due to the use of a dense time model). In our experiments, most of the requirements can be reduced to reachability properties, so we can use on-the-fly model-checking techniques.

We interpret a GTS by a Fiacre process whose parameters consist of all its state and flow variables. Each transition g ⊢evt→ e in the GTS is (bijectively) encoded by a transition that matches the guard g and updates the variables to reflect the effect of e plus the assertions. Each transition can be labelled with time constraints to take into account the **extern** declarations of the node. This translation is straightforward since all the operators available in AltaRica have a direct equivalent in Fiacre. Hence every state/transition in the GTS corresponds to a unique state/transition in Fiacre. This means that the state (reachability) graph of a GTS and its associated Fiacre model are isomorphic. This is a very strong and useful property for formal verification, since we can very easily transfer verification artefacts (such as counterexamples) from one model back to the other. The close proximity between AltaRica and Fiacre is not really surprising. First of all, both languages have similar roots in process algebra theory and share very similar synchronisation mechanisms. More deeply, they share formal models that are very close: AltaRica semantics is based on the product of "communicating automata", whereas the semantics of Fiacre can be expressed using (a time extension of) one-safe Petri nets. The main difference is that AltaRica provide support for defining probabilities on events, whereas Fiacre is targeted towards the definition of timing aspects. This proximity in both syntax and semantics is an advantage for the validation of our tool, because it means that our translation should preserve the semantics of AltaRica on models that do not use extern laws to define probabilities and time. We have used this property to validate our translation by comparing the behaviours of the models obtained using Cecilia OCAS simulation tool and their translation. For instance, in the case of the CAS system of Sect. 4, we can compute the set of cuts corresponding to Safety Property 1 (loss detection) by checking an invariant of the form $((F1.0 = Loss) \vee (F2.0 = Loss) \Rightarrow (F3.0 = Loss))$. In both cases— with and without FDI—we are able to compute the exact same set of cuts than Cecilia OCAS. This is done using the model-checker for modal mu-calculus provided with Tina, which can list all the counterexamples for a (reachability) formula as a graph. More importantly, we can use our approach to compute the timed counterexample described at the end of Sect. 4. All these computations can be done in less than a second on our test machine.

We have used our toolchain to generate the reachable state space of several AltaRica models:[1] RUDDER describes a control system for the rudder of an A340 aircraft [4]; ELEC refers to three simplified electrical generation and power distribution systems for a hypothetical twin jet aircraft; the HYDRAU model describes a hydraulic system similar to the one of the A320 aircraft [8]. The results are reported in Table 1. In each case we indicate the time needed to generate the whole state space (in seconds) and the number of states and transitions explored. We also give the number of state variables as reported by Cecilia OCAS. All tests were run on an Intel 2.50 GHz CPU with 8 GB of RAM running Linux. In the case of model HYDRAU we stopped the exploration after 30 minutes and more than 9.10^9 generated states; the state space is large because this benchmark models the physical a-causal propagation of a leak, so a leak can impact both upward and backward components and trigger a reconfiguration, multiplying the number of reachable states. In all cases, the time needed to generate the Fiacre code is negligible, in the order of 10 ms.

Table 1. State space size and generation time for several use cases.

Model	Time (s)	# states	# trans.	# state vars
RUDDER	0.85	$3.3\,10^4$	$2.5\,10^5$	15
ELEC 01	0.40	512	$2.3\,10^3$	9
ELEC 02	0.40	512	$2.3\,10^3$	9
ELEC 03	101	$4.2\,10^6$	$4.6\,10^7$	22
HYDRAU	1800	—	—	59
CAS	0.40	729	$2.9\,10^3$	6
CAS with Pre	46	$9.7\,10^5$	$4.3\,10^6$	10

Our models also include two versions of the complete CAS system (including the detectors, the alarm and the switch); both with and without the delay functions D1 and D2. The "CAS with Pre" model is our only example that contains timing constraints. In this case, we give the size of the state class graph generated by Tina, that is an abstract version of the state space that preserves LTL properties. Tina can check temporal properties on this example, in particular we can check that F3 has the *loss detection convergence* property. To this end, a solution is to add a Time Observer to check the maximal duration between two events: first, an obs_start event is triggered when the output of F1 or F2 changes to Loss; then an obs_end event is triggered when the output of F3 changes to Loss. The observer has also a third transition (obs_err) that acts as a timeout and is associated with a time interval I and is enabled concurrently with obs_end. Hence, Time Observer ends up in the state yield by obs_err when the output

---

[1] All the benchmarks tested in this paper are available at https://w3.onera.fr/ifa-esa/ content/model-checking-temporal-failure-propagation-altarica.

of F3 deviates from its expected value for more than d units of time, with $d \in I$. We have used this observer to check that the *convergence latency* of the CAS system equals 3, when we assume that the delays are in the time interval $[1, 3]$. The result is that obs_err is fireable for any value of d in the interval $[0, 3]$, while obs_err is not fireable if $I =]3, \infty[$. These two safety properties can be checked on the system (plus the observer) in less than 0.6 s.

6   Conclusion and Related Work

Our work is concerned with the modelling and analysis of failures propagation in the presence of time constraints. We concentrate on a particular safety property, called *loss detection convergence*, meaning that the system applies an appropriate and timely response to the occurrence of a fault before the failure is propagated and produces unwanted system behaviours. Similar problems were addressed in [18], where the authors describe a process to model Failure Detection Isolation and Reconfiguration architecture (for use on-board satellites) that requires to take into account failure propagation, detection, and recovery times. However, these needs are not matched by an effective way to express or check the safety constraints of the system. Our approach provides a solution to model these timing constraints within AltaRica, also providing an automatic transformation from Time AltaRica models in one of the input formats of Tina, showing how two interesting problems—computing "timed cuts" and bounding the convergence latency of a node—can be reduced to a decidable model-checking problem.

Several works have combined model-checking and AltaRica, the archetypal example being the MEC tool [14] that was developed at the same time as the language. More recently, Bozzano et al. [12] have defined a transformation from AltaRica Dataflow to the symbolic model-checker NuSMV. While this tool does not support complex timing constraints, it offers some support for Dirac laws (and implicit priorities) by encoding an ad-hoc scheduler. The use of symbolic model-checking techniques is interesting in the case of models with a strong combinatorial blow up, like for instance model HYDRAU of Sect. 5. Nonetheless, even though Tina also includes BDD-based tools, no approaches allow to combine the advantages of both realtime and symbolic model-checking techniques.

Realtime techniques are central to our approach. We define an extension of AltaRica where timing constraints can be declared using temporal laws of the form law (evt) = "[a,b]", with a semantics inspired by Time Petri nets. As a result, we can apply on AltaRica several state space abstractions techniques that have been developed for "timed models", such as the use of DBM and state classes [5]. In a different way, Cassez et al. [13] have proposed an extension of AltaRica with explicit "clock variables", inspired by Timed Automata, where clocks are real-valued flow variables that can be used inside the guards of events. Their work is mainly focused on the verification of behavioural properties and focuses on the encoding of urgency and priorities between events, two notions that are naturally offered in Fiacre. Also, our extension is less invasive. If we ignore the extern declaration then we obtain valid AltaRica code. More research is still needed to further the comparison between these two approaches in the context of safety assessments.

Aside from these works on AltaRica, recent works centred on combining failure propagation analysis and timing constraints, define an automatic method for synthesising *Timed Failure Propagation Graphs* (TFPG), that is an extension of the notion of cut-sets including information on the date of events [9]. TFPG provide a condensed representation that is easier to use than sets of timed cuts. Therefore, it would be interesting to use this format in our case.

. For future work, we plan to adapt our translation to a new version of the AltaRica language—called AltaRica 3.0, or OpenAltaRica [15]—that imposes less restrictions on the computation of flow variables. We also want to apply our approach to more complex industrial use cases, as the benchmarks involving temporal constraints are rare, due to the lack of tools for verification of temporal properties. We are actually applying our approach to a satellite case study involving reconfiguration time besides failure detection and isolation. In such a model, identifying convergence times for failure detection and isolation, directly influence the working modes of the satellite, as switching modes depends on the reconfiguration time, being a critical tool for safety assessment.

References

1. Arnold, A., Point, G., Griffault, A., Rauzy, A.: The AltaRica formalism for describing concurrent systems. Fundamenta Informaticæ **40**(2–3), 109–124 (1999)
2. Rauzy, A.: Mode automata and their compilation into fault trees. Reliabil. Eng. Syst. Saf. **78**, 1–12 (2002)
3. Guarded, R.A.: Guarded transition systems: a new states/events formalism for reliability studies. J. Risk Reliabil. **222**(4), 495–505 (2008)
4. Bernard, R., Aubert, J.-J., Bieber, P., Merlini, C., Metge, S.: Experiments in model based safety analysis: flight controls. Proc. IFAC **40**(6), 43–48 (2007)
5. Berthomieu, B., Ribet, P.O., Vernadat, F.: The tool Tina - construction of abstract state spaces for Petri nets and time Petri nets. Int. J. Prod. Res. **42**(14), 2741–2756 (2004)
6. Berthomieu, B., Bodeveix, J.-P., Farail, P., Filali, M., Garavel, H., Gaufillet, P., Lang, F., Vernadat, F.: Fiacre: an intermediate language for model verification in the topcased environment. In: Proceedings of ERTS (2008)
7. Bieber, P., Bougnol, C., Castel, C., Christophe Kehren, J.-P.H., Metge, S., Seguin, C.: Safety assessment with AltaRica. In: Jacquart, R. (ed.) Building the Information Society. IIFIP, vol. 156, pp. 505–510. Springer, Boston (2004). doi:10.1007/978-1-4020-8157-6_45
8. Bieber, P., Castel, C., Seguin, C.: Combination of fault tree analysis and model checking for safety assessment of complex system. In: Bondavalli, A., Thevenod-Fosse, P. (eds.) EDCC 2002. LNCS, vol. 2485, pp. 19–31. Springer, Heidelberg (2002). doi:10.1007/3-540-36080-8_3
9. Bittner, B., Bozzano, M., Cimatti, A.: Automated synthesis of timed failure propagation graphs. In: Proceedings of IJCAI, pp. 972–978 (2016)
10. Bouissou, M.: Automated dependability analysis of complex systems with the KB3 workbench: the experience of EDF R&D. In: Proceedings of CIEM (2005)

11. Bouyer, P., Dufourd, C., Fleury, E., Petit, A.: Updatable timed automata. Theor. Comput. Sci. **321**(2–3), 291–345 (2004)
12. Bozzano, M., Cimatti, A., Lisagor, O., Mattarei, C., Mover, S., Roveri, M., Tonetta, S.: Symbolic model-checking and safety assessment of AltaRica models. Electron. Commun. EASST **46** (2012)
13. Cassez, F., Pagetti, C., Roux, O.: A timed extension for AltaRica. Fundamenta Informaticæ **62**(3–4), 291–332 (2004)
14. Griffault, A., Vincent, A.: The Mec 5 model-checker. In: Alur, R., Peled, D.A. (eds.) CAV 2004. LNCS, vol. 3114, pp. 488–491. Springer, Heidelberg (2004). doi:10.1007/978-3-540-27813-9_43
15. Prosvirnova, T., Batteux, M., Brameret, P.-A., Cherfi, A., Friedlhuber, T., Roussel, J.-M., Rauzy, A.: The AltaRica 3.0 project for model-based safety assessment. IFAC Proc. **46**(22), 127–132 (2013)
16. Rauzy, A.: AltaRica dataflow language specification version 2.3. Technical report, Ecole Centrale de Paris, June 2013
17. Teichteil-Königbuch, F., Infantes, G., Seguin, C.: EPOCH probabilistic model-checking. In: Model Based Safety Assessment Workshop, Toulouse, France (2011)
18. Thomas, D., Blanquart, J.-P.: Model-based RAMS & FDIR co-engineering at Astrium satellites. In: Proceedings of DASIA, ESA Special Publication, 720:33 (2013)

A Model-Based Extension to HiP-HOPS for Dynamic Fault Propagation Studies

Sohag Kabir[1]([⊠]), Yiannis Papadopoulos[1], Martin Walker[1],
David Parker[1], Jose Ignacio Aizpurua[2], Jörg Lampe[3],
and Erich Rüde[3]

[1] University of Hull, Kingston upon Hull, UK
{s.kabir, y.i.papadopoulos, martin.walker,
d.j.parker}@hull.ac.uk
[2] University of Strathclyde, Glasgow, UK
jose.aizpurua@strath.ac.uk
[3] DNV GL SE, Hamburg, Germany
{Joerg.Lampe, Erich.Ruede}@dnvgl.com

Abstract. HiP-HOPS is a model-based approach for assessing the dependability of safety-critical systems. The method combines models, logic, probabilities and nature-inspired algorithms to provide advanced capabilities for design optimisation, requirement allocation and safety argument generation. To deal with dynamic systems, HiP-HOPS has introduced temporal operators and a temporal logic to represent and assess event sequences in component failure modelling. Although this approach has been shown to work, it is not entirely consistent with the way designers tend to express operational dynamics in models which show mode and state sequences. To align HiP-HOPS better with typical design techniques, in this paper, we extend the method with the ability to explicitly consider different modes of operation. With this added capability HiP-HOPS can create and analyse temporal fault trees from architectural models of a system which are augmented with mode information.

Keywords: Model-based safety analysis · Fault tree analysis · HiP-HOPS · Dynamic systems · Temporal fault trees

1 Introduction

To overcome the limitations of classical approaches to dependability analysis like Fault Tree Analysis (FTA) and Failure Modes and Effects Analysis (FMEA) [1], in the last two decades, research has focused on simplifying dependability analysis by looking at how dependability artefacts can be automatically synthesized from system models. This has led to the field of model-based safety analysis (MBSA) [2]. MBSA approaches offer significant advantages over classical approaches as they utilise software automation and integration with design models to simplify the analysis of complex safety-critical systems. Over the years, several approaches, e.g., Failure Propagation and Transformation Notation (FPTN) [3], Hierarchically Performed Hazard Origin and Propagation Studies (HiP-HOPS) [4], AltaRica [5], FSAP-NuSMV [6], and AADL

© Springer International Publishing AG 2017
M. Bozzano and Y. Papadopoulos (Eds.): IMBSA 2017, LNCS 10437, pp. 163–178, 2017.
DOI: 10.1007/978-3-319-64119-5_11

with its error annex [7], have been developed to facilitate MBSA of complex systems. An overview of these approaches is available in [8, 9]. These approaches usually combine different classical safety analysis approaches to allow the analysts to perform safety analyses automatically or semi-automatically. For example, HiP-HOPS, a state-of-the-art MBSA approach, enhances an architectural model of a system with logical failure annotations to allow safety studies such as FTA and FMEA. In this way it shows how the failure of a single component or combinations of failures of multiple components can lead to system failures.

Early versions of the HiP-HOPS method used the classical combinatorial model of traditional FTA. In this model, systems failures are caused by logical combinations of component failures as these combine and propagate through the system architecture. However, in modern large-scale and complex systems, system behaviour is dynamic over time. This could be due to their capability to operate in multiple modes, e.g., an aircraft can operate in take-off, flight, and landing modes or it could be because the system behaviour changes in response to different events. This dynamic system behaviour leads to a variety of dynamic failure characteristics such as functionally dependent events and priorities of failure events. It is not only combinations of events that matter but sequences too. As systems are getting more complex and their behaviour becomes more dynamic, capturing this dynamic behaviour and the many possible interactions between the components is necessary for accurate failure modelling.

There are different possibilities to model the dynamic behaviour of a system. On the one hand, it is possible to directly specify the dynamic failure behaviour through dynamic dependability formalisms [9, 10]. One example is Pandora TFTs [10], where dynamic behaviours are modelled using temporal gates and temporal laws are used for qualitative analysis. Pandora can be used in the context of HiP-HOPS for assessing event sequencing in dynamic systems. A difficulty with this approach is that the dynamic operation is not explicitly given in a system design model, but has to be introduced later on in the failure modeling where event sequences are described. This can make application of the method counterintuitive to designers who are used to describing dynamics directly in system models using mode and state diagrams. The difficulty can be overcome by modelling dynamic behaviour in state automata linked to an architectural model of the system and by synthesizing fault trees by traversing the combined model [11]. However, in this approach important information related to the sequencing of events is eventually lost, as the resultant fault trees are combinatorial and do not have temporal semantics. This, however, is not ideal since there are circumstances where the order of two or more events is significant and changes the effects of failure and the capability to recover [10].

The main contribution of this paper is the proposal of a dynamic fault propagation approach which extends the HiP-HOPS technique with explicit representation of system modes and states. The approach generates Pandora temporal fault trees which represent accurately the dynamic failure behaviour of the system without any loss of the significance that the sequencing of events may have. The approach has been illustrated on a model of a twin-engine aircraft fuel distribution system.

2   Background

2.1   An Overview of the HiP-HOPS Technique

Hierarchically Performed Hazard Origin & Propagation Studies or HiP-HOPS [4] is one of the more advanced and well supported compositional model-based safety analysis techniques. It can automatically generate fault trees and FMEA tables from extended system models, as well as perform quantitative analysis on the fault trees. It also has the ability to perform multi-objective optimisation of the system models [12]. It can semi-automatically allocate safety requirements to the system components in the form of Safety Integrity Levels (SILs) which automates some of the processes for the ASIL allocation specified in ISO 26262.

The approach consists of three main phases: (a) system modelling and failure annotation (b) fault tree synthesis and (c) fault tree analysis and FMEA synthesis.

The system modelling and failure annotation phase allows analysts to provide information to the HiP-HOPS tool on how the different system components are interconnected and how they can fail. The architectural model of the system shows the interconnections between the components of the system and the architecture can be arranged hierarchically, i.e., the system consists of different subsystems and subsystems have their own components. Modelling and annotation of the system with dependability information can be done using popular modelling tools like Matlab Simulink or SimulationX. The dependability related information includes component failure modes and Boolean expressions for output deviations, which describe how a component can fail and how it responds to failures that occur in other parts of the system. The expression for the output deviations show how the deviations in the component outputs can be caused either by the internal failure of that component or by corresponding deviations in the component's input. Such deviations can be user defined but typically include omission (O) of output, unexpected commission (C) of output, incorrect output, or too late or early arrival of output [13] (see Fig. 1). If available, quantitative data can also be entered to facilitate quantitative analysis in a later phase through parametric distribution functions (e.g. failure rate or scale and shape parameters of exponential and Weibull distributions, respectively). Note that while annotating components, HiP-HOPS considers that a component has a fixed set of nominal and failure behaviour, and these behaviours do not change over time. For instance, consider the component shown in Fig. 1, where the annotation of the output deviation of component A is shown in Table 1.

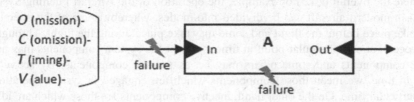

Fig. 1. An example component

Table 1. Annotation of component with static behaviour in HiP-HOPS

Component name	Output deviation	Failure expression
A	O-Out	A.Fail + O-A.In

Once the components in the system model are annotated with failure expressions, the annotated model is used by HiP-HOPS to synthesize fault trees. This process starts with a deviation of system output (top event) and traverses the system architecture backwards, i.e., from the system level outputs to the component level failures, to examine the propagation of failures through connections between components. In this way the process traverses the whole architecture and combines the local fault trees from the individual components until no connected components remain. The result is a single fault tree (or set of fault trees) which represents all the possible combinations of component failure that can lead to the system failure.

In the final phase, the synthesised fault trees are analysed both qualitatively and quantitatively. Qualitative analysis results in minimal cut sets (MCSs), which represent the smallest combinations of failure events that can cause the system failure. In addition to that, FMEA tables are generated automatically showing the connections between component failures and system failures. In quantitative analysis, probability of system failure is estimated based on the failure rate/probability of the basic events.

Generally, temporal dependencies among the events are not considered in FTA. However, HiP-HOPS is able to consider them using Pandora temporal fault trees (TFTs) [10]. Pandora uses temporal gates such as Priority-AND (PAND) and Priority-OR (POR) to represent temporal relations among events. The PAND gate represents a sequence between events X and Y where event X must occur before event Y, but both the events must occur. The POR gate also represents a sequence between the events, but it specifies an ordered disjunction rather than an ordered conjunction, i.e., event X must occur before event Y if event Y occurs at all. In this paper, the symbols '$\lhd$' and '$|$' are used to represent PAND and POR operation respectively in logical expressions. Additionally, '+' and '.' are used to represent logical OR and AND operations.

2.2 Dynamic Behaviour and Challenges in Dependability Analysis

In modern systems, big tasks are often divided into smaller tasks and are processed in different stages of the operation. In this way, resources are utilised in a sequence of different stages, and in each of those stages, a set of different functions are performed to complete the overall task. For example, the operation of the Aircraft Fuelling Systems (AFS) in modern aircraft can be divided into modes, whereby some of the operations may take place before the flight and some may take place during the flight. Throughout the process, at any particular point in time, some of the system components may act as active components and some others may act as passive components. By active at a point in time, we mean those components which are engaged in system operation at that particular time. On the other hand, inactive components are those which are idle or switched off, i.e., not involved in any operation at that point in time and waiting to be reactivated by the system.

Sometimes a system may have to perform a set of variable functions and, to facilitate this, a variable configuration of the system is obtained by deliberately activating and deactivating a selected number of components. A second scenario could be that a system is performing a fixed set of functions, and in the presence of a failure, the system may sacrifice some of its non-critical functions and go to a degraded operational mode by only doing the critical functions with a limited number of components with a different configuration. Additionally, to make the safety critical system tolerant to faults, many systems have fault tolerance strategies built in. As part of such a fault tolerant strategy, in the presence of faults, systems may reconfigure by using spare (cold or hot) components to respond to the faults and continue the nominal behaviour.

If we want to analyse such a system with techniques like HiP-HOPS, we will soon be faced with difficulties caused by the dynamic behaviour of the system. Temporal fault trees capture temporal dependencies, but for multi-state systems, it is difficult to precisely define the nominal behaviour of the system because it has different behaviours in different modes. Therefore, it is equally difficult to define the potential deviations from the nominal behaviour. Another thing to note is that different selections of components are activated and deactivated to obtain a desirable configuration; therefore some of the components may be irrelevant in some of the modes, and thus so are their failure modes. As a result, it is a challenge to take this mode dependent behaviour into account and represent it in an understandable and manageable format to facilitate dynamic failure propagation studies.

3   Dynamic Fault Propagation Studies Using HiP-HOPS

3.1   Representing Dynamic Behaviour Using Mode Charts

As already mentioned, we consider that in the presence of failure a system can behave dynamically by reconfiguring itself to deliver a variable set of functions or a single set of function with some alternative configurations. That means the configuration of the system may be dependent on the mode in which the system is operating, i.e., a distinct configuration/architecture can be associated with a distinct mode of operation. We propose to use mode charts [14] to represent the functional, dynamic behaviour of the systems, where each mode will represent a distinct configuration and the transition conditions will be the events associated with the component failures. Please note that in future work this concept will be applied in a more general sense, i.e., by also considering events that can transition the system state between operational modes; which is out of the scope of this paper.

A mode chart M could be formally defined as:

$$M = (Q, \Sigma, \delta, q_0) \tag{1}$$

where Q is the set of all possible modes, Σ is the set of all possible events, δ is the transition function $\delta : Q \times \Sigma \rightarrow Q$, and q_0 is the initial mode. The initial mode represents the fully functional architecture of the system where all the system components are operative and all functionality of the system is provided. Each of the other modes represents a degraded architecture (a distinct configuration) which is formed due to the presence of some failure, however, this architecture is still able to provide system functionality. We make the distinction between these modes based on the criticality of the configurations they represent:

- *Critical mode*: any further component failure will result in the system failure.
- *Non-critical mode*: the system failure cannot not be reached directly and further configurations can be formed from the present configuration.

Figure 2 shows different modes, M_i, connected via transition events, T_i, which cause mode changes. According to the criticality of the modes, they are classified as non-critical modes = $\{M_1, M_2, M_3\}$ and critical modes = $\{M_4, M_5, M_6\}$.

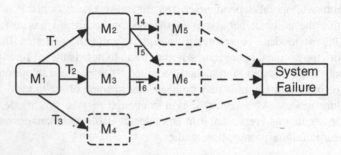

Fig. 2. Concept of mode based behaviour modelling; dashed and solid rounded rectangles represent the *critical* and *non-critical* modes respectively

To describe the dynamic behaviour of a system using mode charts, we would have to identify: (i) all possible functional modes, (ii) all possible conditions that can trigger transitions between those functional modes, and (iii) the *critical* and the *non-critical* modes.

3.2   Annotation of Mode Based Behaviour of Components

As mentioned earlier, for static fault propagation studies, the HiP-HOPS technique considers the system architecture as static and annotates the systems components with a fixed set of failure behaviours. These behaviours are considered the *default* behaviours of the components. However, for dynamic fault propagation studies, we need to annotate the components with mode-based behaviour. In this paper, the system components are regarded as non-repairable and have defined failure behaviour for different *critical modes* as the system failure could be reached directly from those modes. The components are non-repairable to ensure that the mode chart will be loop free, i.e., a directed acyclic graph.

Note that a component does not have to have a failure behaviour for all the critical modes because it may be (i) inactive in a particular mode, (ii) failed prior to entering a mode, or (iii) masked due to the failure of other components. In the first case the failure behaviour of that component is irrelevant in this mode. In the second case, the component has already failed before coming to the present mode; therefore, the failure behaviour of the component is already addressed in any of the prior modes. In the third case, the component itself is not failed; however, its activity does not have any effect in the system because of some other reason, e.g., failure of other components.

For example, let us consider that in a functional mode chart there are three critical modes M_1, M_2, and M_3 respectively; the component A is active in mode M_1 and M_3, but not in mode M_2. Therefore, we have to define the failure behaviour of component A only for modes M_1 and M_3. The annotation can be represented in tabular format as displayed in Table 2, where E_i denotes the i-th failure event of component A. If the failure specification of a component is the same in all its modes, the mode-based behavior reduces to their *default* behaviour as defined in the static analysis.

Table 2. Example of mode-based failure annotation of component

Component name	Output deviation	Failure expression		
		Mode M_1	Mode M_2	Mode M_3
A	O-Out	$E_1 + E_2 + E_3$	N/A	$E_4.E_5$

3.3 Synthesis and Analysis of Annotated System Models

Once the mode chart of the system behaviour and the mode based failure data have been defined, the mode chart and the annotated architectures can then be synthesised using the HiP-HOPS technique. This phase operates by examining how the failure of components propagates through system architecture and through different modes in the mode chart to cause system failure. Therefore, the first task of this phase is to identify the parts of the system model that act as the system outputs, and then define system failures (top events of the fault trees) for each of the *critical* modes in the mode chart. The top event of a mode specific fault tree is represented in the following form:

$$\texttt{Output\_Deviation\_Name}<mode\_name>$$

where the *mode_name* inside the angle brackets defines the mode from which the causes for output deviation defined by the `Output_Deviation_Name` are required to be derived. Similarly, mode specific basic events can be named as:

$$\texttt{event\_name}<mode\_name>.$$

The system operation modes denote non-overlapping system states. Accordingly, the system failure condition is defined as the disjunction of the causes of output deviation in all the critical modes. That is:

$$\texttt{O\_D\_X} = \texttt{O\_D\_X}<mode_1> + \texttt{O\_D\_X}<mode_2> + ... + \texttt{O\_D\_X}<mode_n> \qquad (2)$$

where `O_D_X` denotes the output deviation X.

In the synthesis process, each top event is considered separately and fault trees are generated using the HiP-HOPS technique by traversing both the mode chart and the system architecture. This process differs from HiP-HOPS' static fault propagation studies in that now sets of fault trees are generated for all the *critical* modes whereas in the static studies with a single operation mode only a single set of fault trees was created to represent the failure behaviour of the whole system. The fault tree synthesis process is now divided into two connected phases:

- *Architecture traversal*: represents the causes of system failure from that particular critical mode (as it is done in static studies).
- *Mode chart traversal*: represents the causes of reaching a particular critical mode from the initial mode.

A graphical overview of the fault tree synthesis process is shown in Fig. 3 where *IM* denotes initial mode, *NM* denotes non-critical modes, and *CM* denotes critical modes. We can see that all the *CM* lead directly to the system failure occurrence. Note that the arrows showing the direction of mode-chart traversal are in opposite direction of mode transitions.

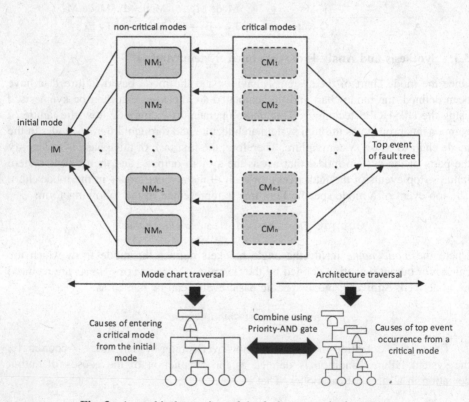

Fig. 3. A graphical overview of the fault tree synthesis process

The two traversal steps generate two interconnected fault trees. The architecture traversal starts with the failure logic of the system output that is defined for this critical mode. It then traverses the static architecture to examine the propagation of failure through the components to the system output. After that, the mode based local fault trees of all involved components are created and this process continues until no connected components remain. Once all the mode based local fault trees are created, they are combined together to obtain a single set of fault trees.

The second set of fault trees is generated by traversing the mode chart. We can consider this as a single source single destination graph traversal problem, where the source is the critical mode under consideration and the destination is the initial mode. This mode-traversal process will be backward from an internal mode towards the initial mode. In every iteration, the process replaces the current mode by its immediately preceding mode(s) and transition conditions from the preceding mode(s) to the current mode. This process will continue until the initial mode is reached. As a result of this process, we obtain all the possible combinations of events (component failures) that cause the system to go to the mode in question from the initial mode. If the initial mode is the critical mode then there is no need to traverse the mode chart.

In order to obtain the complete failure behaviour we need to combine these two sets of fault trees. The system can only fail if it reaches the critical mode of operation first and then from the critical mode to the system failure. Hence, when combining fault tree models generated from mode and architecture traversals, we need to maintain the sequence between them. We can use a PAND gate to combine these two sets of fault trees and define the system failure caused by the mode i denoted top-event, TE_i:

$$TE_i = FTA_i \triangleleft FTA_{architecture} \qquad (3)$$

where FTA_i denotes the fault tree obtained from the mode-chart traversal for the mode i and $FTA_{architecture}$ denotes the fault tree obtained from the architectural traversal.

When fault trees for all the critical modes are obtained, they can be linked with the OR logic to obtain the complete failure behaviour of the system. Let us assume that the system has N critical modes, then the system failure, TE, is defined as:

$$TE = TE_1 + \ldots + TE_i + \ldots + TE_N \qquad (4)$$

where TE_i is defined in Eq. (3).

Qualitative analysis could be performed on the Eq. (4) so as to remove redundant events and minimise the expression into a set of minimal cut sequences (MCSQs). MCSQs are the smallest sequence of events that are necessary and sufficient to cause the top event. In this paper, Pandora temporal fault trees are used to illustrate the idea and the methodologies proposed by Walker [10] to obtain MCSQs are applied. After minimization, the quantitative analysis of MCSQs can be performed using the approaches described in [15, 16], however, it is out of scope of this paper.

4 Case Study

To illustrate the idea of dynamic fault propagation studies, we use the case study of a hypothetical twin engine aircraft fuel distribution system, shown in Fig. 4.

The system has two fuel tanks TL (Tank Left) and TR (Tank Right); three valves VL (Valve Left), VR (Valve Right), and VC (Valve Centre); two pumps PL (Pump

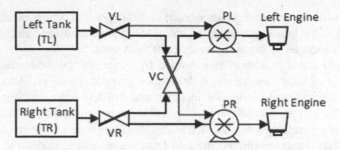

Fig. 4. Architecture of twin engine aircraft fuel system

Left) and PR (Pump Right). Under normal operating conditions, pump PL provides fuel to the Left Engine from tank TL through valve VL and pump PR provides fuel to the Right Engine from tank TR through valve VR. We can denote this as **M_TLTR** mode of system operation and in this mode, the valve VC is kept closed. Now, if we hypothesise a failure such that VR is stuck closed, then fuel flow to the Right Engine from TR is stopped. In this condition, the system can reconfigure itself by opening valve VC, hence continue fuel flow to the Right Engine from TL. We denote this as **M_TL** mode. Similarly, the system can operate in **M_TR** mode by providing fuel to Left Engine from TR in the condition that VL is stuck closed.

In the first stage of dynamic fault propagation studies, we need to annotate the components in the system architecture with mode based behaviour. After that, we have to identify the system output. Provision of fuel to each engine could be considered as the system output, and thus failure to provide fuel to any of the engines could be considered as a hazardous condition. Thus, failures of the engines are not considered here. As the fuel to the Left Engine and the Right Engine is provided in a similar fashion with the opposite set of components, for brevity, we concentrate on the failure of the system to provide fuel to the Left Engine alone.

As mentioned earlier, the system can operate in M_TLTR, M_TL, and M_TR modes. From the architecture in Fig. 4, we can see that the failure of pump PL will cause no fuel flow to the left engine in any mode, hence failure of pump PL can be considered as a single point of failure. For this reason, all the modes are considered as *critical* modes as described in Sect. 3.1. The mode-based annotations of the system components are shown in Table 3. In this table, the value N/A means that the behaviour of the component is not applicable (relevant) in this mode because it has no activity in this mode. We also need to define the mode chart. M_TLTR is the initial mode where all the system components are available. M_TL and M_TR are two degraded modes where the system can provide functionality, in this case, provision of fuel to the left engine, with reduced number of components. A transition from M_TLTR mode to M_TL mode will happen when fuel flow through VR will stop (i.e., O-VR.Out) and the system will enter to M_TR mode from M_TLTR mode when fuel flow through VL stops (i.e., O-VL.Out) (see Fig. 5).

In Table 3, 'O-' stands for *Omission*. It can also be seen that failure expressions of some components are the same in different modes. For example, failure expressions for VL is `VL.Fail + O-TL.Out` for both M_TLTR and M_TL modes. However, we

Table 3. Mode-based annotations of the components of system in Fig. 4

Component	Output deviations	Failure expression		
		M_TLTR	M_TL	M_TR
Left engine	O-Out	O-PL.Out	O-PL.Out	O-PL.Out
PL	O-Out	PL.Fail	PL.Fail + O-VL.Out	PL.Fail + O-VC.Out
PR	O-Out	PR.Fail	PR.Fail + O-VC.Out	PR.Fail + O-VR.Out
VL	O-Out	VL.Fail + O-TL.Out	VL.Fail + O-TL.Out	N/A
VR	O-Out	VR.Fail + O-TR.Out	N/A	VR.Fail + O-TR.Out
VC	O-Out	N/A	VC.Fail + O-VL.Out	VC.Fail + O-VR.Out
TL	O-Out	TL.Empty + TL.Block	TL.Empty + TL.Block	N/A
TR	O-Out	TR.Empty + TR.Block	N/A	TR.Empty + TR.Block

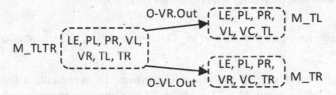

Fig. 5. Mode chart with active components listed in the modes

treat them differently under the assumption that the probability of failure of a component can be different in different modes due to the change in workloads in different modes, e.g. see [17]. Consider, for instance, each of the engines of the system in Fig. 4 consumes X litres of fuel per hour. Therefore, while the system operates in M_TLTR mode X litres of fuel flow through both VL and VR. Now, if for some reason VR gets stuck closed then the system will switch to M_TL mode, meaning that the left tank will provide fuel to both engines. This results in double fuel flow from left tank through the VL, which means the workload on valve VL and tank TL get doubled, and this in turn affects the failure probability of these components. As a result, although having the same failure expression in different modes, the behaviour is still treated differently due to the change in failure probability.

For fault tree synthesis from the annotated system architecture and mode chart, we defined the output deviation of the system as a disjunction of output deviations in all critical modes as follow:

```
O-Left_Engine.Out = O-Left_Engine.Out<M_TLTR>
                  + O-Left_Engine.Out<M_TL>
                  + O-Left_Engine.Out<M_TR>
```

In the above expression, O-Left_Engine.Out represents the output deviation of the system, i.e., omission of fuel flow to the left engine.

O-Left_Engine.Out<*M_TLTR*>, O-Left_Engine.Out<*M_TL*>, and O-Left_Engine.Out<*M_TR*> represent the output deviation in modes M_TLTR, M_TL,

M_TL, and M_TR respectively, which are essentially the top events of fault trees for the respective modes. Fault trees for each of the modes can be synthesised following the process described in Sect. 3.3.

Firstly, for the initial mode, M_TLTR, as mentioned in Sect. 3.3, we need to traverse the system architecture only based on the failure annotations (see Table 3).

$$
\text{O-Left\_Engine.Out} < M\_TLTR> = \text{O-PL.Out} < M\_TLTR>
$$
$$
= \text{PL.Fail} < M\_TLTR>
$$

For modes M_TL and M_TR, as they are *critical* but not initial modes, we need to obtain two fault trees. Consider the M_TL mode: to obtain the cause of system failure, we can start with the following expression (cf. Eq. (3)).

$$
\text{O-Left\_Engine.Out} < M\_TL> = \{M\_TL\} \lhd \text{O-Left\_Engine.Out} < M\_TL>
$$

On the right hand side of the above expression, '$\lhd$' represents a logical PAND operation. The left operand {M_TL} of the PAND operator represents the causes of entering the mode M_TL from the initial mode. On the other hand, the right operand (O-Left_Engine.Out<*M_TL*>) represents the causes of system failure from mode M_TL. Each of these operands represents a top event for two different fault trees and the fault tree can be obtained using the mode chart and architecture traversal process as follows. Data from Table 3 is used in the traversal process.

Mode Chart Traversal

{M_TL}= {M_TLTR}. O-VR.Out<*M_TLTR*>
= O-VR.Out<*M_TLTR*>
= VR.Fail<*M_TLTR*> + O-TR.Out<*M_TLTR*>
= VR.Fail<*M_TLTR*> + TR.Empty<*M_TLTR*> + TR.Block<*M_TLTR*>

Architecture Traversal

O-Left_Engine.Out<*M_TL*> = O-PL.Out<*M_TL*>
= PL.Fail<*M_TL*> + O-VL.Out<*M_TL*>
= PL.Fail<*M_TL*> + VL.Fail<*M_TL*> + O-TL.Out<*M_TL*>
= PL.Fail<*M_TL*> + VL.Fail<*M_TL*> + TL.Empty<*M_TL*>
 + TL.Block<*M_TL*>

Combining the results obtained from above two steps the failure behaviour of the system outputs from the M_TL mode is written as:

```
O-Left_Engine.Out<M_TL>=(VR.Fail<M_TLTR>+
TR.Empty<M_TLTR> + TR.Block<M_TLTR>) ◁ (PL.Fail<M_TL>
+ VL.Fail<M_TL>+TL.Empty<M_TL> + TL.Block<M_TL>)
```

Similarly, the causes of system failure from mode M_TR can be obtained as:

```
O-Left_Engine.Out<M_TR>=(VL.Fail<M_TLTR>+
TL.Empty<M_TLTR> + TL.Block<M_TLTR>) ◁ (PL.Fail<M_TR>
+ VC.Fail<M_TR>+VR.Fail<M_TR> + TR.Empty<M_TR>
+ TR.Block<M_TR>)
```

Now, the complete failure behaviour of the system can be obtained by taking logical OR of the individual failure behaviour in different modes (cf. Eq. (4)).

```
O-Left_Engine.Out= PL.Fail<M_TLTR>+ [(VR.Fail<M_TLTR>
+ TR.Empty<M_TLTR> + TR.Block<M_TLTR>) ◁ (PL.Fail<M_TL>
+ [VL.Fail<M_TL> + TL.Empty<M_TL> + TL.Block<M_TL>)]
+(VL.Fail<M_TLTR>+ TL.Empty<M_TLTR> + TL.Block<M_TLTR>)
◁ (PL.Fail<M_TR> + VC.Fail<M_TR> +VR.Fail<M_TR>
+ TR.Empty<M_TR> + TR.Block<M_TR>)]
```

From a closer look at the architecture of Fig. 4, we can see that the work pattern or workload on pump PL and PR remains the same in all the modes. For this reason, failure behaviour of these components can be considered to be mode independent, i.e., PL.Fail<M_TLTR> ⇔ PL.Fail<M_TL> ⇔ PL.Fail<M_TR> ⇔ PL.Fail. Therefore, the above expression can be written as:

```
O-Left_Engine.Out= PL.Fail+ [(VR.Fail<M_TLTR>
+ TR.Empty<M_TLTR> + TR.Block<M_TLTR>) ◁ (PL.Fail
+ VL.Fail<M_TL> + TL.Empty<M_TL> + TL.Block<M_TL>)]
+ [(VL.Fail<M_TLTR>+ TL.Empty<M_TLTR> + TL.Block<M_TLTR>)
◁ (PL.Fail + VC.Fail<M_TR> +VR.Fail<M_TR> + TR.Empty<M_TR>
+ TR.Block<M_TR>)]
```

This fault tree expression now shows the causes of omission of fuel to the left engine form all the relevant modes. Using a prototype version of the HiP-HOPS tool, the minimal cut sequences to cause the system failure are calculated, and shown in Table 4. In this table, basic events are replaced by their IDs as:

X_1 = PL.Fail, X_2 = VL.Fail<*M_TLTR*>, X_3 = VL.Fail<*M_TL*>, X_4 = VR.Fail<*M_TLTR*>, X_5 = VR.Fail<*M_TR*>, X_6 = VC.Fail<*M_TR*>, X_7 = TL.Empty<*M_TLTR*>, X_8 = TL.Block<*M_TLTR*>, X_9 = TL.Empty<*M_TL*>, X_{10} = TL.Block<*M_TL*>,
X_{11} = TR.Empty<*M_TLTR*>, X_{12} = TR.Block<*M_TLTR*>,
X_{13} = TR.Empty<*M_TR*>, X_{14} = TR.Block<*M_TR*>.

Table 4. Minimal cut sequences that can cause the system failure in Fig. 4.

MCSQs	MCSQs
X_1	$X_2\| X_6. X_2 \triangleleft X_5. X_2\| X_{13}. X_2\| X_{14}$
$X_4 \triangleleft X_3. X_4\| X_9. X_4\| X_{10}$	$X_2\| X_6. X_2\| X_5. X_2 \triangleleft X_{13}. X_2\| X_{14}$
$X_4\| X_3. X_4 \triangleleft X_9. X_4\| X_{10}$	$X_2\| X_6. X_2\| X_5. X_2\| X_{13}. X_2 \triangleleft X_{14}$
$X_4\| X_3. X_4\| X_9. X_4 \triangleleft X_{10}$	$X_7 \triangleleft X_6. X_7\| X_5. X_7\| X_{13}. X_7\| X_{14}$
$X_{11} \triangleleft X_3. X_{11}\| X_9. X_{11}\| X_{10}$	$X_7\| X_6. X_7 \triangleleft X_5. X_7\| X_{13}. X_7\| X_{14}$
$X_{11}\| X_3. X_{11} \triangleleft X_9. X_{11}\| X_{10}$	$X_7\| X_6. X_7\| X_5. X_7 \triangleleft X_{13}. X_7\| X_{14}$
$X_{11}\| X_3. X_{11}\| X_9. X_{11} \triangleleft X_{10}$	$X_7\| X_6. X_7\| X_5. X_7\| X_{13}. X_7 \triangleleft X_{14}$
$X_{12} \triangleleft X_3. X_{12}\| X_9. X_{12}\| X_{10}$	$X_8 \triangleleft X_6. X_8\|X_5. X_8\| X_{13}. X_8\| X_{14}$
$X_{12}\| X_3. X_{12} \triangleleft X_9. X_{12}\| X_{10}$	$X_8\| X_6. X_8 \triangleleft X_5. X_8\| X_{13}. X_8\| X_{14}$
$X_{12}\| X_3. X_{12}\| X_9. X_{12} \triangleleft X_{10}$	$X_8\| X_6. X_8\| X_5. X_8 \triangleleft X_{13}. X_8\| X_{14}$
$X_2 \triangleleft X_6. X_2\| X_5. X_2\| X_{13}. X_2\| X_{14}$	$X_8\| X_6. X_8\|X_5. X_8\| X_{13}. X_8 \triangleleft X_{14}$

5   Conclusion

In this paper, we pointed out that the dynamic behaviour of systems makes it difficult to precisely define the nominal and failure behaviour of systems, thus complicating dependability analysis processes. As a potential remedy to the above problem, we propose the use of mode charts to define dynamic behaviour of systems, and subsequently annotate the components in the system architecture with their mode based behaviour. The proposed approach extends the state-of-the-art model-based dependability analysis approach, HiP-HOPS, by extending the existing phases of the approach for dynamic fault propagation studies.

The annotation phase has been extended by annotating system components with mode-based dynamic behaviour. The synthesis phase has been extended by providing ways to generate temporal fault trees by examining the system model and how the failure of components propagates through the system architecture and the different modes in the mode chart to cause system failure. Finally, in the analysis phase, minimal cut sequences are generated by analysing the temporal fault trees. As a whole, this extension to HiP-HOPS combines the advantages of the existing HiP-HOPS approach — semi-automatic generation of system-wide failure propagation information from an annotated system model — with the benefits of forms of representation better suited to dynamic systems, such as mode charts. This combination allows designers to model more complex dynamic scenarios in a more intuitive way than simply using temporal expressions and logic. It also allows them to perform compositional dynamic dependability analysis of complex systems by generating temporal fault trees. This work enriches the semantics of HiP-HOPS and has the potential to be combined with the other advanced features of HiP-HOPS, such as architecture optimisation, maintenance, safety requirement allocation, and safety case generation for dynamic systems. However, the scalability of this approach for analysis of large-scale systems is yet to be verified. Some of our current work is focused on continuing development of the techniques as part of HiP-HOPS tool.

Acknowledgments. This work was partly funded by the DEIS H2020 project (Grant Agreement 732242).

References

1. Vesely, W.E., Stamatelatos, M., Dugan, J., Fragola, J., Minarick, J., Railsback, J.: Fault Tree Handbook with Aerospace Applications. NASA office of safety and mission assurance, Washington D.C. (2002)
2. Joshi, A., Heimdahl, M.P.E., Miller, S.P., Whalen, M.W.: Model-based safety analysis. NASA Technical report, Hampton, VA, USA (2006)
3. Fenelon, P., McDermid, J.A.: An integrated toolset for software safety analysis. J. Syst. Softw. **21**, 279–290 (1993)
4. Papadopoulos, Y., McDermid, J.A.: Hierarchically performed hazard origin and propagation studies. In: Felici, M., Kanoun, K. (eds.) SAFECOMP 1999. LNCS, vol. 1698, pp. 139–152. Springer, Heidelberg (1999). doi:10.1007/3-540-48249-0_13
5. Arnold, A., Point, G., Griffault, A., Rauzy, A.: The AltaRica formalism for describing concurrent systems. Fundam. Inform. **40**, 109–124 (2000)
6. Bozzano, M., Villafiorita, A.: The FSAP/NuSMV-SA safety analysis platform. Int. J. Softw. Tools Technol. Transf. Spec. Sect. Adv. Autom. Verif. Crit. Syst. **9**, 5–24 (2007)
7. Feiler, P., Rugina, A.: Dependability modeling with the architecture analysis & design language (AADL). Technical report, Carnegie Mellon University (2007)
8. Aizpurua, J.I., Muxika, E.: Model-based design of dependable systems: limitations and evolution of analysis and verification approaches. Int. J. Adv. Secur. **6**, 12–31 (2013)
9. Sharvia, S., Kabir, S., Walker, M., Papadopoulos, Y.: Model-based dependability analysis: state-of-the-art, challenges, and future outlook. In: Software Quality Assurance: In Large Scale and Complex Software-Intensive Systems, pp. 251–278 (2015)
10. Walker, M.: Pandora: a logic for the qualitative analysis of temporal fault trees. Ph.D. thesis, University of Hull (2009)
11. Rauzy, A.: Mode automata and their compilation into fault trees. Reliab. Eng. Syst. Saf. **78**, 1–12 (2002)
12. Papadopoulos, Y., Walker, M., Parker, D., Sharvia, S., Bottaci, L., Kabir, S., Azevedo, L., Sorokos, I.: A synthesis of logic and bio-inspired techniques in the design of dependable systems. Ann. Rev. Control **41**, 170–182 (2016)
13. Papadopoulos, Y., Mcdermid, J., Sasse, R., Heiner, G.: Analysis and synthesis of the behaviour of complex programmable electronic systems in conditions of failure. RESS **71**, 229–247 (2001)
14. Sampath, M., Sengupta, R., Lafortune, S., Sinnamohideen, K., Teneketzis, D.: Failure diagnosis using discrete-event models. IEEE Trans. Control Syst. Technol. **4**, 105–124 (1996)

15. Kabir, S., Walker, M., Papadopoulos, Y.: Quantitative evaluation of pandora temporal fault trees via petri nets. IFAC-PapersOnLine **48**, 458–463 (2015)
16. Kabir, S., Walker, M., Papadopoulos, Y.: Reliability analysis of dynamic systems by translating temporal fault trees into Bayesian networks. In: Ortmeier, F., Rauzy, A. (eds.) IMBSA 2014. LNCS, vol. 8822, pp. 96–109. Springer, Cham (2014). doi:10.1007/978-3-319-12214-4_8
17. Labeau, P.E., Smidts, C., Swaminathan, S.: Dynamic reliability: towards an integrated platform for probabilistic risk assessment. Reliab. Eng. Syst. Saf. **68**, 219–254 (2000)

A Fault Diagnostic Tool Based on a First Principle Model Simulator

Francesco Cannarile[1,2(✉)], Michele Compare[1,2], and Enrico Zio[1,2,3]

[1] Energy Department, Politecnico di Milano, Milan, Italy
francesco.cannarile@aramis3d.com
[2] Aramis Srl, Milan, Italy
[3] Chair on Systems Science and the Energetic Challenge, Fondation EDF,
Ecole Centrale Paris and Supelec, Châtenay-Malabry, France

Abstract. We develop a First Principle Model (FPM) simulator of a solenoid micro-valve of the control system of a train braking system. This is used for failure diagnostic when field data of normal and abnormal system behaviors are lacking. A procedure is proposed to adjust the diagnostic model once field data are available.

Keywords: Fault diagnostics · Feature selection · Wrapper approach · Solenoid valve · Train braking system

1 Introduction

The engineering field that focuses on Detection, Diagnostics and Prognostics is often referred to as Prognostics and Health Management (PHM) [1]. PHM allows for a significant reduction in the system unavailability through an efficient and agile maintenance management, capable of providing the right part to the right place at the right time, together with the necessary resources to perform the maintenance task [1]. This has obviously gained the interest of industry and has resulted in new win-win maintenance service contract models.

This new situation has led several companies of different industrial sectors (i.e., transport, aviation, energy, etc.) to look into PHM first of all simply because having a PHM-equipped system may be the mandatory condition to sell it and, then, because there may be new important sources of income, related to the new opportunities arising if the company is able to sell added values by taking over parts of clients' business risks and other (financial) burdens. In this way, a contractor can diversify his "product" range and may be able to achieve a higher profit.

On the other side, the companies interested in PHM have to balance the risks of PHM due to the lack of experience and the capital expenditures required to purchase the necessary instrumentation, software and specialized knowledge. These risks and costs are larger at the beginning of the development of PHM, when real data of normal and abnormal system behaviors are lacking or scarce, and in case of new systems, when there is no experience on their operation. In these situations, the capability of PHM is

M. Bozzano and Y. Papadopoulos (Eds.): IMBSA 2017, LNCS 10437, pp. 179–193, 2017.
DOI: 10.1007/978-3-319-64119-5_12

difficult to be estimated, and this may lead potentially interested companies to distrust the investment in developing a PHM solution.

One possible way to overcome the initial skepticism of the companies is to propose an adaptive and robust PHM development framework, which allows updating and adjusting the PHM tool on the basis of the Knowledge, Information and Data (KID) that incrementally become available as the development goes on from the design to its operation in different working and aging conditions. This gives the companies the possibility of tracking the development of the PHM and the improvement of its performances, which are, then, partially reassured about the risks undertaken in the different stages.

In this work, we present a case study concerning a solenoid valve mounted on the braking system of trains, which has been proposed by a company of the transportation industry interested in fault diagnostics. The case study is characterized by the fact that real data patterns of both normal and abnormal solenoid valves behaviors are currently unavailable. Thus, to start the PHM development pathway, we have developed a First Principle Model (FPM) simulator, which gives a sound basis for an initial identification of an optimal subset of features for the development of a diagnostic classifier with high classification performance.

This work paves the way to future works, when real signal measurements from the solenoid valve become available: the developed algorithms will be adaptively tuned and their parameters updated to provide more accurate and precise estimates, and, further, field data will be exploited to take into account uncertainty related to un-modelled dynamics. For this, we also sketch the entire development pathway for building a diagnostic tool, from the FPM development up to the tuning of the diagnostic classifier based on real data.

Obviously, the simulator can also be used as a reliability-based design tool, for designing solenoid valves meeting given reliability requirements with a specific confidence, and as a workbench to design tests on the valve.

The paper is organized as follows: in Sect. 2, the FPM-based fault diagnostic tool is presented in details; Sect. 3 details the FPM of the solenoid valve; Sect. 4 illustrates the development of the diagnostic system based on the FPM. Section 5 concludes the work.

2   Diagnostic Tool Based on FPM Simulator

In this Section, we present our methodology for the fault diagnostic issue. The main tasks to be addressed by the diagnostic tool are:

- Detect anomalous conditions at an early stage of the initiation of the degradation processes (Fault Detection), for problem awareness.
- Characterize the detected conditions (Fault Diagnostics), for establishing the correct maintenance action.
- Quantify the uncertainty on the Detection and Diagnostics outcomes.

These tasks are pursued by implementing the procedure detailed in the following Subsections. Notice that in general, fault detection and fault diagnostics are tackled separately, whereas our approach these tasks are properly integrated.

2.1 Fault Detection Procedure

A general procedure to tackle the fault detection issue is made up of the following steps:

(S1) *Building a dataset (data history matrix):* containing the signals corresponding to the normal system operation. To do this while field data are unavailable, either a first principle model (FPM), (i.e., a model based on established laws of physics) or a parametric model (PM), (i.e., a model based on empirical assumption dependent on unknown paramters to be estimated), is developed and simulated in the expected normal operating conditions [1].

(S2) *Feature extraction and selection*: The aims of this step are: (a) the extraction of features from the simulated Condition Monitoring (CM) signals and (b) the selection of an optimal subset of features to be used for fault detection. For more details, see, for example [2].

(S3) *Fault detection*: Two different strategies can be pursued to address the fault detection issue, which are referred to as "Strategy A" and "Strategy B".

Strategy A
This strategy is based on the development of an Empirical Classification Model (ECM), which builds a mapping function between signal features coming from step (S2) and degradation levels (normal condition or abnormal condition).

(S3A) *Fault detection*: Build an empirical detection classification model (e.g., Support Vector Machine (SVM), Fuzzy K-Nearest Neighbors (FKNN), Artificial Neural networks (ANN), etc., [3]) based on the features selected at step S2. The assumption here is that the values of the features corresponding to normal conditions are different from those corresponding to abnormal conditions.

Strategy B
This strategy is based on the development of an Empirical Reconstruction Model (ERM) [4], which reconstructs the values of the features expected in the component normal conditions: features are extracted from signals observed during operation and compared with the reconstruction provided by the ERM; then, abnormal component conditions are detected when the reconstructions are remarkably different from measurements [4].

(S3B) *Normal operation data reconstruction*: the aim of this step is to build an ERM (e.g., based on non-parametric Auto-Associative Kernel Regression (AAKR), Artificial Neural Network (ANN), Self Organizing Maps (SOMs) Fuzzy Similarity Analysis (FSA) [3]) to reconstruct the values of the features corresponding to normal operation based on the optimal subset selected at step S2, even if the measured ones correspond to faulty conditions.

(S3B) *Residual generation;* compute the residuals between the measured data and the normal operation data reconstructed at step S3B.

(S3B) *Fault detection*: develop an algorithm, e.g., Sequential Probability Ratio Test (SPRT) [4], to perform fault detection. The detection is typically alarmed when the distance between the signal feature values corresponding to the normal operating conditions and their actual values achieve a given threshold. Finally, the uncertainty in the distance estimation is also evaluated, which comes from both the lack of knowledge and the stochastic behavior of the signals. This allows controlling the robustness and the confidence on the maintenance decisions made upon the alarm.

(S4) *Fault history matrix update*: as normal operation data is collected on the component/system (in lab experiments or in the field), the data history matrix built at step S1 is updated by appending the new data.

(S5) *FPM calibration*: This activity makes use of as much information as possible from well-designed laboratory or pilot-plant experiments to obtain the most accurate characterization of the fundamental physics of the process involving the continual adjustment of the model and its parameters. The problem of estimating the FPM parameters from real field data can be framed as an inverse problem. The two currently predominant approaches to parameter estimation are those based on Particle Filtering (PF, [5]), and Moving Horizon Estimation (MHE, [6]).

(S6) *Fault detection model updating*: this step requires relaunching the feature selection algorithm in the light of the updated fault history matrix (step S4) and FPM parameters.

(S7) *Uncertainty Analysis*: see Subsect. 2.3.

2.2 Fault Diagnostics

(D1) *Faulty operation data history matrix generation*: while field data are unavailable, inject faults in the FPM to simulate faulty operation data. This allows creating the faulty operation data history matrix generation.

(D2) *Feature extraction and selection:* as described in S2.

(D3) *Fault diagnostics*: build a fault classification model in a similar manner, as illustrated in S3B.

(D4) *Fault data history matrix updating*: As faulty operation data is collected (in lab experiments or in the field), update the data history matrix generated in D1, similarly to what is done in S4.

(D5) *FPM calibration:* as described in S5.

(D6) *Fault diagnostic model: updating* as described in S6.

(D7) *Uncertainty Analysis*: see Subsect. 2.3.

Notice that our approach to fault diagnostics is based on the development of an ECS as in "Strategy A" for fault detection. Therefore, this can be easily integrated with diagnostics by letting steps D1-D2-D3-D4 above be preceded by step S1.

2.3 Uncertainty Analysis

When field data becomes available, i.e., after steps S4 and D4, this can be used to take into account unmodeled dynamics due to epistemic uncertainty related to the nature of the measurement apparatus, assumptions made by the experimenter, and the FPM used to make inferences based on the observed data. Different representations of epistemic uncertainty are possible: probability bound analysis, imprecise probability, evidence theory and possibility theory [7]. Once uncertainty has been represented using the approaches listed above, it must be propagated to the quantity of interest (e.g., the predicted Remaining Useful Life (RUL)). Methods for uncertainty propagation are described in detail in [7].

3   FPM Simulator for Solenoid Valves

The application of our approach to fault diagnostics to a pilot case is proposed in this Section. The equipment considered are solenoid valves mounted on the control system of train backing systems. Steps S1, D1, D2 and D3 of the procedure described above are implemented. Specifically, "Strategy A" for fault detection is applied and integrated with fault diagnostics. Namely, we first develop a FPM model for normal behavior (step S1), which is exploited to simulate the valve behavior and acquire the solenoid current signals. Then, the model of the degradation process due to the accumulation of debris at the valve seat is embedded into the FPM simulator. This mechanism of degradation behaves as a continuous-state stochastic process, and it has been approximated as a discrete-state process.

The simulation of the degradation mechanism together with the valve behavior allows acquiring the signals corresponding to the different behaviors of the solenoid valve in the different degradation states. A FKNN classification algorithm, then, is

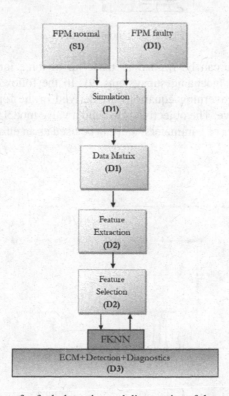

Fig. 1. Scheme for fault detection and diagnostics of the solenoid valve.

developed for diagnostics (steps D2 and D3), based on the simulated solenoid current signals. The development of the classification algorithm (step D3) has been integrated with a wrapper method for optimal feature selection (step D2), based on the Differential Evolution technique (Baraldi et al. 2016). Figure 1 summarizes the application of steps (S1), (D1), (D2) and (D3) of the proposed methodology to the solenoid valve case study.

3.1 Solenoid Valves First Principle Model (Step S1 and D1)

In this Subsection, the FPM of the solenoid valve under study is presented. The solenoid valve here considered is a fast switching spring return 3/2 valve which is used in the Normally Open (NO) setting [8] (Fig. 2).

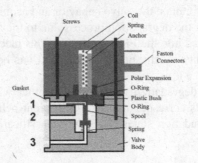

Fig. 2. Solenoid 3/2 valve.

The solenoid valve can be framed as made up of three interacting subsystems: magnetic, electric and mechanic subsystems [9]. In the following, these are deeply investigated and the governing equations are derived in the form of nonlinear state equations for a NO valve. The objective is to build a valve model that is accurate, relies on a reasonable number of parameters, and can be used as an effective simulation tool.

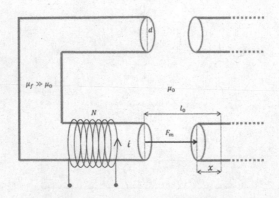

Fig. 3. Model of the magnetic circuit.

3.1.1   Magnetic Subsystem

The magnetic circuit consists of two parts (Fig. 3):

- a fixed core surrounded by N coil turns carrying a current i, and
- a moving part, called cylindrical air gap, which moves under the effect of the exerted magnetic force F_m.

The quantities appearing in Fig. 3 are:

- μ_0: magnetic permeability in the vacuum.
- μ_r: magnetic permeability of the core.
- d: pole diameter of the cylinders.
- l_0: air gap total length.
- N: number of coil turns.
- x: decrease in the length of the air gap due to the magnetic force.

Assuming that the reluctance of the core is negligible ($\mu_f \gg \mu_o$), the magneto-motive force $\mathcal{F}$ can be written as [10]:

$$\mathcal{F} = Ni = \mathcal{R}_{gap}\,\phi \tag{1}$$

where $\mathcal{R}_{gap}$ is the reluctance of the air gap, i is the current carried by the N coil turns and ϕ is the magnetic flux for a cylindrical air gap, the reluctance is given by [10]:

$$\mathcal{R}_{gap} = \frac{l_0 - x}{\mu_0 A} \tag{2}$$

where

$$A = \frac{\pi d^2}{4} \tag{3}$$

The magnetic force in the air gap is given by [10]:

$$F_m = \frac{\phi^2}{2}\frac{\partial R_{gap}(x)}{\partial x} \tag{4}$$

Equations (1) and (2) yield:

$$\phi = \frac{Ni}{R_{gap}} = \frac{Ni\mu_0 A}{l_0 - x} \tag{5}$$

Considering that

$$\frac{\partial R_{gap}(x)}{\partial x} = \frac{-1}{\mu_0 A} \tag{6}$$

it follows that

$$F_m = \frac{\phi^2}{2}\frac{\partial R_{gap}(x)}{\partial x} = -\frac{N^2 i^2 \mu_0 A}{2(l_0 - x)^2} \tag{7}$$

This force acts on the shuttle of the valve, as shown in the mechanical subsystem described in Subsect. 3.1.3.

3.1.2   Electric Subsystem

The equivalent electric circuit of the micro-valve is schematized in Fig. 4.

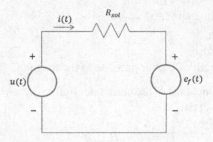

Fig. 4.   Model of the electric circuit.

By applying Kirchhoff's voltage law, the state equation of this subsystem can be written by

$$u(t) = R_{sol}i(t) + e_f(t) \tag{8}$$

in which $u(t)$ is the input voltage, R_{sol} is the solenoid resistance and $e_f(t)$ is the electro-motive force induced by the changing magnetic field. According to Faraday's law, $e_f(t)$ is given by [10]:

$$e_f(t) = \frac{d\lambda}{dt} \tag{9}$$

where $\lambda = N\phi$ is the flux linkage, which is also equal to $L \cdot i$. The inductance of the magnetic circuit, which determines the value of $e_f(t)$, can be derived from the expression of the magnetic flux ϕ in Eq. (5):

$$L(x) = \frac{N^2}{R_{gap}(x)} \tag{10}$$

Then, Eq. (8) can be written as:

$$\frac{di(t)}{dt} = \frac{1}{L(x)}\left(u(t) - R_{sol}i(t) - i(t)\frac{\partial L(x)}{\partial x}\frac{dx}{dt}\right), i(0) = i_0 \tag{11}$$

3.1.3 Mechanical Subsystem

The mechanical subsystem consists of a spring with spring rate K_1, a mass m (i.e., the spool mass) and a second spring with spring rate K_2. The mechanical system is shown in Fig. 5.

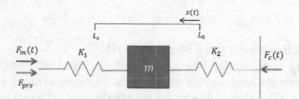

Fig. 5. Model of the mechanical subsystem.

The term $F_c(t)$ in Fig. 5 represents the contact force with the seat [8], which is described by:

$$F_c(t) = F_c^D(t) + F_c^K \tag{12}$$

where

$$F_c^D(t) = D\frac{dx(t)}{dt} \tag{13}$$

D is the damper coefficient, and

$$F_c^K(t) = \begin{cases} K(-x) & \text{if } x < 0 \\ 0 & \text{if } 0 \le x \le L_s \\ -K(x - L_s) & \text{if } x > L_s \end{cases} \tag{14}$$

In Eq. (14), K and L_s represent the (large) spring constant associated with the flexible seats and the maximum movement allowed to the moving mass, respectively, [8]. The force F_{prs} in Fig. 5 is the pressure force, which is approximated by [9]:

$$F_{prs} = (A_1 - A_2)P_{in} + (A_3 - A_2)P_{out} \tag{15}$$

where P_{in} and P_{out} are the pressures at the inlet and outlet ports of the valve and A_1, A_2, A_3 and A_4 are different areas on the spool lands which are affected by P_{in} and P_{out} in different directions. In the valve studied, the areas A_3 and A_4 are approximatively equal [9]. Then, $F_{prs} \cong (A_1 - A_2)P_{in}$. Finally, the equilibrium equation for the mass m is given by

$$m\frac{d^2x(t)}{dt^2} + F_c(t) + D\frac{dx(t)}{dt} + k_2\left(x(t) - x_0^2\right) - k_1\left(x(t) - x_0^1\right) = F_{prs} - F_m \tag{16}$$

$$x(0) = x_0, \frac{dx(0)}{dx} = x_0'\; L_0 \le x \le L_s, L_o \ge 0 \tag{17}$$

In Eq. (17), L_0 represents the displacement of the lower position of the moving mass with respect to its nominal position, i.e., $L_o = 0$. The displacement x refers to the same origin as for L_o.

3.1.4   Degradation Model (Step S0 and Step D1)

In our modelling methodology, the model of the nominal micro-valve behavior is extended to encode the model of the effects of the friction due to the accumulation of debris at the seats of the micro-valve, which has been recognized by our industrial partner FMEA analysis, as the leading cause of performance reduction in the train braking system (step S0). As the debris builds up, it impedes the valve spool movements and prevents it from fully opening [8]. This results in a change in the boundary conditions of the spool valve motion: the larger the degradation level, the larger the value of L_0. We characterize the friction damage by a change in the friction coefficient $r(t)$, and model the damage progression as [8]:

$$\frac{dr(t)}{dt} = \omega_r \left| F_f(t) \frac{dx(t)}{dt} \right|, r(0) = r_0 \tag{18}$$

where ω_r is the wear coefficient, whereas $F_f(t)$ is the friction force [8]. This is defined as:

$$F_f(t) = r(t) \frac{dx(t)}{dt} \tag{19}$$

Notice that the value of ω_r can be estimated from real data, once these become available. Finally, Eq. (16a) is modified to encode the damages due to friction:

$$m\frac{d^2x(t)}{dt^2} + F_c(t) + D\frac{dx(t)}{dt} + k_2\left(x(t) - x_0^2\right) - k_1\left(x(t) - x_0^1\right) = F_{prs} - F_m(t) - F_f(t) \tag{20}$$

From the discussion above, it follows that

$$L_0 = L_0(r(t)) \tag{21}$$

where L_o is a monotone increasing function of the kinetic friction coefficient, that is, the mass can no longer reach the position x where $L_0 = 0$ due to the debris. The maximum elongation allowed to the spool valve

$$L_{s-o} = L_{s-o}(r(t)) = L_s - L_o \tag{22}$$

is a decreasing function of $r(t)$.

4   Development of the Diagnostic Classifier (Steps S1+D1+D2+D3)

In this Section, a classification algorithm is developed to assess the degradation level of the solenoid valve based on the solenoid current signals obtained from the simulator of the FPM described in Sect. 3. The FPM parameters have been set according to our partner knowledge and are reported in Tables 1, 2 and 3 below.

Table 1. Values of parameters μ_0, dl_0, N and R_{sol}.

μ_0	d	l_0	N	R_{sol}
$4\pi \cdot 10^{-7} H/m$	$7 \cdot 10^{-4} m$	$6.5 \cdot 10^{-4} m$	$3210\ ts$	$236\ \Omega$

Table 2. Values of parameters K_1, K_2, x_0^1, x_0^2 and m.

K_1	K_2	x_0^1	x_0^2	m
$367.875\ N/m$	$588.6\ N/m$	$7.13 \cdot 10^{-3} m$	$0.967 \cdot 10^{-3} m$	$5.4957 \cdot 10^{-3} Kg$

Table 3. Values of parameters $D, K, L_s, F_{prs}, i_0, x_0, x_0'$ and ω_r.

D	K	L_s	F_{prs}	i_0	x_0	x_0'	L_0	ω_r
$5\ N \cdot s/m$	$10^8\ N/m$	$0.3 \cdot 10^{-3} m$	$0.7442\ N$	$0\ A$	$0.3 \cdot 10^{-3} m$	$0\ A/s$	$0\ m$	10^{-10}

4.1   Model Simulation (Steps S1+D1)

For the solenoid valve under investigation, we have considered 4 degradation levels: 'normal', 'low damage', 'medium damage' and 'failure', which correspond to an increase in the value of the lower position of the moving mass L_0 and, consequently, to a decrease in the value of the highest position L_s, as reported in Table 4.

Table 4. Threshold values of L_0 and pr characterizing the 4 degradation levels.

Degradation level	$L_0(mm)$	Percentage reduction in $L_{o-s}(pr)$
Normal	$0 \leq L_0 < 0.02$	$0\% \leq pr < 6.67\%$
Low damage	$0.02 \leq L_0 < 0.04$	$6.67\% \leq pr < 13.34\%$
Medium damage	$0.04 \leq L_0 < 0.06$	$13.37\% \leq pr < 20\%$
Failure	$L_0 \geq 0.06$	$pr \geq 20\%$

To simulate different levels of degradation, we need to find the values of the kinetic friction coefficient $r(t)$ associated to the threshold values in Table 5, which refer to the valve spool displacement. To establish the relationships between the displacement and the friction coefficient, we have simulated 2000 solenoid current signals, corresponding to the values $\{1, ..., 2000\}$ of the initial condition r_0 in Eq. (18) with $\omega_r = 0.00001$ and the input voltage coming from real measurements. For each simulated current profile, we have got the corresponding value of L_0: this gives the curve $(r_0, L_0(r_0))$ shown in Fig. 6, which maps the valve spool position onto the degradation model. Different valve spool positions correspond to different flow rate values, and thus different breaking performances. From this, we can derive the upper bounds r_n, r_l and r_m for defining the 'normal', 'low damage' and 'medium damage' degradation levels, respectively (Table 5), which correspond to decreasing flow rate levels and, thus, decreasing valve performance.

Table 5. Kinetic friction value intervals corresponding to the four degradation levels.

I_0 (normal)	I_1 (low damage)	I_2 (medium damage)	I_3 (failure)
$(0, r_n) = (0, 1018)$	$[r_n, r_l) = [1019, 1097]$	$[r_l, r_m) = [1098, 1189]$	$[r_m, 2000) = [1189, 2000]$

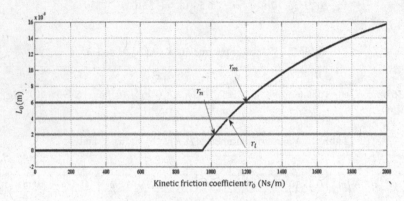

Fig. 6. Kinetic friction coefficient r_0 vs L_0.

4.2 Data History Matrix Generation (Steps S1+D1)

We have randomly generated 200 values of r_0 within each interval (see Table 5), and we have simulated the FPM model. By so doing, we have obtained a total of 800 solenoid current signals, labelled as $g_{1_i}, g_{2_i}, g_{3_i}$ and $g_{4_i}, i = 1, \ldots, 200$, depending on the degradation state in which they are generated: normal, low damage, medium damage and failure, respectively. Finally, we have also added a white noise to all 800 generated current signals, to take into account that real data are expected to be noisy (e.g., owing to current sensor noise).

4.3 Feature Extraction (Step D2)

In the case study proposed in this work, a set of $n = 177$ features have been extracted from each current signal, which include statistical indicators (features 1 to 9), Wavelet Transforms (WPT) using different basis (Biorthogonal 2.4 (features 10 to 51), Reverse Biorthogonal 2.4 (features 52 to 93), Symlet5 basis (features 94 to 135) and Haar basis (features 136–177)) [2].

By so doing, we have obtained a dataset X consisting of 800 patterns in the 177-dimensional space. Since the range of signal values of the entries of the matrix X can widely vary, these have been normalized: the values in every column of X have been re-scaled so that they are (standard) normally distributed with mean equal to 0 and standard deviation equal to 1.

Then, all the available 800 labelled data of X are partitioned into

- A set used for the feature selection task, which is made up of 50% of the total number of patterns, obtained by randomly sampling 100 patterns among the 200 patterns available at each degradation level.
- A validation set, which contains the remaining patterns. These will be used for validating the performance of the diagnostic model after the optimal features subset selection.

4.4 Feature Selection (Step D2)

The problem of selecting from the set of features extracted an optimal subset of features relevant for classification can be framed as a Multi-objective (MO) optimization problem. Namely, the wrapper approach builds a number of candidate features set $z \in \{0, 1\}^n$, where $z(k) = 1$ denotes that feature k is selected, whereas $z(k) = 0$ that it is not selected. The performance of each feature set z is evaluated with respect to a multi-objective fitness function F, which is defined as:

$$F = \left[-F_1(z), F_2(z)\right] z \in \{0, 1\}^n \qquad (23)$$

where $F_2(\cdot)$ counts the number of features (to be minimized) forming the subsets:

$$F_2(z) = \sum_{k=1}^{n} z(k) \qquad (24)$$

whereas $F_1(\cdot)$ represents the classification accuracy of the diagnostic classifier (in Eq. (23) the sign is changed, as we use a DE algorithm for minimization). To calculate this value, the total number of pre-labelled available patterns is randomly subdivided into training set and test set, consisting of 75% and 25% of the data, respectively. The random subdivision of the available patterns in training and test sets is repeated 20 times (i.e., 20 cross-validations): the mean recognition rate, i.e., the average fraction of correct classifications over the 20 cross-validation tests, is then calculated and represents the fitness value F_1 of candidate solution z. Finally, the classification algorithm used in this work is the Fuzzy K-Nearest Neighbor (FKNN) algorithm.

The performance of the MO optimization can be quantified in terms of the *diversity* of the solutions and the *convergence* to the Pareto optimal front [2]. Since in a MO optimization problem, it is typically not possible to simultaneously improve the values of two or more objective functions without causing the deterioration of some other objectives, diversity is a fundamental requirement in a MO evolutionary optimization. In practice, diversity in the population allows improving the coverage of the search space and exploring different evolutionary paths. An indicator of the diversity of a Pareto optimal set is the hyper-volume over the dominated set, which has been defined as the Lebesgue-measure of the hyper-volume with respect to a lower reference bound (normally, the ideal best values of each objective function) [2]: the smaller is the value of such indicator, the better is the performance in terms of objective function evaluations and the wider is the exploration of the search space. In our case, we set $(-1, 0)$ as the smaller reference point (i.e., the feature set characterized by the best possible perform-ances), which corresponds to the situation where the patterns are all classified correctly $(-F_1(z) = -1)$ and $F_2(z) = 0$ features are used.

Figure 7 shows that the optimal Pareto set hyper-volume significantly decreases until (approximatively) generation 200; then, it remains constant. This indicates that the Pareto set becomes stable and no improvement is expected in the solution optimal set by further increasing the number of generations.

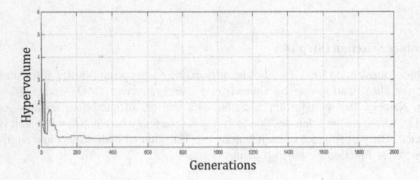

Fig. 7. Hyper-volume values iteration by iteration.

In Table 6, the candidate solutions in the Pareto optimal set are reported.

Table 6. Candidate solutions in the pareto optimal front.

Solution	Classification accuracy (F_2)	Number of features (F_1)
z_1^B	0.9469	1
z_2^B	0.9673	2
z_3^B	0.9781	3
z_4^B	0.9816	4
z_5^B	0.9837	5
z_6^B	0.9847	6
z_7^B	0.9852	7
z_8^B	0.9857	10

We have chosen the solution with best classification accuracy, i.e., solution z_8^B, disregarding the number of features. This choice is motivated by the fact that an incre-ment in the number of features does not significantly increase the computational burden. We have developed the Fuzzy K-Nearest Neighbours (FKNN) to classify the solenoid valve degradation states. After the feature selection task, the solenoid valve classification system has been developed. The overall accuracy of the classification model (i.e., the fraction of patterns correctly classified) has been obtained in a 20-folds cross validation on the data of the validation set (i.e., containing data not previously used during the feature selection) is 0.9671 ± 0.0133 which is satisfactory and corresponds to a percentage 0.78% and 2.51% false and missed alarms, respectively.

5 Conclusions

In this work, we have proposed a diagnostic tool based on FPM simulator to cope realistic case in which field data of the system in normal and abnormal condition are not currently available. To show the procedural steps of the approach, an application has been presented with reference to fault diagnostic of a solenoid valve mounted on the braking system of trains.

Future works will be focussed on the further application of the proposed methodology to the solenoid valve pilot case study, to make use of field data as they become available, for:

1. Updating the fault history matrix, the parameters of the FPM and the diagnostic model (steps D4-D5-D6, respectively).
2. Extend the proposed methodology to fault prognostics and developing a prognostic model for solenoid valve.
3. Making uncertainty analysis (steps D7).

References

1. Zio, E.: Some challenges and opportunities in reliability engineering. IEEE Trans. Reliab. **65**(4), 1769–1782 (2016)
2. Baraldi, P., Cannarile, F., Di Maio, F., Zio, E.: Hierarchical k-nearest neighbours classification and binary differential evolution for fault diagnostics of automotive bearings operating under variable conditions. Eng. Appl. Artif. Intell. **56**, 1–13 (2016)
3. Hastie, T.J., Tibshirani, R.J., Friedman, J.H.: The Elements of Statistical Learning, 2nd edn. Springer, New York (2009)
4. Baraldi, P., Canesi, R., Zio, E., Seraoui, R., Chevalier, R.: Genetic algorithm-based wrapper approach for grouping condition monitoring signals of nuclear power plant components. Integr. Comput. Aided Eng. **18**(3), 221–234 (2011)
5. Kantas, N., Doucet, A., Singh, S.S., Maciejowski, J., Chopin, N.: On particle methods for parameter estimation in state-space models. Stat. Sci. **30**(3), 328–351 (2015)
6. Kühl, P., Diehl, M., Kraus, T., Schlöder, J.P., Bock, H.G.: A real-time algorithm for moving horizon state and parameter estimation. Comput. Chem. Eng. **35**(1), 71–83 (2011)
7. Aven, T., Baraldi, P., Flage, R., Zio, E.: Uncertainty in Risk Assessment: The Representation and Treatment of Uncertainties by Probabilistic and Non-Probabilistic Methods, 1st edn. Wiley, New York (2014)
8. Daigle, M., Goebel, K.: Improving computational efficiency of prediction in model-based prognostics using the unscented transform. In: Proceedings of the Annual Conference of the Prognostics and Health Management Society (2010)
9. Taghizadeh, M., Ghaffari, A., Najafi, F.: Modeling and identification of a solenoid valve for PWM control applications. C.R. Mec. **337**(3), 131–140 (2009)
10. Rizzoni, G.: Principles and Applications of Electrical Engineering, 5th edn. McGraw Hill, New York (2007)

Safety Assessment in the Automotive Domain

Learning-Based Testing for Safety Critical Automotive Applications

Hojat Khosrowjerdi[1], Karl Meinke[1(✉)], and Andreas Rasmusson[2]

[1] School of Computer Science, KTH Royal Institute of Technology,
Stockholm, Sweden
{hojatk,karlm}@kth.se
[2] Scania CV AB, Södertälje, Sweden

Abstract. Learning-based testing (LBT) is an emerging paradigm for fully automated requirements testing. This approach combines machine learning and model-checking techniques for test case generation and verdict construction. LBT is well suited to requirements testing of low-latency safety critical embedded systems, such as can be found in the automotive sector.

We evaluate the feasibility and effectiveness of applying LBT to two safety critical industrial automotive applications. We also benchmark our LBT tool against an existing industrial test tool that executes manually written test cases.

Keywords: Automotive software · Model-based testing · Black-box testing · Learning-based testing · Machine learning · Requirements testing · Temporal logic

1 Introduction

Learning-based testing (LBT) [18,21] is an emerging paradigm for fully automated requirements testing using formal requirement models. LBT uses active machine learning [4,14] to reverse engineer a behavioral model of the system under test (SUT). Behavioral models are typically state machines, to which model-based test generation techniques can then be applied, including model checking from formalized temporal logic requirements. Machine learning is particularly useful when the SUT is a black box. In this case, we can apply model-based testing techniques even when the development process is not (or not fully) model driven. For example, black-box third party components are common in certain industries such as automotive.

For real-time safety-critical applications, such as can be found in the automotive sector, the low test latency[1] of many applications is well matched to the high test throughput that can be achieved by LBT tools. LBT seems to offer a promising automated technology for achieving higher test coverage in shorter time at lower cost, when compared with manual testing. However, this

---

[1] By test latency we mean the average time to execute a single test case on the SUT.

© Springer International Publishing AG 2017
M. Bozzano and Y. Papadopoulos (Eds.): IMBSA 2017, LNCS 10437, pp. 197–211, 2017.
DOI: 10.1007/978-3-319-64119-5_13

promise needs to be carefully evaluated on realistic industrial case studies. For this purpose, we will present two automotive case studies in LBT taken from an extended series we have conducted with Scania CV AB over several years[2]. This series is documented in [16]. Scania CV is an OEM engaged in the production of heavy commercial vehicles, including trucks and buses. The two studies presented here aim to illustrate the basic principles of LBT for requirements testing of safety critical embedded applications. They also give insight into questions of technology transfer for the automotive sector.

The organization of this paper is as follows: in Sect. 2 we consider related work in the fields of behavioral requirements modeling and testing in the automotive sector. In Sect. 3 we give a brief introduction to learning-based testing. In Sect. 4 we present our two case studies. Finally in Sect. 5 we draw conclusions and discuss open research problems.

2   Related Work

A wide variety of formal notations have been proposed to support requirements testing of safety critical systems over the years, an extensive survey is [13]. In the context of embedded systems, considerable attention has been devoted to the use of *temporal logic* [12] for requirements modeling.

In [23] the authors present a large-scale study of modeling automotive behavioral requirements. For this they use the Real Time Specification Pattern System (RTSP) presented in [17]. This pattern system is an extension of the earlier Specification Pattern System (SPS) of [9]. RTSP requirements are semantically mapped into a variety of temporal logics, including linear temporal logic (LTL) [10], computation tree logic (CTL) [10] timed computation tree logic (TCTL) [3] and metric temporal logic (MTL) [3]. The intention of pattern languages such as SPS and RTSP is to allow the semantics of requirements to be easily understood and validated.

Drawing upon five informal requirements documents, [23] assembles a total of 245 separate requirements for 5 different ECU (Electronic Control Unit) applications. Of these, just 14 requirements (3% of total) could not be modeled. The authors conclude that TCTL provides an appropriate temporal logic for behavioral modeling within the automotive domain. However, their proposal has the significant disadvantage that model checking is undecidable for TCTL (see [23]), and hence it cannot be used for automated test case generation. This contrasts with LTL, used in our own research, which has a decidable model checking problem. A later study [11] of RTSP at Scania CV has broadly confirmed these statistics. It estimated the relative frequency of successfully modeled behavioral requirements at about 70%. Just 6% of the requirements could not be modeled. Our own research here seems to suggest that a large proportion of commonly encountered ECU requirements can already be modeled with LTL.

Methods to reverse engineer state machine models of automotive ECUs using similar machine learning techniques to our own have been considered in [24].

---

[2] In the context of the joint Vinnova FFI project 2013-05608 VIRTUES.

Here, the authors used an industry standard test runner PROVEtech [1] to perform hardware-in-the-loop testing of components, and reverse engineer SUT models using their RALT tool. These methods were shown to be effective for third-party software where source code was unavailable. However, in contrast to our own work, formal requirements and model checking were not used. In [25] the effectiveness of machine learning techniques for test case generation has been studied, and it has been shown that machine learning provides significantly better SUT coverage than random testing. This work concurs with results from our own previous investigation in LBT effectiveness [19].

3   An Overview of Learning Based Testing

To understand the results of our case studies, it is important to have some understanding of the design and functionality of a learning-based testing tool. In this section we describe the tool LBTest [22] that was used for our case studies.

3.1   Test Tool Functionality and Architecture

Learning-based testing may be described as *model-based testing without a model*. This is because LBT uses machine learning technology to reverse engineer a model of the SUT from test cases. This model can then be subjected to model-based testing techniques. However, machine learning alone does not solve the oracle problem of generating test verdicts. This is because a reverse engineered model, from SUT behavior, cannot also function as an external reference model[3].

For scalability to large test suites, any test oracle needs to be fully automated and reliable. These two needs can be met by introducing precise behavioral modeling languages to represent test requirements. Then, given an executable version of the SUT and a behavioral requirement, we can apply incremental learning and model checking, in alternation, to build up a model and search it for counter-examples which violate the requirements. From each counter-example we can extract a test case, which may either be: (i) a true negative (an SUT error), or (ii) a false negative (an artifact of an incomplete model). By executing this test case on the SUT, and comparing the actual SUT behavior with its predicted behavior from the model, we can reliably identify all the true negatives, i.e. test failures. Each true negative is returned to the tool-user for post-mortem analysis. The model checker currently used by LBTest for analysis of learned models is the open-source tool NuSMV [7].

Integration of the processes of incremental learning and model checking needs to be organised into a tool architecture. Figure 1 illustrates the current architecture of LBTest, showing the main feedback loop that allows test cases generated by machine learning and model checking to be interleaved. During the test session, the learning algorithm generates a sequence of increasingly accurate SUT

---

[3] The reason here is that an SUT is *by definition* behaviorally correct w.r.t. a model that has been reverse engineered from its behavior. So there is nothing to test.

models $M_1, M_2, \ldots$. This process may terminate with a correct and complete model M_{final} for a simple low latency SUT. For complex, high latency SUTs complete learning may not be possible within any reasonable time frame. In this case, a precise *black-box coverage model* is necessary to characterise the final result of testing.

Figure 1 illustrates the stochastic equivalence checker used to empirically measure *stochastic convergence* of the learned model. This black-box coverage model measures the capability of a learned model M_i to accurately simulate the SUT on a randomly chosen input. A more detailed discussion of this topic can be found in [16].

Finally in Fig. 1 we can observe the *communication wrapper* which forms a test harness around the SUT. This software component, implements mappings between symbolic data types and concrete data types, and marshals test cases into the SUT and observations back to LBTest.

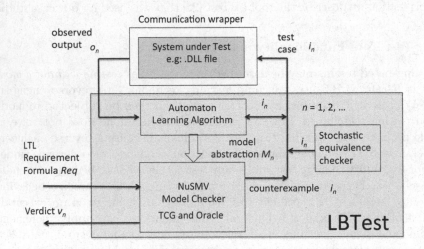

Fig. 1. LBTest architecture

3.2   Behavioral Modeling with Linear Temporal Logic

For behavioral requirements modeling, LBTest makes use of propositional linear temporal logic (PLTL). This language is much more restrictive than TCTL, but has a decidable model checking problem. Furthermore, test case extraction from PLTL counter-examples is fairly straightforward. Among the case studies that we present in Sect. 4 only a small number of behavioral requirements could not be directly modeled in PLTL. The concrete syntax for PLTL that is supported by LBTest is the syntax used by the model checker NuSMV. The most important syntactic constructs needed for our case studies are summarised in Table 1.

Table 1. Propositional and Temporal Operators of PLTL

Proposition forming operators	Intended meaning
x = c	Variable x equals constant c
x != c	Variable x does not equal constant c
p & q	p and q
!p	not p
p | q	p or q
p -> q	if p then q
p <-> q	p if, and only if q
p XOR q	p exclusive or q
Temporal operators	Intended meaning
G(p)	p is true in all future states
F(p)	p is true in some future state
X(p)	p is true in the next state
(p U q)	p is true until q is true
Y(p)	p was true in the previous state
H(p)	p was true in all previous states
O(p)	p was true in at least one previous state
(p S q)	p has been true since q was true

Many re-usable generic requirement patterns have emerged from requirements case studies for embedded systems (e.g. [9,17]). A very common pattern is:

$$G(\texttt{trigger} \rightarrow X(\texttt{response}))$$

which expresses that: *at all times (G-operator) if the situation represented by* **trigger** *holds, then in the next time period (X-operator) the situation represented by* **response** *must hold*. This pattern can generically capture each time-invariant immediate-response requirement on an embedded system.

PLTL is able to express both *safety properties*, i.e. something bad should never happen G(! bad_property), and *liveness properties*, i.e. eventually something good should happen, F(good_property). Notice that counter-examples to liveness properties are infinite execution sequences. To convert these into concrete test cases, finite truncation is necessary, and only a restricted warning verdict can then be issued by the test oracle.

4   Two Automotive Case Studies of LBT

The overall question addressed by our case study research has been: *how useful is learning-based testing for requirements testing of automotive applications?* This general question can only be answered with respect to some concrete LBT tool with specific limitations and capabilities. Therefore, a first refinement of this question is: *how mature is the state-of-the-art in LBT technology for the problem of behavioral requirements testing in the automotive sector?* We begin by clarifying our methodology to answer this question.

4.1 Case Study Methodology

The effectiveness of LBT can be assessed in terms of many different quantitative measures such as test session length, achieved coverage and discovered errors. To structure our case studies, we introduced an observation methodology that addressed four specific questions.

1. Behavioral Requirements Modeling. Given an ECU application, is it possible to identify its informal behavioral requirements, and directly model these requirements using PLTL?

2. Requirements Redefinition. If there are informal behavioral requirements that cannot be directly modeled in LTL, can they be reformulated in a way that can be expressed in LTL? If not, what additional modeling language (e.g. CTL) would be needed?

3. Model Learning. Is it possible for a machine learning algorithm to learn a complete and detailed behavioral model of an ECU application in a reasonable amount of time?

4. Error Discovery Is it possible to model check the learned SUT models and generate test cases that yield reliable true negatives (test failures) within a reasonable time?

These sub-goals have a natural logical order. If an earlier sub-goal fails significantly, it will be less interesting to try to investigate any of the later sub-goals within a particular case study. Ideally, all sub-goals are fully satisfied in every case study, but in practise this is not always so.

4.2 Characteristics of the Case Studies

The two automotive case studies that we describe here were supplied by Scania CV. The first case study is a remote engine start (ESTA) application and the second one is a dual circuit steering (DCS) application. Both applications are in production[4].

ESTA is a simple low latency application. However, both black-box and glass-box safety-critical requirements are involved in the product definition. The testing challenge for ESTA was behavioral modeling of a time dependent system in the presence of somewhat complex temporal sequences. Hence this case study was mainly focused on sub-goals 1 and 2.

The DCS case study arose from a hazard analysis motivated by emerging safety standards such as *ISO26262* to add redundancy in case of high safety integrity levels (SILs). Here the challenge was whether informal requirements

---

[4] This has limited our possibility to disclose all technical details for commercial reasons.

were formalizable directly or needed some restructuring to get the right abstraction level required for black-box behavioral testing. Other aspects of the DCS case study included: (1) investigating the capability of the tool to find undiscovered discrepancies in the SUT, and (2) benchmarking the tool against existing industrial test technology using a mutation testing approach. Therefore, all subgoals 1–4 were involved within the DCS case study.

4.3   Case Study 1: Engine STart Application (ESTA)

Functionality. The remote Engine STart Application (ESTA) is a commonly used functionality that supports starting the engine from outside the driver cabin safely. When ESTA receives a request to activate the remote engine start (signal), it performs a series of safety checks to evaluate the engine start safety conditions. If these so called acceptance conditions are fulfilled then ESTA transmits a CAN message to the engine start manager to start the engine. If the acceptance conditions are not fulfilled before and as long as the start request is valid, ESTA aborts the remote engine start and sends a message to the hazard lights interface to activate them constantly as an indication of an unsuccessful start attempt. Improper start can harm the engine or its environment. Therefore, it is important that the ESTA application meets certain safety and timing requirements to avoid unintended accidents.

System Architecture. From a black-box testing perspective, ESTA is a single ECU application that is implemented as part of the Bodywork ECU software. It has an execution cycle of 10ms. At the ECU level, ESTA reads its required inputs directly from sensors and switches, or indirectly through CAN messages. All outputs at this abstraction level are CAN signals requesting an engine start/stop and a hazard lights visualization.

The application can be viewed as a self-contained unit for black-box testing with respect to user requirements. The architecture of the Fig. 2 shows this abstraction view.

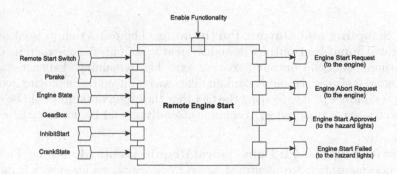

Fig. 2. The architecture of ESTA.

System Interface. Requirements modeling began with identification of the required input and output parameters which describe the ESTA functionality. Depending on the configuration, ESTA has a variable number of inputs. These can be grouped into two main categories, with most in the category *Acceptance_Condition*. The rest of the inputs correspond to the category remote start activation request *Remote_Start_Switch*. Four Boolean outputs were identified for testing, two for the Engine Management Unit and two for the direction indicators' controller unit.

An interface description for ESTA is outlined in Table 2. This is the same interface from both the system and unit testing perspectives. What differs is only the place where the signals are read from, either from the ECU internal variables or from external sources. The types of the input and output variables are either Boolean or enumerated (with finite valid ranges) regardless of the abstraction level. With this relatively large set of input variables, some strategy for a combinatorial choice of test values became necessary.

Table 2. The ESTA interface

Variable	Type	Name	Meaning	Range
0	in	*SelectedGear*	Position of gear	Enum
1	in	*CrankEnabled*	Gearbox allows engine cranking?	Boolean
2	in	*InhibitStart*	Prevent all types of engine start?	Boolean
3	in	*PbrakeApplied*	Parking break applied?	Boolean
4	in	*EngineState*	Engine state	Enum
5	in	*RemoteStartSwitch*	State of remote start switch	Boolean
6	out	*engine_start_request*	Request to start the engine	Boolean
7	out	*engine_abort_request*	Request to abort engine start	Boolean
8	out	*engine_start_approved*	Request to visualize engine start	Boolean
9	out	*engine_start_failed*	Request to visualize failed engine start	Boolean
10	out	*AcceptanceCondition*	Acceptance_condition logic output	Boolean

Input Sampling and Output Partitioning. The restriction to Boolean and enumerated input and output domains greatly simplified construction of the input sample sets and output partition sets. The remaining challenge was the combinatorial size of the input domain. This was reduced by employing pairwise testing techniques [15]. exploiting the fact that the input variables could be classified into two separate groups (Acceptance_Condition and Remote_Start_Switch).

Results for Sub-Goal 1: Behavioural Requirements Modeling. From the ESTA documentation we identified several behavioral requirements in natural language, including both safety and liveness properties of the application. Most of these requirements could be transformed into PLTL without any difficulty. Table 3 shows some examples of this transformation.

Table 3. Formal and informal black-box requirements on ESTA

	Informal and corresponding PLTL black-box requirements
Req b.1	If the security conditions to remotely start the engine are fulfilled and the start button is pressed, a request will be sent to the engine control unit to start the engine
PLTL b.1	`G(RemoteStartSwitch = sw_0 & X(AcceptanceCondition = True & RemoteStartSwitch = sw_1) - >F(engine_start_request = True))`
Req b.2	In case the operator presses the start button without the acceptance criteria being met, a request should be sent to VIS to light hazard lights around the vehicle
PLTL b.2	`G((RemoteStartSwitch = sw_0 & X(RemoteStartSwitch = sw_1 & AcceptanceCondition = False) - >F(engine_start_failed = True))`

Besides black-box requirements, the ESTA documentation also included a state machine as a reference model for the application shown in Fig. 3. From this state machine we were able to extract thirteen grey-box requirements by representing each individual state transition as a PLTL formula. For instance the state transition from SNAL to SFA could be expressed in PLTL as:

```
state = SNAL & switch = sw_1 & ACond = F->X(state = SFA)
```

meaning that if the current state is SNAL (symbolic value for start not allowed) and the start switch is pressed (sw_1) and the acceptance condition (ACond) is false the next state should be SFA (symbolic value for start failed).

Testing requirements derived from a reference state machine model in this way can be seen as an instance of classical model-based testing (MBT) [6]. Therefore, we see that learning-based testing can also be used to perform model-based testing, based on graph coverage concepts.

Results for Sub-Goal 2: Requirement Redefinition. The thirteen requirements derived from the transitions of the ESTA reference machine model provide complete edge coverage of the model. To be able to test these requirements, two additional grey-box output variables were introduced in the communication wrapper which represented the internal state of the application at any specific time and the time period for which the start switch should be active after the engine has been started. Both of these variables are measured inside the wrapper considering their relationship to the black-box signals.

Results for Sub-Goal 3: Model Learning. Given the formalized behavioral requirements from sub-goals 1 and 2, we applied our testing technique to ESTA in a series of experiments to search for any discrepancies. In most cases LBTest terminated testing with no more than 31 learned states and about 220 transitions in less than 5 min. However, it turned out that for some requirements the

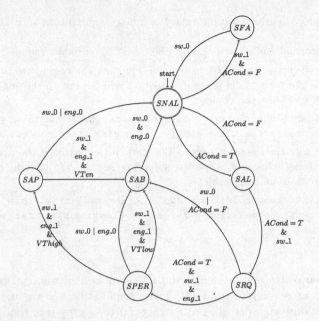

Fig. 3. The state machine reference model of the ESTA application

convergence criteria was not satisfactory. Further investigations revealed that complete coverage of the state space required certain input sequences to happen for a specific period of the execution time. This is due to the fact that LBTest uses random sequences to equivalence-check the learned model with the actual behaviour of the SUT. Our approach to this problem was to freeze some of the input variables to reduce the complexity and as a result the convergence measure increased to an acceptable level.

Results for Sub-Goal 4: Error Discovery. The ESTA application had been developed and maintained for many years and seemed to contain no serious bugs violating the requirements that we tested.

4.4   Case Study 2: Dual-Circuit Steering (DCS)

Functionality. Steering ability can be regarded as even more important than breaking ability in a vehicle. For example: according to safety standards like ISO26262, steering function is regarded as an ASIL D item (maximum criticality), where hazard analysis is highly recommended. This is because both in nominal driving and breaking situations there must always be sufficient steering torque available to avoid life-threatening injuries. From this perspective, failures in the hydraulic system or the engine could render the steering insufficiently responsive. To mitigate this hazard, Dual-Circuit Steering (DCS) backs up the main steering system to maintain the steering availability in case of failures.

System Architecture. What we refer to as DCS in this paper is an application located in the steering-ECU software that controls the secondary steering circuit. According to this definition and from a black-box perspective, the DCS architecture is shown in Fig. 4. In this figure, DCS communicates with its environment through eighteen inputs and outputs. In addition, there is a configuration parameter that specifies if a dual-circuit steering system is installed or not.

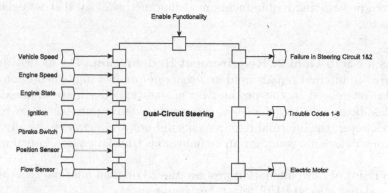

Fig. 4. A unit level software architecture of DCS application

System Interface. DCS was tested as a black-box unit. Hence the testing interface contains exactly the same inputs/outputs shown in Fig. 4. Among the inputs, four CAN signals transfer messages to determine the vehicle and engine status. Other inputs are signals from ignition, position and flow switch sensors.

All output variables are discrete valued with no more than six values. The main outputs include the control signal to the electric motor and two CAN signals determining the working condition of the two hydraulic systems. In addition, there are eight trouble code signals in the outputs (Trouble Codes 1–8 in Fig. 4) which are used for diagnosis.

Input Sampling and Output Partitioning. Four out of seven input variables are discrete valued with a finite number of values. The three remaining input variables are continuous valued (Vehicle/Engine Speed and Position Sensor). The corresponding variable domains were finitely sampled using boundary values specified in the requirement documentation.

There was no need to partition the output domains into equivalence classes since they were small finite sets of discrete values.

Results for Sub-Goal 1: Behavioural Requirements Modeling. Out of the 32 requirements identified in application documents written by engineers at Scania, 9 could not be formalised in LTL. This was due to several reasons. Some were *phenomenon requirements* not describing any relation between inputs and outputs (see e.g. [23]). Other requirements referred to a specific platform for hardware-in-the-loop (HIL) testing. The remaining 23 requirements could be formalized in PLTL. However, they required extensive reformulation, since the informal requirements made use of so called model variables[5]. For black-box testing, these model variables had to be eliminated using their known relationships to each other and the API input and output variables. Therefore, in this case study no direct mapping of informal requirements into PLTL was possible, owing to a pre-existing requirements modeling methodology that was glass-box in character.

Results for Sub-Goal 2: Requirement Redefinition. The model variables all referred to internal signals used in a concrete product implementation. They were also referenced in the product documentation. Recursive elimination of these glass-box model variables was necessary to derive pure black-box requirements. However, the informal requirements did not always systematically model all the corner cases necessary for an unambiguous translation into formal requirements.

As a result of this elimination process, the 23 original informal requirements were translated into 30 PLTL black-box requirements.

Most of the reformulated requirements followed the simple trigger-response pattern described in Sect. 3.2. However, sometimes the relationships between past and future events, as described in the requirements, made reformulation a difficult task without using the PLTL past operators (c.f. Table 1). For example, the specifications require certain events to occur if a self test has been performed previously. However, there is no observable variable capturing the state of the self test in a black-box setting. An equivalent black-box event would be: *"the electric motor had been on while the second sensor had a flow or noflow, since the last engine restart"*, which shows that the self test has been performed. Using past operators in LTL, this requirement could be easily expressed as shown below:

$$(\texttt{emotor = on \& (sensor2 = flow | sensor2 = noflow)}$$
$$\texttt{S ignition = restart)}$$

Results for Sub-Goal 3: Model Learning. In total, the testing procedure took 7 h and 24 min to terminate. The learned model then contained over 60 states and more than 800 transitions since the size of the input alphabet for the automaton model was 14. The estimate of the final model convergence was 97%.

Results for Sub-Goal 4: Error Discovery. Besides warnings resulting from incomplete or ambiguous requirements (which were corrected after further consultation with engineers) LBTest was successful in finding previously unknown

---

[5] Here, a model variable is an internal SUT signal that is not part of the API. Model variables may be defined in terms of other model variables, though recursive definitions are not allowed.

discrepancies between the requirements and the system under test. In total, LBTest found five failed LTL requirements due to errors in the SUT behavior. These five failed requirements were discussed with testing engineers at Scania and proved to be real faults in the SUT, although they were not considered safety critical.

To conclude this case study, we constructed an experiment to evaluate Subgoal 4 for DCS by means of a mutation testing experiment [8]. Mutation testing is an approach to evaluating the quality of a test suite, by estimating the percentage of injected faults (source code mutations) that can be discovered. The aim was to compare the error detection capability of LBTest with an in-house testing tool called piTest. piTest represents a typical automated test framework that executes manually written test cases. Injected mutations included: changed boundary values, mixed up input/output variables and randomly modified Boolean expressions. Table 4 shows the results of this comparison of the two testing tools. Eight out of ten injected mutations were discovered by LBTest, suggesting the enhanced error discovery power of this tool, compared with piTest.

Table 4. DCS mutation testing results and comparison

Fault	piTest	LBTest	Fault	piTest	LBTest
1	Unterminated	**Detected**	6	Unterminated	Undetected
2	Undetected	**Detected**	7	**Detected**	**Detected**
3	**Detected**	Undetected	8	Undetected	**Detected**
4	Unterminated	**Detected**	9	Unterminated	**Detected**
5	Undetected	**Detected**	10	Unterminated	**Detected**

5 Conclusions

We have investigated the problem of automatically testing behavioral requirements on two automotive ECU applications. The goal was to evaluate learning based-testing (LBT) as a solution to this problem. Using two industrial case studies, we have examined issues such as: the ease of modeling informal behavioral requirements using temporal logic, and the success rate of LBT in finding known and unknown errors. We have even conducted benchmark comparisons of LBT against an industrial testing tool by means of mutation testing.

From our own studies, we can see that simple propositional linear temporal logic (PLTL) is already quite viable for modeling many behavioral requirements. For low latency ECU applications, the high test throughput of LBT tools is well suited to construct large black-box test suites on-the-fly. A beneficial side-effect of machine-learning is that models are guaranteed to be consistent with the SUT. This avoids a major source of false positives and negatives found in model-based testing.

An important open research issue is to consider the difficulties of testing more complex high latency applications. To this end, we have begun to investigate parallelised testing on multicore platforms. Another direction of current research concerns virtualised hardware-in-the-loop (VHIL) testing using a hardware emulation platform such as QEMU [5]. Such emulation platforms support fault injection testing (see e.g. [20]) which is highly recommended by safety standards such as ISO 26262 [2].

We acknowledge the financial support of VINNOVA FFI project 2013-05608 VIRTUES. We also acknowledge the generous assistance we received with our case studies from Sophia Bäckström, Christopher Lidbäck, Mattias Nyberg, Sophia Ulke and Jonas Westman.

References

1. Mbtech. www.mbtech-group.com
2. Supporting processes, baseline 17. ISO 26262:(2011)–Part 8 Road vehicles—functional safety, International Organization for Standardization (2011). https://www.iso.org/obp/ui/#iso:std:iso:26262:-8:ed-1:v1:en
3. Alur, R.: Techniques for Automatic Verification of Real-time Systems. Ph.D. thesis, Stanford, CA, USA (1992). uMI Order No. GAX92-06729
4. Balcázar, J.L., Díaz, J., Gavaldà, R., Watanabe, O.: Algorithms for learning finite automata from queries: a unified view. In: Du, D.Z., Ko, K.I. (eds.) Advances in Algorithms, Languages, and Complexity, pp. 53–72. Springer, Boston (1997). doi:10.1007/978-1-4613-3394-4_2
5. Bellard, F.: QEMU, a fast and portable dynamic translator. In: Proceedings of the FREENIX Track: 2005 USENIX Annual Technical Conference, pp. 41–46 (2005)
6. Broy, M., Jonsson, B., Katoen, J.P., Leucker, M., Pretschner, A.: Model-Based Testing of Reactive Systems: Advanced Lectures. LNCS. Springer Inc., New York (2005)
7. Cimatti, A., Clarke, E., Giunchiglia, E., Giunchiglia, F., Pistore, M., Roveri, M., Sebastiani, R., Tacchella, A.: NuSMV 2: an opensource tool for symbolic model checking. In: Brinksma, E., Larsen, K.G. (eds.) CAV 2002. LNCS, vol. 2404, pp. 359–364. Springer, Heidelberg (2002). doi:10.1007/3-540-45657-0_29
8. DeMillo, R.A., Lipton, R.J., Sayward, F.G.: Hints on test data selection: help for the practicing programmer. Computer 11(4), 34–41 (1978). http://dx.doi.org/10.1109/C-M.1978.218136
9. Dwyer, M.B., Avrunin, G.S., Corbett, J.C.: Patterns in property specifications for finite-state verification. In: Proceedings of the 1999 International Conference on Software Engineering, pp. 411–420, May 1999
10. Emerson, E.A.: Temporal and modal logic. In: van Leeuwen, (ed.) Handbook of Theoretical Computer Science. Volume B: Formal Models and Sematics (B), pp. 995–1072. MIT Press, Cambridge (1990)
11. Filipovikj, P., Nyberg, M., Rodriguez-Navas, G.: Reassessing the pattern-based approach for formalizing requirements in the automotive domain. In: 2014 IEEE 22nd International Requirements Engineering Conference (RE), pp. 444–450, August 2014
12. Fisher, M.: An Introduction to Practical Formal Methods Using Temporal Logic, 1st edn. Wiley Publishing, Chichester (2011). http://cds.cern.ch/record/1518490

13. Hierons, R.M., Bogdanov, K., Bowen, J.P., Cleaveland, R., Derrick, J., Dick, J., Gheorghe, M., Harman, M., Kapoor, K., Krause, P., Lüttgen, G., Simons, A.J.H., Vilkomir, S., Woodward, M.R., Zedan, H.: Using formal specifications to support testing. ACM Comput. Surv. **41**(2), 9:1–9:76 (2009). http://doi.acm.org/10.1145/1459352.1459354
14. De la Higuera, C.: Grammatical Inference: Learning Automata and Grammars. Cambridge University Press, Cambridge (2010)
15. Jorgensen, P.C.: Software testing (2008)
16. Khosrowjerdi, H., Meinke, K., Rasmusson, A.: Automated behavioral requirements testing for automotive ECU applications. Technical report, KTH Royal Institute of Technology (2016)
17. Konrad, S., Cheng, B.H.C.: Real-time specification patterns. In: Proceedings of the 27th International Conference on Software Engineering, ICSE 2005, pp. 372–381. ACM, New York (2005). http://doi.acm.org/10.1145/1062455.1062526
18. Meinke, K.: Automated black-box testing of functional correctness using function approximation. In: Proceedings of the 2004 ACM SIGSOFT International Symposium on Software Testing and Analysis, ISSTA 2004, pp. 143–153. ACM, New York (2004). http://doi.acm.org/10.1145/1007512.1007532
19. Meinke, K., Niu, F.: A learning-based approach to unit testing of numerical software. In: Petrenko, A., Simão, A., Maldonado, J.C. (eds.) ICTSS 2010. LNCS, vol. 6435, pp. 221–235. Springer, Heidelberg (2010). doi:10.1007/978-3-642-16573-3_16
20. Meinke, K., Nycander, P.: Learning-based testing of distributed microservice architectures: correctness and fault injection. In: Bianculli, D., Calinescu, R., Rumpe, B. (eds.) SEFM 2015. LNCS, vol. 9509, pp. 3–10. Springer, Heidelberg (2015). doi:10.1007/978-3-662-49224-6_1
21. Meinke, K., Sindhu, M.A.: Incremental learning-based testing for reactive systems. In: Gogolla, M., Wolff, B. (eds.) TAP 2011. LNCS, vol. 6706, pp. 134–151. Springer, Heidelberg (2011). doi:10.1007/978-3-642-21768-5_11
22. Meinke, K., Sindhu, M.A.: LBTest: a learning-based testing tool for reactive systems. In: Proceedings of the 2013 IEEE Sixth International Conference on Software Testing, Verification and Validation, ICST 2013, pp. 447–454. IEEE Computer Society, Washington (2013). http://dx.doi.org/10.1109/ICST.2013.62
23. Post, A., Menzel, I., Hoenicke, J., Podelski, A.: Automotive behavioral requirements expressed in a specification pattern system: a case study at BOSCH. Requirements Eng. **17**(1), 19–33 (2012). http://dx.doi.org/10.1007/s00766-011-0145-9
24. Shahbaz, M., Shashidhar, K.C., Eschbach, R.: Specification inference using systematic reverse-engineering methodologies: an automotive industry application. IEEE Softw. **29**(6), 62–69 (2012). http://dx.doi.org/10.1109/MS.2011.159
25. Walkinshaw, N., Bogdanov, K., Derrick, J., Paris, J.: Increasing functional coverage by inductive testing: a case study. In: Petrenko, A., Simão, A., Maldonado, J.C. (eds.) ICTSS 2010. LNCS, vol. 6435, pp. 126–141. Springer, Heidelberg (2010). doi:10.1007/978-3-642-16573-3_10

Verification of Component Fault Trees Using Error Effect Simulations

Sebastian Reiter[1]([✉]), Marc Zeller[2], Kai Höfig[2], Alexander Viehl[1],
Oliver Bringmann[1], and Wolfgang Rosenstiel[1]

[1] FZI Forschungszentrum Informatik,
Haid-und-Neu-Str. 10-14, 76131 Karlsruhe, Germany
{sreiter,viehl,bringman,rosenstiel}@fzi.de
[2] Siemens AG, Corporate Technology,
Otto-Hahn-Ring 6, 81379 Munich, Germany
{marc.zeller,kai.hoefig}@siemens.com

Abstract. The growing complexity of safety-relevant systems causes an increasing effort for safety assurance. The reduction of development costs and time-to-market, while guaranteeing safe operation, is therefore a major challenge. In order to enable efficient safety assessment of complex architectures, we present an approach, which combines deductive safety analyses, in form of Component Fault Trees (CFTs), with an Error Effect Simulation (EES) for sanity checks. The combination reduces the drawbacks of both analyses, such as the subjective failure propagation assumptions in the CFTs or the determination of relevant fault scenarios for the EES. Both CFTs and the EES provide a modular, reusable and compositional safety analysis and are applicable throughout the whole design process. They support continuous model refinement and the reuse of conducted safety analysis and simulation models. Hence, safety goal violations can be identified in early design stages and the reuse of conducted safety analyses reduces the overhead for safety assessment.

1 Introduction

The growing number and complexity of safety-relevant embedded systems poses new challenges, in many application domains such as the automotive domain with the rapidly evolving advance driver assistance systems. Along with the growing system complexity, also the need for safety assessment and its associated effort is drastically increasing. Safety assessment is a mandatory part in order to guarantee the high quality demands, imposed by the market. However, this is contrary to industry's aim to reduce costs and time-to-market.

In different application domains, safety standards, such as the IEC 61508 [10] or its automotive adaption ISO 26262 [11] define the safety assurance process. The goal of the safety assessment process is to identify all failures that cause hazardous situations and to demonstrate that their probabilities are sufficiently low. Traditionally, the analysis of systems in terms of safety consists of bottom-up safety analysis approaches, such as *Failure Mode and Effect Analysis (FMEA)*,

© Springer International Publishing AG 2017
M. Bozzano and Y. Papadopoulos (Eds.): IMBSA 2017, LNCS 10437, pp. 212–226, 2017.
DOI: 10.1007/978-3-319-64119-5_14

and top-down ones, such as *Fault Tree Analysis (FTA)*. Both provide structured procedure models to identify failure modes, failure causes and the effects on the system safety goals. The early identification of safety goal violations is crucial for a cost-efficient development process.

The quality of the safety assessment strongly depends on the correctness and completeness of the safety analysis model, describing the failure propagation and its transformation through the system. In current industrial practice, the quality of the safety analysis models in terms of completeness and correctness needs to be guaranteed manually by model reviews, which are very time-consuming tasks. Since such reviews are required after the initial construction of the safety analysis model as well as after each modification, the effort for maintaining its quality during the whole design time is significant. Applying a development strategy with frequent changes, such as agile methods, drastically increases this maintenance effort, endangering the success of the development.

Since system-level simulations enable the simultaneous analysis of software and digital/analog hardware, the application of simulations for safety evaluations attracted growing attention [2–4, 14–17]. However, the focus of most of these approaches is either the verification of fault tolerance mechanisms or the identification of failure modes as well as their effects. The determination of the analyzed fault space, as well as the integration in the still required safety assessment process is neglected. The main contribution of this paper is the synergistic combination of both methodologies. We present an approach for the verification of a failure propagation specification in form of a *Component Fault Tree (CFT)* methodology [12] with an *Error Effect Simulation (EES)* approach. Test cases are automatically generated from CFTs, which serve as input to inject faults into a system simulation. Additionally a test oracle, for failure effect detection, is created automatically. Thus, it is possible to discover gaps and errors in the failure propagation specification. This increases the quality while simultaneously reduces the effort for the manual safety model review drastically.

Since system simulations can be performed at different levels of granularity and CFT elements can be reused in different contexts, our approach is applicable throughout the design process. Hence, iterative and agile development strategies are supported by speeding up the analysis of the current system design abstraction. Thereby, only the refined parts of the system must be modified.

The paper is organized as follows: In Sect. 2 relevant related work is briefly summarized. The Sect. 3 presents the underlying method. The concept of CFTs is presented in Sect. 4. The EES infrastructure is presented in Sect. 5. The Sect. 6 outlines how test cases can be automatically generated from CFTs as input for the EES in order to review the safety analysis model. In Sect. 7 the benefits of our approach are demonstrated. The paper is concluded in Sect. 8.

2   Related Work

As already mentioned, there exist manifold approaches that utilize simulation-based fault injection (SFI), such as [2–4, 14–17]. These approaches use system simulations combined with fault injection for enhancing safety analyses. They focus on the efficient execution of the fault injection and the determination of error effects. Randomly generated parameters are used in a large number of simulation runs. However, in order to get meaningful results, which can be used as evidence in a safety case, the number of test runs must be extremely high. Still these approaches cannot guarantee that all relevant faults are injected into the simulation. Previous approaches are missing a methodology to combine the presented techniques with established safety assessment processes, which are still required for system qualification/certification. SFI mitigates the new challenges, but cannot replace safety assessments such as FTA or FMEA.

Such an FMEA integration is presented in [6]. It presents a simulation-assisted FMEA by formalizing the FMEA structure and deriving a system simulation. With the help of such an approach, the fault catalogues used during FMEA are reused by the SFI. We utilize a similar approach for FTA, by mapping the FTA components to simulation components of a SFI. By provision of both a component-based FTA and a component-based SFI, the concept of reusable databases is extended to reusable safety analysis artifacts.

The formalization of the FTA and the SFI structure are realized with the UML. Approaches such as [5,20] are also using the UML to support safety assessment. Reference [5] provides a model-to-model transformation to map a UML specification to a executable model based on the *Action Language for Foundational UML*. However, the derivation or construction of FMEA tables are neglected.

In [13] Simulink-based simulation models are generated based on an EAST-ADL description of the system. Safety analysis is explicitly targeted by this approach, but it cannot be used to verify safety analysis. Similar to other SFI approaches, it is not described how input for the fault injection is generated.

3   Methodology

The goal of the safety assessment process is to identify all failures that cause hazardous situations and to demonstrate that their probabilities are sufficiently low. In the application domains of safety-relevant systems, the safety assurance process is defined by the means of safety standards (e.g. IEC 61508 [10]). Figure 1 illustrates typical activities and their relation to the development process. Moreover, it outlines the used models and their interactions. As a first step, all relevant hazards of the system are identified and the associated risks are assessed during the so-called *Hazard Analysis and Risk Assessment*. Top-level safety requirements are the result of this step. Based on the system requirements the architecture of the system is designed in a model-based way using UML. Based on this system specification, the safety engineer is developing a safety analysis to identify failure modes, their causes, and effects with impact on the system safety. The results of the safety analysis as well as results of verification activities are used as evidences to evolve safety requirements to a safety case. Finally, the system safety is assessed based on the safety case and a certificate is issued in case of a positive assessment result.

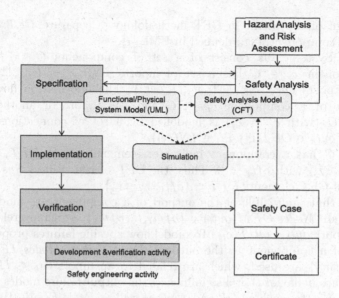

Fig. 1. Overview over the proposed methodology to verify safety analysis models

In our approach, we use the CFT methodology as a model- and component-based approach for fault tree analyses to enable modular and compositional safety analysis. Thereby, fault tree elements are related to their development artifacts (defined in UML) and can be reused along with them. Based on the available system specification in UML a system level simulation can be generated automatically. Since safety artifacts are associated with design artifacts of the system architecture, a straightforward mapping between the entities in the generated system simulation and the safety analysis model is given. Hence, test cases with fault injection and test oracles are automatically generated from CFTs. This way it possible to check whether the specified failure propagation is correct, using the system-level simulation. This enhances the quality of the CFT-based safety analysis model in terms of correctness, since failure modes as well as failure mitigation mechanisms can be discovered, which the safety engineer overlooked. Moreover, failure propagation paths, which are not yet know, e.g., caused by emergent behavior on system level, can be discovered.

4   Component Fault Trees

Component Fault Trees are Boolean models associated with system development elements such as components [8,12,22]. It has the same expressive power as classic fault trees, which are described in [19]. Like classic fault trees, CFTs are used to model failure behavior of safety-relevant systems. This failure behavior, including their appearance rate, is used to document the absence of unreasonable risk of the overall system. In addition, it can also be used to identify drawbacks of the design of a system. In CFT methodology, a separate *CFT element* is related to a component, e.g., defined in UML [7].

Let the System Sys consist of a set of components $C = \{c_1, ..., c_n\}$. Each component $c_i \in C$ has a set of inports $IN(c_i) = \{in_1, ..., in_p\}$ and a set of outports $OUT(c_i) = \{out_1, ..., out_q\}$. The information flow between the outport of a component $c_i \in C$ and the inport of another component $c_j \in C$ (with $c_i \neq c_j$) is modelled by a set of connections $CON = \{(out_x, in_y) | out_x \in OUT(c_i), in_y \in IN(c_j)\}$.

If $c_i \in C$ has a component fault tree element $cft_i \in CFT$, then it is $C\tilde{F}T(c_i) = cft_i$ with $cft_i \neq \emptyset$. Thus, the CFT of the system Sys is defined by the set of CFT elements $CFT = \{cft_1, ..., cft_n\}$.

Failures that are visible at the outport of a component are modeled using *Output Failure Modes* $OFM(out_l) = \{ofm_1, ..., ofm_t\}$, which are related to the specific outport $out_l \in OUT(c_i)$. To model how specific failures propagate from an inport of a component to the outport, *Input Failure Modes* $IFM(in_k) = \{ifm_1, ..., ifm_s\}$ are used, which are related to an inport $in_k \in IN(c_i)$. The internal failure behavior that also influences the output failure modes is modeled using Boolean gates such as *OR* and *AND* as well as *Basic Events*. Basic Events $B(cft_i) = \{b_1, ..., b_r\}$ represent failure modes that originate within a component. Each Basic Event can be assigned a failure rate, e.g., the *Mean Time Between Failure (MTBF)* or the *Failure in Time (FIT)*. In case of an OR gate a failure propagates if at least one of the inputs is active, while an AND gate propagates failures only if all input failures are active.

A library, which contains CFT elements for all system components, eases the reusability of safety artifacts. Hence, it is possible to create different CFTs by just changing the assembly of the CFT elements. Every CFT can be transformed to a classic fault tree by removing the input and output failure mode elements.

5   Error Effect Simulation

The EES consists of a *Device Under Test (DUT)* and its test bench. The DUT models software, hardware and analog system parts. We use the IEEE standard *SystemC* [9] because of its support of various simulation domains and its comprehensive support of different abstraction levels. The EES uses an approach similar to [18]. It consists of a modular, parameterizable system simulation that is used to assess error effects. One simulation instance is assembled of parameterizable *Simulation Entities (SEs)*. To facilitate the analysis of different DUT characteristics, the framework uses dynamic configuration that is supplied during runtime. This covers the DUT architecture as well as the SEs parameterization.

The EES requires *fault injectors*, which cause a discrepancy within the DUT. We provide injection capability by replacing simulation primitives with an injectable container that encapsulates the original simulation primitive. This container provides an interface to change the value of the simulation primitive. The design of the injectors is particularly suited to support simulation models of different abstraction levels with their different modeling primitives. A centralized injection control module stimulates the safety case by controlling the injectors.

The so-called *Behavioral Threat Models (BTM)* specifies the injected behavior. A BTM is based on *Timed Automata (TA)*. A TA consists of a finite set of locations L, actions Σ and a set of clocks C, which can be reset individually. An edge $(l_i, \sigma, g(C), r(C), l_j) \in E$ is a transition from location l_i to location l_j with an action $\sigma \in \Sigma$, a time dependent guard $g(C)$ and a clock reset $r(C)$. For fault modeling the TA approach is extended in a way that guard statement $g(C, \mathbb{W}_s, \mathbb{W}_l, \mathbb{E})$ can additionally depend on the state of the simulation $\mathbb{W}_s$, the state of BTM local variables $\mathbb{W}_l$ and a set of events $\mathbb{E}$ that are used to synchronize multiple BTMs. Actions $\sigma(\mathbb{W}_s, \mathbb{W}_l)$ are extended to modify the simulation state $\mathbb{W}_s$ or local variables within the BTM $\mathbb{W}_l$. The centralized injection control module interprets a BTM dynamically and stimulates faults.

For failure detection, the virtual prototype is extended with *failure monitors*, which compare the behavior of one variable with a previous simulation run. Using an error free simulation run as reference enables the detection of failures that are caused by the fault injection. Reference [1] presents a general failure mode characterization, which cover *content failures, early failures, late failures, halt failures* as well as *erratic failures*. The proposed failure monitors detect these standard failure modes by default. Besides the detection of these standard failure modes it is possible to specify queries that are checked both on the reference and error trace. A *Computation Tree Logic (CTL)* expression specifies the queries. This enables the detection of application specific failure modes.

A graphical specification of the EES based on the UML supports the user by conducting analyses. It reduces the manual overhead by code generation steps and increase the usability. The graphical specification consists of the specification of the SEs, their instantiation, parametrization and interconnection. Moreover, the placement of fault injectors, failure monitors and fault behavior is specified.

With these extensions of the system simulation the question still remains, at which location to inject faults (fault injector placement), how does the injected behavior look like (BTM specification) and where to detect deviations from the reference trace (monitor placement).

6 Verification of CFTs Using Error Effect Simulation

In order to verify the failure behavior specified as CFT, test cases for the EES are generated automatically. A test case covers the fault specification and the fault injector placement. Additionally it includes a test oracle, which is realized by a failure monitor. The test cases are derived from the CFT. For this purposes, we define a so-called *scope S* of the CFT that involves only a certain amount of the components with $S \subseteq CFT$. Thus, it is possible to verify both the entire failure propagation model as well as only a part of it. A scope $S \subseteq CFT$ provides a set of inputs and outputs. The inputs of the scope $IN_S \subseteq \bigcup_{c_i \in S} IN(c_i)$ are used to enter a test scenario. The outputs $OUT_S \subseteq \bigcup_{c_i \in S} OUT(c_i)$ are used to measure the results of a test scenario. The inner CFT logic can be simplified to a CFT element for the scope S, which only contains the gates and basic events, input and output failure modes that are related to the scope (cf. Reference [21]). Internal input and output failure modes are omitted. Hence, for a scope $S \subseteq CFT$, the CFT element related to S is $CFT_S \subseteq CFT$. It contains failure modes related to the inports and outports and have a connection outside of the scope. Let

$$IFM(S) = \{in \mid \exists(a,b) \in CON, a \in OUT(A), A \notin S,$$
$$b \in IN(B), B \in S, in \in IFM(B)\}$$

be the input failure modes of the scope S and

$$OFM(S) = \{out \mid \exists(a,b) \in CON, a \in OUT(A), A \in S,$$
$$b \in IN(B), B \notin S, ut \in OFM(A)\}$$

be the output failure modes of the scope S. Moreover, let

$$B(S) = \bigcup_{c_i \in S} B(c_i)$$

be the set of basic events of the scope S.

In order to determine a set of test cases, we apply the methodology of *Minimal Cut Set Analysis (MCA)*. A MCA is a representation of a tree using a disjunction of conjunctive terms that cannot be reduced further [19]. For a scope S, let

$$mc_i(t) = x_1 \wedge \cdots \wedge x_n, t \in OFM(S), x_i \in IFM(S) \cup B(S)$$

be all cut sets that result in the occurrence of the output failure mode $t \in OFM(S)$ of the scope $S \subseteq CFT$. Moreover, let

$$MCA(t) = mc_1(t) \vee \cdots \vee mc_m(t), t \in OFM(S)$$

be the minimal cut set analysis of the output failure mode t and scope $S \subseteq CFT$. Since in general multiple combinations of input data leads to different output data for the same test case, typical measures can be applied here to further reduce the set of test cases like equivalence class testing.

Thus, the results of the MCA are used to generate input for the fault injectors. For each input failure mode ifm_i a set of BTMs is generated $BTM(ifm_i) = \{btm_{i,1} \ldots btm_{i,m}\}$ to control the fault injector at the inports IN_S of the respective component. Similar for each Basic Events b_i a set of BTMs is generated $BTM(b_i) = \{btm_{i,1} \ldots btm_{i,n}\}$ to inject faults by the modification of the component state. In this work, we use sets of predefined BTMs that match the failure behavior of the input failure modes and Basic Events within the CFT. An approach with a BTM-library is used and the generation process parametrizes these predefined fault behaviors. The generated inputs stimulate the DUT and lead to a discrepancy from the intended behavior. Since the output failure modes $OFM(S)$ of S can be observed at the outports OUT_S, failure monitors are placed within the EES. These monitors detect general failure modes by default but can also be extended to detect application specific failure modes. With this the the CFT can be verified by the EES.

7   Case Study

We illustrate the benefits of our approach using an automotive case study namely a coasting assistant. This assistant calculates driver hints such as acceleration or braking with regard to an energy efficient driving strategy. The system is designed for electric vehicles, where in case of a deceleration the driver has the choice of freewheeling or braking with recuperation. The coasting assistant displays the optimal driving choice w.r.t. energy efficiency in the Head-Unit. Therefore, the coasting assistant ECU uses maps annotated with speed limits but also a video-based speed limit detection to adjust to undocumented limits such as road works. This speed limit detection will be the focus of the case study.

7.1   Overview

The coasting assistant functionality is distributed over multiple Electronic Control Units (ECUs), which are interconnected by different communication channels. Figure 2 shows the involved ECUs and communication channels. The camera ECU records the road in front of the vehicle and sends this image to a circle detection algorithm using the synchronous channel of a MOST bus. In the next processing step, circles are detected and the containing image segments are forwarded to a speed limit classification. The image segments are forwarded via the dynamic segment of the FlexRay bus. Information about the estimated distance of the potential speed sign is sent with a separate CAN message to the coasting assistant ECU. The cropped circles are classified and the results are sent to the coasting assistant via CAN. The coasting assistant uses the received information on the next speed limit as well as the estimated distance and an internal look-up table to calculate an energy efficient driving strategy.

Focus of the safety analysis in early development stages is the actual functionality itself. The communication between simulation entities is abstracted by function calls. The logical system architecture, specified with the CFT architectural model, is shown in Fig. 3. The data exchange is modeled using ports.

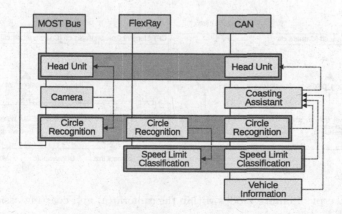

Fig. 2. Overview of the case study

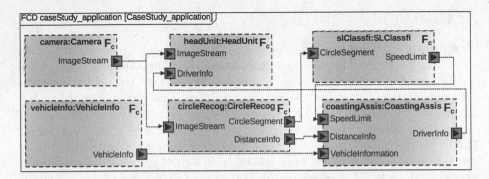

Fig. 3. Functional architecture of the exemplary system

7.2 CFT-Based Analysis

For each of the components within the system architecture a CFT element is specified. Figure 4(a) shows the CFT element describing the failure behavior of the camera ECU. Basic Events model the different internal failures. Each of them is associated with a specific failure rate. The CFT element of the camera specifies failure modes like a frozen image stream, a corruption of the image pixels, the omission of the complete images or a variation in the sampling time of the camera. These failure modes are propagated via the components' outports to other components. This way the failures originating from the camera induces the failure modes in the head unit and the Circle Detection ECU. Figure 4(b) shows the failure modes within the coasting assistant ECU. The input failure modes represent that a speed limit is reported too late that an erroneous speed limit is reported or that speed limit is missing. The output failure modes depend on the input failure modes and the Basic Events of the component. The output failure modes determine the input failure modes of the next component - in our case study the ones of the head unit.

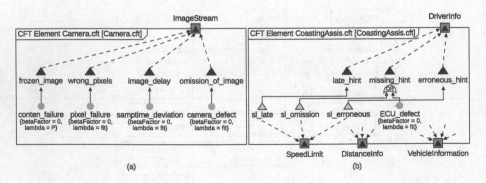

Fig. 4. Excerpt of failure modes within the camera (a) and coasting assistant (b)

With the specification of the CFT elements for all components of the system architecture it is possible to calculate the complete fault tree or different fault trees w.r.t. a restricted scope. Table 1 shows a few of the generated test cases with different scopes. One example path in the fault tree would be that `camera.content_failure OR camera.pixel_failure` can cause the failure mode `coastingAssis.erroneous_hint`, when the HMI is excluded from the analyzed scope.

Table 1. Excerpt of the generated test cases

Scope	Fault injection	Failure monitor
camera	camera_defect	omission_of_image
	content_failure	frozen_image
coastingAssistant	sl_omission OR di_omission OR ECU_defect	missing_hint
	sl_errornous	erroneous_hint
camera, circleRecog, slClassfi, coastingAssis	camera.content_failure OR camera.pixel_failure	coastingAssis.erroneous_hint
complete System	camera.content_failure OR camera.pixel_failure	HMI.image_content_failure
	camera.samptime_deviation	HMI.sl_late

7.3 Simulation-Based Verification

After generation of the relation between input failure modes and output failure modes, these relations are verified using simulations. The EES shows if the caused-by-relation specified in the safety analysis model is observed in the simulation. In case of OR-relations, the simulation has to provoke an error effect if any of the faults is injected. In case of an AND-relation, the error effect should only manifest if all input faults are injected simultaneous. For each component in the CFT, a corresponding SE exists in the simulation. Figure 5 shows the graphical specification of the simulation configuration. It contains the same components as the CFT system architecture and for each of the components a CFT element is specified. Model-to-model transformations enable the mapping of CFT elements to simulation components. The simulation specification contains additional information that is not specified within the CFT system architecture or the CFT, such as the SE parametrizations or the SEs of the test bench. Thus, it is no bijective transformation. In the context of this work the developer is supported by automated model-to-model transformations, but still manual extensions, e.g., to specify the component parametrization or to extend the configuration with sole simulation components, are required to create the simulation. This approach offers the benefit that the system architecture or the CFT is not polluted with information, which is only required for the simulation.

The fault injection targets mainly the internal information of the components. The failure modes specified in the CFT element of the Camera (cf. Fig. 4) target the internal storage of the transmitted image. The failure mode `frozen_image` is represented by altering the sampling time of the camera, the `wrong_pixels` fault by altering the image payload. A camera defect (`omission_of_image`) is modeled by an infinite sampling time. If two failure modes are affecting the same injector, e.g., the camera defect and the frozen image, the user have to assure the interaction between the two failures modes is desired. The simulation contains therefore fault injectors that are associated with the payload array and with the sampling time variable. Figure 6 (above) shows the BTMs to inject a pixel failure and Fig. 6 (below) shows the behavior of the content failure. It can be seen that both BTMs control the injector `VPvar('m_Camera.pixel')`. In the context of the CFT the different failure modes determine the selection of the BTMs ($BTM(ifm_i)$ or $BTM(bi)$). In this case study, for each input failure mode or Basic Event in the CFT a set of BTM are created. For instance, the BTM in Fig. 6 (below) is generated for the `camera.content_failure` solely. For the `camera.pixel_failure` different BTMs that stimulate different corruption patterns are created. Figure 7 illustrates three effects of the generated BTMs. The picture on the left shows the pixel corruption limited to a horizontal line, the middle one to a vertical line and the picture on the right shows a random pixel corruption over the complete image.

Each output failure mode within the CFT is presented in the simulation by a monitor. The case study adds a monitor at the received speed limit in the coasting assistant, corresponding to the output failure mode specified in the CFT element of the coasting assistant. Before each fault simulation, a reference trace is generated without fault injection. Based on this generated reference trace the monitors classify the current trace, altered by the fault injection.

In this example, the traces indicate a late failure. The reference trace reports a speed limit at 28.8 s but the injection trace first at 29.1 s. This is based on the fact that the speed sign is recorded in sequence of images, while the vehicle drives towards the sign, and that the first classifications is

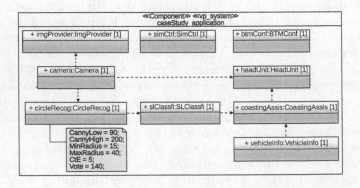

Fig. 5. Specification of the system simulation for the case study

```
1   <ESname> eInit <EStype> initial
2   <ESname> eFree
3   <ESname> eState
4   <ETsrc> eInit <ETtgt> eFree
5     <ETaction> ids = [id for id in range(719*200,719*210)]
6   <ETsrc> eFree <ETtgt> eState
7     <ETguard> BTMclock('OKTime').read()==sc_time(23, sc_time_unit.SC_SEC)
8     <ETaction> [VPvar('m_Camera.pixel')[id].force(0x00) for id in ids]
9   <ETsrc> eState <ETtgt> eState
10    <ETaction> [VPvar('m_Camera.pixel')[id].release() for id in ids];
11               [VPvar('m_Camera.pixel')[id].force(0x00) for id in ids]
```

```
1   <ESname>errFree, <EStype>initial
2   <ESname>errState1
3   <ETsrc>errFree <ETtgt>errState1
4     <ETguard> BTMclock('OKTime').read()==sc_time(22,sc_time_unit.SC_SEC)
5     <ETaction> VPvar('m_Camera.pixel')[0].force(
6                VPvar('m_Camera.pixel')[0].read())
```

Fig. 6. BTM for image corruption (above) and a freeze frame failure (below)

Fig. 7. Effect of different pixel corruption strategies

prevented based on the pixel corruption within the image. In this fault scenario, the horizontal line is injected, blocking the speed limits far away. This situation was overseen during the creation of the CFT. As mentioned earlier a `camera.content_failure` OR `camera.pixel_failure` can cause the failure mode `coastingAssis.erroneous_hint`. The simulation has shown that this is a very unlikely case, because the classification will most likely return no classification at all instead of the wrong classification. Resulting in a late failure mode because a sequence of images is taken from the actual speed limit sign and most likely, a subsequent image will be classified correctly. The nearer the speed limit the more robust is the classification against pixel errors. Subsequent to the EES, the CFT, particularly the classification component, is adjusted in a way that the `classification.erroneous_circle_recognition` input failure additionally causes `classification.speed-limit_information-too-late` output failures. This case is a very good example how the none-complete simulation approach and the deductive safety analysis in form of a CFT complement each other. A very large number of simulation runs would be necessary to reproduce the behavior of corrupted speed limit information within the coasting assistant based on a pixel corruption in the camera. Therefore, the safety analyst can specify this case manually in the fault tree after verifying the CFT using an EES.

On the other hand when solely using the top-down safety analysis (in form of a CFT), the safety experts could have missed the propagation of a pixel corruption to a late speed limit failure mode.

Besides the verification of existing failure propagation paths of the CFT, it is also possible to verify if failure propagation exists that are not represented in the CFT. Therefore, the input failure modes and Basic Events, respectively the generated fault behavior, are combined with different output failure modes, respectively their failure monitors. Thus, missing propagation paths within the CFT can be revealed using the EES. With increasing complexity of safety analysis models, the effort to verify all combinations of fault injection and monitors is rapidly increasing. One benefit of our approach is that different failure monitors can be used within one simulation run in order to examine different failure propagation paths at once.

7.4   Analyses Refinement

In later stages of the design process, the models will be refined. In this case study, only the communication between the components is refined. In a first refinement step, the communication is mapped to abstract transaction models and in a second step to detailed bus models of CAN, FlexRay and MOST. With each more detailed abstraction level, new failure sources are added and the CFT is extended with CFT elements of the corresponding components. This will enable more detailed safety analyses of the system. On the other hand, the already verified CFTs and simulation models of the application are reused with each refinement step. This is an example of the benefit of using a modular, compositional approach for the safety analysis and the simulation.

Another benefit is the reuse of components (CFT, EES) within a single system configuration. For example, the models of the transaction-based communication are required at different locations of the system. Through a single CFT- and simulation-element it is possible to create multiple instances. This way the effort is reduced and the failures are automatically applied at different system parts.

8   Summary

The presented approach enables the verification of failure propagation models in form of Component Fault Trees (CFT) by an Error Effect Simulations (EES). Automatic generation steps are provided to generate the injected fault behavior, required for the EES, as well as a test oracle to classify the monitored failure behavior. It is shown how the verification of the safety analysis model is applied during different phases of the development process. In particular, after each change of the system design, including modifications or refinements of the system architecture. Since the inputs of the fault injection as well as the test oracle are generated automatically, the repeated verification of the failure propagation model can be performed efficiently.

Supporting a safety analysis technique, like CFT, with a non-complete simulation-based analysis reduces the weaknesses of both methodologies. The results of the CFT-based analysis are only as good as the system knowledge of the involved experts. Especially, the safety analysis model of large-scale, complex systems might be incomplete. The system simulation on the other hand offers a method to enable different stakeholders, in particular IP providers, to contribute their system knowledge. Such simulation models offer a good basis to support safety analysis, since they enable a quantitative assessment of failure mitigation mechanisms. On the other hand, only selective use cases are analyzed and the detailed assessment of failure rates can cause a huge simulation effort. By the automatic generation of fault injection input and test oracles for the simulation from the CFT these weaknesses are reduced. Hence, our approach enables the verification whether the specified failure propagation is defined correctly within a CFT-based safety analysis model. Moreover, additional failures on system level as well as additional failure mitigation mechanisms can be discovered. It is also possible to discover failure propagation paths, which are not know yet. Another benefit is that in most cases the simulation does not have to be executed with a random fault injection based on very small failure rates. Firm fault combinations are injected and the propagation is evaluated by the EES. The probabilistic analyses is then executed on the verified CFTs, reducing the simulation effort drastically.

Acknowledgement. This work has been partially supported by the German Ministry of Science and Education (BMBF) in the project ASSUME under grant 01IS15031 and EffektiV under grant 01IS13022.

References

1. Avizienis, A., Laprie, J.-C., Randell, B., Landwehr, C.: Basic concepts and taxonomy of dependable and secure computing. IEEE Trans. Dependable Secure Comput. **1**(1), 11–33 (2004)
2. Ayestaran, I., Nicolas, C.F., Perez, J., Larrucea, A., Puschner, P.: Modeling and simulated fault injection for time-triggered safety-critical embedded systems. In: IEEE 17th International Symposium on Object/Component/Service-Oriented Real-Time Distributed Computing (ISORC), pp. 180–187 (2014)
3. Becker, M., Kuznik, C., Mueller, W.: Virtual platforms for model-based design of dependable cyber-physical system software. In: 17th Euromicro Conference on Digital System Design (DSD), pp. 246–253 (2014)
4. Bolchini, C., Miele, A., Sciuto, D.: Fault models and injection strategies in SystemC specifications. In: 11th EUROMICRO Conference on Digital System Design Architectures, Methods and Tools (DSD), pp. 88–95 (2008)
5. Bonfiglio, V., Montecchi, L., Rossi, F., Lollini, P., Pataricza, A., Bondavalli, A.: Executable models to support automated software FMEA. In: 2015 IEEE 16th International Symposium on High Assurance Systems Engineering (2015)
6. Chaari, M., Ecker, W., Novello, C., Tabacaru, B.A., Kruse, T.: A model-based and simulation-assisted FMEDA approach for safety-relevant e/e systems. In: 2015 52nd ACM/EDAC/IEEE Design Automation Conference (DAC), June 2015

7. Adler, R., Domis, D., Höfig, K., Kemmann, S., Kuhn, T., Schwinn, J.-P., Trapp, M.: Integration of component fault trees into the UML. In: Dingel, J., Solberg, A. (eds.) MODELS 2010. LNCS, vol. 6627, pp. 312–327. Springer, Heidelberg (2011). doi:10.1007/978-3-642-21210-9_30
8. Höfig, K., Zeller, M., Heilmann, R.: ALFRED: a methodology to enable component fault trees for layered architectures. In: 41st Euromicro Conference on Software Engineering and Advanced Applications (SEAA) (2015)
9. IEEE Computer Society: IEEE 1666–2011 Standard SystemC Language Reference Manual (2011)
10. International Electrotechnical Commission (IEC): IEC 61508: functional safety of electrical/electronic/programmable electronic safety related systems (1998)
11. International Organization for Standardization (ISO): ISO 26262: road vehicles - functional safety (2011)
12. Kaiser, B., Liggesmeyer, P., Mäckel, O.: A new component concept for fault trees. In: Proceedings of the 8th Australian Workshop on Safety Critical Systems and Software, SCS 2003, vol. 33, pp. 37–46 (2003)
13. Marinescu, R., Kaijser, H., Mikučionis, M., Seceleanu, C., Lönn, H., David, A.: Analyzing industrial architectural models by simulation and model-checking. In: Artho, C., Ölveczky, P.C. (eds.) FTSCS 2014. CCIS, vol. 476, pp. 189–205. Springer, Cham (2015). doi:10.1007/978-3-319-17581-2_13
14. Misera, S., Vierhaus, H.T., Sieber, A.: Fault injection techniques and their accelerated simulation in SystemC. In: 10th Euromicro Conference on Digital System Design Architectures, Methods and Tools (DSD), pp. 587–595 (2007)
15. Oetjens, J.-H., Bannow, N., et al.: Safety evaluation of automotive electronics using virtual prototypes: state of the art and research challenges. In: 51st ACM/EDAC/IEEE Design Automation Conference (DAC), pp. 1–6 (2014)
16. Perez, J., Azkarate-Askasua, M., Perez, A.: Codesign and simulated fault injection of safety-critical embedded systems using SystemC. In: European Dependable Computing Conference (EDCC), pp. 221–229 (2010)
17. Reiter, S., Pressler, M., Viehl, A., Bringmann, O., Rosenstiel, W.: Reliability assessment of safety-relevant automotive systems in a model-based design flow. In: 18th Asia and South Pacific Design Automation Conference (ASP-DAC) (2013)
18. Reiter, S., Viehl, A., Bringmann, O., Rosenstiel, W.: Fault injection ecosystem for assisted safety validation of automotive systems. In: 2016 IEEE International High Level Design Validation and Test Workshop (HLDVT), October 2016
19. Vesely, W., Goldberg, F., Roberts, N., Haasl, D.: Fault Tree Handbook. US Nuclear Regulatory Commission, Rockville (1981)
20. Weissnegger, R., Schuß, M., Kreiner, C., Pistauer, M., Römer, K., Steger, C.: Seamless integrated simulation in design and verification flow for safety-critical systems. In: Skavhaug, A., Guiochet, J., Schoitsch, E., Bitsch, F. (eds.) SAFECOMP 2016. LNCS, vol. 9923, pp. 359–370. Springer, Cham (2016). doi:10.1007/978-3-319-45480-1_29
21. Zeller, M., Höfig, K.: Confetti component – fault tree-based testing. In: Podofillini, L., Sudret, B., Stojadinovic, B., Zio, E., Kröger, W. (eds.) Safety and Reliability of Complex Engineered Systems: Proceedings of the 25th European Safety and Reliability Conference (ESREL), pp. 4011–4017 (2015)
22. Zeller, M., Höfig, K.: INSiDER: incorporation of system and safety analysis models using a dedicated reference model. In: 2016 Annual Reliability and Maintainability Symposium (RAMS) (2016)

A Model-Based Approach to Dynamic Self-assessment for Automated Performance and Safety Awareness of Cyber-Physical Systems

DeJiu Chen[1(✉)] and Zhonghai Lu[2]

[1] Mechatronics, Machine Design, School of ITM,
KTH Royal Institute of Technology, 10044 Stockholm, Sweden
chendj@kth.se
[2] Electronics and Embedded Systems, School of ICT,
KTH Royal Institute of Technology, 164 40 Kista, Sweden
zhonghai@kth.se

Abstract. Modern automotive vehicles represent one category of CPS (Cyber-Physical Systems) that are inherently time- and safety-critical. To justify the actions for quality-of-service adaptation and safety assurance, it is fundamental to perceive the uncertainties of system components in operation, which are caused by emergent properties, design or operation anomalies. From an industrial point of view, a further challenge is related to the usages of generic purpose COTS (Commercial-Off-The-Shelf) components, which are separately developed and evolved, often not sufficiently verified and validated for specific automotive contexts. While introducing additional uncertainties in regard to the overall system performance and safety, the adoption of COTS components constitutes a necessary means for effective product evolution and innovation. Accordingly, we propose in this paper a novel approach that aims to enable advanced operation monitoring and self-assessment in regard to operational uncertainties and thereby automated performance and safety awareness. The emphasis is on the integration of several modeling technologies, including the domain-specific modeling framework EAST-ADL, the A-G contract theory and Hidden Markov Model (HMM). In particular, we also present some initial concepts in regard to the usage performance and safety awareness for quality-of-service adaptation and dynamic risk mitigation.

Keywords: Cyber-physical systems · Commercial-Off-The-Shelf · Uncertainties · EAST-ADL · Contract · Probabilistic inference · Safety · Performance

1 Introduction

One key technological aspect of a modern automotive vehicle is its embedded E/E (Electrical/Electronic) system, consisting of sensor and actuator devices, ECUs (Electronic Control Units) and communication networks (e.g. CAN, LIN, MOST). By means of digital software and hardware, the embedded system allows both more

© Springer International Publishing AG 2017
M. Bozzano and Y. Papadopoulos (Eds.): IMBSA 2017, LNCS 10437, pp. 227–240, 2017.
DOI: 10.1007/978-3-319-64119-5_15

effective realization of advanced functionalities and better achievement of performance and flexibilities in a way that is impossible with traditional mechanical and electrical solutions. Currently, the industry shares the view that the embedded system constitutes the most important technology for the advances in sustainability, road safety, and novel traffic solutions. The key innovation areas include ADAS (Advanced Driving Assistant Systems) and AD (Autonomous Driving) [1], with further enhancement by V2V (Vehicle-to-Vehicle) and V2I (Vehicle-to-Infrastructure) communication for cooperative behaviors [2]. Because of such features, an automotive vehicle becomes cyber-physical in nature by having, on one hand, physical dynamics and energy flows under control, and, on the other hand, the corresponding perception, control and cognitive loops within the embedded E/E system.

The evolution of automotive vehicles relies strongly on the technological developments and innovations in the electronics industry that are driven by consumer products. For automotive, the adaptation of generic purpose COTS (Commercial-Off-The-Shelf) solutions, ranging from camera, radar and other sensors for traffic perception, to speech recognition and augmented-reality displays for human-machine interactions, and to wireless and telecommunication services for V2V and V2I connectivity, has been advocated as a necessary means for shortening the innovation loops and enabling efficient product evolution. Unfortunately, there are often big gaps between the quality expectations of automotive vehicles and the quality assurance by generic purpose COTS. One reason for this is that the COTS solutions are developed for different use cases or operational conditions differing from the automotive ones. For example, the reliability targets of automotive components differ considerably from those of consumer products. The expected lifetime for electronics components would be up to 15 years for automotive vehicles, in comparison to a length in 2–5 years for consumer products [3]. Meanwhile, the operational temperature ranges are normally $-40 \sim 160$ °C for automotive vehicles and $0 \sim 40$ °C for consumer products. Moreover, as a failure of a COTS solution for automotive vehicles could result in system hazards, a systematic management of the risks according to the safety standard ISO26262 becomes necessary [4]. The information of concern typically includes not only a specification of its functional behaviors, but also a complete definition of its assumed failure modes, adopted quality assurance measures, and expected system-wide measures for fault tolerance and treatment. This is not a trivial task for separately developed COTS.

This paper presents a novel model-based approach to system operation monitoring and self-assessment in regard to the operational uncertainties and thereby automated performance and safety awareness. The approach emphasizes an integration of several modeling technologies, including the domain-specific modeling framework EAST-ADL for modularity design, the A-G contract theory for module specification, and Hidden Markov Model (HMM) for probabilistic inference of operation conditions. The ultimate goal is to support effective integration and management of separately developed services and components in safety critical CPS by means of quality management services for post-deployment operation- and life-cycle management. The rest of this chapter is structured into the following sections: Sect. 2 provides an overview of the overall methodology. Section 3 introduces the modeling support for modularity design and module specification for successful management of COTS solutions, including the EAST-ADL modeling framework and the A-G contract theory. Section 4 focuses on the dynamic self-assessment through probabilistic inference based on Hidden Markov Model (HMM), while describing the related software services and design considerations for self-assessment and self-management. An overview of related technologies is given in Sect. 5. The paper concludes with Sect. 6 by elaborating the future research directions.

2 Overview of the Methodology

The overall methodology is shown in Fig. 1. Following the *knowledge-in-the-loop* paradigm proposed in [5], the approach emphasizes an integration of the models that describe system requirements, design solutions, verification and validation cases, and the software services that are embedded for operation monitoring, *compositionality* and composability assessment, diagnostics and anomaly treatment.

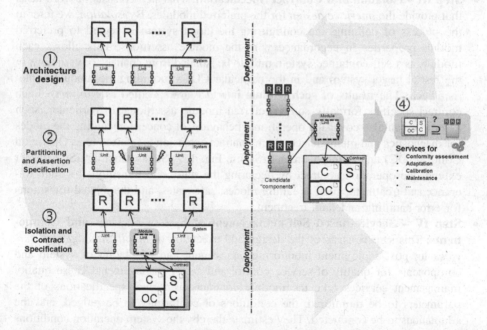

Fig. 1. The overall methodology for a model-based contract and service for self-managed system service and components. ① Step I – Architecture design; ② Step II – Partitioning and Assertion Specification; ③ Step III – Isolation and Contract Specification; ④ Step IV – Service-based Self-Management of System Services and Components. R- Requirement; C- Contract; OC-Operation Contract; SC-Safety Contract.

As shown in Fig. 1, the methodology consists of the following four main steps with the activities ranging from modularity design to automated post-deployment services:

- **Step I – System architecture design:** This step consists of work tasks that focus on the *overall design* of a particular cyber-physical system. The issues of concern include the expected operational environments, the functional and technical constituent units, the expected behaviors and quality constraints, the corresponding verification and validation cases, etc. As the outcome, it provides a system view that stipulates the design-space with compositional variants and restrictions.

- **Step II – Partitioning and assertion specification:** This step consists of work tasks for system *modularity design*, which is centric on partitioning the target system into modules and thereby refining the system design-space for external COTS solutions. In effect, the design results in a restructuring of the target system so that some of its constituent units can be developed and managed independently. As a self-contained unit, each system module should not violate the functional and technical requirements of the corresponding services and components being composed. We specify such top-level module constraints as the *module assertions* (e.g., the accepted types and resolutions of input and output signals, the allowed range of execution time, and the criticalities of failure modes).

- **Step III – Isolation and Contract Specification:** This step consists of work tasks that provide the *interface design* for the preferred modules. By *isolation*, we refer to the process of defining and configuring the target system in regard to preferred module properties in accordance with the module assertions. This allows each module, as a self-contained system unit, to be isolated from changes or variations in the rest of target system and in the particular COTS providing the module implementation. The results of such module interface are specified as *contracts*. Each contract specifies formally some preferred module assertions. In particular, such assertions can also cover the operational behaviors of concern, including the modes for diagnostics and maintenance. Such contract extension is referred to as Operation Contract (OC) and Safety Contract (SC) in Fig. 1. A Safety Contract (SC) further extends the operation contract by declaring the states and transitions for fault tolerance and treatment, such as failure modes, safe states, and the related transitions for error handling and fault treatment.

- **Step IV – Service-based Self-management of System Services and Components:** This step consists of the design and execution of *quality management services* for post-deployment monitoring, assessment and adaptation of system and components for quality-of-service control and safety management. These quality management services take the module contracts as formal specifications of the parameters to be monitored, the conditions of conformity to be judged, and the adaptations to be conducted. They estimate thereby the system operation conditions by probabilistic inference with Hidden Markov Model (HMM). The adaption planning is centered on the condition-action reasoning based on some deterministic or probabilistic decision models. For the service realization, a key issue is related to how to enable the run-time monitoring and control through integration with system run-time environment and maintenance infrastructure.

3 Modeling Support for Modularity Design and Module Specification

3.1 EAST-ADL for Modularity Design

ADL (Architecture description language) is a modeling technology for structuring and managing the engineering information of a system in particular in regard to the overall system design. As a domain-specific approach, the EAST-ADL represents a key European initiative towards a standardized description of automotive embedded E/E systems [6, 7]. In our approach, the EAST-ADL system model, together with the associated requirements and constraints, constitutes a basis for effective but still very flexible modularity design. That is, given the models capturing the system wide inter-dependencies, a particular modularization task can be driven at any specific abstraction level in accordance with the particular preferences of modules. For example, the modules given by features (*EAST-ADL Vehicle Level*) provide a structuring of the externally visible functionalities of the target system and allow a service-oriented composition of external functions. Meanwhile, module definitions can also be done based on software components (*EAST-ADL Implementation Level*) to allow a component-based engineering of software solutions. In both cases, the EAST-ADL system model constitutes a useful means for systematically reasoning about the corresponding module coupling and cohesion, both in regard to the functional interactions (which are given by communication links in the same level of abstraction) and technical implications (which are given by realization links across the abstraction levels).

3.2 A-G Contract for Module Specification

Following the contract theory defined in [8, 9], we use formal contracts to specify the expected functional and technical properties of a system module. Fundamentally, a system module M is defined by its variables, behaviors as well as some related quality constraints as follows

$$M = (\mathbb{V}, \mathbb{F}, \mathbb{Q}) \tag{1}$$

with $\mathbb{V}$ for all variables $\mathbb{V} = \mathcal{U} \cup \mathcal{X} \cup \mathcal{Y} \cup \mathcal{K}$, where $\mathcal{U}$ denotes the input variables, $\mathcal{X}$ the internal state variables, $\mathcal{Y}$ the output variables, and $\mathcal{K}$ the configuration variables; $\mathbb{F}$ for all functional behaviors over the variables $\mathbb{F} = [\![\mathcal{F}(\mathcal{U}, \mathcal{Y}, \mathcal{X}, \mathcal{K}) = 0]\!]$; and $\mathbb{Q}$ for all quality constraints over the functional behaviors $\mathbb{Q} = \{\mathbb{P}, \mathbb{R}, \ldots\} = \{[\![\mathcal{P}(\mathbb{F}) = 0]\!],$ $[\![\mathcal{R}(\mathbb{F}) = 0]\!], \ldots\}$ with $\mathbb{P}$ for all performance constraints and $\mathbb{R}$ for all reliability constraints, etc. For successful system integration, all COTS solutions implementing a module implementation need to satisfy the expected module properties given by M, under certain environmental conditions. Such a requirement is formally defined by module contract $\mathcal{C}$ in terms of the pair:

$$\mathcal{C} = (\varepsilon_c, \mathcal{M}_c) \tag{2}$$

with $\mathcal{M}_c$ for all COTS solutions satisfying the M; and ε_c for all the legal environmental conditions. A contract is consistent if $\mathcal{M}_c \neq \emptyset$ and compatible if $\varepsilon_c \neq \emptyset$. A component $M_{comp} \vDash \mathcal{C}$ if and only if $M_{comp} \in \mathcal{M}_c$; An environment $E \vDash \mathcal{C}$ if and only if $E \in \varepsilon_c$.

An A-G (Assume-Guarantee) contract is a formalism for the description of contract $\mathcal{C}$ without directly referring to the actual COTS solutions $\mathcal{M}_c$. Normally, it is used for behavioral specifications of components, with A for the constraints on acceptable behaviors of the environment and G for the guarantees in terms of the corresponding component behaviors (as in e.g. [9]). Here, we use the A-G contract formalism in a more generic sense for all constraints that are characterized by logical or technical causalities from some environmental conditions (A) to some consequential module properties (G). Formally, an A-G module contract $\mathcal{C}$ is a pair of assertions (A, G) over some module variables, defined as:

$$A \Rightarrow G \tag{3}$$

with A for the constraints on the acceptable environment conditions; and G for the corresponding constraints on the properties to be guaranteed by module implementations. There is a logical or technical causality between A and G. That is, a module M satisfies the contract $\mathcal{C}$ if it has the same variables as $\mathcal{C}$ and satisfies the guarantee G whenever subjected to the assumptions A, (i.e. $A \cap M \subseteq G$). Currently, we use STL (Signal temporal logic) [10] and PrSTL (Probabilistic Signal temporal logic) [20] for the constraint specification.

System architecture models constitute the basis for the contract design. For example, an automotive vehicle braking system has been introduced in [7] as a case study for the modeling support. In the system, there is an ABS (Anti-lock Braking System) controller and an electromagnetic brake actuator at each wheel of the vehicle. For the braking control, a global brake controller receives the driver braking request and then sends brake force request to each ABS controller. Figure 2 shows an excerpt of the system architecture model (*SystemModel*).

A timing model augments the system model with information about the executional events and their timing constraints. The declarations are also shown in Fig. 2. An executional event defines the occurrence of data arrival on a port (e.g. *pStimuli_PedalPosIn*), or the triggering of function execution (e.g. *E_p1*). An event chain binds then together events to establish synchronization relations between the events e.g. to capture a complete end-to-end flow timing requirement from sensor inputs to actuator outputs. For example, the event chains *End-to-End Braking Response_FL* and *End-to-End Braking Response_FR* capture the timing requirement from driver braking request (*pStimuli_PedalPosIn*) to the brake torque actuation on the FL and FR wheels (*pResponse_ForceActuation_FL*, *pRsponse_ ForceActuation_FR*) respectively. The timing model also captures the timing constraints within the end-to-end flow, such as the preferred delay (A) from the braking request (*pStimuli_PedalPosIn*) to the arrival of torque request on the receiving port (*driverRequestedTorque_gbc_in*).

This EAST-ADL specification of timing properties is converted to A-G contracts for the integration of modules implemented by separately developed services or components. Suppose the entire braking system will be based on COTS, the A-G contract C_{com_1} shown in Fig. 3 stipulates the end to end communication and timing

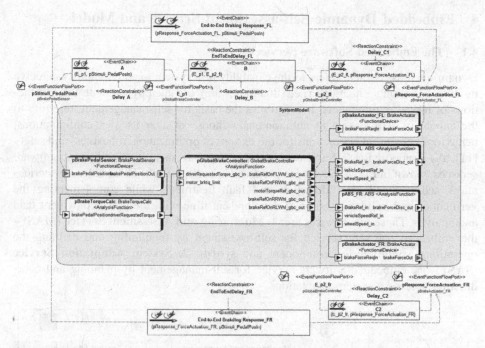

Fig. 2. The architecture model of an automotive vehicle braking system and the timing specification in EAST-ADL (implemented with the DSM Workbench MetaEdit+)

in a service-oriented way. The contract first declares the related executional events as contract variables: x for *pStimuli_PedalPosIn*, y_1 for *pResponse_ForceActuation_FL*, y_2 for *pRe sponse_ForceActuation_FR*. All these events are of the type *control* and *latency critical*. Given the assumption x about its *size*, *periodicity* and *priority*, each separately developed solution for the braking system needs not only to guarantee the preferred size and periodicity y_1 and y_2, but also to satisfy the delays $x \rightarrow F_{[0..\#delay_{y_1}]}y_1$ and $x \rightarrow F_{[0..\#delay_{y_2}]}y_2$ for the *End-to-End Braking Response_FL* and *End-to-End Braking Response_FR* respectively.

$$C_{com\_1}: \begin{cases} \text{messages:} \begin{cases} \text{in:}\, x \\ \text{out:}\, y_1, y_2 \end{cases} \\ \text{message\_types:}\, x, y_1, y_2 \in (Control, Latency\_Critical) \\ \text{assumptions:}\, x = (\#size_x, \#periodicity_x, \#priority_x) \\ \text{guarantees:}\, y_1 = (\#size_{y_1}, \#periodicity_{y_1}), y_2 = (\#size_{y_2}, \#periodicity_{y_2}), \\ \quad G\left(x \rightarrow F_{[0..\#delay_{y_1}]}y_1\right), G\left(x \rightarrow F_{[0..\#delay_{y_2}]}y_2\right), \ldots \end{cases}$$

Fig. 3. The A-G contract for the operation of vehicle braking. Here, we use STL (Signal temporal logic) [10] to denote the behavioral constraints, with the operator G for always (globally) and F for eventually (in the future).

4 Embedded Dynamic Self-assessment Service and Models

4.1 The Embedded Software Services

Dynamic self-assessment refers to the capability of a system to autonomously perceive its own operational situations (i.e. situation-aware) and thereby estimate the satisfactions of related requirements. It constitutes the basis for self-management, referring to the capability of a system to autonomously choose or alter its own configurations, behaviors, or external interactions for the reasons of optimization, robustness and safety [11]. As a support for self-assessment and self-management, two additional software services, shown in Fig. 4, have been proposed in our approach. These software services allow self-managed error detection and fault treatment, while complementing the verification and validation effort at development time with the post-deployment data and analysis. These two services are: **1. Monitoring and Assessment Service (MAS)** – the embedded software service for self-assessment by monitoring and defining the operational conditions of component and system; **2. System Adaptation Service (SAS)** – the embedded software service for self-management by planning and coordinating necessary system adaptations.

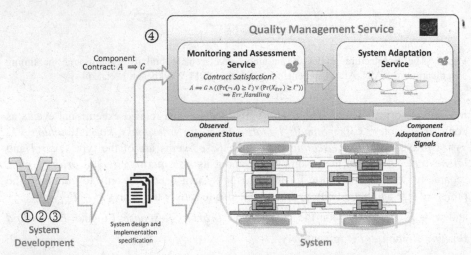

Fig. 4. The architecture of software services for self-management system services and components. (Note, ① ② ③ ④ are for the methodological steps as depicted in Fig. 1.)

Contracts are used for the decision-making in the MAS. For example, for a critical component, this embedded service monitors the actual external conditions (A) and tracks the internal error states (X_{Err}); it then triggers appropriate error handling behaviors ($ErrHandling$) by the adaptation service SAS when necessary. This is given by the expression: $A \Rightarrow G \wedge ((\Pr(\neg A) \geq l') \vee (Pr(X_{Err}) \geq l'')) \Rightarrow Err\_Handling$, in Fig. 4, where two probability assertions with the operator Pr specify the corresponding probabilistic fault assessments in regard to two acceptance levels (l' and l''). The decision-making of the SAS requires built-in knowledge about the configuration variability and the related rules for deciding and planning changes (e.g., mode switches). For system dependability, the ability of inferring the causing factors of anomalies or other undesired conditions plays a key role for the success.

4.2   Contracts and Models for Operation Assessment

The embedded service MAS tracks the component operational behaviors based on some observed evidences in terms of sensor measurements and system service feedbacks. Such behaviors evolve dynamically over time, while exhibiting stochasticity. The stochasticity could be due to varying workloads, emerging failures, as well as the actions of quality of service adaptation, error handing and fault treatment. Accordingly, the reasoning of such behaviors is supported by Markov Model (MM), which is a special type of DBN (Dynamic Bayesian Network) with a chain structured states in time series [12]. We assume here that the target system or component satisfies Markov Property (i.e. its future state is only affected by its present state).

In particular, we use the Operation Contract (OC) and Safety Contract (SC), (shown in Fig. 1) for capturing the operation concerns of module. The key content is related to the constraints of nominal and error states as well as the conditional probabilities of the transitions among these states. For example, assume that one component *BrakePedalSensor* operates with a simple normal mode and a simple error mode, shown in Fig. 5. We denote the operational states with X given by two state variables: $X = \{Norm, Err\}$, where *Norm* – Normal Mode, and *Err* – Timing Error. The overall operational behavior is characterized by the Markov Model as a set of chain structured states in discrete time series: $(X_1, X_2, ..., X_{k-1}, X_k, X_{k+1}, ...)$. At a time instance k, the conditional probabilities of state transition outcomes are given by the values of $p(X_k \mid X_{k-1})$. For instance, the conditional probability of state transition from *Norm* at X_1 to *Err* at X_2 equals to *0.01*, which corresponds to the component reliability requirement; while the conditional probability of state transition from *Err* at X_2 to *Norm* at X_2 equals to *0.03*, which corresponds to the requirement on component error recovery. With such constraints, each particular execution exhibits a sequence of state conditions in time series, such as $(X_1 = Norm, X_2 = Norm, X_3 = Err, X_4 = Norm, ...)$. For a component in general, the probability figures can be estimated from related experience or laboratory testing in regard to particular operational conditions (e.g. failure rates in different temperature levels and repair rates by related component services). Figure 6 shows the corresponding specification with two probabilistic temporal assertions as the fault contract extension: $(\tau) = 0.99, Pr(Next(\neg\tau) = \tau) = 0.03$.

Given the contracts for operation and safety constraints, the service MAS (Sect. 4.1) monitors the system operation and thereby estimates the component status for situation awareness, performance and dependability management. The estimation is supported by Hidden Markov Model (HMM) [12], which consists essentially of two pieces of Markov Model: one for the conditional probability of operational states $p(X_k|X_{k-1})$, and another one for the conditional probability of external observation given a system state $p(Y_k|X_k)$. Here, Y_k refers to the variables of observation given by the target system architecture and component interfaces, while X_k and X_{k-1} refer to the operational state at time k and $k-1$ respectively. As the conditional probability $p(Y_k|X_k)$ plays a key role in the status estimation, it is preferred that such information is

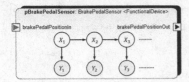

Guarantee:	X_{k-1}	X_k	$p(X_k|X_{k-1})$
G1	Norm	Norm	0.99
G2	Norm	Err	0.01
G3	Err	Norm	0.03
G4	Err	Err	0.97

Fig. 5. The component *BrakePedalSensor* and its operational behavior in terms of Markov Model given by a chain-structured discrete-time states: $(X_1, X_2, X_3, ...)$. The table for conditional probabilities $p(X_k \mid X_{k-1})$ defines the probabilities of state transitions. The Markov model representation is extended with the indicators $Y_1, Y_2, Y_3, ...$ to form a Hidden Markov Model.

$$C_{comp\_1}: \begin{cases} \text{messages:} \begin{cases} \text{in: } v_{in} \\ \text{out: } s_{out} \end{cases} \\ \text{message\_types: } v_{in}, s_{out} \in (Control, Latency\_Critical) \\ \text{assumptions: } v_{in} = \left(\#size_{v_{in}}, \#periodicity_{v_{in}}, \#priority_{v_{in}}\right) \\ \text{guarantees: } s_{out} = \left(\#size_{s_{out}}, \#periodicity_{s_{out}}\right), \quad \tau = G\left(v_{in} \rightarrow F_{[0..\#delay_{s_{out}}]}s_{out}\right) \\ Pr(\tau) = 0.99, Pr(Next(\neg\tau) = \tau) = 0.03 \end{cases}$$

Fig. 6. The Operation and Fault Contract for a brake pedal sensor with additional probabilistic assertions. Here, *Vin* and S_{out} denote the input and output events respectively. We use *PrSTL* (Probabilistic Signal Temporal Logic) [20] to denote the probabilistic behavioral constraints, with the operators **Pr** for the probability assertion, **Next** for next state, and ¬ for negation.

available in the contracts (i.e. *OC* and *SC*) as operation observability or diagnostics constraints. Otherwise, additional efforts for the elicitation of such constraint through analysis, testing and machine-learning would be necessary. The definition of state variable X of a module depends on the needs of situation awareness and quality management. The state variable could include non-observable analytical states, for which the HMM models support the inference. For example, due to some technical or managerial constraints, the embedded service MAS for a distributed system would only be deployed on the network switches. The indicators Y_k then provide information about the timing and resource utilization at the switches at time k. By such info, the service MAS would estimates the end-to-end communication deadlines and related timing failures for some messages based on the knowledge of $p(Y_k|X_k)$ and $p(X_k \mid X_{k-1})$. One experimental result is shown in Fig. 7. See e.g. [12] for the further details about the algorithms for hidden state inference.

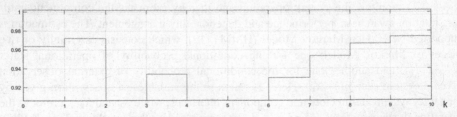

Fig. 7. Estimated probability of state *Norm* of $p(X_k \mid X_{k-1})$ according to a specific sequence of emissions Y_k.

4.3   Contracts and Models for System Performance and Safety Awareness

One key aspect of performance and safety awareness is related to the estimation of component operational conditions and then their system-wide impacts. Such a task is supported in our approach by the service MAS. By observing the system operation and inferring local conditions of components, the risks of violating a component contract is assessed according to the actual probability of being in particular error states. Moreover, by composing the estimated local operational conditions, the service also estimate the corresponding system-level operational conditions and thereby assess the risks of violating system-level performance and safety constraints.

Given a distributed E/E system with switched Ethernet for the communication of messages in mixed criticalities, the system performance levels can be analyzed and derived using Stochastic Network Calculus [13, 14]. The corresponding timing constraints in regard to the arrival patterns of messages, resource utilizations and end-to-end performances can be captured by contracts. In operation, the MAS observes the arrival processes of messages to a network switch and thereby estimates the overall performance. The service detects certain combinations of performance levels of messages that may cause exceptionally high interference to critical messages.

For the safety awareness, fault models capturing the overall system failure logic in terms of FTA and FMEA [15, 16] play a key role. They allow effective safety reasoning by reusing the results of regular safety analysis in regard to the system-wide consequences of local errors. Current EAST-ADL technology allows a multi-viewed approach to safety engineering [17], where error models capturing the plausible anomalies in terms of local faults and failures and their permeations across the system are synthesized automatically from nominal architecture models. The analysis engine for FTA and FMEA is given by the HiP-HOPS tool [18, 19]. For example, pre-calculated minimum cut-sets can be used to quickly determine the system-wide effects of particular component errors. An alternative way is to learn and create a Dynamic Bayesian Network (DBN) for capturing the system-wide effects of local errors. In regards to functional safety, the estimated probability of system failure represents the uncertainty that the target system has in regard to the related functionality. Such a functionality, when subjected to safety requirements, has associated safety integrity levels (i.e. ASIL), representing essentially the degree of (in) tolerance in regard to the failures. For example, given some safety requirements: 1. *SafetyGoal#1*: *ASIL A, the ... control function shall not cause a clash ... when the vehicle has speed in 15 km/h*; 2. *SafetyGoal#2: ASIL D, the ... control function shall not cause a clash ... when the vehicle has speed in 45 km/h*. The requirement *SafetyGoal#1* with ASIL A has better tolerance to uncertainties by system failures. For a system, the estimated failure probabilities by the embedded service MAS provides a dynamic justification of the overall system uncertainty in regard to its control actions. Such an estimated awareness in regard to safety makes it possible to avoid control actions with unacceptable high risk.

5   Related Technologies

In recent years, generic and domain specific modeling frameworks have been developed for model-based development (MBD) of cyber-physical systems in many industrial domains, such as SysML [21], AADL [22] and EAST-ADL [6, 7]. All these technologies focus on the support for system description and information management only during the development time. For dealing with the partially unknown or inaccurate system properties, the specification of systems with abstract goals, probabilistic properties and contracts together with the provision of related intelligent services and platform support will be necessary. For example, a mission goal description based approach to the identification of required capabilities for the constituent system, operations, connections, emergent behavior, among other elements of system-of-systems has been proposed in [23]. A contractual description of constituent systems interfaces, to address the imprecision and uncertainty inherent in the description of constituent systems is given in [24]. For quality assurance and certification, such contractual support needs to be defined and managed seamlessly along with the life-cycles of system development, componentization and maintenance. A great many techniques have been developed and explored for advanced verification and validation of complex systems, both statically at design-time and dynamically at run-time. One particularly promising type of model checking is the so-called on-line model checking, as explored in [25]. In this approach, the resulting combined state space is continuously monitored against critical safety properties, or used to compute safe trajectories. Another approach that combines model-checking with dynamic model validation and creation based on machine-learning is learning-based testing (LBT) [26]. New methodological approaches to operational risk assessment include statistical analysis of near-miss and incident data using related Bayesian theories to estimate operational risk value and the dynamic probabilities of accidents sequences having different severity levels [27]. In regard to all these above mentioned approaches, our work aims to provide a framework for facilitating the industrial adoptions.

6   Conclusion

This paper presents a novel approach that aims to enable advanced operation monitoring and self-assessment and thereby automated performance and safety awareness. The ultimate goal is to support the adoption of generic COTS solutions in cyber-physical systems without violating the overall system requirements. To these ends, the approach emphasizes an integration of the domain-specific modeling framework EAST-ADL, the A-G contract theory, and Hidden Markov Model (HMM). With EAST-ADL for the overall system modeling, the provision of appropriate contract formalism allows dynamic self-assessment and adaptations with embedded software services. The approach also addresses the stochasticity of system and component operation. With HMM, the software services estimates the operational status, including non-observable analytical states, for the situation awareness, performance and dependability management. Currently, we are looking into how to effectively integrate the modeling technologies.

References

1. SAE International, SAE Information Report: (J3016) Taxonomy and definitions for terms related to on-road motor vehicle automated driving systems
2. European Commission: Intelligent transport systems. https://ec.europa.eu/transport/themes/its_en
3. PwC Semiconductor Report: Spotlight on Automotive. PwC, September 2013
4. ISO: ISO 26262 Road vehicles – Functional safety
5. Chen, D., et al.: A knowledge-in-the-loop approach to integrated safety & security for cooperative system-of-systems. In: IEEE 7th International Conference on Intelligent Computing and Information Systems, ICICIS 2015, Cairo, Egypt, 12–14 December 2015
6. EAST-ADL: EAST-ADL Domain Model Specification, Version M.2.1.12 (2014)
7. Kolagari, R., et al.: Model-based analysis and engineering of automotive architectures with EAST-ADL: revisited. Int. J. Conceptual Struct. Smart Appl. (IJCSSA) 3(2), 25–70 (2015). IGI Global Publishing, Hershey, USA
8. Benveniste, A., et al.: Multiple viewpoint contract-based specification and design. In: 6th International Symposium on Formal Methods for Components and Objects, FMCO 2007 (2007)
9. Benveniste, A., et al.: Contracts for system design. Report RR-8147, Inria, November 2012
10. Maler, O., et al.: Monitoring temporal properties of continuous signals. In: Formal Techniques, Modelling and Analysis of Timed and Fault-Tolerant Systems, Joint International Conference on FORMATS/FTRTFT (2004)
11. Anthony, R., et al.: Context-aware adaptation in DySCAS. Electronic Communications of the EASST: Context-Aware Adaptation Mechanism for Pervasive and Ubiquitous Services (CAMPUS), vol. 19. European Association of Software Science and Technology (EASST) (2009). ISSN 1863-2122
12. Ghahramani, Z.: An Introduction to Hidden Markov Models and Bayesian Networks. Hidden Markov Models: Applications in Computer Vision. World Scientific Publishing Co. Inc., River Edge (2001)
13. Liu, Y., et al.: A calculus for stochastic QoS analysis. Perform. Eval. 64(6), 547–572 (2007)
14. Jiang, Y., Liu, Y.: Stochastic Network Calculus. Springer Publishing Company, Heidelberg (2008)
15. Vesely, W.E.: Fault Tree Handbook. US Nuclear Regulatory Committee Report NUREG-0492, US NRC, Washington, DC (1981)
16. Palady, P.: Failure Modes and Effects Analysis. PT Publications, West Palm Beach (1995). ISBN: 0-94545-617-4
17. Chen, D., et al.: Integrated safety and architecture modeling for automotive embedded systems. e&i Elektrotechnik und Informationstechnik 128(6), 196–202 (2011). doi:10.1007/s00502-011-0007-7. ISSN: 0932-383X
18. Chen, D., et al.: Systems modeling with EAST-ADL for fault tree analysis through HiP-HOPS. In: 4th IFAC Workshop on Dependable Control of Discrete Systems, York, U.K., 4–6 September 2013
19. Papadopoulos, Y., McDermid, J.A.: Hierarchically performed hazard origin and propagation studies. In: Felici, M., Kanoun, K. (eds.) SAFECOMP 1999. LNCS, vol. 1698, pp. 139–152. Springer, Heidelberg (1999). doi:10.1007/3-540-48249-0_13
20. Sadigh, D., Kapoor, A.: Safe control under uncertainty with probabilistic signal temporal logic. Robotics: Science and Systems (RSS), June 2016
21. SysML: OMG Systems Modeling Language (OMG SysML™), OMG

22. Feiler, P.H., Gluch, D.P.: Model-Based Engineering with AADL: An Introduction to the SAE Architecture Analysis & Design Language. SEI Series in Software Engineering series. Addison-Wesley Professional, Boston (2012). ISBN: 10: 0-321-88894-4

23. Silva, E., et al.: A mission-oriented approach for designing system-of-systems. In: Proceedings of the 10th System-of-Systems Engineering Conference (SoSE), pp. 346–351, May 2015

24. Bryans, J., et al.: SysML contracts for systems of systems. In: IEEE Systems of Systems Engineering Conference 2014, June 2014

25. Althoff, M., et al.: Online verification of automated road vehicles using reachability analysis. IEEE Trans. Robot. **30**(4), 903–918 (2014)

26. Meinke, K., Sindhu, M.A.: Incremental learning-based testing for reactive systems. In: Gogolla, M., Wolff, B. (eds.) TAP 2011. LNCS, vol. 6706, pp. 134–151. Springer, Heidelberg (2011). doi:10.1007/978-3-642-21768-5_11. IEEE Trans. Robot. 30(4), 903-918 (2014)

27. Meel, A.: Plant-specific dynamic failure assessment using Bayesian theory. Chem. Eng. Sci. **61**, 7036–7056 (2006)

Case Studies

Application of Model-Based Safety Assessment
to the Validation of Avionic Electrical Power Systems

Orlando Ferrante, Luigi Di Guglielmo, Valerio Senni, and Alberto Ferrari[(✉)]

Advanced Laboratory on Embedded Systems, United Technologies Research Center,
Piazza della Repubblica, 68, 00185 Rome, Italy
{orlando.ferrante,luigi.guglielmo,valerio.senni,
alberto.ferrari}@utrc.utc.com

Abstract. System safety assessments are integral part of system development
as indicated by the ARP4754A standard. These activities are usually performed
manually and rely on reviews and engineering judgments with limited use of
models to support the assessment phase. In this paper we present an application
of Model-Based Safety Assessment to the validation of an Aircraft Electrical
Power System (EPS). Safety assessment is a fundamental part of the development
for aircraft systems and the use of model-based techniques provides an effective
method for the formalization and analysis of such complex systems. A toolchain
that integrates the Formal Specs Verifier and the xSAP toolsets is presented and
results of the application of the toolchain to the EPS use case are shown.

1 Introduction

Model-Based Design is a methodology that relies on models to represent different views
of the system under design. The use of models is an enabler to reduce cost and time to
market without impacting the high quality and reliability that avionics systems require.
Recent efforts have been made to use formal analysis for the validation of avionics
systems using both run-time and formal verification methods. Concrete application of
formal methods to the verification of software components have been performed in the
past [2–4]. System safety assessments are integral part of system development as indicated by the ARP standards [1]. These activities are usually performed manually and
rely on engineering reviews and analysis leveraging the experience and the domain
knowledge of the analyst with limited use of models to support the assessment phase.
However, the increasing complexity of requirements and functionalities of industrial
cyber-physical systems impacts the effort required for exploring all the possible effects
of failure in the system due to the large number of cases to be taken into account. The
combination of model-based design and formal engines is a recent research and innovation area that leverages the model-based approach to help the safety engineer during
the safety assessment providing benefits in terms of reduced development time in presence of increasing system complexity [9–13].

In this paper, we focus on the application of Model-Based Safety Assessment on
Electrical Power Systems (EPS). These systems expose specific challenges due to their

© Springer International Publishing AG 2017
M. Bozzano and Y. Papadopoulos (Eds.): IMBSA 2017, LNCS 10437, pp. 243–254, 2017.
DOI: 10.1007/978-3-319-64119-5_16

criticality as the trend to have More Electrical Aircraft (MEA) continues [5]. The verification and validation of EPS, including safety aspects, has been already tackled by several works in literature. In [6] the authors define a Domain-Specific Language for the specification of EPS and an encoding of the system to a Boolean satisfiability problem to analyze some topological aspects. In [7] the authors describe a method and tools for the automatic synthesis of EPS controllers from a requirement specified as LTL properties. In [8] a methodology framework based on contract-based design is presented for the design and validation of several aspects of EPS design ranging from design space exploration to protocol synthesis.

In this paper we focus on the application of a Model-Based methodology to the safety assessment of EPS leveraging state-of-the-art formal engine and expanding the applicability of existing toolchains to this set of systems.

The results presented in this paper shows that MBSA can be successfully applied to such type of systems using industrial strength languages for the specification of the system behavior. The main contributions of the paper are the following: (1) the description of a toolchain that integrates the Simulink modeling language [16] and the state-of-the-art xSAP formal safety analysis platform [14, 15]; (2) the identification of a prototype EPS architecture evaluation methodology that leverages the results of the analyses to refine the architecture and (3) the application of the proposed methodology and toolchain for the improvement of an Electrical Power System example architecture.

The paper is organized as follows: in Sect. 2 we illustrate the EPS use case, in Sect. 3 we discuss the Safety analysis methodology and the toolchain used to perform the analysis, in Sect. 4 we describe the application of the methodology and toolchain to the use case, and in Sect. 5 we sketch ideas for the next steps of this work.

2   Electrical Power System Use Case

We consider an example design, taken from [27], of an Electrical Power System (EPS) for an aircraft. An EPS is a safety-critical system designed to ensure generation, transmission and distribution of power in the aircraft. Its principal components are Generators (producing Alternating Current), AC/DC Power Buses, Rectifier Units (ensuring conversion of Alternating Current to Direct Current), and Loads. Switch components are used to reconfigure the EPS topology according to the aircraft needs.

The principal objective of an EPS is to ensure that the power flow is maintained constant to the loads requiring it (Invariant 1). Furthermore, the EPS must ensure that no reconfiguration will ever lead to short-circuiting of two power generators (Invariant 2). Given the large number of loads, generators and buses in modern airplanes, the design of an EPS topology, the positioning of the switches and the correct control logic to ensure the above mentioned system-level invariants can be challenging. The complexity raises even more if we require system robustness with respect to faults. Indeed, in this latter case, the above mentioned invariants shall be maintained despite failure of selected components.

We adopt an illustrative example, represented in Fig. 1 and taken from [27], where there are two generators, two power buses (split into AC and DC branches), and eight switches to allow reconfiguration of the system. The allowed reconfigurations include, for example, (1) powering both power buses with a single generator and (2) bypassing a failed rectifier. That paper addresses the challenge of defining an optimal control for the switches in terms of minimal number of switch changes to reach a desired configuration (under the constraint that only one switch at a time is actuated) and ensuring the satisfaction of the invariants in any intermediate state. In our work we adopt the same architecture and the control configurations as provided in [27] and we improve the architecture to make it *robust to any single failure of a switch*. The key challenge is to improve robustness without limiting the system reconfiguration capabilities, i.e. without further constraining the provided control behavior, while keeping the invariants satisfied.

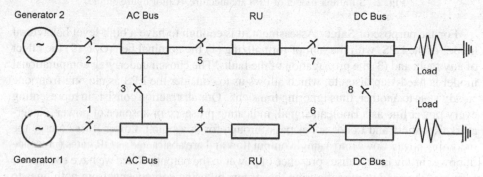

Fig. 1. The EPS conceptual architecture.

In our case study we assume that the switches are the only components that are affected by faults in the EPS architecture. A typical fault of switches is to remain stuck at an Open or Closed position. Let us assume, for example, that Switch 3 in Fig. 1 is stuck at closed position. There are some system configurations where this fault has no effect on the system Invariants 1 and 2, such as in the configuration where Generator 1 provides power to both buses. On the contrary, this fault leads to a violation of Invariant 2 in the case where both Generators are active, and there is no way to control the system in order to avoid this violation. Our purpose is to model the EPS provided in Fig. 1 and use the xSAP tool to identify every Minimal Set of Failures that lead to the violation of the Top Level Events identified by Invariants 1 and 2. Then we will use these failures to identify the sources of weakness and improve the robustness of the EPS. Our target is to achieve robustness to a single Switch stuck-at failure, of either Open or Closed type, so we are going to focus on Minimal Sets of Failures of size one.

Figure 2 illustrates the Simulink model of the EPS architecture. It replicates faithfully the conceptual architecture: in green the Generator blocks, in blue the AC/DC Buses, in purple the Rectifiers and in gray the Switches. The light blue squares group together the following functionalities: the Gen-2-AC power routing, the AC power routing and the DC power routing logics, respectively.

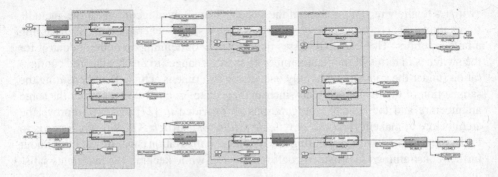

Fig. 2. Simulink model of EPS architecture. (Color figure online)

For the purpose of Safety Assessment, it is enough to have a high-level behavioral model of the EPS, with the aim of formalizing (1) the nominal behavior, (2) the effect of any fault, and (3) the propagation of the faults. The chosen underlying computational model is fixed-step discrete, which allows us to consider the EPS as moving from one steady state to another, thus ignoring transients. Our abstraction consists in representing every power line as a Boolean signal, indicating presence or absence of power. Generators, Rectifiers and Loads act as pass-through for this signal. Power Buses merge the incoming power flows into a single output flow and are abstracted as OR gates (presence of power in any input causes presence of power in the output). Since we have two power lines and the need of reconfiguring the system by using components from both lines to supply/transfer power, each bus has two inputs in our model. A Switch is controlled by a Boolean input that causes switch opening and closing. On change of the Switch control input there is a one-step delay in propagation of the switch configuration, which is an abstraction of the actual physical delay in switching. In the case of stuck-at (Open/Closed) failure, the Switch control input has no effect, thus leaving the switch stuck at Open or Closed position. We have two variants of the switch: Single and Two Way. Single Way switches are used when the power flow happens in one direction only. Two Way switches are used when the flow is bi-directional, as in the case where we bridge the two Power Lines.

The model inputs consist of the generators status and the Switch control inputs. Generators are assumed to be always active, while Switch control inputs can only take admissible configurations, as they are constrained by the given EPS control logic. The model of assumptions on generators and Switch control configurations is not visible in Fig. 2 but consists in an encoding of the control configurations as provided in [27]. For the purpose of Safety Assessment we ignore the order of these configurations.

In the model there are several From/Goto blocks that allow to observe the status of the EPS system in several points of the network. This is required to formalize the EPS invariants. Invariant 1 is formulated as: "When the Generators are active, the AC Buses and the DC Buses shall be powered". Invariant 2 is formulated as: "Neither AC Bus 1 nor AC Bus 2 shall be powered by the two Generators at the same time".

In terms of Safety Assessment these formulas are called Hazardous Condition of the system. Thus, their violation leads to a critical condition for the EPS and, thus, for the aircraft.

3 System Design Methodology and Toolchain

3.1 Methodology Overview

To evaluate the EPS architecture using a model-based approach, we employ a methodology represented in Fig. 3. We start from a preliminary architecture that is usually derived from initial trade studies. The System High Level Requirements (HLRs) are the inputs for an initial iteration of the system design step producing as output a refined system architecture and the corresponding system control algorithm.

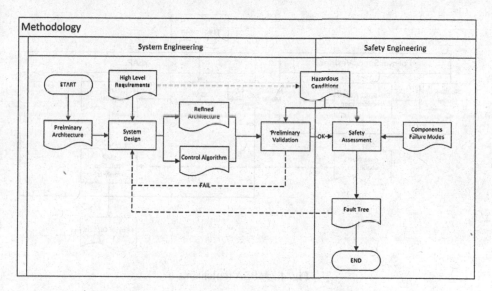

Fig. 3. Architecture evaluation methodology

These items are modelled and validated using formal methods (e.g. as described in [5]) to verify that in absence of faults the Hazardous Conditions specified in the HLRs are always verified. In case a violation of one or more HLRs is found, a new system design iteration is required to obtain an architecture or a control scheme that guarantees the compliance with HLRs. In case of HLRs compliance the architecture and the control algorithm models can be handed-off to the safety engineering team to perform the Model-Based Safety Assessment (MBSA) step. The MBSA can be performed extending the input models taking into account components failure modes and elaborating such extended model to produce the system fault tree artifacts. These artifacts are then reviewed by the team and in presence of unexpected results, an interaction with the system engineering group is required to refine the design or identify potential misinterpretation of the HLRs.

In this methodology, models represent *a unique and formal artifact* exchanged between the system design and safety teams. Further artifacts from both sides are produced starting from these formal and shared reference models. In our view the use of models impacts positively the communication between the engineering and safety teams reducing time to develop the required artifacts (requirements, fault trees, architectures and algorithms) and enabling the possibility of deriving part of them by using automatic techniques, hence reducing overall development costs.

3.2 Toolchain

To perform a full, Model-Based Safety Assessment flow for the EPS use case, we have developed a toolchain, represented in Fig. 4. The toolchain is based on the combination of the Formal Specs Verifier and the xSAP frameworks.

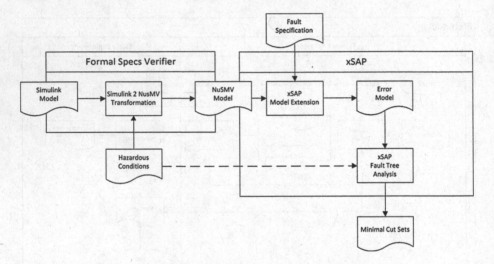

Fig. 4. MBSA toolchain.

The input is a MATLAB Simulink model, formalizing the nominal behavior of the system under analysis and using an abstraction of the architecture of the EPS by following an approach similar to the one described in [6]. As discussed in Sect. 2, power sources and buses are abstracted using Boolean values (true for "power is present" and false for "power not present") and the status of each Switch ("open" or "closed") corresponds to the presence of a link ensuring the power flow. In addition to the system nominal behavior, the model contains a specification of the Hazardous Conditions as invariant properties. The input model is translated using the Formal Specs Verifier Framework to a semantically equivalent nuXmv model [18].

Formal Specs Verifier (FSV) [21, 22] is an ALES-UTC Framework that translates models adopting a restricted subset of Simulink blocks to a semantically equivalent formal model that is amenable to be processed by state-of-the art model checkers. An abstract representation of FSV internals is given in Fig. 5.

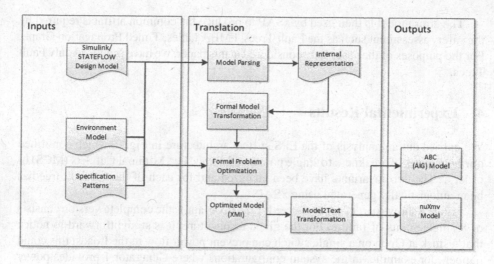

Fig. 5. Formal specs verifier transformation flow

The transformation is based on three steps: model parsing, internal model optimizations and model to text transformation. In the parsing phase the input is processed by using a MATLAB API-based parser that reproduces the model using an internal formal intermediate representation [17]. During this phase, the tool detects unsupported blocks or unsafe constructs, if present. The internal representation is processed and optimized with the objective of producing a formal model that encodes the input model as a finite state machine. In addition, (1) a set of assumptions on the primary input of the system (Environment model) and (2) the property to be verified are translated and processed by the optimization phase as specification patterns [19]. Finally, the model-to-text step produces artifacts that can be processed by state of the art model checking tools such as nuXmv and ABC [18, 20].

The FSV framework has been used in several industrial and research projects [5], and extensions have been presented for the verification of embedded systems [23], synthesis of failure scenarios [13], automatic test generation [24, 25], requirements validation [26] as well as applications to concrete industrial size cases [24, 25].

After the translation phase the produced formal model is processed by the nuXmv model checker to verify that the nominal model does not violate the HLRs (including Hazardous Conditions). This step is necessary to guarantee that only an injection of faults can lead to the top-level events, and to ensure the production of meaningful results in terms of generated cut sets.

The validated model is then processed by the xSAP platform [14, 15]. First, a Fault Specification file (FEI specification) is produced to formalize how the different components can fail. This file is used to automatically produce a new model, called the error model (or Extended Model, according to xSAP terminology), that combines the original nominal behavior with the faulty ones as specified in the FEI for each instance of each component of the system under analysis. This step is fully automatic and relies on the capabilities provided by the xSAP framework.

The error model is then used by xSAP to produce the common artifacts required by the safety assessment such as the Fault Trees, FMEA tables, Timed Propagation Graph. For the purposes of the case study considered in this paper, we have produced only Fault Trees.

4   Experimental Results

We carried out an analysis of the EPS system architecture in Fig. 2, which confirmed our hypothesis of weakness to single points of failures, i.e., Minimal Cut Sets (MCS) of order 1. The two invariants have been analyzed and for each of them a fault tree has been automatically generated using xSAP.

Figure 6 shows part of the fault tree for the Invariant 1: the complete version consists of 8 single points of failure. For the given architecture, it is straightforward to notice that a stuck at Open on a single switch can prevent power flow to the Loads: this could happen, for example, in the system configurations where Generator 1 provides power to both the Buses, and a stuck at Open on Switch 1 breaks the power flow.

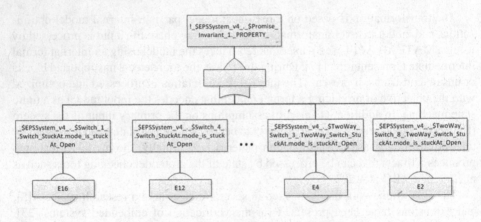

Fig. 6. EPS architecture: fault tree for Invariant 1

Figure 7, instead, shows the fault tree generated for Invariant 2. It consists of 3 single points of failure. A stuck at Close on one of the switches Switch 1, Switch 2 and Switch 3 may lead the short-circuiting of the two power generators. This can happen, for example, in the system configurations where only Generator 1 provides power to both the Buses, and a stuck at Closed event on Switch 2 causes the short-circuiting.

As previously stated, our target is to achieve robustness to a single switch stuck-at failure (of either Open or Closed type) without constraining the provided control behavior, while keeping the invariants satisfied. Thus, we need to refine EPS architecture to remove the sources of weakness by introducing redundancies among the switches.

To avoid that a single stuck at Closed on a switch causes short-circuiting (i.e., violation of Invariant 2), the switch can be replaced by two switches connected in series and controlled by the same input command: in case of a fault stuck at Closed on one of those switches, the power flow would be interrupted by the non-faulty one. Notice that even

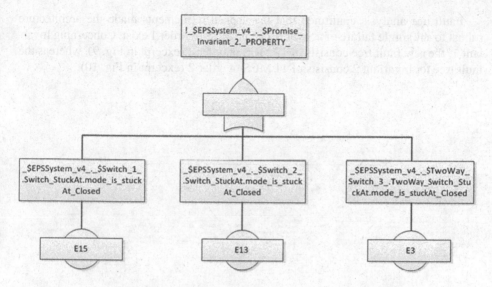

Fig. 7. EPS architecture: fault tree for Invariant 2

if this solution is robust to stuck at Closed events, it cannot avoid a stuck at Open event to interrupt power flow to the Loads. This means that further redundancy would be needed. Robustness to stuck at Open events can be achieved by replacing a single switch with two switches connected in parallel and controlled by the same input command, i.e. the power will flow through the non-faulty switch in case one of them is stuck at Open. Combinations of these patterns can be used to improve switches robustness to both stuck at Open and Closed at the same time at the cost of increasing architecture complexity.

The fault tree analysis results generated for the EPS architecture of Fig. 2 guided us to choose the appropriate combination of the patterns described above to refine the EPS architecture. In particular, each of the switches of the Gen-2-AC power routing group has been replaced by two pairs of switches connected in parallel. The pairs are then connected to each other in series. On the contrary, each switch in the AC power routing and DC power routing groups has been replaced by two switches connected in parallel. Figure 8 provides an overview of the refined EPS architecture.

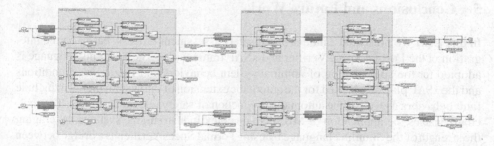

Fig. 8. Refined EPS architecture

Fault tree analysis confirmed that the applied refinements made the architecture robust to any single failure of a Switch, i.e., no MCS of order 1 exist. Concerning Invariant 1, the new fault tree consists of 12 MCS of order 2 (excerpt in Fig. 9), whereas the fault tree for Invariant 2 consists of 11 MCS of order 2 (excerpt in Fig. 10).

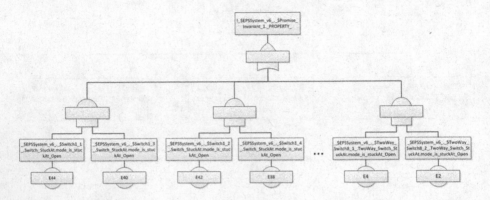

Fig. 9. Refined EPS architecture: fault tree for Invariant 1

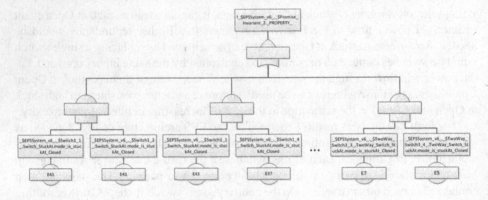

Fig. 10. Refined EPS architecture: fault tree for Invariant 2

5 Conclusions and Future Work

In this paper we presented a model-based safety assessment process, based on the integration of the Formal Specs Verifier and xSAP frameworks. The Simulink language is adopted for the specification of nominal system behaviors and Hazardous Conditions and the xSAP platform is used for the automatic extension of the system model to include fault behaviors as well as the automatic production of safety relevant artifacts. The toolchain enables the application of MBSA to complex industrial-size systems, leveraging the strength of the Simulink language by using Formal Specs Verifier as a bridge between the input model and the formal engine. The method has been demonstrated by applying it to an Electrical Power System use case and showing promising results in terms of application to industrial-sized models.

This work can be extended in several directions. First, the scalability of the identified method and toolchain shall be further analyzed and engineered to tackle EPS of increasing topological complexity, still maintaining the Boolean modeling abstraction for component behaviors. Second, we plan to model the system by using less coarse abstractions, taking into account transient behaviors. An analysis of the impact of such modeling constructs to the effectiveness of the formal algorithms is required to tackle industrial relevant models. Finally, the application of novel algorithms for the automatic synthesis of diagnosers represents an exploration area that is enabled by the presented toolchain.

References

1. SAE: ARP4761 Guidelines and Methods for Conducting the Safety Assessment Process on Civil Airborne Systems and Equipment, December 1996
2. Miller, S.P., Whalen, M.W., Cofer, D.D.: Software model checking takes off. Commun. ACM **53**(2), 58–64 (2010)
3. Dutertre, B., Stavridou, V.: Formal requirements analysis of an avionics control system. IEEE Trans. Software Eng. **23**, 267–278 (1997)
4. Hamilton, D., Covington, R., Kelly, J., Kirkwood, C., Thomas, M., Flora-Holmquist, A.R., Staskauskas, M.G., Miller, S.P., Srivas, M., Cleland, G., MacKenzie, D.: Experiences in applying formal methods to the analysis of software and system requirements. In: Proceedings of the 1st Workshop on Industrial-Strength Formal Specification Techniques, p. 30. IEEE Computer Society, Washington, D.C. (1995)
5. Ferrante, O., Scholte, E., Pinello, C., Ferrari, A., Mangeruca, L., Liu, C., Sofronis, C.: A methodology for increasing the efficiency and coverage of model checking and its application to aerospace systems. In: SAE ASTC Conference, Hartford (2016)
6. Xu, H., Oszay, N., Murray, R.: A domain-specific language for reactive control protocols for aircraft electric power systems. In: Hybrid Systems Computation and Control (HSCC) (2013)
7. Xu, H., Topcu, U., Murray, R.: Specification and synthesis of reactive protocols for aircraft electric power distribution. IEEE Trans. Control Netw. Syst. **2**(2), 193–203 (2015)
8. Nuzzo, P., Xu, H., Ozay, N., Finn, J., Sangiovanni-Vincentelli, A., Murray, R., Donze, A., Seshia, S.A.: Contract-based methodology for aircraft electric power system design. IEEE Access **2**, 1–25 (2013)
9. Peikenkamp, T., Cavallo, A., Valacca, L., Böde, E., Pretzer, M., Hahn, E.M.: Towards a unified model-based safety assessment. In: Górski, J. (ed.) SAFECOMP 2006. LNCS, vol. 4166, pp. 275–288. Springer, Heidelberg (2006). doi:10.1007/11875567_21
10. Joshi, A., Heimdahl, M.P.E.: Model-based safety analysis of simulink models using SCADE design verifier. In: Winther, R., Gran, B.A., Dahll, G. (eds.) SAFECOMP 2005. LNCS, vol. 3688, pp. 122–135. Springer, Heidelberg (2005). doi:10.1007/11563228_10
11. Bozzano, M., Cimatti, A., Katoen, J.-P., Nguyen, V.Y., Noll, T., Roveri, M.: Safety, dependability and performance analysis of extended AADL models. Comput. J. **54**(5), 754–775 (2011)
12. Güdemann, M., Ortmeier, F., Reif, W.: Using deductive cause-consequence analysis (DCCA) with SCADE. In: Saglietti, F., Oster, N. (eds.) SAFECOMP 2007. LNCS, vol. 4680, pp. 465–478. Springer, Heidelberg (2007). doi:10.1007/978-3-540-75101-4_44

13. Marazza, M., Ferrante, O., Ferrari, A.: Automatic generation of failure scenarios for SoC. In: ERTS2 2014, Tolouse (2014)
14. Bozzano, M., Cimatti, A., Fernandes Pires, A., Jones, D., Kimberly, G., Petri, T., Robinson, R., Tonetta, S.: Formal design and safety analysis of AIR6110 wheel brake system. In: Kroening, D., Păsăreanu, C.S. (eds.) CAV 2015. LNCS, vol. 9206, pp. 518–535. Springer, Cham (2015). doi:10.1007/978-3-319-21690-4_36
15. Bittner, B., Bozzano, M., Cavada, R., Cimatti, A., Gario, M., Griggio, A., Mattarei, C., Micheli, A., Zampedri, G.: The xSAP safety analysis platform. In: Chechik, M., Raskin, J.-F. (eds.) TACAS 2016. LNCS, vol. 9636, pp. 533–539. Springer, Heidelberg (2016). doi:10.1007/978-3-662-49674-9_31
16. http://www.mathworks.com/products/simulink/
17. http://www.omg.org/spec/QVT/index.htm
18. Cavada, R., Cimatti, A., Dorigatti, M., Griggio, A., Mariotti, A., Micheli, A., Mover, S., Roveri, M., Tonetta, S.: The NUXMV symbolic model checker. In: Biere, A., Bloem, R. (eds.) CAV 2014. LNCS, vol. 8559, pp. 334–342. Springer, Cham (2014). doi: 10.1007/978-3-319-08867-9_22
19. Ferrante, O., Ferrari, A., Mangeruca, L., Passerone, R., Sofronis, C.: BCL: a compositional contract language for embedded systems. In: 19th IEEE International Conference on Emerging Technologies and Factory Automation, Barcelona (2014)
20. Brayton, R., Mishchenko, A.: ABC: an academic industrial-strength verification tool. In: Touili, T., Cook, B., Jackson, P. (eds.) CAV 2010. LNCS, vol. 6174, pp. 24–40. Springer, Heidelberg (2010). doi:10.1007/978-3-642-14295-6_5
21. Carloni, M., Ferrante, O., Ferrari, A., Massaroli, G., Orazzo, A., Petrone, I., Velardi, L.: Contract-based analysis for verification of communication-based train control (CBTC) system. In: Bondavalli, A., Ceccarelli, A., Ortmeier, F. (eds.) SAFECOMP 2014. LNCS, vol. 8696, pp. 137–146. Springer, Cham (2014). doi:10.1007/978-3-319-10557-4_17
22. Carloni, M., Ferrante, O., Ferrari, A., Massaroli, G., Orazzo, A., Velardi, L.: Contract modeling and verification with FormalSpecs verifier tool-suite - application to Ansaldo STS rapid transit metro system use case. In: Koornneef, F., Gulijk, C. (eds.) SAFECOMP 2015. LNCS, vol. 9338, pp. 178–189. Springer, Cham (2015). doi:10.1007/978-3-319-24249-1_16
23. Ferrante, O., Benvenuti, L., Mangeruca, L., Sofronis, C., Ferrari, A.: Parallel NuSMV: a NuSMV extension for the verification of complex embedded systems. In: Ortmeier, F., Daniel, P. (eds.) SAFECOMP 2012. LNCS, vol. 7613, pp. 409–416. Springer, Heidelberg (2012). doi:10.1007/978-3-642-33675-1_38
24. Ferrante, O., Ferrari, A., Marazza, M.: An algorithm for the incremental generation of high coverage tests suites. In: 19th IEEE European Test Symposium (2014)
25. Ferrante, O., Ferrari, A., Marazza, M.: Formal specs verifier ATG: a tool for model-based generation of high coverage test suites. In: ERTS (2016)
26. Mangeruca, L., Ferrante, O., Ferrari, A.: Formalization and completeness of evolving requirements using contracts. In: 8th IEEE International Symposium on Industrial Embedded Systems (SIES) (2013)
27. Christalin, B., Colledanchise, M., Ogren, P., Murray, R.: Synthesis of reactive control protocols for switch electrical power systems for commercial application with safety specifications. In: IEEE Symposium on Computational Intelligence in Control and Automation (2016)

Timed Failure Propagation Analysis for Spacecraft Engineering: The ESA Solar Orbiter Case Study

Benjamin Bittner, Marco Bozzano[(⊠)], and Alessandro Cimatti

Fondazione Bruno Kessler, Trento, Italy
{bittner,bozzano,cimatti}@fbk.eu

Abstract. Timed Failure Propagation Graphs (TFPGs) are used in the design of safety-critical systems as a way of modeling failure propagation, and to support the evaluation and implementation of functions for Fault Detection, Isolation, and Recovery (FDIR). TFPGs are a very rich formalism: they enable modeling Boolean combinations of faults and events, and quantitative delays between them. Several formal techniques have been recently developed to analyze them as stand-alone models or to compare them to models that describe the more detailed dynamics of the system of reference, specifically under faulty conditions.

In this paper we present several case studies that apply TFPGs to Solar Orbiter, an ESA deep-space probe under development by Airbus. The mission is characterized by high requirements on on-board autonomy and FDIR. We focus on three possible application areas: hardware-to-software propagations, system-level propagations, and propagations across architectural hierarchies. The case studies show the added value of TFPGs for safety analysis and FDIR validation, as well as the scalability of available analysis tools for non-trivial industrial problems.

1 Introduction

Modern complex engineering systems, such as satellites, airplanes and traffic control systems need to be able to handle faults. Faults may cause failures, i.e. conditions such that particular components or larger parts of a system are no longer able to perform their required function. As a consequence, faults can compromise system safety, creating a risk of damage to the system itself or to the surrounding infrastructure, or even a risk of harm to humans. Faults can also affect the availability of a system, for instance by causing service outages. In some applications such as telecom satellites or intelligence infrastructure, such outages might be unacceptable. For these reasons, complex system needs to tolerate faults – either passively, for instance through robust control laws, or actively, implementing a Fault Detection, Isolation and Recovery (FDIR) subsystem.

B. Bittner was partially supported by ESA NPI contract No. 4000111815/14/NL/FE.

M. Bozzano and Y. Papadopoulos (Eds.): IMBSA 2017, LNCS 10437, pp. 255–271, 2017.
DOI: 10.1007/978-3-319-64119-5_17

The first step in developing an FDIR architecture is to identify the faults and their effects on the system. Standard analyses employed for this task include Fault Tree Analysis (FTA) [16] and Failure Modes and Effects Analysis (FMEA) [10]. For a review on the state-of-the-art in modeling and tools we refer to [15]. These techniques however don't have a comprehensive support for timing of failure propagations and are specialized to specific discrete analyses that make it difficult to obtain a global integrated picture of the overall failure behavior of a system. This in turn makes it difficult to develop a coherent set of detailed FDIR requirements and to check whether a given FDIR architecture is able to handle all possible faults and their propagation effects.

To address these issues, *Timed Failure Propagation Graphs* (TFPGs) [1,12] were recently investigated as an alternative failure analysis framework. TFPGs are labeled directed graphs that represent the propagation of failures in a system, including information on timing delays and mode constraints on propagation links. TFPGs can be seen as an abstract representation of a corresponding dynamic system of greater complexity, describing the occurrence of failures, their local effects, and the corresponding consequences over time on other parts of the system. TFPGs are a very rich formalism: they allow to model Boolean combinations of basic faults, intermediate events, and transitions across them, possibly dependent on system operational modes, and to express constraints over timing delays. In a nutshell, TFPGs integrate in a single artifact several features that are specific to either FMEA or FTA, enhanced with timing information.

TFPGs have been investigated in the frame of the FAME project [4,8,9], funded by the European Space Agency (ESA). Here, a novel, model-based, integrated process for FDIR design was proposed, which aims at enabling a consistent and timely FDIR conception, development, verification and validation. More recently, [3,5,6] have investigated TFPG-based validation and formal analyses. In particular, [6] focuses on the validation of TFPGs, seen as stand-alone models, using Satisfiability Modulo Theories (SMT) techniques; [5] addresses TFPG validation, and tightening of TFPG delay bounds, with respect to a system model of reference; finally, [3] develops algorithms for the automatic synthesis of a TFPG from a reference system model.

In this paper we present several case studies that apply TFPGs to an ESA deep-space probe design under development by Airbus, whose mission is characterized by high requirements on on-board autonomy and FDIR. These case studies were produced during a 10-month research stay at ESA-ESTEC, in which we studied the application of TFPGs for failure analysis in the "Solar Orbiter" (SOLO). We present three TFPG case studies for SOLO: one looking at error propagation from hardware to software, one studying failure propagation during detection and isolation activities on system-level, and one considering propagation across architectural layers. Based on the case studies, we make some observations on how TFPGs can improve our understanding of system failure dynamics and how they can be used to validate and tune FDIR design coverage. Finally, we describe how the analyses helped to raise five issues that were submitted to the FDIR critical design review. Four of them were classified as major, one as minor.

The case studies show the adequacy and added value of TFPGs for safety analysis and FDIR validation, as well as the scalability of available analysis tools for non-trivial industrial problems. Moreover, the issues we found led to an improvement of the available design documentation, and in one case triggered a modification of the design, as the analyses unveiled a missing consistency check.

The rest of the paper is structured as follows. Section 2 describes in detail the syntax and semantics of TFPGs. In Sect. 3 we present the main TFPG-related analyses available in the xSAP tool for model-based safety analysis and used for the case studies. Section 4 contains a detailed discussion of the case studies. We conclude with a summary and outlook on interesting directions in Sect. 5.

2   Timed Failure Propagation Graphs

TFPGs – first described in [11,12] – are directed graph models where nodes represent *failure modes* (root events of failure propagations) and *discrepancies* (deviations from nominal behavior caused by failure modes). Edges model the temporal dependency between the nodes. They are labeled with propagation *delay bounds*, and *system modes* indicating the system configurations in which the propagation is possible. TFPGs are formally defined as follows.

Definition 1 (TFPG). *A TFPG is a structure* $G = \langle F, D, E, M, ET, EM, DC \rangle$, *where:*

- *F is a non-empty finite set of failure modes;*
- *D is a non-empty finite set of discrepancies;*
- *$E \subseteq V \times D$ is a non-empty set of edges connecting the set of nodes $V = F \cup D$;*
- *M is a non-empty set of system modes (we assume that at each time instant the system is in precisely one mode);*
- *$ET : E \to I$ is a map that associates every edge in E with a time interval $[t_{min}, t_{max}] \in I$ indicating the minimum and maximum propagation time on the edge, with $I \in \mathbb{R}_{\geq 0} \times (\mathbb{R}_{\geq 0} \cup \{+\infty\})$ and $t_{min} \leq t_{max}$;*
- *$EM : E \to 2^M$ is a map that associates to every edge in E a set of modes in M (we assume that $EM(e) \neq \emptyset$ for every edge $e \in E$);*
- *$DC : D \to \{\texttt{AND}, \texttt{OR}\}$ is a map defining the discrepancy type;*

Failure modes never have incoming edges. All discrepancies must have at least one incoming edge and be reachable from a failure mode node. Circular paths are possible, with the exception of self-loops or zero-delay loops.

As an example we consider *ForgeRobot*, a robot working in a hypothetical industrial forge. The robot is either in standby in a safe area, or performs work in a critical area that has high heat levels. It moves around using its locomotion facilities. To prevent overheating in the critical area, a cooling system is used. The TFPG in Fig. 1 shows possible failures of the robot and their effects over time. Two modes are used to differentiate the operational context: S for safe area, and C for critical area. The locomotion drive of the robot can fail (f_{loc}), causing

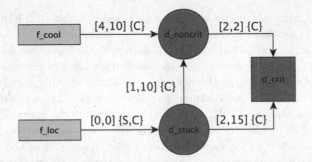

Fig. 1. TFPG for the ForgeRobot example. Rectangles are failure mode nodes, squares are AND nodes, and circles are OR nodes.

the robot to be stuck (d_{stuck}). The cooling system can fail (f_{cool}), decreasing the performance of heat protection. f_{cool} and d_{stuck} can both independently cause a non-critical overheating of the robot ($d_{noncrit}$) in mode C. In case both happen, they cause a critical overheating (d_{crit}). The time ranges on the propagation edges represent the different propagation speeds, influenced by the variable amount of workload and of heat in the critical area.

According to the semantics of TFPGs [1], a TFPG node is activated when a failure propagation has reached it. An edge $e = (v, d)$ is active iff the source node v is active and $m \in EM(e)$, where m is the current system mode. A failure propagates through $e = (v, d)$ only if e is active throughout the propagation, that is, up to the time d activates. For an OR node d and an edge $e = (v, d)$, once e becomes active at time t, the propagation will activate d at time t', where $t_{min}(e) \leq t' - t \leq t_{max}(e)$, with $t_{min}(e)$ (resp. $t_{max}(e)$) representing the t_{min} (resp. t_{max}) parameter of edge e. Activation of an AND node d will occur at time t' if every edge $e = (v, d)$ has been activated at some time t, with $t_{min}(e) \leq t' - t$; for at least one such edge e we must also have $t' - t \leq t_{max}(e)$, i.e. the upper bound can be exceeded for all but one edge. If an edge is deactivated any time during the propagation, due to mode switching, the propagation stops. Links are assumed memory-less, thus failure propagations are independent of any (incomplete) previous propagation. A maximum propagation time of $t_{max} = +\infty$ indicates that the propagation across the respective edge can be delayed indefinitely, i.e. it might never occur at all. This is a useful over-approximation when the real t_{max} value is not available; it is also necessary when the propagation depends on some unconstrained input or other dynamics not captured by the TFPG.

3   TFPG Analysis with xSAP

Building a TFPG can be an error-prone and time-consuming activity. Just as it is difficult to get fault trees and failure mode and effect tables right, it is difficult to build TFPGs, possibly even more so as we combine several of their features and furthermore add timing information. There is therefore a clear need for a comprehensive framework to analyze and validate TFPGs. Such framework is provided by the xSAP safety analysis platform [2].

TFPG analyses implemented in xSAP cover validation of TFPGs as stand-alone models, or validation against a model of reference, i.e. a more detailed model representing the system's dynamic behavior. Validation of TFPGs as stand-alone models include analyses such as possibility, necessity, consistency and refinement checks [6].

Validation of TFPGs against a model of reference has the objective to make sure that no important failure behavior that is possible in the system is overlooked (i.e. not modeled) in the TFPG. Likewise, we want to make sure that the TFPG contains as few spurious behaviors as possible, even though it might be impossible to exclude all such behaviors, due to the approximate nature of the TFPGs. We define the following TFPG properties: *completeness* guarantees that all failure propagations possible in the system are captured by the TFPG; *edge tightness* guarantees that the time and mode constraints of propagations are as accurate as possible. The corresponding analyses in xSAP are called *behavioral validation* (completeness check) and *edge tightening* (generation of tighter bounds for TFPG edges, that preserve completeness) [5]. These analyses are implemented as verification problems in temporal logic model-checking. If the properties are violated, diagnostic information for debugging is provided.

In a second scenario, a TFPG can be automatically derived from the corresponding system model. This analysis is called *TFPG synthesis* in xSAP [3]. Synthesizing TFPGs may be preferable over manually creating them, in particular when it is not possible to leverage the results of previous safety analyses, or when the engineer performing the analysis does not have a sufficiently deep understanding of the system behavior under faults. Obviously the main burden then lies on the system modeler, but it is arguably easier to create a model that specifies the behavior of individual parts of the system, how they interact, and how they can fail locally, than it is to directly model the failure behavior that *emerges* from these local behaviors and interactions.

xSAP provides a set of algorithms to *automatically* derive TFPGs from the corresponding system models in a way that guarantees by construction a number of formal properties. The engineer needs to provide as input the system model, the set of failure modes, and the set of discrepancies and monitors that should be included in the end result. The link between the TFPG and the system of reference is defined by means of a trace-based semantics, which enables the comparison of TFPG behaviors (those compatible with the TFPG constraints) to behaviors that are possible in the system. Based on the traced-based semantics, TFPGs are formally defined as abstractions of system behavior. As an example, Fig. 2 shows a TFPG trace and the corresponding system trace in the *ForgeRobot* example. The algorithm for TFPG synthesis [3] is structured in three parts: generation of an initial verbose graph topology; simplification of the graph structure for improved readability; finally, tightening of the edge parameters for obtaining accurate propagation constraints.

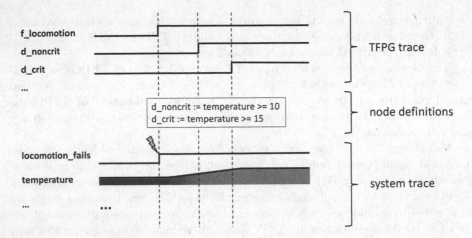

Fig. 2. Example of trace abstraction for ForgeRobot. Square signals are used to model Boolean values over time.

4   Case Studies

Solar Orbiter (SOLO) is a Sun-observing satellite under development by the European Space Agency, planned to be launched in October 2018 [13]. It will orbit the Sun to perform various scientific observations which are very difficult or impossible to do from Earth. The FDIR requirements on SOLO are much more stringent than on typical Earth-observing satellites, especially due to the intensity of solar radiation. Many faults are highly time-critical as they can quickly cause considerable damage to the spacecraft. Detection, isolation, and recovery need thus to be performed in extremely short time frames.

Due to the mission's general complexity and time-critical faults, SOLO is an ideal context to evaluate the use of TFPGs in space systems engineering. Three case studies on timed failure propagation analysis were performed. To support system and TFPG modeling we referred to the project documentation related to FDIR (mostly FMECA and FDIR design coverage documents) and the general software/hardware architecture (for instance the Control Algorithm Specification). These documents were at a pre-CDR (Critical Design Review) level and thus contained considerable design details.

Collecting the necessary information for the case studies was very challenging especially due to the huge amount of documentation, which was several hundreds of pages just for the documents effectively used. Additionally we found that the information needed for the case studies was scattered throughout the documents, and collecting and interpreting everything required substantial work and several interactions with engineers. This gives an intuition of how difficult it is, for instance, to manually validate the FDIR design of the *whole* spacecraft and to verify that the overall FDIR design is coherent and covers all possible (and reasonably probable) effects of faults. A formal and structured approach to interpret this information, for instance by using TFPG modeling, is thus a clear benefit and increases the confidence in the completeness of the analysis.

The proprietary information that we used for our study is subject to non-disclosure, and therefore cannot be quoted literally. However, we remark that the models created for the case studies are generic; the problems the case studies deal with are quite universal and do not apply only to SOLO.

4.1   Hardware-to-Software Propagation

The first case study involved modeling and analysis of the gyroscope channel processing software function, which reads different types of raw gyroscope sensor data coming from the inertial measurement unit (IMU), retrieved over the bus and stored in the datapool. From these values the function computes the rotation rate around the axis on which the channel's gyroscope is positioned, along with health flags signaling data corruption. In total the function has 7 inputs and 13 outputs.

The function runs on the main computer and is called cyclically at fixed intervals. It is composed of several smaller subfunctions, some of which have internal state variables (in total 8) to store values computed in previous cycles for various purposes. Time elapses by one unit during tick events. After each tick, the values in the datapool are updated and the function uses them to compute, through various consecutive steps, the new output values.

For this function we created a model representing various computational steps on an abstract level. Variables with values in the reals are abstracted to discrete domains, such as "normal", "degraded", and "erroneous". For degraded data readings we assume that the internal checks might or might not detect the corruption, thus including the possibility of detectable and undetectable levels of data corruption due to selected thresholds. Based on the IMU FMECA, 13 hardware faults where defined, which influence the values stored in the datapool. In the analysis we follow the single-fault assumption of FMECA. The faults are constrained to occur at the beginning of a cycle, such that we can analyze how many cycles (ticks) a fault needs to propagate to the function outputs. Failure modes are the 13 faults. We chose two discrepancies of interest expressed over the output values: degraded (and possibly undetectable) output measurements, and a Boolean data health flag indicating data corruption. The goal was to understand the temporal relationship between faults, the health flag, and degraded rate estimations.

The resulting model has in total 16 Boolean input variables and 84 Boolean state variables. The diameter of the corresponding reachable state-space is 105; this is the upper bound on the least number of transitions that need to be taken to reach any state from the set of initial states. In total 3488 states are reachable. Certain states can only be reached after executing the function several times, and since the function itself also consists of several steps, the overall execution can be quite long. This is important for the performance of model-checkers, which typically decreases with an increasing model depth. The complexity could be

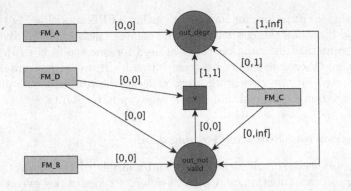

Fig. 3. Extract of TFPG for the gyroscope processing function. Multiple simultaneous faults and mode-switching are not considered.

avoided by collapsing several computational steps into a single atomic transition, but this would also make modeling more difficult.

We ran the synthesis and tightening procedures on the problem instead of manually building the TFPG, as we didn't have a clear expectation on the propagation behavior. Figure 3 shows part of the synthesized TFPG. Most failure modes have the same edge as "FM_B", and we don't show them here for clarity. The following observations can be made based on the synthesized TFPG.

- "FM_B" and the failure modes not shown immediately trigger the health monitor and can thus be recognized and adequately handled by the overall IMU processing (if the flag is used correctly by subsequent functions); the fault doesn't lead to degraded output (but always erroneous output, not shown here).
- Also "FM_D" immediately triggers the health monitor; furthermore, after exactly one cycle, it will also reach the rate estimation (edge from the virtual AND node).
- "FM_C" will affect the rate estimation within one cycle; it might, depending on the fault magnitude, also trigger the monitor, but this is not guaranteed ($t_{max} = +\infty$).
- Finally, "FM_A" immediately results in degraded estimations; furthermore, the edge from "out_degr" to "out_not_valid" shows that, after at least one cycle, also the health monitor may trigger, but again this is not guaranteed.

These results concisely show the different propagations possible in the gyroscope channel processing function, and give formal support to the informal predictions made in FMECA and FDIR design coverage documents. The information shown in the TFPG goes beyond what can be described by FMECA tables and also fault trees, giving detailed insight into how faults evolve over time and affect possible monitored variables.

As for XSAP tool performance, we notice that, on an average desktop computer, synthesis and simplification was completed in 4 s by using the BDD-based synthesis engine, whereas tightening takes 43 min. The efficiency of the quantitative timing analysis thus clearly needs to be improved to enable faster iterations.

4.2 System-Level Propagation

The second case study focused on a time-critical propagation scenario. The analysis scope is very different w.r.t. the first case study. We model the scenario shown in Fig. 4, where a thruster valve is stuck-open, causing a rotation of the spacecraft that might jeopardise the safe zone of the spacecraft attitude. In the case of Solar Orbiter this relates to the requirement to keep the heat-shield pointing towards the Sun. The analysis is focused on one axis only, which is a reasonable constraint. Note that for other missions similar requirements exist, i.e. keeping the high-gain antennas always pointing to Earth in order to maintain ground contact.

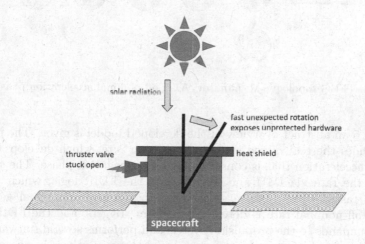

Fig. 4. Failure scenario

The goal of the case study was to formally validate a timing analysis done by hand, which is the basis for estimating the worst-case spacecraft off-pointing. The chosen scenario was well understood from a discrete perspective: it consists of fault occurrence, detection, and several isolation phases. We developed the TFPG shown in Fig. 6; the nodes A1 to A5 are different acceleration phases corresponding to different fault propagation stages, up to the point where fault isolation completely stops the propagation; the node M is a monitor that is used to trigger the fault isolation. The TFPG also contains delay bounds – derived from the documentation – whose precision is in tenths of milliseconds and whose values range from milliseconds to several seconds. For this TFPG we aimed at performing a completeness check, which would confirm the worst-case timing estimates made by engineers.

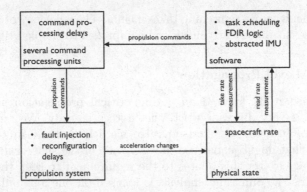

Fig. 5. System model

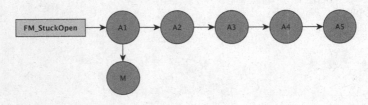

Fig. 6. TFPG topology (M: monitor; A1-5: off-nominal acceleration phases).

In Fig. 5 an abstract overview of the developed model is given. The physical state includes the real-valued spacecraft rotation rate, which develops according to an acceleration that is constant in each propagation phase. The software measures the rate via IMU and feeds it into the FDIR logic, which consists of several tasks. These tasks are scheduled together with nominal activities. When an off-nominal rate is detected, an alarm triggers, and the FDIR sends several commands to the propulsion system and performs several software operations. The propulsion system includes several thruster valves, in one of which the fault can occur. The spacecraft acceleration is set according to the current configuration of the propulsion system. Delays incur in all parts of the model, from task scheduling to data transmission via communication infrastructure and propulsion system reconfiguration. All basic delays and acceleration constants are modeled in the same detail as found in the documentation, and the model is thus representative for the real physical behavior. We also remark that these modeling principles are applicable to many generic spacecraft designs that face similar challenges. Thruster-valve-stuck-open is a well-known failure mode that is critical in all missions where high-pointing accuracy is required. Overall the model consists of 7 Boolean and 1 real input variables, as well as 18 Boolean and 5 real state variables.

A first completeness check was run with bounded model-checking to have a quick feedback on the delay bound estimates. This check showed that they were not fully accurate with respect to the developed model (the completeness check failed), and the t_{max} bound on some segments needed to be increased. In other words this meant that the isolation phase took longer in the model than we expected.

As the automatic tightening procedure in xSAP assumes a TFPG that is complete to begin with we couldn't use it to identify valid over-approximations of the delay bounds. We performed a number of manual iterations based on bounded model-checking to identify time bounds that made the completeness test pass, proceeding in an ad-hoc manner until finding a solution that was precise down to millisecond level. This manual interaction with the model-checker took a couple of hours.

The completeness check on the final TFPG using the IC3 model-checking engine in NUXMV was able to prove the established bounds, with a runtime of 30 min on a high-end workstation. This is a relevant result not only from an application perspective, giving feedback on worst-case behavior in a critical scenario, but also from an analysis performance perspective. Indeed they show that it is feasible to analyse very focused but highly accurate propagation problems and prove respective TFPG properties.

The analysis made it possible to raise two issues at the FDIR critical design review of SOLO. The modeling of this scenario and the TFPG analysis showed that the documentation was not clear on whether the complete duration of the last propagation edge in the TFPG was considered in the worst-case analysis for spacecraft off-pointing. The issue was raised during CDR, and worst-case off-pointing estimates as reported in the documentation were confirmed as accurate. Furthermore, the spacecraft can be in several operational modes, and thus in principle the TFPG mode labels should cover all of them. The issue was raised whether mode-switching is of relevance to the propagation scenario. A corner case was identified by the review panel and confirmed not to influence propagation dynamics, and hence to be covered by FDIR.

4.3   Architectural Propagation

The objective of the third case study was to develop a TFPG model as a way to perform failure propagation analysis at various architectural levels, which is usually done with Failure Modes and Effects Analysis. FMEA (or FMECA, when also criticality is considered) is the primary type of failure analysis used in aerospace [7], and serves as a central point of reference in defining and validating FDIR architectures. Going beyond the scope of FMECA, we also wanted to integrate in the TFPG the set of monitors defined in the FDIR design, in order to assess their completeness w.r.t. possible failure propagation paths. We focused on propagations originating from the IMU, reaching subsystem (AOCS) and system (spacecraft) levels, and furthermore focused only on one system mode.

Identification of TFPG Nodes. The first issue was to decide what information from the FMEA should be imported in the TFPG as failure mode and discrepancy nodes. The natural candidates here are the failure modes and the corresponding failure effects. In cases where the failure mode is associated to a function, as opposed to a hardware or software component, the failure effect is usually identical to it, especially at unit level. In our case this was applicable to all unit-level failure modes, and for them we added a single node to the TFPG, declared as TFPG failure mode node.

At subsystem level the identification was more challenging. Each row in the subsystem table had one associated failure mode, but often more than one failure effect. While the failure modes represented a consolidated list of items (at all levels), the failure effects were less structured. Identifying propagation events thus required interpretation of the informal textual description of what effects a certain failure mode has, in order to extract a consolidated set of propagation events. A specific challenge here was that certain events were mentioned in various parts of different FMEA tables, but the textual description slightly differed, and thus unambiguous integration was not straightforward. Another challenge consisted in the fact that it seemed to be possible to derive distinctive propagation events from both failure mode and failure effect column entries. Whether a failure mode at subsystem level should be modeled in the TFPG as a separate event needed to be assessed by looking at the individual case.

A number of discrepancies were thus derived at subsystem level, declared as OR nodes due to the single-fault assumption. We assume here that all failure events at subsystem level can be traced back to events at unit level, and thus don't introduce dedicated TFPG failure mode nodes at subsystem level.

Finally we integrated also standard and functional monitors – SMON and FMON, respectively. The former are simple Boolean expressions over observable state variables, and the latter are Boolean combinations (OR/AND) of those standard monitors. Standard monitors can be seen as fault symptoms, and functional monitors, which are used to trigger recoveries, as slightly more complex diagnosers. Note how the semantics of the monitors matches the notion of TFPG discrepancies. They are conditional on the occurrence of a linked fault, otherwise false alarms would be possible.

Even though in this case study we didn't create a system model to compare the TFPG against, it became clear that a considerable difficulty would be in defining certain TFPG nodes. It seems to be pretty straightforward at the unit level, in our case with clear effects on the IMU hardware. However, at the subsystem level the FMEA uses terms such as "fast", "slow", and "high", without a formal definition being available in the project documentation. For a precise definition, which we would need for TFPG validation or synthesis, additional interaction with engineers would be necessary. Also the validation of the overall FDIR design would benefit from such a formal description.

Identification of TFPG Edges. The next question to consider was how to connect the nodes. Two approaches to link failure mode and discrepancy nodes were identified based on the FMEA tables: "forward linking" by considering the columns for failure effects at the higher architectural level (chosen for the case study), and "backward linking" via the possible-cause column. By "forward" we mean following the same direction as the propagation, and by "backward" the opposite direction as the propagation. For forward linking we focus on one FMEA table row and look at the prediction of failure effects at the next level. These should ideally match with the failure effects of some failure mode at the higher level. Relating table rows was possible this way but not fully straightforward, due to the less structured content of failure effect table cells and inconsistent use of effect names across levels. We were thus able to match rows of different FMEA levels. However, since the FMEA rows at subsystem level in our use case correspond to more than one node in the TFPG, additional interpretation of the nature of individual events and interaction with engineers were necessary to establish the exact temporal ordering via TFPG edges. This additional knowledge allowed us to create a clearer propagation model compared to how the FMEA tables represent propagation.

Backward linking of FMEA rows can in principle be done through the possible-cause column. However we found this to be conflicting with our choice of forward linking, because in the available tables this backward perspective had an implicit assumption of fault isolation. It indicated failures at a lower level that are not detectable or recoverable at that level, thus excluding all failure modes for which monitors and recoveries were defined there. It seems thus that two different implicit and possibly conflicting propagation models are present in the FMEA tables: one where FDIR fails or is not executed and the failure thus propagates further to the next level (forward linking), and one where FDIR cannot, by design, prevent a propagation (backward linking).

Edges towards monitor discrepancies were established based on "Failure Effect Summary List" (FESL) tables, which associate the standard and functional monitors to individual FMECA rows. Based on this and the precise definitions of the monitors it was possible to establish the edges from failure effect nodes to SMON nodes; edges from SMON to FMON nodes directly followed from the definition of FMON monitors.

We didn't model refined time bounds on the propagations, as this would have required more intense interaction with project engineers. Compared to FMEA the TFPG makes it clear that, without further information, we need to assume for all TFPG edges that propagation can be instantaneous ($t_{min} = 0$) or might never occur at all ($t_{max} = +\infty$), forcing engineers to be explicit about timing aspects. Note how instantaneous propagation is worst-case for propagations towards (unobservable) failure effects, as there is no time to react, and infinite delay is worst-case for propagations towards monitors, as the monitor will never trigger.

The TFPG resulting from our analysis is shown in Fig. 7.

Evaluation of FDIR Design Coverage. The general problem that drove the case studies was the validation of FDIR design coverage. Typically based on FESL tables and supporting documentation, engineers try to investigate the following two questions: how are the monitors related to the failure mode row; what happens if FDIR at this level fails to detect and isolate the propagation. The experience with SOLO shows that both questions are not trivial when working with the classical approach.

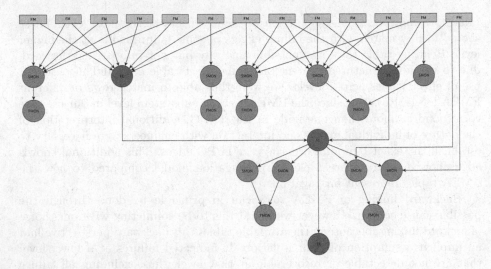

Fig. 7. TFPG of the IMU-to-AOCS case study. FM: failure mode; FE: (unobservable) failure effect; SMON: standard monitor; FMON: functional monitor.

Each failure mode row may contain more than one distinct event which have to be identified by interpreting the textual description in the row cells. Furthermore, if multiple monitors are assigned to the row, then there is no information in the table on which exact event each monitor is associated with. Furthermore, the structure of FMECA tables is driven by the failure modes, whereas the failure effects are typically presented more informally. FDIR monitors however, arguably, relate to the failure effects and not the more abstract concept of failure mode, which makes a comparison of the monitor and the related failure effects challenging.

TFPGs, instead, force the engineer to clearly describe what the events of interest are and how we assume them to be related in a temporal sense among themselves and w.r.t. monitors. From a purely qualitative point-of-view, coverage can thus be assessed by checking what monitors are reachable from every (unobserved) failure event. With the delay bounds TFPGs give also additional information not contained at all in FESL tables, and allow to compare fastest propagation time to the next event against the slowest propagation time towards the monitor (upper detection delay bound).

The second important question is also not straightforward to answer with FESL tables, being directly derived from FMECA tables: What will happen in terms of propagation when the FDIR fails to detect a failure mode or to recover from it, and is a fall-back monitor/response layer in place to capture the propagation? In the case study described here we showed that propagations between different architectural layers can be represented in TFPGs, thus connecting local information into a global propagation model. This then allows to precisely assess, by analyzing the graph, how many and which failure events with associated monitors a propagation has to go through before reaching a point where no further monitors (and recoveries) exist.

Contributions to FDIR Critical Design Review. The modeling efforts described
in this section raised several questions that were forwarded to the FDIR critical
design review panel. A first question regarded the rationale behind the hierarchical placement of two failure modes at subsystem level, as their direct effects
influence the whole system. This issue was identified as our modeling goal was
to explicitly link various levels. Thus it was not fully clear how many moni-
tor/response layers were in place to prevent propagation to system level. It was
clarified during the review that while the failure effects influenced the whole
system, the failure modes were placed at subsystem level because detection, isolation, and recovery was limited to that subsystem. This experience showed that
TFPGs can help to visually analyze escalation levels and compare them to safety
layers implemented in the architecture.

Furthermore, during our analysis we discovered one failure mode at unit-
level that, according to the unit FMECA, was not detectable at unit-level. In
the design coverage tables however, which group explicit failure modes into more
abstract ones, all unit-level failures are detectable at unit-level with the proposed
monitors. It was confirmed during the review that in fact detection of the identified failure mode is possible at unit-level, and that the unit FMECA table was
incomplete. The documentation was updated accordingly, and the association
with subsystem-level monitors was clarified.

Finally, by trying to model the IMU-to-AOCS TFPG we identified an ambi-
guity on the exact ordering of propagation events; this situation was clarified as
well during the review. The problem is that propagation is supposed to connect
failure effects at various levels. As shown in the case study, identifying those
events and connecting them based on FMECA results and other documentation
can be tricky.

5   Conclusion

Typically TFPGs are studied to *implement* fault management or FDIR with
a model-based approach, see e.g. [1,14]. Our experience in developing the case
studies shows that TFPGs can be also a valuable *design-time* analysis tool. They
provide formal rigor, native support of temporal propagation delays, the ability
to unambiguously integrate local propagation patterns into a global model of
failure behavior, as well as formally linking propagation effects to monitors used
to trigger recoveries. These are clear advantages w.r.t. classical analysis tools
such as FMEA and FTA, and the case studies show how these result in a better
understanding of system-level failure behavior, which in turn makes deriving
precise FDIR requirements or validating an FDIR design easier.

We conclude with a selection of interesting directions for future work in
terms of evaluating the use of TFPGs for spacecraft systems engineering. It
became clear while developing the case studies that, due to the fact that TFPGs
integrate various FDIR-related information, it should also be possible to use
them to support several common FDIR tuning problems.

A usual first step of recovery procedures on spacecraft is to disable, upon monitor triggering, a subset of other monitors to avoid execution of other potentially conflicting recoveries. We want to investigate the usability of TFPG models for deciding exactly what monitors need to be considered, which should in principle be possible with a mode-sensitive reachability analysis on the graph. Furthermore, a common principle in FDIR designs is to execute the recovery of the first monitor that triggers. To guarantee that the desired recovery is triggered for each anticipated failure, filters can be used to delay the effective triggering. It would thus be interesting to see if the timing information in TFPGs can be exploited to derive globally consistent filter values. Finally we want to study the use of TFPGs to tune individual monitor thresholds and assess the impact on the detection delay in relation to other TFPG nodes. Not only should such an analysis show how the delay changes, but it might also show a change in reachability of failure effects due to its impact on the FDIR reactivity, in case the isolation and recovery logic is included as well in the system model.

References

1. Abdelwahed, S., Karsai, G., Mahadevan, N., Ofsthun, S.: Practical implementation of diagnosis systems using timed failure propagation graph models. IEEE Trans. Instrum. Meas. **58**(2), 240–247 (2009)
2. Bittner, B., Bozzano, M., Cavada, R., Cimatti, A., Gario, M., Griggio, A., Mattarei, C., Micheli, A., Zampedri, G.: The xSAP safety analysis platform. In: Chechik, M., Raskin, J.-F. (eds.) TACAS 2016. LNCS, vol. 9636, pp. 533–539. Springer, Heidelberg (2016). doi:10.1007/978-3-662-49674-9_31
3. Bittner, B., Bozzano, M., Cimatti, A.: Automated synthesis of timed failure propagation graphs. In: Proceedings of the Twenty-Fifth International Joint Conference on Artificial Intelligence (IJCAI 2016), pp. 972–978 (2016)
4. Bittner, B., Bozzano, M., Cimatti, A., Ferluc, R., Gario, M., Guiotto, A., Yushtein, Y.: An integrated process for FDIR design in aerospace. In: Ortmeier, F., Rauzy, A. (eds.) IMBSA 2014. LNCS, vol. 8822, pp. 82–95. Springer, Cham (2014). doi:10.1007/978-3-319-12214-4_7
5. Bittner, B., Bozzano, M., Cimatti, A., Zampedri, G.: Automated verification and tightening of failure propagation models. In: Proceedings of the 30th AAAI Conference on Artificial Intelligence (AAAI 2016) (2016)
6. Bozzano, M., Cimatti, A., Gario, M., Micheli, A.: SMT-based validation of timed failure propagation graphs. In: Twenty-Ninth AAAI Conference on Artificial Intelligence (2015)
7. ECSS-Q-ST-30-02C: Space product assurance; failure modes, effects (and criticality) analysis (FMEA/FMECA). Technical report (2009)
8. European Space Agency: Statement of Work: FDIR Development and Verification and Validation Process, Appendix to ESTEC ITT AO/1-6992/11/NL/JK (2011)
9. FAME: FAME project web page (2016). http://es.fbk.eu/projects/fame
10. McDermott, R., Mikulak, R.J., Beauregard, M.: The Basics of FMEA. Steiner-Books, Great Barrington (1996)
11. Misra, A.: Senor-based diagnosis of dynamical systems. Ph.D. thesis, Vanderbilt University (1994)

12. Misra, A., Sztipanovits, J., Underbrink, A., Carnes, R., Purves, B.: Diagnosability of dynamical systems. In: Third International Workshop on Principles of Diagnosis (1992)
13. Müller, D., Marsden, R.G., Cyr, O.S., Gilbert, H.R., et al.: Solar orbiter. Solar Phys. **285**(1–2), 25–70 (2013)
14. Ofsthun, S.C., Abdelwahed, S.: Practical applications of timed failure propagation graphs for vehicle diagnosis. In: 2007 IEEE Autotestcon, pp. 250–259. IEEE (2007)
15. Ruijters, E., Stoelinga, M.: Fault tree analysis: a survey of the state-of-the-art in modeling, analysis and tools. Comput. Sci. Rev. **15**, 29–62 (2015)
16. Vesely, W., Goldberg, F., Roberts, N., Haasl, D.: Fault Tree Handbook (NUREG-0492). Division of Systems and Reliability Research, Office of Nuclear Regulatory Research, US Nuclear Regulatory Commission, Washington, DC (1981)

Author Index

Printed in the United States
By Bookmasters